COSTUME LANGUAGE
A DICTIONARY OF DRESS TERMS

COSTUME LANGUAGE

A DICTIONARY OF DRESS TERMS

Compiled and illustrated by
STEPHANIE CURTIS DAVIES

CRESSRELLES PUBLISHING COMPANY LIMITED
MALVERN

© Copyright Stephanie Curtis Davies, 1994
First published in 1994 by
Cressrelles Publishing Company Limited

10 Station Industrial Estate, Station Road, Colwall.
Herefordshire   WR13 6RN

ISBN 0 85956 066 X   (case bound)

ISBN 0 85956 069 4   (limp cover)

Printed in the U.K. by
BPC Wheatons Ltd, Exeter

To 'RUTHERS

for the inspiration to begin

and MY FAMILY

for the encouragement to finish

Foreword

I am greatly indebted to the gifted authors, specialists and researchers of costume history, notably C. Willett Cunnington, Phillis Cunnington, Doris Langley Moore, James Laver and others, whose publications are listed separately in the bibliography. They have been of much assistance in attempting to compile this book. I hope it will bring concise, apt, as well as international, information to all students of this fascinating subject. Over many years, I have collected information which I had not found in existing reference books. It is as up to date as I could make it.

In some cases I have listed sources, or reasons, for similar names, of popularity of certain garments, which have appeared in different parts of Europe and elsewhere, at the same time.

Stephanie Curtis Davies

Adams Hill West, Hereford. 1990

Publisher's Note

Stephanie Curtis Davies died in 1990. She had carefully revised the manuscript but never saw galley proofs. It was intended to add more illustrative drawings to give an even balance throughout the book. Sadly, this did not happen. A few drawings, not specific to the text, have been used to embellish the ends of chapters. Mr G. S. Harris kindly assisted in reading the proofs.

ADONIS WIG - *bushy white wig 'like the twigs of a gooseberry bush in deep snow'. The London Magazine, 1734.*

AAL *Hindustani.* Red dye produced from Morinda bush and used in fabric printing.

ABA, ABAYAH, ABBA *Masc.* Simple square blanket, usually of wool, occasionally of silk, worn by Moslems in Africa, Persia and Turkey. Square, with openings for neck and arms.

ABACA Filipino name for hemp from banana stalk, used in the making of straw hats and fabrics. In present use.

ABALONE Californian mollusc with shell lined with mother-of-pearl. Used for buttons, beads and dress ornaments.

ABAYA *Fem.* Silk headcovering or scarf worn by working women in Arab countries.

ABBE *Fr. Masc.* Title of respect given to secular clergy. The cape of his cloak falls in three tiers.

ABENET *Masc.* Long sash worn by Jewish High Priest.

ABOLLA ACADEMIC GOWN Long gown with flowing sleeves, usually black, worn by students, fellows and graduates of colleges and universities. Properly accompanied by cap or mortar-board headdress.

The hood, a separate cape-like attachment hanging at the back, indicates the rank or degree of the wearer.

ACCORDIAN PLEATING Form of small ribbed pleating applied to material, allowing garment to stretch with movement. Used in sleeves and frills. Fashionable in skirts, 1920s, and as fashion dictates since then.

ACETATE One of the first man-made fibres produced in the U.S.A. by the Celanese Corporation.

ACRILAN Liquid derivative of natural gas and air used in the making of modern lightweight fabrics.

ACUS Roman hairpin of bone, silver or copper. The Saxons used a similar pin called a "hair needle".

ADELAIDE BOOTS *Fem.* Boots trimmed with fur or fringed around the top edge. Named in honour of Adelaide of Saxe-Coburg and Meiningen whom William IV married in 1818. Worn from about 1830-1860.

ADONIS *Masc.* Long wig of white or grey hair. 18th Cent.

AESTHETIC Term applied to fem. clothes adopted by an influential intellectual group in the 1870s. Characterised by studied simplicity, flowing skirts and neutralized colours. Much satirised in the Press because

1

features of the fashion gave a limp, listless appearance. Until c1882.

1878 - 1882 A.D.

AESTHETIC DRESS   A revival of 14th Cent. costume by a small section of artistic English society. The feminine dress style was long and flowing, with long sleeves puffed at the shoulders. Both male and female apparel aimed at an over-relaxed, intense appearance. The illustration was inspired by a contemporary drawing in Punch *by Du Maurier.*

AGABANEE   Cotton material woven in Syria and embroidered in silk.

AGBADA   *Masc.* West African cape of brilliant colours and designs. Worn over lightweight loose-cut trousers.

AGLET, AIGLET, AIGUILETTE   The metal tag of a lacing. Tagged point hanging from some uniforms. Also previously used from 15th-17th Cent. when replaced by buttons and hooks.

AGRAFE, AGRAFFE   Hook fastening to a ring, used for fastening a garment. Originally used as a clasp or buckle for armour until 18th Cent. Name later applied to jewellry hooks.

AIGRETTE, EGRET   Fine feathers usually used for women's headdresses made from plumes of egrets (white heron) or ospreys.

AILE DE PIGEON   *Masc.* Periwig with top and sides plain and smooth but with one or two horizontal rolls above the ears. 1750-1760.

AINYI   (See BURMA)

ALAMODE   Thin light glossy black silk. 17th Cent.

ALB   Long white vestment, originating from the long tunic of Roman Empire period. Now worn by priests and by some consecrated royal persons.

ALBANIAN   *Masc.* High-crowned hat with up-turned brim decorated by plume. Worn notably by Henry IV of France, 16th Cent.

ALBERT   Prince Albert of Saxe-Coburg-Gotha, 1819-1861. Married Queen Victoria 1840.

ALBERT BOOTS   Boots, laced at side, made of cloth with patent toes. Sometimes with front decoration of small mother-of-pearl buttons. Worn for about thirty years, 1840-1870.

ALBERT CAPE   Driving cape made with seamless back, 1860. Also known as SAC.

ALBERT CLOTH   Double-sided reversible, all-wool material requiring no lining.

ALBERT COLLAR   *Masc.* Separate starch-stiffened collar, fastened by button attached to shirt. 1850s.

ALBERT CRAPE   A superior quality of black silk or crape used for mourning. Made in 1862; later of silk and cotton in 1880.

ALBERT JACKET   *Masc.* Single-breasted short coat with no breast pockets, slightly waisted, 1848.

ALBERT TOP FROCK   *Masc.* Shaped overcoat of heavy material, with a velvet collar, flapped pockets on hips, short waist and long skirts, 1860-1900.

ALBERT WATCH CHAIN   Heavy chain, usually of gold, worn across the front of the waistcoat from one pocket to another opposite. The chain, with a small metal guard rod, passed through a buttonhole; the watch was held on the other end and slipped into the pocket. In common use from 1870s.

ALENCON LACE   Handmade needle point lace named after the small French town where it was made. Characterised by the floral design outlined by a heavy thread upon a fine net. From 17th Cent.

ALEXANDRA JACKET   *Fem.* Jacket fashionable in 1863, named after Princess Alexandra of Denmark, who married Prince Albert Edward in that year. A shaped short day-coat with no centre seam. Small revers and collar. The sleeves had epaulets and cuffs.

ALICULA   *Masc.* Hooded cloak worn by huntsmen and travellers in ancient Roman period. Usually red.

'A' LINE   *Fem.* Triangular silhouette dress style, first inaugurated by Yves St. Laurent, 1958. This was evolved from the Trapeze line and later became the Tent shape.

ALIZARIN, ALIZARINE   A purplish red dye from madder root, in use since 1831. Now produced synthetically.

ALL-IN-ONE   *Fem.* Corselet, a heavily-boned combination garment of corset and brassiere which first appeared in the 1920s. It evolved, in the 1930s, into a lighter one-piece body garment made of two-way stretch elastic "lastex".

ALLOUTIENNE *Fr.* Slubbed strong silk material used for fine formal evening gowns.

ALMAIN COAT *Germ. Masc.* Short tight jacket with flared skirt and long hanging sleeves. Worn over doublet. 1450-1500.

ALMAIN HOSE *Germ. Masc.* Full paned hose with silk-lined gaps. Late 16th Cent.

ALMUCE, AUMUCE *Masc.* Fur or fur-lined hood worn by priests and clergy in severe weather. 13th-15th Cent. Also known as MONKSHOOD.

ALNAGE An ell, or forty-five inches (1.40m), an Early English measurement for cloth.

ALOHA SHIRT *Masc.* Brilliantly-patterned and coloured shirt worn outside trousers. Inspired by comfortable, present century, Hawaiian wear popular with cruising visitors to the islands.

ALPACA Shiny springy textile of silk and of wool from alpaca goat. Invented in 1838 by Sir Titus Salt.

ALPARGATA Lightweight sandal worn in Mediterranean coastal countries. Hemp sole with attached strapping. Also called Espadrilla.

ALPINE HAT *Masc.* Soft felt hat with low round crown and circular depression. 1890s.

ALPINE JACKET *Masc.* Double-breasted jacket with centre back pleat, vertical side pockets. Fastening to the neck. 1876.

ALUTA LAXOR Heavy leather boots worn by the ancient Romans.

'AMAZON' Riding Costume as seen in La Mode de Paris, 1834.
Top hat with loosely attached veiling; coat and voluminous skirt.

AMADIS SLEEVE Feminine style made with tight cuff at the wrist. Fashionable for day wear in the 1830s and again in the 1850s when buttons were added from wrist to elbow. cf. Mousquetaire.

AMALIA *Fem.* Greek national costume. Low-fronted silk dress over fine chemise with embroidered front showing at neck. Over this is worn a tight gold-embroidered waist-length velvet jacket. From 1830.

AMAZON Female warrior of Greek and Asiatic legend. Name passed into European languages to signify horsewoman or one of strong tall build. *Fr. Fem.* Long riding-skirt, mid-19th Cent.

AMAZON CORSAGE *Fem.* High bodice buttoned to throat, with plain small collar and cuffs. 1842.

AMAZON CORSET *Fem.* Corset designed for horsewomen. Elastic lacings. It could be shortened by pulling a hidden cord. 1850s.

AMICE *Masc.* White lined hood of religious orders - until 13th Cent. the priest covered his face with this hood upon mounting the altar. A badge worn on left arm by French canons, in the 16th Cent. A grey fur, possibly squirrel.

AMERICAN INDIAN Originally garments were made from skins, furs, feathers and soft bark. All were skilfully dyed, decorated and embroidered and sometimes beaded. Skins were fringed, tied with throngs. Leggings of deerskin worn by both sexes. Masculine hair or head styles varied according to area. Feminine styles favoured long braided hair occasionally with fringe. Principal garments - head band or headdress consisting of porcupine quills, beads, feathers; trousers; mantle or cloak; moccasins. New England men wore breech-clout of skin; women wore a wrap-round skirt.

AMERICAN SHOULDERS *U.S. Masc.* (Fr. Epaules Americaines). Padding placed under shoulders of coats and jackets to give a 'square' broad appearance. Worn from 1875 to beginning of World War II.

AMERICAN TROUSERS The material of the trousers is gathered into a narrow waistband which has adjustible strap and buckle at the rear, obviating need for braces. 1857 on.

AMISH DRESS *U.S.* Dark or black-coloured clothes worn by the Christian Mennonites or "Plain People". There is no ornamentation and garments are fastened by hooks and eyes.

ANADEM, ANADEME Wreath or chaplet of flowers worn on the head. Late 16th to early 17th Cent.

ANALACE An early civilian dagger.

ANGLESEA HAT *Masc.* Hat with high crown and flat brim, 1830s. Later, in the 1900s, name was given to a curling brim in men's hats.

ANGLETERRE or ENGLISH EDGING Edging made from needlepoint. Loops of braid or cord worked along an edge.

ANILIN, ANILINE Product of indigo, the source of many brilliant dyes, obtainable from coal tar. Colours produced include aniline red, fuchsia, magenta, malachite green, martino yellow, victoria green. (Also mauve).

ANGLO SAXON (12th Century) Both men and women wore super tunics. Married women wore veils over long hair. Men carried swords, often richly decorated.

ANKLE-JACKS *Masc.* Boots worn in 1840s, short and laced up the front. Worn a great deal in poorer working areas of London.

ANORAK Hip-length jacket with hood attached, worn in Arctic regions. The modern anorak is an adaption of the Scandanavian PARKA, and is made of lightweight weather and water resistant cotton or silk and is worn for sports.

APPLIQUE *Fr. - "applied".* Motifs of fabrics-lace and so on - sewn upon other material by hand.

APRON *Of. napperon.* Protection for dress, usually tied at waist by strings, 13th Cent. onwards. Aprons worn by men-artisans, blacksmiths, gardeners and the like often made of leather. Check material was worn by barbers, blue by tradesmen, green by porters and furniture removers from 16th Cent., and in some degree the traditional look is still to be seen. Early use of homespun and linen was made by farm wives and housekeepers. Fine and transparent materials used for decorative aprons by fashionable women from the end of the 16th Cent. to 18th Cent. "Pinny" - name given to a dainty apron of beautiful workmanship pinned over the gowns worn by ladies-in-waiting at Court,

17th and 18th Cents. In 1870, a small black silk apron, sometimes embroidered, and referred to as a "fig-leaf" became fashionable.

AQUERNE Name of squirrel's fur. 1200 A.D.

ARANEOUS LACE Laraneida - araneu spider. A term used in the Middle Ages for embroidery. Later it became descriptive of thin delicate cobweb-like lace which used the lines of a cobweb.

ARGENTAN LACE "Point de France" Needlepoint lace from Alencon, France.

ARISAD *Fem.* Long gown of plaid worn in Scotland.

ARMAZINE, ARMOZINE A 17th Cent. strong, silk-corded material used for waistcoats, still in use for scholastic and clerical robes.

ARMENIAN CLOAK *Masc.* Fashionable cloak made of one piece of cloth with a velvet collar, 1850-1860s.

ARMENIAN MANTLE *Fem.* Loose cloak with lace or gimp trimming in front. 1847-1850.

ARMET Medieval helmet with iron flap to protect back of neck.

APPLIQUE Women from Archangel - 19th Century. Dress in rich materials. Kokochniki-Headdress decorated with jewels and embroidery.

ARMOUR Protective body covering worn in battle, from ancient times to the Renaissance. The Greeks wore a cuirass of leather, covered with metal plates and shoulder plates and greaves. European armour of mail

4

and plate - used from 12th-14th Cents. Complete plate armour - 15th-17th Cents. Decorative armour - after 1600-1700. Sturdy leather body covering such as buff-coat, gauntlets and long protective boots made cimberson metal unnecessary.

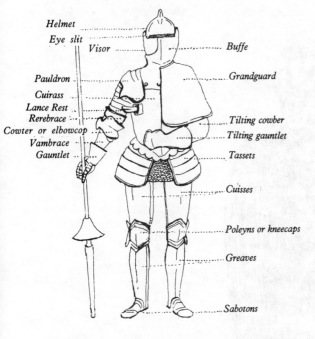

Helmet
Eye slit
Visor
Buffe
Pauldron
Grandguard
Cuirass
Lance Rest
Rerebrace
Cowter or elbowcop
Tilting cowber
Vambrace
Tilting gauntlet
Gauntlet
Tassets
Cuisses
Poleyns or kneecaps
Greaves
Sabotons

ARMOUR as worn for Tournaments, Pageants, Jousting. 16th Century Armour was lined with leather and cloth and worn over doublets and other garments. It was hinged with hooks, screws and straps at the joints. 'Parade' armour was often decorated with designs made by etching and a process known as Damascening, when strands of gold and silver were inlaid into the steel. Embossing, or raising from underneath, was also used.

'How a man schall be armyd at his ese when he schal fighte . . . He schal have noo schirte up on him but a dowbelet of ffustean lyned with satene cutte full of hoolis . . .' 15th Century manuscript.

ARRAS   Town of northern France, famous for tapestries in 14th Cent. and for beautifully tooled leathers. Cloth from English and Scottish wool was also woven here and sent to the East.

ARRAS LACE   Bobbin lace made in Arras.

ART DECO   Fashionable style created by dress designer, Paul Poiret, in early 1900s. Inspired by the Orient and followed his Empire line.

ARTIFICIAL SILK   Produced commercially in the U.S.A. in 1910 and called RAYON. A textile woven from cellulose fibre.

ART NOUVEAU   Decorative style influenced by Pre-Raphaelite floral patterns and their artists of 1890.

ARTOIS   *Masc.* Long cloth coat with three or four short capes, made fashionable by Comte d'Artois, later Charles X of France, 1824-1830. The style lasted for a long time, in use especially as a coachman's box coat.

ARTOIS BUCKLE   Very large shoe buckle worn by fashinable men between 1775 and 1788.

ASCOT   *Masc.* Double knot cravat with wide square ends folded over, held in place with a pin. *Fem.* Worn as a stock or neckcloth with riding-habits. First used in 1850s.

ASCOT TIE   *Masc.* Plain form of made-up scarf as a cravat, from 1876 onwards. The "ASCOT PUFF" with wide puffed centre also appeared. Some were self-tied, some ready-made of plain and patterned silk.

ASTRAKAN   Close curled wool from skin of lambs, from Astrakan, Russia. Used for collars, coats and hats.

ASWASH   *Masc.* Garment worn draped diagonally across the body instead of hanging down. Cloaks were worn in this way in 17th Cent.

ATEF   High rounded cone-like shape of the crown of the Kings of Egypt, 3000 B.C. Made of felt and decorated with the Royal Asp or Uraeus.

ATTABY   Simple silk textile, later colled TABBY. 14th Cent.

ATTIFET   *Fem.* Heart-shaped wire bonnet and coiffure, with a point over the centre of the forehead. Worn in white by Mary, Queen of Scots, and in black by Catherine de Medici, 1550s. (See BARBETTE).

ATTIRE   Headdress of gems and gold or silver from 15th Cent. onwards. Later shortened to "TIRE". In present use as "TIARA". (See TIARA).

AUMONIERE, ALMONER   Small pouch or purse suspended from girdle and worn by medieval nobility, presumably for giving of alms. *O.E.* - oelmysse; *M.E.* - aumoner; *Fr.* - aumone - alms.

AUNE   Old measure for fabric, forty-five inches wide, used in France.

AUSTRIAN KNOTS   Heavy silk braid ornamentation, usually black, inspired by Austrian military dress. Imitated by European armies in the 19th Cent.

AZO   Dye stuffs which dye cotton in one process, discovered by Greiss, a brewer's chemist.

AZUR   *Masc.* Hungarian great-coat made of felt or sheepskin, with wool turned to the inside. With huge sleeves which are used to carry personal belongings. The wide lapels are extended to form a collar at the back. Elaborately decorated on the outside. Contemporary.

ART NOUVEAU JEWELLERY worn by Sarah Bernhardt. Late 19th Century.

ARMENIAN CLOAK

Fashionable 1850s-1860s.
With velvet collar and side seams.

BLOOMERS 1852

BABET BONNET *Fem.* Tulle headdress in bonnet style for evening wear, to cover back of head and ears. Decorated with small roses and lace. 1838-1839.

BABET CAP *Fem.* Daytime version of bonnet. Usually of muslin with ribbon trimming. Worn indoors. 1836-1840.

BABICHE Name denoting leather thong or thin strap, from the Algonquinian Indian tribes around the Ottawa River, Canada.

BABOUCHE Heel-less, richly embroidered slipper from Arabia.

BABY STUART CAP 1) *Fem.* Small cap resembling a baby's bonnet, worn over a coiffure with shoulder-length side curls. After 1600. 2) Children's lace cap with decorative edging. Example - painting by Van Dyck. 1634.

BACHLICK, BACKLIK, BACHELIK *Fem.* Short cape or fichu with tasselled hood. A revived style, worn over daydress. 1868. Also in France and the Balkans, since 1900.

BACINET, BASCINET, BASINET *Masc.* Light-weight helmet with conical point, usually with mail curtain (aventail) laced to its lower edge, protecting throat and neck. 14th Cent. By 15th Cent. became more rounded, with plate gorget. Until 16th Cent. Worn when fighting on foot.

BACKSTERS Leather boots on wooden platforms, worn by dyke-makers, for walking over soft mud. Worn in East Anglia. Also known as MERSEA PATTENS. From 16th Cent. Still in use.

BADGE Distinctive mark, crest, device or arms displayed and employed by nobility, especially during Middle Ages.

BADGER 1) Hawker, dealer, huckster, in corn, butter, eggs, fish. From 16th Cent. *'Certain persons upon Humber side who . . . buy great quantities of corn, two of whom were authorised badgers.'* - State Papers, 1565. 2) Heavily furred mammal. Its durable, coarse hair used for collars, cuffs, trimming. Black mixed with grey, white or fawn.

BADINE *Fem. Fr. - switch, playful.* Fashionable stick. An adaptation of shepherdess's crook. 18th Cent.

BAFT Coarse cotton fabric, undyed or red and blue. 16th Cent.

7

BAG (See AUMONIERE, MUSETTE, RETICULE).

BAG BODICE *Fem.* Day-blouse with pouched front falling low over waistband. 1883.

BAG BONNET *Fem.* Day-bonnet with loosely-gathered crown. 1800-1810.

BAG HOLLAND Fine quality linen used for shirt-making. 17th Cent.

BAGGING SHOE Countryman's footwear, consisting of strong shoe, with separate knee-high legging of leather, cloth or wool, tied at top and bottom of shin. Late 16th and 17th Cents.

BAGNOLETTE *Fem.* Short cape with hood. Early 18th Cent.

BAGPIPE SLEEVES *Masc. and Fem.* Full hanging sleeves gathered into cuff. Distinctive feature of the HOUPPELANDE gown of the 15th Cent.

BAGS *Masc.* Casual term for trousers. 19th and 20th Cents.

BAGWIG *Masc.* A powdered wig with queue or tail tied in a black silk bag having a drawstring at back of neck, which was concealed with stiff, black bow. Rows of rolled curls, called 'pigeon's wings', were sometimes added above the ears. Also used to cover growing hair. 1720-1790.

BAHUT *Masc. Fem.* Domino or masquerade dress. 18th Cent.

BAIGNEUSE *Masc. and fem. Fr.* Originally cap for protecting hair when bathing. Late 18th Cent. *(cf. Fr. Fem. - Dormeuse - for sleeping).*

BAINBERG *Ger. Bein bergen* - shinguards. Greaves used for protection. Examples - effigies in Temple Church, London, including Gilbert Mareschal, Earl of Pembroke, died 1241. The use of these greaves led to adoption of plate armour. (See GREAVES).

BAISHAN *Masc.* Chinese sleeveless coat. 20th Cent.

BAIZE Thick woollen cloth, first used for servants' clothing. Made at Colchester in 16th Cent., but originally from Spain. Also BAYS or BAISE, a thin serge introduced by Walloon refugees, 1561.

BAJU *Masc.* Loose white cotton jacket usually with short sleeves and breast pocket. Worn with cotton breeches, Malaysia. 20th Cent.

BAKELITE Trade name of synthetic hard resin resembling hard rubber, invented by L. H. Baekeland (1863-1944). Used for costume accessories such as buckles, buttons, pendants.

BAKU Fine straw made from leaf stalks of talipont palm from Malabar and Ceylon. Used in making fine quality hats.

BAL, BICYCLE BAL *Fem.* Shortened term for BALMORAL, with reference to style of ankle shoe or boot, worn for bicycling. Low-heeled and with lacing from toecap to top of footwear.

BALACLAVA *Masc.* Thick woollen headpiece with neck-cuff, knitted for serving men in World Wars I and II. The style has been generally adopted for wearing in severe weather and for some sports. Named after Balaklava, on the Crimean Coast, the scene of the Charge of the Light Brigade, 1854.

BALAGNIE *Masc. Fr.* Fashionable cape with deep collar, usually of arm-length. It was worn draped over one shoulder and tied under collar with cords, during reign of Louis XIII, King of France, 1610-1643.

BALANDRANA *Masc.* Voluminous coat or mantle worn for travelling. From 12th Cent. *Masc. or Fem.* A protective cloak with hood, 16th-17th Cent.

BALAYEUSE *Fem.* Stiff muslin hem frilling, sewn to protect the underside of fashionably trailing long skirts worn in 1870s.

BALBRIGGAN Unbleached cotton fabric with fleecy back. First made in Balbriggan, Ireland. When dyed in greys and browns, used for masculine underwear, hosiery, sweaters. Garments of the material were known as BALBRIGGANS.

BALDEKIN, BANDEKIN Rich silken fabric resembling brocade, woven with addition of gold thread. Medieval.

BALDRIC, BALDRICK, BANDRIKE, BAUDRY *Masc.* Plain or ornamental belt worn diagonally across body from shoulder to waist, for suspending horn, dagger or sword. Reputedly named after Baldrick, Chancellor of William the Conqueror, who wore one of 'uncommon magnificence'. A fashion which continued, with variety such as suspended bells, pendants, rings, until the reign of Henry VII, 1485-1509. Re-appeared in English Restoration period, 1660. Seen also in modern ceremonial and service dress. Also BALTEUS, BANDOLEER.

BALEEN Horny substance from the jaw of a whale. Used in armour. Also as strips for stiffening garments, from 16th Cent.

BALERNOS Soft, silky fabric of mohair. 1874.

BALINE Coarse woollen or cotton fabric used for packing. When made of jute or hemp, used for stiffening in modern feminine handbags.

BALISTA Abbreviation of ARCUBALISTA - Crossbow whose arrows were 'a cloth yard long'. Also PRODDS.

BALKAN BLOUSE *Masc.* Long waisted tunic-blouse gathered into a hip-band, with wide full sleeves ending in tight wrist cuffs. *Fem.* Fashion evolved after Balkan War, 1913 and persisted for decades. Materials popular - fine voile, cambric or lawn, and often embroidered with red, blue and black cross-stitch.

BALLERINA *Fem.* 1) Traditional dress with tight bodice and short full skirt, called tutu, made of layers of tulle or gauze standing away from the body. Worn by ballet dancers usually with tights and block-toed shoes, 19th-20th Cent. 2) *Fem.* Evening dress, not long, popular in years following World War II. Elegant and full in skirt, worn when men wore business suits, not full formal attire. A fashion originated by American couturiere, Valentina.

BALLET SLIPPERS Low flat shoes of cotton or

silk, with well boxed toes for support in toe-dancing. Laced, up ankles and legs, with ribbon ties.

BALLIBUNTL, BALIBUNTAL Hat worn with straw of light-weight palm leaf stems from Luzon, Philippine Is.

BALLOON HAT *Fem.* Very large hat, with ballooned full crown of gauze, supported by light wire foundation. Wide brimmed, with ribbon or wide band. Created and fashionable as result of notoriety of Lunardi and his balloon. 1780s.

BALLOON SLEEVE *Fem.* Fashionable sleeve with full rounded and lined puff from shoulder to elbow; the forearm fitted close from elbow to wrist. 1890s.

BALL-ROOM NECKCLOTH *Masc.* White starched neckcloth with ends crossing in broad folds in front, and secured to braces. Held in place with brilliant pin or brooch at neck, 1830s. Predecessor of formal evening neck wear.

BALMACAAN *Masc.* Comfortable, loose flaring coat with neat standing collar and slashed pockets. Usually just below knee length. Of Scottish origin. 1850.

BALMAIN, PIERRE (See COUTURE)

BALMORAL The Royal Castle of Queen Victoria and Prince Albert in Scotland, after which many new clothes and ideas were named. 1853.

BALMORAL BOOT *Masc. and Fem.* Short laced boot with closed throat, worn with country or walking dress. 1860s.

BALMORAL CLOAK *Fem.* Short hooded cloak; sleeveless. 1852.

BALMORAL JACKET *Fem.* Daytime jacket with pointed fronts resembling a waistcoat. Buttoned to throat. 1867. Later tailored version, belted and cuffed. 1870.

BALMORAL MANTLE *Fem.* Outdoor cape of cashmere, cloth or velvet. Similar to Inverness. 1866.

BALMORAL PETTICOAT *Fem.* Woollen, red and black striped underskirt. Worn under a walking dress. 1860-1880.

BALTEUS Form of baldric worn in ancient Rome. (See BALDRICK).

BALZO *Fem.* Italian turban or large round toque worn to conceal hair. Based on padded circle of leather or metal. 15th and 16th Cents.

BAMBINO HAT *Fem.* Off-the-face hat. Brim in halo style. Named after Italian round plaques of Christ Child by Lucia de la Robbia. Fashionable 1930s. Also called HALO HATS.

BAMS Protective leather gaiters worn by sailors and quay workers. 19th Cent.

BAND Collar of white linen or cambric surrounding the neck, sometimes stiffened with starch. If allowed to fall upon shoulders, called 'falling band', becoming 'turned-down collar.' An upstanding collar, without a turn-over, was called a 'standing band'. 16th and 17th Cents. Still worn by some clergy. (See BAND-STRINGS)

BANDANA, BANDANNA Silk and later cotton square or handkerchief, imported from India. Named from Hindu 'bandhnu' - dyeing; brilliant coloured spots on dark ground. Used in 18th Cent. for neckclothes and for snuff handkerchiefs.

BANDBOX Round lightweight box made originally for holding bands and collars in immaculate condition. 16th Cent.

BANDEROLLE Small flag or streamer placed near the head of a lance.

BANDITTI Small arrangement of feathers for decoration on feminine bonnet; early 19th Cent.

BANDLE Old word used in Scotland and England for cloth measurement two feet wide. Also Irish linen or homespun of same width.

BANDOLEER, BANDOLIER Woven fabric webbing or belting used for military bands and sportswear. (See BALDRICK)

BANDORE AND PEAK *Fem.* Widow's headdress. A black bonnet which curved to point over forehead and was completed by flowing black veil at the back. Early 18th Cent.

BANDSTRINGS Laces, cords or ribbons used to fasten bands around the neck, often as hanging bow or tassels. Shown in illustrations of 'Cries of London', in time of Charles II, as being sold. Some woven to resemble backbone of snake and were called 'snake-bone bande stringes'. 17th Cent.

BANGKOK Lightweight, fine straw used for making hats, so named from the vicinity of Bangkok.

BANGS Straight cut fringe of hair over forehead, constantly appearing throughout history for men and women.

BAN LON Name used as trademark for 20th Cent. crimped machine-knit yarn.

BANNER Standard or ensign, held aloft at the head of an army, decorated by the arms of that army; or cloth flag used as standard of emperor, king, lord or knight.

BANNOCKBURN A tweed cloth used for suiting and coats made in Bannockburn, Scotland.

BANYAN, BANIAN *Masc.* Indian inspired loose-skirted coat fastened in front. Became very fashionable indoors and even out of doors in 1780s. In early 18th Cent. style was adopted as a dressing-gown. Often made in high quality materials.

BARATHEA 1) Medieval material with weave resembling chain armour, also called ARMURE. 2) Twilled worsted in silk or wool. From 1840s.

BARBE *Fem.* A covering of white linen surrounding the face, encircling the chin and falling in fine pleats halfway to the waist. Worn by religious women and widows, 14th - 16th Cents. Also term for ribbon or lace millinery adornment worn in 18th and 19th Cents.

BARBETTE *Fem.* French term for wimple and band worn under the chin, usually covered by a fillet. 12th -14th Cents.

BARBETTE and FILLET over FRET. 13th Century Details from Brass, Beddington Church, Surrey, showing woman wearing fur-lined mantle and head-covering of Barbette. The child has a simple veil and plain cloak. 15th Century.

BARBUTE Helmet of the 14th Cent. of Italian origin with large cheek pieces. Originally had high pointed crown but later was rounded.

BARCELONA Soft twilled Spanish handkerchief used as a neckscarf. Early 18th Cent.

BAREGE *Fr.* Silky gauze made originally in Baregas, France. Semi-transparent with open mesh. 1819.

BARMCLOTH Barme cloth, barmhatre. *O.E. barmlap.* An apron.

BARMFELL, BARMSKIN Leather apron worn by workmen from 14th Cent.

BARMILLION Fustian material in Manchester. 17th Cent.

BAROQUE Extravagant stylistic tendencies which lasted throughout the 17th Cent. Based on Classical ideals originating in Italy. The period is characterised by rich decorative effects and much use of rounded contours. Richly embossed silver, colourful exuberant embroideries, dramatic jewellery and pearls are manifest in the costume and paintings of this style and time.

BAROUCHE COAT *Fem.* Three-quarter length fitted outdoor coat styled with full sleeves, girdle and front fastening, worn when riding in a barouche - a four-wheeled carriage with collapsible half-head. In fashion the early part of the 19th Cent.

BARRACAN, BARRAGAN *Masc.* Cloth made in British Isles from goat or camel hair. Used for cloaks in Asiatic countries.

BARRAS Dutch linen imported and used for neckcloths in 17th and 18th Cents.

BARREL HOSE *Masc.* Very full breeches, 16th Cent. Gradually controlled, by pleating or gathers, from waist to lower part.

BARREL SNAPS Small barrel-shaped metal fastenings in gilt for cloaks and pelisses.

BARRET *Masc. and Fem.* Flat headgear of soft material, round or square, 15th and 16th Cents. Sometimes decorated with embroidery and feathers.

BARETINO Italian word for bonnet. Long stocking cap of knitted wool. A style much copied and worn in many ways.

BARRETTE *Fem.* Long bar-shaped clip or brooch. Much used in late Victorian period for holding hair above the nape of the neck.

BARROW Infant's wrapper of flannel, with turned-up closure over feet, 19th Cent. Modern versions in colours and as fashion dictates.

BASE COAT *Masc.* Jerkin with pleated skirt to just above knees. Short sleeves and square neck. Worn under gown. 1490-1540.

BASELARD Ornamental dagger, worn centrally on the girdle by gentlemen and pretenders to gentility, 15th Cent.

BASES *Masc.* Pleated or circular skirts of coats worn by knights on horseback. Very late 15th and early 16th Cents. When worn with armour, were separate garments. Term is also applied to hose. 1607. Made of padded segments.

BASINET, BACINET (See BACINET)

BASQUE *Fem.* Short skirt-like band or continuation of upper bodice of garment. Fashionable, 1870s.

BASQUE BELT *Masc.* Corset worn to give the required fashionable small waist. Mid-19th Cent.

BASQUE BERET Small round headgear of the Basques. *Fr.* Became extremely fashionable everywhere in the 1920s. Still worn today.

BASQUE-HABIT *Fem.* A bodice with square-cut basques. 1860s.

BASQUE WAISTBAND *Fem.* Bodice with five van-dyked tabs on waistband. Attractive styling for afternoon dress. 1867.

BASQUIN BODY *Fem.* Day-bodice cut to include basque in one piece with the upper portion. 1850s.

BASQUINE 1) *Masc.* Fitted padded doublet fastening down centre front. 2) *Fem.* Fitted hip-length garment worn with full petticoat, 17th Cent. A pad tied around the waist above the petticoat to produce the fashionable elliptical appearance. (See paintings of Royal princesses, Valasquez, 1656). These garments, masculine and feminine, were worn with tightly laced corsets. 3) *Fem.* Coat with fringed basques, a bertha collar and pagoda sleeves. 1857. The name also given to a new styled outdoor jacket, 1860. (See VASQUINE).

BAST HAT Hat made of plaited bass or bast, which is the pliable inner bark of lime. Mentioned in 17th Cent.

BASTON A truncheon or small club used in the tournament instead of the mace.

BATHING DRESS 1) *Masc.* Voluminous flannel gowns were worn at public bathing places such as Bath, 18th and 19th Cents. After rail travel became available and seaside bathing popular, black and grey sleeveless suits reaching below the knee were worn. Striped knee-length bathing suits appeared in the early 20th Cent. Later, when competitive sports were encouraged, less restrictive styling was allowed and brief shorts have since been universally accepted. 2) *Fem.* Before mid-19th Cent., loose flannel gown with sleeves was worn. After this, a one-piece garment of dark blue or brown came into vogue and a knee-length skirt was added. By 1880 a combination style of dress of stockinette, sometimes decorated with frills, was worn with black stockings. After 1918 a clinging knitted one-piece more abbreviated costume became fashionable. In the 1930s a two-piece suit of top and shorts, later called a 'bikini', evolved.

BATIK Method of dyeing designs on fabric by use of wax repellent. From Java. The attractive, oriental, bright coloured silks are much admired in the Western World.

BATISTE A fine lightweight material of linen or cotton resembling cambric. Named after the inventor, Baptiste Cambrai, a French weaver of the 13th Cent.

BATTENBURG JACKET *Fem.* Outdoor short jacket. 1880s.

BATTLEDRESS JACKET Usually masculine. Comfortable waist-length single-breasted woollen bloused jacket gathered into waistbelt of same material. Used by service men and women in World War II. Style adapted later for general and sports wear by men and women.

BATTS Heavy shoes of black leather laced in front, with tongue over which leather straps were buckled. Medium heel. Worn in British Isles by country and working folk; also shipped to American colonies. Worn with home-knitted stockings. 17th Cent.

BATWAT *Masc.* Small padded cap worn by knights of the Middle Ages to relieve pressure of metal helmet.

BAUDEKYN, BAUDEQUIN Sumptuous tissue of silk and gold thread originally made in Baldeck or Babylon and later in Cypress and Palermo. Brought back by the Crusaders. Henry III is supposed to have been the first English monarch to use the 'cloth of Baudekin for his vesture'. (Strutt - *Dress and Habits*). Used by European royalty for robes and throne drapery, 12th - 16th Cents.

BAUDELAIRE Small knife carried in the girdle or on the person.

BAUSON SKIN Skin of a badger, so named 16th Cent.

BAUTTA *Ita.* Black hooded cloak.

BAVARIAN DRESS *Fem.* 1) Dress with rows of bands decorating the front from top to bottom. 2) Pelisse. Robe adorned in front with two descending lines of trimming from shoulder to hem. Both these garments were in vogue during the Napoleonic wars.

BAVOLET *Fem. Fr.* Headdress of peasants and commoners. A piece of white linen, about two metres long and half a metre wide, with fringed ends. This was folded and pinned to the cap. The back ruffle or curtain on any bonnet was called a bavolet, 16th Cent. The fashion was revived, 19th Cent. (See FANCHON).

BAVARETTE Child's bib. Early 17th Cent.

BAYADERE Fabrics and ribbons, silk and velvet laid flat to trim garments with horizontal stripes. Much worn 1850s.

BAYEUX LACE (See BLACK LACE)

BAYONET Dagger affixed to the end of a gun. Takes its name from Bayonne in Spain where they were first made. Introduced during the time of Charles II and used in the reign of William - 17th Cent.

BAYS (BAIZE) (see BAIZE)

BAZNA SASH *Fem.* Length of silk worn round waist of Algerian women.

BEADLE In England, ceremonial officer of church, college, etc., *M.E. - bedel; Fr. - bedel.*

BEADLE   Costume worn by
Town's Beadle,
Stratford on Avon.

BEANIE, BEANY *Fem.* Very small flat beret-type hat, fashionable in United States at intervals from the 1930s.

BEARD The manner of wearing the masculine beard has changed from epoch to epoch. The shape or lack of a beard expresses fundamental attitudes or beliefs of a period. Razors have been found among prehistoric remains and shaving was a convention among the Romans. After A.D. 117, the beard began to re-appear in spite of Greek and Roman influence. In Eastern Europe it was regarded as a sign of saintliness. In the Middle Ages it was merely clipped to suit current fashions. Later, in France at the Court of Louis XIV, beards became out of keeping with luxuriant wigs, but in the 16th Cent. Spanish influence introduced many styles of beard. Rulers and monarchs often set the fashion.

Some outstanding styles:

FRASE: Earliest trimmed beard, introduced by Semites into Babylon, sideburns, but no moustache.

CONVENTIONAL RENAISSANCE: Short fringe over forehead and short clipped beard.

SPADE BEARD: Broad, with curved sides to point below. Of martial appearance. Late 16th Cent.

MARQUISETTO, CADIZ, ROUND: Late 16th Cent.

POINTED - STILETTO, 1621: PEAK 1623: French version of GOAT BEARD - HENRI QUATRE, always worn with moustache, 17th Cent. PICK-A-DEVANT, 1688.

HAMMER or ROMAN: Straight tuft under lower lip and horizontal moustache, 1618-1650.

SIDE WHISKERS: originated in England at the end of 18th Cent.

FAVORIS: Long sideburns around the cheeks. Very popular, 1800 -1850.

CATHEDRAL BEARD: Broad, square-cut, worn by churchmen and learned persons. 19th Cent.

IMPERIAL: A pointed tuft with small moustache, as worn by Napoleon III, 19th Cent. Also KNEBELBART.

DUNDREARY WHISKERS: Full, with shaven chin. 19th Cent.

FRANZ-JOSEF: Thick side whiskers without beard or moustache. European. 19th Cent.

Pointed beards were worn by followers of Garibaldi and shaggy 'existentialist' beards by Fidel Castro's men. 20th Cent.

ENGLISH MOUSTACHE: Close-clipped style worn by film stars - Clark Gable, Menjou and others. 1930s.

BEARER *Masc.* Stiffening used for boot hose tops. Mid-17th Cent. *Fem.* Padded rolls placed under skirt, either to give width or heighten skirt, as fashion dictated. End of 17th Cent.

BEARSKIN PANTS *Masc.* White bearskin fur pants worn by the men of Thule, N.W. Greenland, now a U.S. strategic base. (*Note:* Thule was the name given by Greeks and Romans to an island (Iceland, Norway, Shetlands) in the then-known world.)

BEAR'S PAW *Masc.* Padded footwear. 16th Cent. (See SOLLERET)

BEATLE HAIRCUT *Masc.* Hair style with longer than ear-depth coiffure, made famous by the four young British entertainers in the 1960s. Its popularity led to longer hair-dressing for most men after the more military short style worn from the time of the First World War, 1914.

BEAU Term used to describe a gentleman most particular and fastidious as to dress. More distinguished than a fop. Beau Brummel, 1778-1840; Beau Fielding, 1712; Beau Nash, 1674-1761.

BEAU CATCHER *Fem.* Curl dressed in the centre of a women's forehead, fashionable 18th Cent.

BEAUDOY Worsted material for stockings. 18th Cent.

BEAUTY PATCHES (See PATCHES)

BEAVER, BEVOR Face-guard of a helmet, consisting of several wide bars attached to projecting umbril or peak, allowing it to be drawn up for protection. The term is used for the helmet itself, e.g. Shakespeare - Henry IV, Part 1, Act IV, Sc. 2; in Richard III; in Hamlet, Act 1, Sc. 2; and in Henry IV, Part 2, Act IV, Sc. 1.

BEAVER Rich brown fur found in U.S.A., Canada, Russia and Siberia. Imitations are made from Australian opossum and coney rabbit. Sheared beaver is used for trimmings.

BEAVER CLOTH Sheared thick heavy woollen material of fine quality originally made in England. Eminently suitable for uniforms, overcoats and some hats.

BEAVER HAT *Masc. and Fem.* In 14th Cent. hats were made of beaver skin, but with the production of the fine felted beaver wool, the beaver hat became a stylish item of dress. In 16th Cent. it was called a CASTOR and cost £3 or £4. (See *Portrait of a Laughing Cavalier* by Frans Hal). A demi-castor was inferior, as it was often made partly of coney. In 19th Cent. the prepared beaver nap was placed over a strong felt base.

BECK Beak-shaped central projection from a hood worn at the turn of the 16th Cent. It hung like a beak over the forehead. It was a mourning accessory to the English hood, 1500-1525.

BEEFEATER'S HAT *Masc.* Black beaver hat trimmed with black, white and red ribbon around the crown. 16th Cent. Worn by the Yeomen of the Guard and Warders of the Tower of London.

BEEHIVE COIFFURE *Fem.* Hairstyle piled very high over backcombed base. 1950s.

BEEHIVE HAT, BEEHIVE BONNET *Fem.* Straw bonnet or hat with tall rounded crown, hive-shaped and with a small narrow brim, sometimes tied with ribbon under the chin. 1780-1820.

BEGUIN *Fem.* Three-piece, close-fitting head covering, 12th Cent. Later worn by the Beguines, a sisterhood of the Netherlands. It was also worn by clergy and under nobles' crowns; when under a helmet it was made of leather. Worn by the laity, it was made of fine or coarse linen depending on the status of the wearer. Red felt or velvet material replaced the linen coif, 15th Cent. Worn under a wig in the 18th Cent. and still retained under the wig of a British barrister in the 19th Cent. (See also BIGGIN, BIGGON; also BONET).

BELCHER *Masc.* Neckerchief of blue with large white spots, each dotted with a dark blue spot - named after a famous pugilist of the early 18th Cent.

BELETTE A jewel or ornament. 1300-1600.

BELL BOTTOMS Flaring trousers worn by seamen who manned sailing ships, allowing for vigorous movement required aboard such vessels.

BELL BOY'S CAP Stiffened small round cap of colour, matching buttoned livery of young hotel worker or bell boy. (See also PAGE BOY)

BELL HOOP *Fem.* Under-petticoat formed into bell shape by whalebone hoops. 1710-1780.

BELLOWS POCKET *Masc.* Patch pocket for sports jacket with inward pleated folds, capable of expanding to give added space. A buttoned flap keeps the pocket closed. Usual in Norfolk jackets from 1890.

BELLS *Masc. Fem.* Small bells were fashionable as decoration on dagged edges in 14th and 15th Cent.; also suspended from girdles, belts and around the neck (especially in Germany).

BELT *Masc. Fem.* Band made to encircle waist or hips.

BENDS Ribbons or bandages for the head, in imitation or instead of circles of gold. Known from 1000 A.D., and termed 'Bindae' by the Normans. A fillet or band worn on the head or hat. To the end of the 15th Cent.

BENDIGO *Masc.* Fur cap of poor grade skin, worn for warmth by the poor. 19th Cent.

BENGAL Thin mixed silk hair and cotton fabric, for feminine wear. Very popular in stripes. 17th Cent.

BENGALINE Light mohair fabric, sometimes brocaded with small flowers, 1869. Originally from Bengal, India.

BENJY *Masc.* Slang term for waistcoat, possibly inspired by decorative apparel worn by Benjamin Disraeli. 19th Cent.

BENOITON CHAINS *Fem.* Silver or gold chains of jet or metal, worn suspended from the head over chignon towards the waist. Popularised from the play *La Famille Benoiton* by Sardou. 1866.

BENTS Pieces of whale bone or stiff rushes, used to enlarge farthingales. Late 16th Cent.

BERET Early simple form of headgear made of shrunk round piece of wool felt, which reached Europe via Basque Country, from early Greek traders.
Fem. Large flat brimless hat-style with extensive adornment, often made of velvet and worn with evening dress. Early 19th Cent.
Masc. Service military headdress; similar style worn by men and women with sports and holiday clothes. 20th Cent.

BERET SLEEVES *Fem.* Short shoulder sleeve of evening dress cut to imitate shape of the fashionable beret headdress of early 19th Cent. It was stiffened by muslin to retain the large flat look. 1829.

BERGERE HAT *Fr. - shepherdess. Fem.* Large brimmed straw hat with tiny flat crown, 18th Cent. Style renewed, and fashionable again, in 1860.

BERLIN GLOVES Knitted plain strong cotton gloves, worn by lower Middle Classes. 1830 to early 20th Cent.

BERLIN or GERMAN WOOL Yarn prepared for embroidery, made from wool of merino sheep in Saxony. Usually dyed in very bright strong colours. 'Berlin work' was a popular handicraft in the latter part of the 19th Cent.

BERMUDA SHORTS *Fem.* Knee-length pants worn for sports, etc., from 1930s. Made of drill or suitable weight cotton material.

BERNHARDT MANTLE *Fr.* An out-of-door or short cape named after that worn by the famous French actress; loose-falling front, high turned down collar, shaped back and slung sleeves. 1886. (See SLING SLEEVE)

BERSAGLIERE *Ital. Bersaglio - mark, target. Masc.* Black felt brimmed hat with chinstrap, decorated with cock feathers at the side. Worn by Italian riflemen.

BERTHA *Fem.* Deep cape-like collar, usually of lace, which resembles the palatine fashion introduced into France in 1671 by the second wife of the Duc d'Orleans. A style reviving interest upon shoulder and neck adornment was introduced in 1839, sometimes encircling the then fashionable low decolletage. Term is still used for deep falling collar to low-necked dress. (See also PALATINE, PELERINE)

BERTIN, ROSE Dressmaker to Queen Marie Antoinette. The first couturiere of standing in France. She maintained an establishment for English clients in London. Late 18th Cent. (See COUTURE)

BESAGUE Horn-like staff or club used by knights until the end of the 14th Cent.

BESPOKE TAILORING Term used for individually made-to-measure clothes by high class tailors.

BESSHE, BISE, BISSHE Fur of small animal, as squirrel. 13th Cent.

BETEN Medieval term for embroidery work on garments.

BETHLEHEM HEADDRESS worn by Moslem women. A Tarboosh with coins and chain. Married women wear white veils over cap.

13

KHURKEH *Bethlehem gown,
with bolero and veiled Tarboosh
and a folded silk sash at the waist.*

BETSIE, BETSY or CHERUSSE Collar fashion originating in England in the 16th Cent., named for Elizabeth I. Consisted of small ruff with several rows of fluted lace. Leroy, the famous dressmaker to the Empress Josephine, used the style in France in 1819. (See CHERUSSE)

BEVOR (See BEAVER)

BEWDLEY CAP (See MONMOUTH CAP)

BIAS, BYESSE Term for line running diagonally across the warp and weft of woven material. Material cut 'on the cross' was used to ensure a good fit for leg garments and close body-fitting garments. Since 15th Cent.

BIAS BINDING Binding material cut in strips may be purchased to apply to curved edges and lingerie wear. 20th Cent.

BIB Piece of material placed below and fastened around the neck. Upper part of apron, above the waist.

BIB-CRAVAT *Masc.* Bib-like cravat, often edged with lace. Late 17th Cent.

BIBI BONNET *Fem.* Headgear in bonnet shape, with brim at the side projecting upwards and forwards. Also known as ENGLISH COTTAGE BONNET. Early 19th Cent.

BICE Blue or green pigments made from hydrocarbonate of copper. Term in use since reign of Arthur.

BICORNE *Masc.* Hat which was a simplified two-sided shape, supplanting the three-cornered hat in the 1790s. Usually worn with peaks pointing forwards and back or carried under the arm. Early 19th Cent. (See CHAPEAU BRAS)

BICYCLES Two-wheeled vehicle built from the late 1870s, the use of which influenced the styling of more comfortable dress for men and women.

BICYCLE BAL Leather or canvas laced ankle boot made for cycling. The term 'bal' was short for 'Bal-moral', the castle built for Queen Victoria in Scotland. (See BALMORAL BOOT)

BIEDERMEIER *Ger. Bieder - trusty, honest. Meier - farmer, bailiff.* Name given to period of interior decoration, dress and furniture in Germany, 1815-1850. The style emerged gradually as standards of craftsmanship were lowered by use of mechanical means. Consumers were complacent and content with imitations of quality goods. Fashion became independent of social status, although the influence of the Second Empire in France and the tailors of quality in London set certain fashion trends suitable for regional character and taste. This period, which coincided with the literary movement - the Romantic Revival, was characterised by certain fashions.

Masc. Black, blue or brown frockcoat; elaborately knotted cravats; short fanciful waistcoats. Faces - clean-shaven until 1830s.

Fem. High collars, large sleeves, small waists, cone-shaped skirts which reached maximum circumference about 1835; pantalettes, low-heeled shoes, cashmere shawls. Hairstyles included plaits, side-curls and ringlets until 1840. The name of BEIDERMEIER conveyed the image of a sober upright person who was, however, lacking in polish.

BIETTA *sp.* Bright scarlet cloth used for uniforms Brought to America and much admired by the Indians, who traded or fought to obtain it.

BIFID BEARD *Masc.* Saxon beard parted in the centre.

BIGGEN, BIGGIN, BIGGON As BEGUIN; term used in Tudor times.

BIGOUDEN *Fr. Fem.* Mobcap, vertical mobcap of Port l'Abbe.

BIKINI *Fem.* Two-piece abbreviated bathing dress. It appeared in the 20th Cent. in 1947, but Sicilian and Roman mosaics of 406 A.D. show ladies wearing identical garments.

BILBOQUETS Small rollers of pipe cleaners, heated and used for winding hair of wigs. 17th and 18th Cents.

BILLES, BILLS Long metal spear-like weapons, used by infantry until the pike came into use. They were carried by watchmen in the 16th and 17th Cents.

BILLIMENT, BILIMENT, BILLMENT, ABILLE-MENT, HABILLEMENT *Fem.* Delicate decorated border to 16th Cent. headdress or hood. Usually of jewels, with beads worked with gold thread and lace.

BILLICOCK, BILLYCOCK *Masc.* Hard felt hat with low crown and curving brim, worn and made popular by Coke, Earl of Leicester, of Holkam in Norfolk. 1754-1842.

BIRDSEYE Small regular pattern with central dot, resembling a bird's eye, used in fine lightweight materials.

BIRD FEATHERS Use initiated from ceremonial capes of New Zealand in 1835-1911. Worn on masculine ceremonial hats; also on feminine capes, boas, hats and bonnets. Mid-Victorian to date, whenever fashionable.

BIRETTA   Square, cap-like headcovering, often furnished with a pom-pom, worn by the priesthood from about the 15th Cent. Cardinals - red; bishops - purple; priests - black; abbots and canons - white.

BIRRUS, BYRRUS   Heavy all-purpose cloak with cowl, worn in the Middle Ages by commoners. Similar to ancient Roman hooded cape.

BIS   Silky linen interwoven with gold threads. 17th Cent.

BISHOP'S SLEEVE   Long full sleeve gathered into a band at the cuff. Feminine form recurring, fashionable 1900 onwards, based on Anglican clergyman's rochet.

BLACK LACE   Made fashionable by royal Spanish Infanta on her marriage to Louis XIV, 1660. Sometimes called BAYEUX LACE as made in that area.

BLACK TIE   *Masc.* Conventional 20th Cent. black bow worn with soft white shirt and dinner jacket, usually on semi-formal occasions when full formal evening-dress was not required, although since 1970 its use has become less frequent.

BLACKJACK   (See BOOT)

BLACKWORK   Counted black thread embroidery worked on white linen or cotton. 16th and 17th Cents. English.

BLANCHET   *Masc.* Doublet of white cotton, with collar and sleeves; sometimes fur-lined. 14th Cent.

BLANKET CLOTH   Woollen West of England cloth used for overcoats. 19th-20th Cents.

BLAZER   Lightweight buttoned jacket, usually of flannel, with stripes, or of solid colour, proclaiming membership of a club, college, school, etc. Adapted from regimental sportswear after Great War and much favoured for sporting wear. Masculine and feminine since 1920s. In the 1970s, a falling-off in popularity with use of more comfortable lightweight garments of manmade fibres. Again fashionable 1986-.

BLIAND, BLIAUS, BLIANT, BLIAUNT   *Masc. Fem.* Outer shirt-type dress, slit up the sides, or with pleats allowing freedom of movement, especially on horseback. Precursor of shirt or blouse. 12th Cent.

BLOOMERS   *Fem.* Knee-length loose knickers. Designed and worn by Mrs. Amelia Bloomer, a social worker in the U.S.A., 1850. Worn for athletics and cycling.

BLOUSE   *Fem.* Upper lightweight garment, usually reaching below the waist, but of varying lengths; evolved from the bliand and worn tucked into or over a skirt.

BLUCHER   *Masc.* Short laced leather boot, named after Field Marshall von Blucher, Prussian Commander, 1742-1819. The sides were laced to tie in front over a tongue.

BLUE BONNET   *Masc.* Scottish traditional dark blue cap, tufted and worn with ribbon cockade and feathers to signify wearer's rank. (See BALMORAL, GLENGARRY).

BOA   *Fem.* Long scarf or neckpiece of feathers, fur, tulle or lace, usually about 2 metres long and tied with ends hanging below the knees. Late 19th Cent. and periodically revived 1930s and 1960s.

BOATER   *Fr. -canotier. Masc.* Stiff oval straw hat, coated with shellac, which became fashionable for summer wear in 1900s in Europe and U.S.A. Worn when punting or boating and in summer resorts. Used by filmstars, actors and actresses, notably Harold Lloyd, Buster Keaton, Maurice Chevalier, Frankie Vaughan, as part of their stage dress and act. Tradesmen in United Kingdom adopted the hat, notably butchers and fishmongers, and often its wearing combined with blue-and-white striped apron. No longer fashionable after 1930s but retained as part of uniform by some British public schools.

BOB   *Fem.* Short hair style, adopted after Great War in 1920s by Paul Poiret for the mannequins in his dress shows; also by dancers in Isadora Duncan's troupe, with Dutch boy straight-all-round style. The shingle style followed with hair trimmed to a 'V' at the back and later by a slightly longer style called the 'page boy', with the ends rolled under.

BOB WIG   *Masc.* Everyday short wig. Quakers and clergy often wore a curled fuller white wig. 18th Cent.

BOBBIN   Small cylinder or pin used in the making of lace.

BOBBIN LACE, PILLOW LACE   Lace made on a pillow with the design marked by pins. The bobbins, with thread, are woven over and round the pins.

BODICE   *Fem.* Upper part of dress. Term used from Middle Ages, when one layer or 'body' of canvas and another layer or 'body' of softened boiled leather were boned and hooked together. This garment was laced tightly, thus forming a corset or under-bodice.

BODKIN   Long bone or bronze pin used as hairpin from ancient times. Used by Saxons for fastening on cloaks. Later, term given to large-eyed blunt-ended sewing needle.

BODY STICHET   *Fem.* Rigid corset worn in Tudor period.

BODY STOCKING   Finely-knit body garment, usually of stretch manmade fibre eliminating use of other supporting wear. Evolved for exercise and dancing, etc. From 1960s.

BOEMIO   *Masc.* Cape worn in Spain. 16th Cent.

BOISSON   *Fem.* Short hooded cloak. Late 18th Cent.

BOKASYN   Type of fustian material. 15th Cent.

BOKILL   A buckler name. Early 16th Cent.

BOLERO   Tailored, short open jacket or waistcoat ending above or at waist. Spanish in origin. Introduced into feminine dress 1850 and re-appearing at intervals.

BOLLINGER   *Masc.* Hat worn by cab-drivers. Bowl-shaped crown with knob or button at centre top, narrow, circular brim. Late 19th Cent.

BOMBACHAS   S.A., Uruguay. *Masc.* Long full pantaloon breeches gathered into a band at the ankle.

Usually held in place at waist with decorated silver and leather belt. Worn by cowboys, or gauchos. To date.

BOMBAST Cotton padding and stuffing much used in Europe, 16th Cent., for shaping doublets, especially in Court fashions. *Masc.* In Spanish peascod-shape breeches, 1545-1620.

BOMBAZINE 1) Cotton twilled fabric made in the Middle Ages. Later mixed with wool and silk. Usually black. 2) Twilled silk and worsted introduced in Norwich by Flemings, 1570s. 3) In 18th Cent. name was given to a silk woven in France and Italy.

BONDED FABRIC Fabrics bonded back-to-back to make one material, thus reducing need for lining when fashioned into garments.

BONET (See BONNET).

BONGRACE *Fem.* Headdress, flat and square in shape, dipping in peak over forehead, free at back, with veil. Sometimes decorated with suspended jewel in front. Late 15th-17th Cents.

BONNET, BONET *Fem.* Any soft head-covering with strings tying under the chin, from Medieval times.

BONNET BEEHIVE *Fem.* Plain straw hat, made in shape of a beehive, trimmed with a ribbon tying under the chin. Early 19th Cent.

BONNET CABRIOLET *Fem.* Bonnet shaped like a folding top of a cabriolet, collapsible, with bows tying under chin. 18th-19th Cents.

BONNET PAMELA *Fr. Fem.* Straw bonnet with tall crown, trimmed with daffodils, and rose-coloured ribbons which tied under chin. 1820.

BONNET POKE, COAL SCUTTLE *Fem.* Hat of straw with crown and scuttle-shaped brim. Worn over a cap and tied with ribbons. Late 18th Cent. Also called CAPOTE.

BONNET-SHAPED CAP *Fem.* Head-fitting cap with frills framing face. From 18th Cent.

BONNET SUGAR LOAF *Fr. Masc.* High cap worn with bobbed hair. Mid-15th Cent.

BONNET WATTEAU (See WATTEAU).

BOOT BLACK JACK *Masc.* Short heavy boot of black tarred leather. 17th Cent. **BLUCHER** (See BLUCHER). **BOTTINE** *Fem.* (See JEMIMA) **BRODEQUIN** (See COTHURNUS below) **BUCKET TOP** *Fr. Masc.* Cavalier style with spur leather. 17th Cent. **BUSKIN** 1)High platform-soled boot, initially worn in Greek drama to give height to wearer. 2) *Masc. Fem.* High kneeboots, often of silk. Court wear. Middle Ages.3) *Masc. Fem.* Leather for riding. 16th Cent. **CAVALIER** *Masc.* High unsupported leather boots with wide funnel or bucket tops which were worn over lace-edged boot hose. With spur leathers and spiked rowels. 17th Cent. **CHUKKA** *Masc. Fem.* Ankle-high boot with two eyelets, worn with legged riding breeches known as jodhpurs. Styled from India. 19th, 20th Cents. **COTHURNUS** Decorated Roman boot development of Greek buskin. With fur trimmings fringed from top. The medieval Sc. **BRO-**

DEQUIN was made of soft leather, or costly fabric, and embroidered. **COURREGES** *Fem.* Long white real or imitation leather boot, designed by French fashion artist, worn with very short skirts for warmth and style in winter. 1960s. **COWBOY** *Masc.* Calf-high boot, with high heel to hold foot in the stirrup. Often decorated. **CRACKOWE or POULAINE** *Masc.* Mid-calf-length boot with upward curling and long pointed toes. Those with extreme lengths needed chains attached to knees or ankles. Originated in Krackowe, Poland, and thus called 'Crackowes' in England and 'Poulaines' in France after Poland. Lengths beyond the toes of 2 ft. allowed to noblemen; 1 ft. to gentlemen and 6 inches for commoners. Mid-14th Cent. **FLIGHT BOOT** *Masc.* Worn by aircraft service men in World War II, chukka-like in style with non-skid sole. **GUARD OFFICER'S BOOT** As NAPOLEON, WELLINGTON. **HESSIAN, HUSSAR or SOUVAROFF** *Masc.* A tassel hung from a dip below the knee. Worn by Messian mercenaries fighting the American Colonists. Style adopted in late 18th Cent. for civilian wear. **JACKBOOT** *Masc.* Heavy large boot. Lined with pockets and made of jack leather, mostly worn in 17th and 18th Cents. **NAPOLEON also WELLINGTON** *Masc.* Military officer's boot, heavy black leather, with square top cut out behind the knee. Lined with chamois. 19th Cent. **PERO** Thonged leather boot worn by peasants, 12th and 13th Cents. Term from Roman patrician's shoe. **POULAIN** (See CRACKOWE above) **SOUVAROFF** (See HESSIAN above) **TOP BOOT** Riding boot of leather with light flesh-colour side turned over as contrast. Strapped around knee. Late 18th Cent. **WADERS or WADING BOOT** Hip-length rubber boots for fishing and wading. Modern. **WELLINGTON** As NAPOLEON **WELLINGTON HALF-BOOT** *Masc.* Short boot worn with breeches which were fastened under the sole with a strap. 1820-1860.

BOOTHOSE *Masc.* Legwear of white linen with wide lace frills which hung over leather top of boots. Initially protection for costly silk hose worn by cavaliers. 17th Cent.

BO PEEPER Name given to 17th Cent. mask.

BORSALINO Elegant fur-felt hat made in Italy. From early 19th Cent.

BORATO, BURATO Thin silk and worsted material resembling bombazine. 16th Cent.

BOTTINE (See JEMIMA)

BOTTLES *Fem.* Small bottles for holding water to keep flowers fresh as a dress adornment. Usually flat and four inches long. Late 18th and early 19th Cents.

BOU BOU (See NIGERIA).

BOUCLE *Fr.* Looped, curled, woven or knitted soft fabric. Invented 1886. Used for sports suits and jerseys. 20th Cent.

BOUDOIR CAP *Fem.* Lace-edged cap of soft material, worn over undressed hair. Late 18th-19th Cents.

BOUFFANT *Fr. - puffed, puffy.* Applied to full skirts, particularly 18th Cent. Also used of hair styles. 20th Cent.

BOURDALOU Ribbon surrounding hat at base of crown. Traditional since 17th Cent.

BOURETTE Yarn of cotton, linen or silk with uneven nubbed thread, causing woven fabric of same name to have an interesting rough-looking texture.

BOSSES *Fem.* Decorative cauls or box-like covers for thick coils of plaited hair arranged on each side of head. Worn with coverchief or veil. 13th and 14th Cents. (See TEMPLERS)

BOURRELET *Masc.* Circular padded headroll, sometimes used as base of Chaperon. 15th Cent. *Fem.* Version of farthingale in shape of a roll of felt which was worn under the gown at the waist, notably by Marguerite de Valois. 15th Cent.

BOURSE A purse.

BOUTIQUE *Fr.* Shop having available ready-made clothes, accessories, perfumes, etc., usually under the aegis and name of a famous dressmaker.

BOUTONNIERE *Fr. - buttonhole. Masc.* Fashion in France at the time of Louis XV. Re-adopted, by a single fresh flower. Still worn at weddings. 20th Cent.

BOWDY Name of scarlet dye peculiar to a dye house in Bow. 17th Cent.

BOWKNOT *Masc.* Black ribbon bow securing the looped-back hair of cadogan wig. 1770s. The term is also used for bow ornament on leather pumps and slippers.

BOWLER Hard dome-shaped hat designed by an English hatter, William Bowler, in 1850. Worn in Great Britain when the top hat became fashionable. Evolved as a compromise between the top hat and felt hat. The Earl of Derby wore one to the races and it was thereafter called a 'derby' in the U.S.A. Made of hard felt, it was worn with riding-habits, offering head protection. 19th Cent. and first half of 20th Cent.

BOWTIE *Masc.* Small tie for day wear with two loops and two ends. For evening wear, black bowtie is worn with a dinner jacket and a white bowtie with a tailcoat for formal occasions.

BOX CLOTH Heavy woollen fabric with surface resembling felt. Much used for driving-coats.

BOX COAT *Masc.* Heavy coachman's overcoat, worn for warmth and protection on the box of a coach. From 1830s to end of 19th Cent.

BRACCAE, BRACCATAE, BRAES Early form of trousers, 2nd to 7th Cent. A.D. Simple wrapped forms worn until 13th Cent. Developed from banded leg covering used as protection from the cold. The Roman invaders of the Franks, Gauls and Celts described the wearers as 'breeched' people. Later, the invaded northerners copied the short woollen tunic of the Romans, together with cross-garterings made of leather or cloth strips on the leg-coverings.

BRACELET Arm or wrist-band usually of metal in ring or chain form.

BRACES Braid with fastenings used to hold up male trousers. Also known as 'suspenders' in U.S.A. From late 18th Cent. Also GALLOWSES.

BRACCONIERE *Masc.* Hoop-shaped steel plates overlapping to form hip-length skirt in a suit of armour. 14th and 15th Cents. Not after 17th Cent.

BRAGOU-BRAZ *Fr. Masc.* Large full knee breeches of Breton peasant worn with wide sash, vest and short jacket. Dark blue and shirred to waist and into knee cuffs. Traditional and still worn.

BRAGUETTE *Fr. term* -Cod piece.

BRAID Flat woven strips of material or ribbon, used for trimming, binding or applique work on garments, etc. Types include military, rickrack, soutache.

BRAIES *Masc.* Leg underwear worn at the time of William the Conqueror. (See also BRACCAE).

BRANC *Fem.* Smock worn in 15th Cent.

BRANDENBURG *Masc.* Loose-fitting overcoat style worn by Prussian troops in 1674, decorated by braided loops and buttons. The name passed to the characteristic trimming of twin buttons linked by cords or laces. This trimming was much worn by men and women on tightly buttoned jackets. 1820-1840. Also periodically on feminine styles. It still appears on men's dressing gowns and pyjama jackets.

BRASSARD, BRASSART *Fr. - arm.* Medieval armour for the arm. Today a band of black for mourning.

BRASSEROLE *Fem.* Type of camisole worn by young girls, 14th-17th Cents. Also, a quilted jacket for warmth, 17th Cent.

BRASSIERE, BRA *Masc. Fem.* Short sleeveless night-garment. 14th-17th Cents. *Fem.* Undergarment to support and shape the breasts. 20th Cent. Paul Poiret designed first modern type, 1912.

BRATT *Irish.* Shawl or cloak for infant. 9th and 10th Cents. Mentioned by Chaucer, 14th Cent.

BREACAN-FEILE Traditional type of Scottish Highland dress, worn until 1746; a folded plaid cloth about 2 yards by 6 yards. Pleated and fastened around the hips. The lower part formed the kilt, the upper half worn over the left shoulder. Used by the wearer as cloak by day and blanket by night.

BREECHES *Masc.* Short trousers fastened below knee, used especially for riding or court costume. Types are: PETTICOAT or RHINEGRAVE Worn in 1650s in France, kilt-like, of generous cut and trimmed with ribbons; designed to display silk stockings newly fashionable in latter part of 17th Cent. PUMPHOSE or GALLIGASKIN *German.* Knee-length, padded or flat. 16th Cent. HEERPAUKE or ROUND HOSE Influenced by late 16th Cent. Spanish fashions. SLOPS Worn straight and loose throughout late 16th Cent. and early 17th Cent. TRUNK HOSE Slashed, puffed, padded breeches of simple cut, but generous size, late 16th Cent.

BRELOQUE *Fem.* Trinket, charm, attached to chatelaine. *Masc.* Seal from watch chain.

BRETELLE *Fr. Masc. Fem.* Brace, strap, suspender (i.e. of skirt or trousers). 19th Cent.

BRETON SAILOR Hat of straw, felt or fabric with wide all-round turned-up brim. Worn by and copied from Breton peasants' headwear.

BREWER'S CAP *Masc.* Traditional knitted woollen stocking cap worn for protection when loading.

BRIDAL DRESS *Fem.* White wool, symbolizing virginity, was worn in ancient Rome by a pagan bride, with a girdle which was untied by her husband. The customary modern white dress dates back to the early 19th Cent. A shoulder-length headdress or even a hat are often worn in place of the earlier style long lace train or veil. Orange blossom, denoting chastity, was worn traditionally as a chaplet to hold the veil in place.

BRIGANDINE Piece of body armour consisting of overlapping metal plates, which were pierced and sewn between layers of canvas, linen and leather. It was probably the first form of corset. Soldiers wearing them were known as 'Brigands' and the companies as 'Brigades'. 15th Cent.

BRILLIANTINE Very light textile of silk and cashmere wool. 1836. Also, masculine hair-dressing oil.

BRISTOL DIAMOND Rock crystals found in Bristol area and cut to resemble diamonds. 18th Cent.

BRISTOL RED West of England cloth dyed red at Bristol. 16th Cent.

BRITISH WARM *Masc.* Short warm coat used in World War II. Later, surplus coats became available to general public and were extremely popular. A more casual style known as a DUFFLECOAT, coloured khaki, fawn, or navy, is still manufactured and is fastened with toggles and loops.

BROADCLOTH Woollen plain woven cloth of high quality, used mostly for men's wear. Made of finest felting wool, always in a wide width, thus giving it its name.

BROCADE Rich silk fabric woven with raised patterns, often with addition of gold and silver threads.

BRODEQUIN (See BOOT - Cothurnus)

BRODERIE ANGLAISE *Fr. - English embroidery.* Open work embroidery on white cambric or linen. Much used on blouses and dresses during the years of the First World War, 1914-1918.

BROELLA Coarse cloth worn by monks and country men. Medieval.

BROGUE, BROGAN Strong leather low shoe for country wear, originally of untanned leather, of Gaelic origin. From 16th Cent.

BROOCH Ornamental hinged pin for fastening garment, used from early times.

BRUMMAGGEM Old name for Birmingham. Applied to early cheap jewellery manufactured there.

BUCKET TOP (See BOOT)

BRUMMEL BODICE *Masc.* Corset worn by dandies in imitation of Beau Brummel, 1810-1820.

BRUNSWICK GOWN *Fem.* Sack-backed gown with loose sleeves to wrists and front-buttoned bodice. 1760-1780. (See GERMAN GOWN)

BUCKLE Clasp with metal rim having a spiked hinged tongue for fastening of leather belts, and early armour. Shoes and slippers were decorated with buckles set with pearls and diamonds, real and false, in 1650s. Round and oval shapes were worn in the 18th Cent and have since then been used in many ways as fashionable accessories.

BUCKLER Popular small round shield held in the left hand by means of a crossbar on the inside. 16th Cent.

BUCKRAM Glue-sized coarse linen used from the 16th Cent. for stiffening. Originally made as floor covering under fine carpets and rugs brought from Bukhara, from which area the name is derived.

BUCKSAIN *Masc.* Padded overcoat fashionable in 1850s.

BUCKSKIN Genuine buckskin is made from small deer of the American continent. It is yellowish, or grey-white, made soft and pliable. Also the name for a leather riding gaiter, l9th Cent. Used for military uniforms and fine equipment. From late 18th Cent.

BUDGE Old English for lambskin dressed with its fine wool intact, used for trimming edges, and linings.

BUFF Dull yellow velvety soft leather of buffalo or oxhide.

BUFF COAT *Masc.* Military coat or jerkin worn by soldiers. Of buffalo hide as proof against sword cuts. Deep skirted, sometimes sleeveless, and thong-laced. Those of officers often decorated, or even embroidered. 16th - 17th Cents.

BUFFIN Inferior form of mixed material used for doublets and gowns of poorer people. 16th Cent.

BUFFONT *Fr. bouffer - puff.* Large gauze scarf worn above low-necked gown. Puffed out over bosom. Late 18th Cent.

BUGLE Tube-shaped glass bead sewn on dress for ornament.

BULGHA Egyptian soft leather slippers worn by village people.

BULL'S HEAD FRINGE Woman's hairstyle with fringe, about 1640.

BULLION Fringe of gold and silver thread twists.

BULLION LACE Lace of gold and silver threads used for Court robes or church vestments.

BULLYCOCK *Masc.* Type of bowler hat, late 19th Cent.

BULLY-COCKED *Masc.* Broad brimmed cocked hat worn by street bullies. Early 18th Cent.

BUMROLL *Fem. Fr.* Padded bolster worn under farthingale. 1560.

BUNAD Term given to revived folk dress, Norwegian.

BURANO LACE Version of Venetian point lace made on nearby island of Burano.

BURIDAN Horizontally-striped silk in tones of one colour. 1836.

BURMA, BURMESE *Masc. Fem.* Both wear wrapround skirt or LONGYI, loose or pleated, to the ankles. *Fem.* Worn wrapped around the bosom and over this a double-breasted buttoned blouse or jacket called AINYI. *Masc.* Single-breasted jacket is called TAIKPON. Headwear includes turbans, caps, widebrimmed straw hats. All garments are of pleasing bright colour, not garish. Also TAMEIN - sari; LUNGI or LUNGEE - long cotton cloth used by East Indians as turban, scarf or loincloth.

BURNOUS, BURNOOSE Arabian, Moorish hooded cloak, or mantle, worn when travelling. In Europe, a shortened sleeved copy became fashionable for men and was distinguished by a hood weighted with a silk tassel. Mid-1800s.

BURNSIDES (See SIDEBURNS, SIDE WHISKERS)

BUSBY *Masc.* Tall fur cap worn ceremoniously by Hussars. Also bearskin worn by British Brigade of Guards, from 18th Cent.

BUSHJACKET Traditional African bush safari jacket, usually of water-repellent material. Furnished with useful pockets, and now popular for general casual wear.

BUSK Rigid strip to stiffen corset front.

BUSKIN (See BOOT)

BUSTLE *Fem.* Pad or frame puffing out upper part of woman's back skirt. Replaced the crinoline in 1869. The wide hemline disappeared by 1870 and "tied back" look came into fashion. In the 1880s, it was wired and padded, beneath a draped skirt and formed a protuberance at the back. This extreme look disappeared in the 1890s.

BUSTLE 1870-1876. Fullness of material was drawn to the back of the dress and much trimming was used. The bustle shape reappeared from 1882-1889.

BURBERRY Waterproofed cloth; coat made by British firm of that name. A lighter cloth is called ROSEBERRY.

BURE *Fr. - drugget.* Coarse heavy brown woollen cloth worn originally by Roman slaves. Served later as covering for chests; chests, as furniture, were made larger and named 'bureaux'.

BURGONET, BURGANET, BOURQUINOTTE Bonnet-like helmet with cheek pieces and occasionally a nose piece. First worn by Burgundians in 15th Cent. Distinguished by brow piece or umbril to protect the eyes. In use until 17th Cent.

BUTCHER'S LINEN Coarse homespun linen often blue-and-white striped, used for butchers' and fishmongers' aprons, etc.

BUTTERFLY HEADDRESS *Fem.* Term used in 16th Cent. for the headdress worn in late 15th Cent. resembling the wings of a butterfly. This consisted of a light framework which supported a veil falling and spreading out on each side with a V-shaped dip above the forehead. The whole was fastened to a small cap worn slightly to the back of the head.

BUTTERFLY SPUR LEATHERS *Masc.* Large butterfly-shaped pieces of leather worn over front of instep of boots and holding spurs at the back, 17th Cent.

BUTTON BOOTS *Masc. Fem.* Early 1830s. Fastened on outside with small black or mother-of-pearl round buttons. Still worn early 1900s.

BYE COCKET HAT *Masc.* Hat with long peak in front, upturned brim at back with long cone-shaped crown. 15th Cent.

BYRNIE *Masc.* Linked chainmail coat worn in N. Europe under linen tunic, 13th Cent.

BYRON TIE *Masc.* Narrow short necktie, similar to shoe-string. 1840-1850s.

BYRRUS (See BIRRUS)

BYZANTINE Byzantium, later called Constantinople, and now Istanbul, was capital of the Roman Empire, 400-1100 A.D. In the 6th Cent. A.D., momks returning from the East brought back silkworms, and formed a silk industry. One of the fabrics produced was SAMITE, a rich costly material with gold and silver threads. Costume of this period included:

JUPPE *Masc.* Basic garment - a sleeved tunic robe. The Roman toga was abandoned for a cloak. **CAMISSIA** *Masc. Fem.* White under-garment or shirt of linen; usually knee-length for men, ankle-length for women. The wearing of the two garments together became common. The'look' of the dress worn during the Byzantine Empire was outstanding for splendour and colour and for the emphasis placed on the concealment of the human body.

Garments worn by the Emperor included:

1) STOLA - a long tunic of white or gold silk.

2) CHLAMYS - a cloak, usually purple, fastened by a jewelled brooch.

3) TRABEA - a wide scarf crossed over the chest.

4) TABLION - an oblong panel encrusted with jewels which adorned the front of the robe.

5) CROWN - an open crown or coronet set with jewels and hanging strings of pearls and gems.

Those worn by the Empress included:

1) TUNIC - a long white garment, adorned with embroidered vertical band.

2) MANIAKIS - jewelled and embroidered band draped over the shoulders.

3) a fringed short-sleeved robe belted with jewels.

4) STEPHANOS - a diadem set with precious stones and long strings of pearls hanging on each side.

6) - red shoes of soft embroidered leather.

Knitting was known. Leggings, hose and under-drawers were worn by upper and lower classes.

From the 4th Cent. A.D., the affluent, elaborate and sumptuous influence of the Byzantine style spread its influence over Medieval and Renaissance Europe, even becoming the foundation of costume in Russia. It was at the height of its glory in the 6th Cent. during the reign of the Emperor Justinian and his wife, Theodora.

One of three kings bearing gifts to Christ BYZANTINE TROUSERS topped by tunic fastened between legs. The wrap, or Lacernae, held with a clasp. Detail from mosaic, Church of St. Apollinare Nuovo, Ravenna, dating from 6th Century A.D.

The Empress Theodora presenting a piece of Church Plate.

BYZANTINE COSTUME as portrayed in mosaic at the
Church of San Vitale, Ravenna, 6th Century, A.D. The central
figure, the Empress, wears a jewelled crown with hanging rows of
pearls. She and her attendant, wear cloaks and gowns of richly
decorated fabrics. The robe of the man shows a breaking away
from the Roman toga shape and having the appearance of the
oriental caftan, which style was gradually adopted by the 12th
Century.

COPOTAIN 1583

CABASET *Masc.* High crowned-helmet with narrow straight brim. 16th Cent. (See MORION)

CABBAGE RUFF *Masc.* Large informal ruff. Starched, but unpleated. 17th Cent.

CABRIOLET *Fem.* Bonnet with curved crown, similar to folding cabriolet carriage top. 18th Cent.

CACHE-FOLIES Fem. Fr. Small wig worn to hide short hair styles of the Revolution. 1800s.

CACHEMIRE Blended textile of wool and silk with eastern designs and colouring. Late 19th Cent.

CADANELLE, CADANETTE *Masc.* Hair style with pigtail, copied from Marshal Cadanet at time of Louis XIII. 17th Cent. Known in England as LOVELOCK.

CADDICE, CADDIS Name for worsted yarns, at time of Shakespeare, 16th Cent.

CADDICE GARTER Garter made of rough silk, usually by servants or attendants. 16th Cent.

CADOGAN *Masc.* Style of wig named after Earl of Cadogan. Popular with young men of fashion called 'Macaronies', in England, 1770s. Hair looped up and tied back. Sometimes held in net by small comb.

CAFFA, KAFFA Silk material from Al Kufa, an Arabian town, 16th - 18th Cents. Name also given to painted Indian cotton, 16th and 17th Cents.

CAFTAN, KAFTAN *Mas. Fem.* Long coat-like garment worn in the Levant. *Masc. Fem.* Adaptations in modern world for casual and leisure wear from 1960s.

CAGE *Fem.* Voluminous petticoat, tied round the waist and stiffened with increasing widths of wire or whalebone. 1850s, 1860s. Versions - AMERICAINE Lighter in weight. 1862-1869. EMPIRE Shaped, increasing in width downwards for wearing at balls, important functions. 1861-1869. From 1868, the size decreased. A garment named CRINOLETTE was introduced and preferred. (See CRINOLETTE).

CAI-AO *Masc. Fem.* Long tunic of silk worn in Vietnam. Standing collar, long-sleeved and buttoned at side. *Fem.* Slit from mid-hip to hem.

CAIQUAN Light-weight trousers worn in Vietnam. *Masc.* Usually white linen. *Fem.* Black silk or velvet.

CAIRNGORM Yellow, smoky brown, or wine-coloured semi-precious stone found in Cairngorm

Mountains, Scotland. Often set in handsome hand-crafted jewellry.

CAKE HAT   *Masc.* Soft felt hat with low rounded crown, having slight circular depression. Similar to ALPINE hat. 1890s.

CALAMANCO   Variations of woollen textile from 16th - 19th Cents. Glazed cotton or wools, plain or twilled until 1790s. Woven for quilts, as well as garments, 19th Cent.

CALASH, CALÈCHE   *Fem.* Large black silk collapsible hooped hood, with whalebone arches. Named after French carriage Calèche. Worn to protect high hairstyles and headdresses in 1770-1790, and again 1820-1839.

CALCARAPEDES   *Masc.* Self-adjusting rubber overshoes or galoshes. 1860s.

CALCEUS   Italian sandal. (See CARBATINA)

CALEÇONS   Drawers worn by Saxons and Franks in Europe, 9th Cent. *Mas.* Of white linen for wearing under breeches, 17th Cent. *Fem.* In France and Italy, a garment was newly introduced for riding, 17th Cent., but otherwise unusual. When transparent Empire gowns became fashionable in early 19th Cent., French and English fashion journals referred to a new kind of underwear, a type of drawers, but was not generally adopted until the 1830s.

CALEDONIAN SILK   Silky surfaced material similar to poplin, with small chequered pattern on white ground. Early 19th Cent.

CALF, CALFSKIN   Fine grained leather made from very young cattle. Finished with high polish, or used as suede, patent leather, for fine quality goods.   Jesters used to wear a calfskin jacket buttoned down the back. Constance says to the treacherous Archduke of Austria - *Thou wear a lion's hide! Doff it for shame, and hang a calf-skin on those recreant limbs.'* Shakespeare, King John III, I.

CALICO   Cotton material from Calicut, India, where printed cottons were first manufactured in mid-19th Cent. Flat buttons, made of calico-covered rings with eyelets in the centre, were first made and used for underclothes from 1840.

CALIGA   Heavy-soled leather sandal worn by Roman centurions. Sometimes nail-studded, but always gartered and thonged with leg lacing, above the ankle. Forerunner of legwear worn by men until end of 12th Cent.

CALIMANCO   (See CALAMANCO)

CALLOT, CALOTTE   *Masc.* Small round undercap originally from Ancient Greece. Later, under hood or crown, worn by clergy, made in scarlet material to cover tonsure, 15th Cent. (See ZUCCHETTO). A plain skull-cap worn under hat. 17th Cent.

CALPAC   High astrakan cap of shape worn by Russian Cossack officer. From 16th Cent.

CALVES   *Masc.* Pads worn at back of legs inside stockings to improve the shape. 17th - 19th Cent.

CALYPSO CHEMISE   *Fem.* Simple gown of coloured muslin worn under a loose robe. Late 18th Cent.

CAMAIL   *Masc.* Chain-mail hood fastened over an iron skull-cap with steel circlet. 13th Cent. *Fem.* Waist length, or slightly longer, cloak or cape. Small falling collar and armholes. Lined or wadded. 1842.

CAMARGO, Marie   *Fem.* French dancer, 18th Cent. Following garments were named after her -
1) CAMARGO   Small evening hat, with brim raised in front. 1836.
2) CAMARGO PUFF   A skirt made by looping up the back of a pannier dress. 1868.
3) CAMARGO JACKET   Worn over a waistcoat, with basques draped on the hips. 1879.

CAMBRIC   Fine white linen or cotton made in Cambrai, France; also in Flanders. From 16th Cent.

CAMBRIDGE COAT   *Masc.* Lounge coat, with three or four buttons, centre back seam, and opening. 1870. Later, with patch pockets and buttoned flaps. 1876-1880.

CAMBRIDGE PALETOT   *Masc.* Large knee-length overcoat with full sleeves and deep turned-back cuffs. Wide cape collar and lapels. 1855.

CAMEL HAIR, CAMEL'S HAIR   The hair is not shorn or plucked but is gathered by caravan owners when the animal is shedding it in clumps. The wool is sorted into three types - the soft short downy kind from next to the hide; the coarse fleece between outer and downy layers; and the tough wiry darker outer hair. From Africa, Asia and Mongolia.

CAMELEONS   *Fem.* Boots, and sometimes shoes, with perforated uppers which daringly allowed coloured stockings to be seen through the holes. 1859.

CAMEO   Ornamental carving on precious or semi-precious stone in relief. The opposite of incised carving or intaglio. Of eastern origin, cameo cutters of Greece and Rome executed beautiful work on onyx and sardonyx. At the time of the first Roman Emperor, small cameo portraits became renowned and much worn until the Middle Ages and the Renaissance. In the 19th Cent., cameos were cut in coral, shells and jet. Paste copies were made by James Tassie and others in Wedgwood jasper ware.

CAMIKNICKERS   *Fem.* Undergarment combining shoulder-strapped bodice and panties or knickers, usually of silk or light pretty materials, dating from 1920s.

CAMISIA   *Italian, CAMISA; Spanish, KAMI. Masc. Fem.* Basic white undergarment or shirt worn between heavy robes and the body. Term still in use for white shirt or blouse.

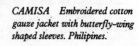

CAMISA   *Embroidered cotton gauze jacket with butterfly-wing shaped sleeves. Philipines.*

CAMISOLE *Fem.* Underbodice, with or without sleeves, worn over corsets to give smoother-looking appearance and protection to outer dress. 1820s.

CAMLET Originally a material of mixed fibres from Turkey, using camel or goat's hair with wool or silk. Later produced in England near River Camlet with half silk, half hair - 16th and 17th Cents. A plain or twilled fabric used by American colonists for cloaks, hoods and under petticoats in 18th Cent.

CAMMAKA Quality Eastern material woven from silk and camel hair, used for Royal and ecclesiastical garments. 14th Cent.

CAMOCA Rich patterned silk originally from China but later obtained from Persia. 15th and 16th Cents.

CAMPAGNUS *Masc.* Half boot, or high shoe, laced at the instep. Byzantine in origin. For walking, country or travelling. From 1st Cent. A.D.

CAMPAIGN COAT *Masc.* Long coat worn by foot-soldiers, early 17th Cent. Style of garment, when tattered and aged, worn by beggars, gypsies and travelling men to gain sympathy.

CAMPAIGN WIG *Masc.* Worn by campaigners and for travelling. Bushy, fairly full top, shorter side pieces, with the back hair or queue tied behind in black silk bag. Favoured by elderly men. Late 17th Cent. to middle 18th Cent.

CANDLEWICK Rough material worn by menservants. 1400. Tufted cotton modern material with velvety finish used for feminine dressing-gowns, casual wear and bed-covers. From mid-20th Cent.

CANDYS *Pers.* A garment of linen or wool with sleeves sewn into pleats at the back of the arm. The first recorded robe with a set-in sleeve. The pleats were repeated in the skirt. c. 7th - 4th Cents., B.C.

CANE *Masc. Fem.* Distinct from walking-stick. Made from stem of small palm or strong reed. Fashionable in 17th and 18th Cents., varying lengths. From 1750, very long ones were 'in style'. Reduced to a 'useful' size, 1762.

CANEPHORUS In Ancient Greece, sculptured figure of a youth or maiden bearing a basket on the head. Represented by participants in processions and festivals.

CANEZOU *Fem.* Feminine dress-bodice usually white. 1820-1830s. It then developed into cape-like shape but not covering the arms. By 1850, it took the appearance of an elaborately decorated fichu of muslin with lace and ribbons.

CANICHE *Fr.* Poodle. Tufted curly cloth used for small jackets and baby bonnets. An imitation of French poodle dog's coat.

CANIONS, CANNONS, CANONS *Masc.* 1) Breeches worn underneath the trunk hose reaching to the knee. Stockings were drawn up over them. Late 16th Cent. 2) Stockings with wide frilled tops worn with breeches not confined to knee. The frills fell downwards over garters below the knee. Late 17th Cent.

CANNETILLE Twisted gold and silver thread used for embroidery. Also, lace made with such threads.

CANNON SLEEVES *Fem.* Wide gown sleeves sloping to closed wrist. Padded and stiffened. Late 16th Cent. to early 17th Cent.

CANONICAL DRESS Appropriate garments worn by the clergy. Also CANONICALS. Robes of other professions.

CANOTIER *Fr.* Straw sailor's hat. A style fashionable for men and women, late 19th Cent. Also BOATER.

CANTALOON 1) A variety of worsted material. c.1600. 2) Fine Plain West of England cloth. 18th Cent.

CANTON CREPE Light-weight durable fabric originally from China. Silk with pebbled surface, used for light-weight dresses and linings. Today, also copied with man-made fibres.

CANVAS *Lat. cannabis - hemp.* Coarse fabric known from 16th Cent. Of linen, cotton, jute or hemp, with square mesh.

CAP Head covering. Brimless headdress. 1) *Mas.* Worn in 16th Cent. as symbol of service. Later varieties - Bellboy, Flatcap, Forage, Gob, Liberty, Monmouth, Montero. 2) *Fem.* An indoors domestic cap worn from 1500 - early 20th Cent. Varieties - Capadüsli, Dormeuse, Juliet, Mob, Night, Pulteny, Quaker, Ranelagh and others.

CAP-AND-BELLS Headwear of Medieval jester or fool.

CAP AND GOWN Full academic dress of university tutor, student or master.

CAP OF MAINTENANCE Anciently dignified headdress of a Duke. The fur cap of the Lord Mayor of London, worn on occasions of State.

CAPA, CAPPA *Sp.* Cape or cloak. Ecclesiastic, academic. Also cape of toreador.

CAPADÜSLI *Fem. Swiss.* Small gold-trimmed cap.

CAPE Short sleeveless cloak worn as separate garment, or as added shoulder piece of longer coat or cloak. Known ecclesiastically as COPE, 12th - 14th Cents.

CAPELINE *Fem.* Wide brimmed hat, worn over a lawn cap and tied with wide, usually velvet, ribbons under chin, 1750-1800s. Also light-weight hood with attached cape for country wear.

CAPESKIN Glacé-finished soft leather. Produced formerly in Cape of Good Hope; now similar comes from other countries.

CAPOT, CAPOTE *Masc.* Long military overcoat, from Levant, 18th Cent. *Fem.* 1) Cloak worn in Medieval times. 2) Bonnet with soft crown and stiff brim around the face. 1830s. Also named POKE BONNET.

CAPPA MAGNA *Masc.* Ceremonial vestment, cape of silk hooded with fur or silk.

CAPRI PANTS *Fem.* Fashionable loose and tapered trousers. In U.S.A. called 'pedal'pushers'. Ending at mid-calf. Mid-20th Cent.

CAPUCH *Masc. Fem.* Hood attached to cloak. 17th Cent.

CAPUCHE *Fem.* Muslin silk-lined sun-bonnet. 1850s.

CAPUCHIN, CAPUCHON *Fr. Capuchon - hood.*
1) *Masc. Fem.* Hooded cape. Medieval. 2) *Fem.* Named after CAPUCE, or pointed cowl worn by Franciscan friars. Fur-lined or fur-edged for winter wear. When in scarlet or cardinal red, called 'Red Riding Hood'. 1740s. Forerunner to CHAPERON.

CAPUCINE *Fr.* Nasturtium flower, in bright flamed-coloured red and orange shades. Popular, fashionable colour. Late 18th and early 19th Cents.

CAPULET *Fem.* Betasseled short cape and hood introduced from the Pyrenees. Early 19th Cent.

CAPYBARA Large South American rodent. The pliable skin, similar to pigskin, is used for gloves and leather goods.

CARACAL *Turkish - blackear.* Lynx fur of mediocre quality.

CARACO *Fem.* Thigh-length waisted jacket worn as a bodice with skirt, to form the 'caraco dress'. Late 18th Cent. In 19th Cent. retained with varying styles and worn in the daytime.

CARACUL *Russian.* Kind of astrakan fur, or cloth imitation. Also KARAKUL.

CARAVAN *Fem.* Small collapsible bonnet preceding the later larger CALASH. Supported with hoops of whalebone, covered with white veiling. 1765.

CARBATINA, CARBATINE Simple Italian sandal consisting of single piece of rawhide kept in place by leather thongs. Worn by early Mediterraneans and Europeans. More sophisticated form known as CALCEUS. Also KARBATINE.

CARCAILLE *Masc. Fem.* High flared decorative collar reaching chin and ears. Characteristic detail of the ground-length houppelande or overgown. 14th Cent.

CARCAN *Fr.* Iron collar used for prisoners. Suppressed and abandoned. 1832.

CARCANET *Fr. Fem.* Jewelled or beaded collar; high neck piece of precious stones. Late 19th Cent.

CARDIGAN *Masc.* Knitted woollen jacket named after Earl of Cardigan. 1855. Later versions had short roll collars.

CARDINAL *Fem.* Three-quarter length hooded cloak, usually red. Late 18th Cent. Worn throughout Europe and further afield.

CARDINAL'S HEADWEAR Originally black brimmed hat worn by all clergy. Tied under chin with cord. When off the head, it hung at back. Pope Innocent IV ordained red hats for cardinals, with rank denoted by the number of tassels, 13th Cent. Later additional - red zucchetto and biretta, 17th Cent.

CARDOWS *Masc.* Tasselled cords adorning a ceremonial robe. Late 16th and 17th Cents.

CARELESS *Masc.* Loose warm overcoat with wide collar and full cape. 1830s.

CARMAGNOLE *Masc.* Short jacket worn by Italian workers from Carmagnola. The style was adopted by French revolutionaries. Turned down collar, front

buttons and pockets. 1790s.

CARMEILLETTE *Fem.* Short evening cloak with hooped hood and long sleeves, for out-of-doors wear. 1837.

CAROLINE Queen and wife of British George IV, 1820-1830.

CAROLINE HAT *Masc.* Hats made of beaver fur imported from Carolina, U.S.A. Usually worn by men-servants, as the quality was inferior to the French beaver fur from Canada. Late 17th Cent. to 1850.

CAROLINE SPENCER *Fem.* A fashionable variety of the very short jacket invented by Lord Spencer in 1790s. In black velvet or fine white woollen material, lined with pale blue, it was named for Queen Caroline.

CARPOTE *Fem.* Small hat set high on head, tied under chin. Victorian. 19th Cent.

CARRANES Leather footwear found in Ireland and the Isle of Man.

CARRICK A coach named after John Carrick, British. *Masc.* Greatcoat for driving. Usually in fawn, double-breasted with high deep collar and two or three shoulder capes. *Fem.* Long dustcoat, also double-breasted and with capes. 1850s to end of century.

CARROTING Treatment of hat furs, in preparation for felting, with nitric acid and quicksilver.

CARTHAGE CYMAR *Fem.* Silk or net scarf with raised gold border, attached to one shoulder of evening dress to hang at the back to knee level. 1807-1809.

CASAQUE *Fr. Cassock, cloak.* Sleeveless short jacket worn over armour, and also by general populace for extra warmth. Adapted by Charles II. *Fem.* Neat fitted jacket buttoning to neck, with deep basque, 1850s. *Masc.* Brilliantly coloured silk jacket worn by modern French jockeys.

CASAQUIN *Fem.* Short dressing-jacket or negligée with sacque back, worn over petticoats, at home. 18th Cent.

CASAQUIN BODICE *Fem.* Tailored tight-fitting bodice shaped and buttoned at front; worn with un-trained skirt which reached two inches above ground. The outfit included a waistcoat, actual or simulated. Late 1870s.

CASAWECK *Fem.* Short quilted jacket, sleeved and with contrasting high velvet collar. Bordered with velvet or fur. 1836-1850.

CASCADE *Usually feminine.* Lace or soft frill hanging vertically from neck.

CASCADE WAISTBAND *Fem.* Neat decorative belt fringed with jet beads arranged in vandyke points. 1860s.

CASHMERE Material woven from fine soft wool of goats from Kashmir and Tibet.

CASHMERE SHAWL *Fem.* Square piece of cashmere designed for warmth over light-weight gowns. Some fringed, and of fine workmanship, from Lyons, France and Paisley, Scotland. Early 19th Cent. Larger sizes became popular in 1860s.

CASQUE Protective helmet or headpiece in armour. Medieval.

CASQUETEL Open helmet without visor.

CASQUETTE *Fem.* Neat-looking straw hat with crown slightly higher in front than the back and a low brim at front and behind. Trimmed with feather and black velvet band. 1863-1864.

CASSENET Summer-weight dress material with diagonal twill; the warp of cotton and the weft of fine wool, or silk and wool mixed. Early 19th Cent.

CASSIMERE Thin fine cloth patented by Francis Yerbury of Bradford-on-Avon in 1766. Plain and twilled, somewhat similar to CASHMERE.

CASSOCK *It. casacca -horseman's coat. Fr. casaque -coat. Masc.* Outer coat of foot-soldiers and horsemen. Buttoned in front, knee-length and slightly flared. 17th Cent. Clerical full-length garment has standing collar. Worn under a surplice. Still contemporary.

CASSOCK MANTLE *Fem.* Three-quarter length cloak with short sleeves. Gathered at centre back and on shoulders. 1880s.

CASTELLATED BORDER Square-cut crenellated edge given to garments in Middle Ages. A fashion echoing the design of castle tower parapets. (See also DAGGED).

CASTOR *L. Beaver.* Hat made of beaver fur. 17th and 18th Cents. By the end of 19th Cent felt was introduced.

CATAGAN *Fem.* Hair-dressing or chignon of ringlets or plaited hair, tied with a wide bow, hanging at the back of the head. Late 19th Cent. Similar to male CATOGAN of the 18th Cent.

CATAGAN NET *Fem.* A snood or hairnet used to cover and support a plaited catagan hair-dressing.

CATER-CAP *Masc.* Four-cornered cap worn by scholars and academicians. 16th and 17th Cents.

CATHEDRAL BEARD *Masc.* Broad long beard. Mid 16th - 17th Cents.

CATHERINE WHEEL FARTHINGALE *Fem.* Hooped support for skirt producing a tub-shaped hang to the gown. The wheel shape was slightly tilted behind the waist and the skirt placed over this and then allowed to fall vertically to the ground. Also called Italian, and Wheel, Farthingale.

CATOGAN *Masc.* Wig with broad flat tail or queue, which was turned up and tied with black ribbon. Late 18th Cent.

CATRINTA *Fem.* Decorative aprons worn both at front and back of skirt. Rumania.

CAUDEBEC HAT *Masc.* Black felt hat originally styled and made in Caudebec, Normandy. Treated to look like beaver. Late 17th-18th Cent.

CAUL 1) *Fem.* Medieval. Trellis work headdress of gold or silver cord, or metal work, often lined with silk. 14th-16th Cents. Called a FRET, also CREPIN, CRESTINE, CRESPINETTE, TRESSURE, TRESSOUR. 2) *Masc.* Network foundation or cap on which a wig was built. Late 16th-17th Cents. 3) *Fem.* Soft crown of cap or bonnet. 18th and 19th Cents.

CAULIFLOWER WIG *Masc.* Closely curled bob-wig worn by coachmen. Late 18th Cent.

CAVALIER *Masc.* Mounted soldier. Member of loyalist country gentry who fought for King in English Civil War, 1642-1652. Their elegant dress included much wearing of lace, embroidered gloves, high leather boots and large plumed hats.

CAVALIER SLEEVE *Fem.* Sleeve worn on daygowns. Full to the elbow and then close to the wrist. Seamed and closed on the outer side by a series of ribbon bows. 1830s.

CAVALRY TWILL Hard-wearing fabric of twill with diagonal weave. Suitable for hard wear, tropical uniforms and sporting garments.

CAXON *Masc.* White simple tie-wig usually worn by professional men. Late 18th Cent.

CEINT *Masc. Fem. Fr.* Name for sash, girdle or belt. 14th and 15th Cents.

CEINTURE, CEINTURON *Fr.* Girdle. 20th Cent.

CELTIC BROOCH Early pieces discovered in Ireland were of gold, used for fastening shawls or cloaks of animal skins. Most common form - open circle with long pin fastening.

CENDAL *Med.* Costly silk fabric still in existence in 17th Cent. Resembled an open weave sarcanet fabric. Woven light or heavy with slightly glazed surface or sheen. By 17th Cent., used only for linings.

CEPKEN *Masc. Turkish.* Sleeveless jacket resembling a bolero. Richly embroidered, worn with wide sash over a white shirt.

CEREVIS *Masc. Germ.* Brimless cap worn by some university corps. Early 19th Cent.

CEREVIS

CERUSE *Mas. Fem.* Cosmetic used for whitening the appearance of the face; it was thought that the white hair powder, used in early 18th Cent., dulled the look of the brightest complexion. Some washes, and wash-balls of that period were very injurious, containing white lead, even quicksilver boiled in bismuth and water, which damaged the skin. 16th, 17th and 18th Cents.

CESTUS *Fem.* Mythological sash of Venus, portrayed in Greek and Roman sculpture. Placed around waist and tied to hang down in front. *Masc.* Roman fighter's strapped glove, reinforced with pieces of iron.

BRITISH CHIEF *in war dress, carrying a bronze shield.*

The Anglo-Saxons wore simple garments. The men wore Braies and the women a long tunic or Stola. The long shawl or scarf worn by all was called a Palla. There were no hats.

THE CELTS IN THE 7th CENTURY

British Bard

CEYLON Island in Indian Ocean, became independent republic 1972. (See COMBOY - part of Ceylon national dress). Now SRI LANKA.

CHACONNE *Mas.* Ribbon cravat or neckcloth, not tied, but hanging over chest. Late 17th Cent.

CHADAR *Fem.* Covering black mantle worn by some Persian women in public. Before 1920s. Now seen in modern materials.

CHAFFERS *Fem.* Embroidered side-pieces, or lappets, of the gable-shaped English hood.

CHAIN Necklace of small links, or ornament pieces. Worn with medallions of great quality, 16th Cent. Still revived and used for insignia of office, or fashion.

CHAIN BUCKLE *Masc.* Buckle or curl. A type of curled wig. 1750s.

CHAINE DE FORÇAT *Masc. Fr. -convict.* Heavy gold linked chain for securing watch or monocle, usually over black velvet waistcoats. Early 19th Cent.

CHAIN HOLE *Mas.* Vertical hole, placed between two buttonholes of waistcoat, allowing watch-chain to pass through and giving added security. Introduced in lounge suits from 1880s.

CHAINMAIL A mesh of interlaced metal links. Used to make the first protective armour.

CHAINSE *Mas. Fem.* Simple body garment. Of varying materials according to means of wearer. Medieval. Later called CHEMISE. Predecessor of shirt.

CHALLIS, CHALEY Lightweight twilled fabric originally of silk and camel hair from India, 1831. Today, made of wool with rayon or cotton. Printed in colours.

CHALON Medieval fabric mentioned by Chaucer. Napped or friezed on both sides.

CHALWAR *Fem. Pers.* Wide, long loose trousers gathered to just above the ankles. Worn until 1870. Also in Turkey and the Balkans. A jacket called ETEK, often beautifully embroidered, worn over a blouse, accompanies this costume.

CHAMARRE *Masc. Fr. Chamarrer - bedeck, bedizen.* Full, loose gown of fine rich material; embroidered, jewelled, fur-lined, decorated with braid. First appeared in Europe, 1485-90. Worn over doublet and hose, often with sash around the waist. Shortened to knee-length in 1520s, with puffed sleeves, introducing the square appearance of the 16th Cent.

CHAMBORD Ribbed woollen cloth used for mourning garments. Sometimes includes silk or cotton fibres.

CHAMBRAY Strong cotton gingham used for making sunbonnets. Made first in Cambrai, France. 1880s.

CHAMMA *Masc. Fem.* Ethiopian outer garment made from a long piece of white cotton material. *Fem.* Sometimes bordered with colourful embroidery. Traditional, but still worn.

CHAMMER *Masc.* Academic robe usually in black, 14th and 15th Cents. Distinguished formal gown, with sleeves, sometimes in velvet trimmed with fur. 16th Cent. Also CHYMER, SHAMEW.

CHAMOIS Soft leather made from the skin of small goat-like antelope of Europe and the Caucasus. Also from sheep or goats when grain is removed. Used for gloves, pockets, and interlinings. Chamois cloth is a yellow-dyed thick cotton fabric made to simulate the leather.

CHANARRE *Masc.* Jerkin with lattice-work design of criss-cross bands. Late 15th Cent, early 16th Cent.

CHANCELLOR *Masc.* Full-bottom wig. 18th Cent.

CHANEL, GABRIELLE Influential French 20th Cent. couturier, who introduced styles and fabrics which are still copied. The elegant suit or 'tailleur', with casual-appearing hip-length jacket and matching skirt have been worn for decades and persist in spite of the fashions of the '60s, '70s and '80s emphasising and manufacturing separate garments.

CHANG FU *Masc. Chinese* Basic simple long robe with standing collar, the style worn for several centuries. 1644-1912.

CHANG-OT *Fem.* Korean outer cloak with full sleeves. Worn with draped silk skirt.

CHANG SHAN *Masc.* Chinese long gown for formal wear. Accompanied with a black jacket, if needed.

CHAPARAJOS *Masc. U.S.* Large protective leather leggings worn over trousers when riding, to protect from prickly bush and vegetation. In California, the deerskin hides are left with the hairy pelt untouched to give added warmth and protection. A 19th-20th Cent. cowboy style.

CHAPARAJOS Batwing leather leg-chaps worn by cowboys when riding in brush or scrub in California. 19th Cent.

CHAPE *Masc.* Heavy cape. 12th Cent.

CHAPEAU À BORNE *Fem. Fr. Swiss* Large circular straw hat worn by grape pickers near Lake Geneva.

CHAPEAU BONNET *Fem. Fr.* Richly decorated hat with bonnet appearance. Worn with veil tying under chin. 18th Cent.

CHAPEAU BRAS *Masc.* A bicorne hat which gradually replaced the three-cornered tricorne of the late 18th Cent. It folded flat for placing under the arm. Used in France with court dress. Retained as part of ceremonial uniform in British, American and French Navies. *Fem.* Satin calash or folding hat. Early 19th Cent.

CHAPEL DE FER *Masc.* Helmet worn over a hood of chainmail. 13th and 14th Cents. *Fem.* Peasant's hat with rolled brim. 16th Cent. Re-appearance as MONTAUBAN, 17th Cent.

CHAPERON *Masc.* Head and shoulder covering in form of hood and shoulder cape, universally worn from 12th to 16th Cents. The pointed pendant end of the hood was elongated into a tail called Liripipe. This was arranged in many ways, sometimes twisted around the head or left hanging. Worn in Europe and Britain by churchmen, nobility and commoners.

CHAPERONE *Fem.* Small soft hood tying under the chin, worn informally. 17th Cent.

CHAPELET 1) Garland or wreath of flowers worn on festive occasions since early times. 2) Jewelled metal circlet worn on head, Medieval. 3) Decorated, twisted or padded roll of silk or satin, 14th and 15th Cents.

CHAPS (See CHAPARAJOS)

CHAQUETA *Masc. Sp.* Leather jacket worn by cowboys in U.S.A.

CORDAY, CHARLOTTE *Fr.* Woman revolutionist who stabbed Marat to death in 1793.

CHARLOTTE CORDAY BONNET *Fem.* In late 19th Cent. in England, many feminine articles of dress were given names with French association. This bonnet, for outdoor wear, had a high soft crown with narrow frilled brim. Decorated by a broad ribbon band with the lo g ends hanging down at the back.

CHASUBLE *Masc.* Long sleeveless cloak worn by priests.

CHATELAINE *Fr. châtelaine -lady of a castle.* Chain or clasp fastened at the waist securing items such as keys, scissors, trinkets, etc. which the mistress of a household would use. Early examples were made in gold, silver, enamel, cut steel. In late 18th Cent. Wedgwood jasper cameos were mounted and added as ornaments. In late 19th Cent. they were little used except as ornament. After World War II, a fashion of wearing two brooches joined by chains across the dress front lasted for a short time. Also TROUSSOIRE, 16th and 17th Cents.

CHATTA East Indian umbrella.

CHAUSSEMBLES *Masc.* Hose, with leather soles stitched under feet, requiring no overshoes or boots; worn by nobility from mid-14th Cent. to mid-15th Cent.

CHAUSSES Norman hose cut out of wool or linen cloth from 11th Cent., prior to knowledge of knitting in the reign of Elizabeth I of England. Sometimes strapped and the forerunner of stockings. The Anglo-French term gave way to that of 'hose' which had been used in British Isles since 11th Cent.

CHAUSSETTE *Fr.* Socks.

CHEATS *Masc.* Waistcoats with fronts of rich material, but with cheap backing. 17th Cent.

CHECHIA *Masc. Algeria.* Deep-crowned soft cap of felt with tassel. Headwear of Zouave, French Light Infantry Corps. 19th Cent.

CHEESECLOTH Thin, soft, unsized cotton of plain weave. *Fem.* In 1970s, peasant and ethnic full length dresses of simple cotton were much worn.

CHEKLATON Brilliant red textile, later of gold. 13th and 14th Cents.

CHELE Fur from the stonemarten's throat area. Medieval.

CHEMISE *Masc. Fem.* Undermost or body garment dating from Ancient Greek and Roman periods. A development from the CHAINSE into the later SHERTE, 13th Cent. Made of soft linen or wool. *Fem.* By 19th Cent., it was the forerunner of lingerie, worn under the corset, of fine white cotton or silk. By the end of the 19th Cent., lace, tucks and frills were added. In 1890s, the garment was replaced by combinations.

CHEMISE À LA REINE *Fr. Fem.* Simply styled lightweight dress of finest cotton or silk, introduced by Marie Antoinette, 1781.

CHEMISE DRESS *Fem. Fr.* Chemise-like fashion gown with drawn-in deep decolletage; tied at waist with sash; and with long tight sleeves. Full, without fastenings, put on over the head, 1783 until 1790s. The 'Perdita' chemise worn in England, named after the famous actress Perdita Robinson, had a close-fitting bodice with V-neck. This style was either closed in front by a series of ribbon bows, or buttons. The sash worn with it was tied to fall down the back. 1783-86. The later London 'Calypso' chemise was worn with a loose robe over it. 1799.

CHEMISETTE *Fem.* Underbodice, usually of white lawn or muslin, with or without sleeves, to 'fill-in' low-cut neckline of dress. Late 19th Cent., early 20th Cent.

CHENILLE *Fr. - caterpillar.* A yarn with upstanding fibres resembling tufts from a caterpillar. It has many uses - embroidery, fringes, etc. When woven, it has a silky luxurious appearance like plush.

CHEONGSAM *Fem.* Modern version of Chinese straight gown or sheath. High collar, short-sleeved, with slit at side of skirt which varies from eight to ten inches, and does not extend more then four inches above the knee. Silk or cotton.

CHERUSSE *Fem.* Small, high dress collar of several rows of gathered lace or frills. Early form of ruff, which started in England, and worn by Queen Elizabeth, after whom it was named. Adopted also in Europe. Examples can be seen in female portraits of the period, e.g. Anne of Austria, Queen of Spain, by Sanchez Coello, 1571. Kunsthistorisches Museum, Vienna. The collarette style was used again in gowns at the beginning of the 19th Cent., when sometimes six or seven rows of frills were included.

CHESTERFIELD *Masc.* Elegantly styled overcoat named after the 6th Earl of Chesterfield, 1830-40. Knee-length at first but gradually grew longer. Slightly waisted with centre-back seam and short back vent. No seam at the waist. Usually with velvet collar. S-B or D-B, with five front buttons, sometimes under a fly-facing. *Fr. TWINE, PARDESSUS, 1850s.*

CHEVERIL Kid leather used for gloves. Medieval.

CHEVESAILLE *O.F.* Decorative border around the neck of a garment. Term used by Chaucer. Medieval, 1400.

CHEVEUX-DE-FRISE *Fr.* Curled piece of hair. Name given to narrow lace edging with vandyked edge. 18th Cent.

CHEVIOT Woollen cloth woven from shaggy wool of sheep from the Cheviot Hills in Northumberland.

CHEVRON *M.E., O.F. Chevron.* Inverted 'V' motif used on heraldic shields and on sleeve of service uniform indicating rank. *Fem.* Zigzag trimming above hem of skirt. 1826 and on.

CHIFFON Semi-transparent lightweight material usually of silk. Durable, although flimsy.

CHIGNON *Fem.* A knot, mass, or twist of hair worn at the back of the head. A style repeated throughout history. *Fr. CHIGNON FLOTTANT* was an arrangement of loops or ringlets hanging from the back over the neck, late 18th Cent. Dressed over false hair, with rows of curls, the chignon often weighed five ounces, in the late 19th Cent. The bulk of the hair-dressing was in keeping with the mass of material used in the dresses of the period, especially in the late 1860s.

CHIL KAT BLANKET *Masc.* The outstanding feature of the Tsimshian Indians of Alaska and British Columbia. Fringed, ornately decorated, it was used as a wrap and woven from goathair and cedar bark. Accompanying this colourful robe was a cloak of beautifully matched white ermine furskins arranged in tiers and on the head, an elaborate headdress or high hat of smooth fine fur, topped with upstanding feathers, quills and front decoration.

CHIMERE *Masc. O.F. Chamaire - a loose gown.* Sleeveless robe, worn over the white lawn rochet, by bishops.

CHIMNEY POT HAT *Masc.* Irreverent name for tall tophat worn in 19th Cent. from 1830. It replaced the high-crowned Beaver hat worn in late 18th Cent.

CHINCHILLA Costly fur of a small South American rodent. Blue-ish grey with black markings. It was used by the Incas for robes. Muffs of this fur were fashionable as early as 1823. It is now bred in U.S.A. and Canada but continues to be rare.

CHIN CLOUT Muffler, or diagonally-folded material worn over chin or mouth, 16th and 17th Cents.

CHINÉ SILK *Fr.* Chinese silk using a technique of colouring warp threads which gave a variegated mottled effect. 1820.

CHINESE DRESS Basic items. (See BAISHAN, CHEONGSAM, SHAN).

CHINESE EMBROIDERY Painted designs of high standard worked over by satin-stitches using silk floss and metal threads.

CHIN SCARF *Fem.* White linen scarf, or barbette, worn under stiff linen toque, around and under the chin. Medieval. From 16th Cent.

CHIN STAYS *Fem.* Frills of lace added to bonnet strings, forming a frill around chin when tied. (See MENTONNIERES)

CHINO Stout, twilled cotton fabric used for uniforms and sports clothes in Far East. 'Dust' colour.

CHINTZ Printed calico from India, 12th Cent. Today, a cotton cloth, usually glazed, with exotic, colourful bird-motifs and flowers. Used for interior decoration and periodically for fashion garments, jackets, handbags.

CHIRINKA *Fem.* Silk square embroidered with gold or silver threads, fringed. An accessory when attending church or ceremony in old Russia.

CHIL KAT Ornately patterned blanket worn by Tsimshian Indians of Alaska and British Columbia. Fringed and woven from goathair and cedar bark, it is accompanied by a tiered cape of beautifully matched white fur skins.

CHIRIPA *Masc.* South American skirt worn for riding. A large square blanket with central hole for putting over head, and arranging around waist. Held in place by elaborate silver belt.

CHIRIPA. S.A. Masc. Skirt worn over pantaloons. Made from square blanket with centre hole cut out for waist.

CHITON *Masc. Fem.* Basic garment of Ancient Greece, made from rectangle of linen or wool. (See GREEK COSTUME)

CHITTERLINGS *Masc.* Decorative frills on front of shirt, which protruded below the chin. Late 18th Cent. and 19th Cent.

CHLAINE *Masc. Gk.* Woollen cloak. Homeric.

CHLAMYS *Masc.* Short cloak of soldiers of Ancient Greece. Worn leaving the right arm uncovered.

CHOGA *Masc.* East Indian Mohammedan tailored outer coat, slightly fitted. Usually of handsome materials - velvet, silk, linen or wool. Small standing collar; knee-length, slightly flared with side slits; buttoned at centre front. (See NEHRU TUNIC) *Fem.* Style used in London and Paris for fashionable coats, usually of black silk. 1967.

CHOKER *Fem.* High collar of fur, fabric, or necklace.

CHOLA DERBY *Fem. S. Amer.* Bowler hat adopted at the beginning of 20th Cent. by Chola Indian women of Bolivia. Previously, the national headwear was of hard white felt, but the factory-made hat in black, brown or beige colours is now worn. The U.S. term for the British bowler is DERBY.

CHOLI *Fem.* Short-sleeved cotton blouse worn under the sari by Hindu women. Sometimes accompanied by full skirt, or IHENGA.

CHOPINES Wooden clogs or overshoes sometimes covered with leather. Thick, high soles of cork or wood on stilts or pegs for protection from mud. Popular in Italy and Spain. Not used extensively in Northern Europe. Much worn by the ladies of Venice. 16th Cent.

CHOU Rosette of tulle, ribbon, velvet, used for ornamental decoration on hats, or neckwear. Late 19th Cent.

CHOUX *Fem.* Term given to large chignon of hair in late 17th Cent.

CHRISOM Child's white robe, signifying innocence, used at baptism.

CHUDDAR Hindu shawl.

CHUKKA East Indian. Ankle-high boot worn with fitted riding breeches called JODHPURS. *Masc. Fem.* Now in modern use.

CHURRIDAH *Fem.* Modern silk or cotton leggings.

CHYMER (See CHAMMER)

CICISBEO Knot of ribbons or silk attached to fans, parasols, walking-sticks, umbrellas.

CICLATON (See CYCLAS)

CIDARIS *Masc.* Tiara of Jewish high priests. Royal headwear of ancient Persian kings.

CILICE *Masc.* Shirt of harsh haircloth once worn by monks as penance.

CIMIER *Masc.* Ornament or decoration worn above helmet in ancient times. Examples - plumage, floating scarf, horses' tails, carved animals or birds which moved when wearer was in action. Also LAMBREQUIN, COINTISE.

CINQUECENTO *Ital.* Renaissance period in 16th Cent. Italy, particularly with respect to its art and literature.

CINQUEDEA *Ital. - Five fingers.* Large dagger, or short sword with flat triangular blade, about five fingers in width. A civilian weapon, sometimes etched and gilded. Late 15th and early 16th Cents.

CIOPPA *Fem.* Elegant, brightly coloured gown with embroidery. High-waisted, with decorative sleeves and train. Worn over more simple, long main dress called GAMURRA. Renaissance. See paintings of Domenico Ghirlandaio, Italian, 1449-94.

CIRCASSIA A European region in southern U.S.S.R. on the coast of the Black Sea. Part of the Ottoman Empire until 1829, when it was ceded to Russia.

CIRCASSIAN A member of a group of tribes, some of whom moved into Turkish territory and whose women were remarkable for their beauty. 19th Cent.

CIRCASSIAN BODICE *Fem.* Bodice of gown with folds from shoulders, crossing at the waist. 1829.

CIRCASSIAN WRAPPER *Fem.* Loose day-wrap of muslin and lace. The sleeves made with strips of lace and muslin forming alternating bands. 1813.

CIRCASSIENNE GOWN *Fem.* A variation of the POLONAISE, in a bell shape, with three puffed panniers, which were held up by silk cords. Made in two colours and of ankle length. 1780.

CIRCINGLE Girdle worn with cassock. (See SURCINGLE)

CISELÉ VELVET Quality fabric with satin ground and raised velvet pattern. 1876.

CLARENCE *Masc.* Type of boot with triangular gusset of soft, folded leather. Lacing and eyelet holes allowed ease of wearing. A forerunner of elastic-sided boot. 19th Cent.

CLASP Metal contrivance for fastening brooch or buckle; used from earliest times.

CLAVI Purple badges or stripes placed on toga and tunic indicating an ancient Roman's rank and profession.

CLAW-HAMMER *Masc.* English name given to riding-coat with two long tapering tails at back of garment, 1811. Later seen in evening dress.

CLAYMORE Two-edged large sword anciently used by Scottish Highlanders.

CLERICAL VESTMENTS White: Emblem of purity, worn on feasts, saints' days, and sacramental occasions.
Red: The colour of blood and fire, for the days of martyrs, and Whit Sunday. Green: Only on days which are not feasts nor fasts. Purple: The colour of mourning. Advent Sundays, Lent, and Ember days.
Black: On Good Friday.

CLIP, CLIP-BROOCH *Fem.* A decorative brooch or clasp, fastened to lapel, collar or neckline by a strong clip. 20th Cent.

CLOAK *O.F. cloke; Fr. cloche-bell* Bell-shaped, loose, sleeveless garment, which evolved from mantles worn by the early Greeks and Romans of the Mediterranean area. Easily removable, and gave protection against inclement weather conditions. Many styles through the generations include ARMENIAN, BALAGHIE, INVERNESS, KERRY, OPERA.

CLOAK BAG PORTMANTEAU Essential receptacle, used when travelling, for packing valuable cloaks. 16th and 17th Cents.

CLOAK BAG BREECHES *Masc.* Full, baggy oval-shaped trousers closed in above the knees. Decorated with bands of metal-tipped laces. Early 17th Cent.

CLOCHE *Fr. cloche-bell* 1) Travelling cloak. Late 13th Cent. - 15th Cent. 2) *Fem.* Small bell-shaped hat. In plain colour and usually trimmed with band of contrasting broad grosgrain ribbon above narrow brim. Evolved to wear on popular short hair style, the shingle, of 1920s -mid-30s.

CLOCK 1) Originally a gore, or insertion, in sewing terms. 2) Embroidered arrow or line of decoration on ankles of female stockings; also at end of seams above pleats.

CLOCHE HAT *Fashionable mid-1920s, over short hair.*

CLOGS, CLOGGES 1) Overshoes with wooden soles to walk above muddy conditions; similar to, and also known as, PATTENS. 17th Cent. 2) *Fem.* Leather-soled overshoes, with straps across foot, to match indoor shoes. Late 18th Cent. 3) All-wooden shoes worn by country and hard-working people. The Lancashire, England, clogs had wooden soles with an iron horse-shoe fitted to the heels and leather uppers fastened on with brass studs. They were worn for industrial work in 19th Cent. but now retained for clog-dancing.

CLOISSONÉ One of the most ancient forms of enamelling, using cloisons or network of raised metal enclosures. Today, usually applied to bracelets, necklets and buttons.

CLOQUÉ *Fr. - Blister, swelling.* Material treated or stitched to give a blistered, raised surface.

CLOSE-HELMET Close-fitting, visored helmet enclosing the head. With chinpiece and visor pivoting at the sides. 16th Cent. Different from the earlier ARMET which had hinged cheek-pieces fastening at the chin.

CLOUD *Fem.* Triangular headscarf of light-weight material, for winter evening wear. Early name was CLOUT, 17th Cent. Also in long scarf form of lace, net, thin silk. Late 19th Cent.

CLOUDED CANE A malacca cane clouded or spotted with age or use. Extremely fashionable early 19th Cent.

Sir Plume of amber snuff-box justly vain,   And the nice conduct of a clouded cane.

Pope: *Rape of the Lock, IV, 123.*

CLOWN The dress of the clown, seen in circus and present theatrical life, is possibly a relic of medieval miracle plays, and also of the traditional costume of the Italian Commedia dell'Arte. Succession of fools and jesters, in courts of kings, also contributed to distinctively exaggerated apparel with voluminous trousers, pom-poms and frills, the peaked hat and bold make-up.

CNEMIS *Masc.* Protective leggings of hard leather, bronze or brass worn above sandals by Greek and Roman soldiers. Also GREAVES.

COACHMAN'S COAT *Masc.* Long heavy coat with many overlapping capes. Originally worn on the box of a coach. Known also as BOX COAT. It was also adapted for walking. Early 19th Cent.

COALMAN'S HAT *Masc.* Protective head gear usually of strong felt, shaped with deep protective fantail at back. 19th Cent.

COAL TAR COLOURS Dyes obtained in the manufacture of coal-gas - aniline, phthaleins, indigo and alizarin. Discovered by Sir W.H. Perkin, English chemist, 1838-1907.

COAT Sleeved outer garment of various lengths according to purpose. (See COTE, COTTE).

COAT OF ARMS Originally a tunic worn by knights over their armour, decorated by recognisable devices. First used in England by Crusaders from the Holy Land, who had protected their armour from the sun. The devices and rules were codified and HERALDRY was born.

COBURG Twilled lightweight material of wool or cotton originally from Germany. 1840.

COBWEB LAWN Very fine linen, suitable for cuffs, ruffs and kerchieves. Early 17th Cent.

COCK *Masc.* Turn-up of brim of hat. Named varieties include DENMARK, DETTINGEN, MONMOUTH. Late 17th Cent. - early 19th Cent.

COCKADE Rosette of pleated ribbon, used on military hats. A badge worn on the head-dress of men servants of Royalty or those holding commission. 18th and 19th Cents.

COCKED HAT *Masc.* Military, bicorne hat with side brim turned up and fastened to crown with cockade. In Europe and England - ANDROSMANE, KEVENHULLER. Worn by American generals. 1780.

COCKERS, COKERS Knee-high boots worn by working people, 14th-16th Cents. Later, of greater length, used for wading, by fishermen. 17th Cent.

COCKLE 1) The shell worn by pilgrims in their hats. It was also used for begging. 2) *Fem.* Term for ringlet or curl. 17th Cent.

COCKLE HAT A pilgrim's hat, especially worn to the shrine of St. James of Compostela, Spain. The symbol of the Saint was a scallop-shell.

COCKTAIL DRESS *Fem.* Semi-formal dress worn for late afternoon and evening occasions. 1940s.

CODOVEC *Masc.* Trade name for type of CASTOR beaver hat. 17th Cent.

CODPIECE *Masc.* Bag or box of fabric worn to conceal the front opening of breeches. Trunkhose and codpiece were secured to doublet by lacings. Of Spanish origin and sometimes constructed to hold money and extras.

COGGERS *Masc.* Firm leather or stiffened cloth gaiters buttoned at side and with a strap under the instep. 18th and 19th Cents.

COIF *Masc.* 1) Close-fitting cap worn under helmet by knight. 2) A simple close-fitting linen piece, covering the ears and tied under the chin. Worn by serjeants-at-law in form of a white hood and also by learned professions. 13th-15th Cents. 3) *Fem.* An undercap, 16th Cent. Later, often embroidered and curved over the ears. 16th-18th Cents.

COIFFE *Fr. - Head-dress.*

COIFFEUR *Fr. - Hair-dresser.* **COIFFURE** A style of dressing the hair.

COIN DE FEU *Fem.* Short jacket with wide sleeves and high closed neck. Of velvet or cashmere and worn indoors for warmth. 1848.

COINTISE A long scarf worn over a lady's head-dress which, when presented to a knight on horseback, was worn from his helmet. 13th and 14th Cents.

COKE *Masc.* A bowler hat, so-named by London tailors, after Thomas William Coke, Earl of Leicester. Mid-19th Cent.   Also BILLYCOCK

COLBERT Jean-Baptiste (1619-83). Chief minister to Louis XIV, who promoted great re-organisation of trade. He equipped a royal workshop for 200 workers near Paris for production of silk stockings; and founded a technical school so that the trade could be learned and maintained.

COLBERTINE *Fr.* An open lace resembling net. Named after famous French minister, Colbert. 17th Cent.

COLLAR 1) Neckchain of knighthood. 2) Band of linen, lace, completing upper portion of costume. Neckband, upright or turned over shirt, dress, coat. Extravagant or not according to period. In late 16th and 17th Cents., referred to as BAND. Many types, but French Revolution caused frills and lace to be abandoned. However, the collar retained significance as a symbol of Class Distinction until mid-20th Cent.

COLLAR TYPES DUTCH: Plain, flat, with rounded or pointed corners. ETON: Schoolboy's plain, stiff white linen. GALLILA. GOLILLA: *Sp.* Plain, upstanding white. GLADSTONE: High-standing, with points, over bow or scarf-tie. MANDARIN: Standing band to close-fitting neckline. MASHER: High all-round stand collar. 1880-1890s. MEDICI: Standing, wired, pleated fan-shape from low neck. 16th-17th Cents. MOAT: Narrow standing collar on bateau neckline. O.F. 13th Cent. MOURNING: Black velvet worn by French refugee aristocrats. NAPOLEON: High-standing, folded over with wide revers, worn with black cravat. Early 19th Cent. PRUSSIAN: Shallow stand-fall with ends nearly meeting in front. 19th Cent.   ROBESPIERRE: Very high-standing, deeply folded over, with broad lapels. Late 18th Cent. SAILOR: Broad, square and flat at back, narrowing in front to 'V'. ROLL: Long, without indentations. WING: Standing, stiff with turned back tabs. Formal. Late 19th Cent.

COLLAR LACE Term for imported Venetian point laces, with simple design and Van Dyke outline. Early 17th Cent.

COLLAR OF ESSES 'S's A decorative collar composed of a series of golden 'S's jointed together. Originally the badge of the House of Lancaster, 1360. Restricted to the Lord Chief Justice, the Lord Mayor of

Collar Styles

Dutch Collar. 17th Cent.

Gladstone Collar. 1850s. Upright standing, worn with silk scarf by W.E.Gladstone.

Eton Collar. Starched white linen. Worn at Eton College. From 1820.

Medici Collar. Italian. High, wired, from low décolletage. Worn by Medici women.

Spanish golilla or whisk. 1630s.

Robespierre Collar. High-standing, with deep fold and broad pointed revers with lawn jabot.

London, Heralds, Serjeants-At-Arms and Serjeant Trumpeter.

COLLECTIONS, COSTUME   (See separate listing.)

COLLEGIANS *Masc.* Short boots, with cut-out wedge-shaped piece removed from sides to allow easier donning and removal. 1830s.

COLLET MONTE *Masc. Fem.* Standing high collar worn after the ruff was abandoned. In lace and lawn, 1580-1620. (See COLLAR, MEDICI)

COLLEY-WESTONWARD *Masc.* Fashion of wearing jacket, or tabard, askew or sideways, usually with one sleeve in front and the other behind. 16th Cent.

COLLETIN *Masc.* Shoulder and collar piece of armour. Middle Ages.

COLOUR The seven fundamental colours of the spectrum are: violet, indigo, blue, green, yellow, orange, red. The Primary colours, which cannot be obtained by mixing other colours, are: RED, YELLOW, BLUE. Secondary colours result from the mixture of two or more primary colours, such as orange (red plus yellow); green (blue plus yellow); purple (blue plus red). From early and Biblical times, colours used came from natural sources, or mixtures obtained in dyeing. Natural colours: white, black, red, yellow and green. Around the world, some colours attain special and yet very different significance - in Brahmanism, yellow is a sacred colour; brides wear yellow in India; the Chinese connect royalty and deity with it. In Europe, in the Middle Ages, heretics were forced to wear yellow.

From Biblical times, dyeing merchants in Canaan used pomegranates and saffron for a lovely yellow; madder-root and safflower for fiery red; woad for blue, and ochres and red chalk for more subtle colours. The murex sea-snail provided purple and the Phoenicians created an industry for its extraction. Not only were textiles patterned and coloured but hair dyes and face-painting were influenced by Israel's delight in adornment and love of colour. Henna, powdered lapis-lazuli for eye make-up, ivory ointment boxes, and mixing jars have been found in ruins of Israelite cities.

In past history, colours have been associated with assigned meanings. Symbolic colour became,and still is, important to religious art. After the Renaissance, the Church, artists and makers of clothes, gradually went their separate ways. It was not until after the discovery and use of aniline dyes in the 19th Cent. that the German scientist, Wilhelm Ostwald, 1853-1932, devised a colour system which helped to bring attention to the order and relationship of different hues to each other.

COMB-MORION (See MORION)

COMBINATIONS *Masc. Fem.* One-piece garment combining vest and drawers introduced second half of 19th Cent. to provide more warmth with less bulk.

COMBOY *Masc. Fem.* Skirt-like garment worn in Sri Lanka, previously Ceylon. *Masc.* Wrapped around and gathered into belt, with short-sleeved jacket. *Fem.* Wear is combined with sari.

COMMODE *Fem.* Silk-covered wire frame on which high hair-dressing and high cap called Fontanges was arranged. Originated from France and also known as TOWER. Late 17th Cent. - early 18th Cent.

CONCH *Fem.* European. Enveloping full-length cloak usually black. Hooped with bones or wires to form a protecting conch-shell shape from the waist upwards. Worn as mourning cloak. 1580s-1620.

CONEY Name given by garment trade to rabbit fur.

CONFIDANTS, CONFIDENTS *Fr. Fem.* 1) Small curls arranged close to ears. Often tied with small velvet bows. 2) Silk hood tied under the chin. Both late 17th Cent.

CONGRESS SHOE *Masc. U.S.* Short leather boot with silk uppers and elastic side pieces which neatly eliminated the opening. 1850s.

CONTOUCHE *Fem.* Comfortable morning gown or wrap. 18th Cent.

COOLIE HAT China. Conical shaped hat of straw worn for protection from the sun by hired labouring persons.

COPE *Masc.* Semi-circular cape or cloak worn by priesthood.

COPOTAIN *Masc. Fem.* Hat with high conical crown and small to medium-sized brim. Popular 1560-1620. Style revived as SUGARLOAF hat, 1640-1665.

COPPED SHOES *Masc. Fem.* Shoes with long points stretching beyond toes. Late 14th Cent., and again late 15th Cent. Also PIKED, CRACOWES.

COQUARD *Masc. Fr.- old cock.* Bonnet worn by German and Swiss knights. Of satin with many ostrich plumes around the crown. 16th Cent.

COQUARD   Distinctive Headwear. A bonnet worn by Swiss and German knights. 16th Cent. See LANSQUENET.

COQUILLE *Fr.- shell.* Shell-like ruching used for trimming on neckwear and bonnet edgings.

CORAZZA *Masc. It.- cuirass, armour plate.* A shirt made to button at the back, fitted to shape of body. 1845.

CORDELIÈRE *Fr.* 1) Girdle of cotton rope with knotted ends, worn by Franciscan friars. 2) Silk and wool fabric. 1846.

CORDOVAN *Sp.* Cordwain-leather. Cordwainer. Shoemaker. Fine grained soft leather made from goatskin in Cordova. High quality, dark brown and durable. Today other types of skins also used. Also CORDWAIM Med.

CORDUROY *Fr. - Cord du Roi.* Thick corded cotton with pile like velvet. 18th Cent.

CORDWAIN (See CORDOVAN)

CORK 1) Bark of the cork oak. 2) Used for sole of very early galosh and patten.

CORKING PINS Pins of large size used by ladies to keep curls fixed in place. Also called CALKIN pins because of similarity to nails used for fitting horseshoes.

CORK RUMP *Fem.* A bustle in the form of a crescent, padded with cork. 15th Cent.

CORKED SHOES *Masc. Fem.* Shoes with wedge-shaped cork heels. 16th Cent. and early 17th Cent.

CORK WIG *Masc.* Used in making of wigs. Late 18th Cent.

CORNED SHOE Broad-toed shoe. First half of 16th Cent.

CORNER CAP *Masc.* Square-shaped velvet cap worn with academic robes. 14th Cent. Sometimes triangular.

CORNET *Fem.* Large spreading white headdress worn by Sisters of Charity. Also in varying styles from 14th Cent. to late 17th Cent.

CORNETTE *Fem.* 1) *Fr.* Large piece of stiffened lace rolled into point, e.g. Breton. 2) A white day cap tied under the chin. Early 19th Cent.

CORNO *Masc.* Ducal bonnet worn by Venetian doge. Of brocade, satin or velvet, decorated with embroidery and jewels. Worn over a white cap tied with strings. 15th and 16th Cents.

CORONA *Lat.* Crown, garland. Bestowed as an honour.

CORONAL The open crown of nobility. 14th Cent.

CORONEL Lance used for jousting. M.E.

CORONET Small crown implying lower rank to that of sovereign. (See CROWN)

CORSAGE 1) Small bouquet of flowers to be worn upon shoulder, bosom, or waist of gown. 2) Bodice or waist of fem. gown.

CORSELET 1) Seen in paintings and mosaics in Ancient Crete. A short jacket laced below the bare breasts in corset style. Not after 1400 B.C. 2) *Fem.* Introduced in Europe over gown, late Medieval. 3) *Masc.* Piece of armour covering body. 15th Cent. Also CORSLET, CORSSELET. 4) Comfortable, smaller corset, only slightly stiffened or not at all. 20th Cent.

CORSET *Fr. corps - body.* 1) Fitted under bodice of boiled leather or stout canvas. 14th and 15th Cents. 2) Basquine, a fitted hip-length tunic of leather was worn by all, over a quilted underbodice, 16th Cent. 3) This garment was reinforced with wire during Renaissance and later with whalebone after 1600. 4) After French Revolution, English tailors became recognised for style and quality in masculine wear. *Masc.* Tightly fitted and boned bodices were worn in early 19th Cent. 5) Fem. styles, tightly fitted, followed shapes that emphasised current fashions. At the end of the 19th Cent., a heavy cotton corset, with basks and suspenders, helped to produce the fashionable wasp-waist favoured at that time. 6) By the 1920s, this formidable garment has been simplified, with the approval of the great couturier, Paul Poiret, who designed simple body undergarments and brassieres for the mannequins showing his dress styles. The introduction of modern Latex has made

bones and stays unnecessary and now form-shaping garments, easily washable, can be worn next to the body.

CORSICAN TIE *Masc.* Violet coloured necktie, narrow at back of neck with wider ends brought to front, and crossed without tying. Fastened to braces or under arms. 1830.

CORSLET Piece of armour covering body. 15th Cent.

COSMETICS Preparations designed to improve and beautify hair, skin and general appearance. Creams, oils, ointments, pastes, powder, lotions.

COSSACK OFFICER *Masc.* Cavalry officer of Russian Army, World War I, 1914-1918. Uniform consistd of greatcoat with flaring full sleeves and skirt. Leather belted with sword and dirk. Cartridge pockets on chest and black satin muffler worn at throat. Full trousers, leather boots, astrakhan cap called CALPAC.

COSSACK OFFICER 1914-1918 World War 1. Astrakhan cap, dark cloth coat with breast pockets for cartridges; black muffler; leather belt with dirk and sword; leather boots.

COSSACKS *Masc.* Wide trousers, pleated into waist-band, and pulled round the ankles with a drawstring. The Cossacks accompanying the Czar of Russia at the Peace Celebrations of 1814, evoked much admiration. The adopted fashion, in simpler style with straps under the instep, lasted until 1840s. This garment was called PLEATED TROUSERS.

COSTERMONGERS Costumes worn by Pearly King and Queen at the Costermonger's Harvest Festival, St Martin's in the Fields, London.

COSTERMONGER London seller of fruit, fish, etc., from street barrow. From Costard - large, ribbed apple. *Masc.* Cloth caps, neckcloths, cord waistcoats, topcoats, bell-bottomed or plain trousers. *Fem.* Black bonnets, silk kerchiefs, skirts, decorative and sometimes buttoned boots. Garments became covered with mother-of-pearl buttons arranged in complex designs. At beginning of 20th Cent., fem. bonnets gave way to the large feathered hats of Edwardian period. Worn now only for special occasions.

COSTREL A pilgrim's bottle; a bottle with handles or ears for hanging from a cord or sling.

COSTUME *Fem.* A dressmaker's term for a day dress made of one material, used for a specific outdoor activity. 1860s. By early 20th Cent., this term also used for separate coat and skirt or dress in matching material.

COSTUME COLLECTIONS (See separate listing)

COSTUME JEWELLERY Jewellery made from glass, metal, ceramics, semi-precious stones, leather, or synthetic materials. Such pieces depend on the novelty and suitability of design and are not intended as imitation of real jewellery. Coco Chanel launched a fashion in the 1920s for crystal and coloured glass, with necklaces of pearls and semi-precious stones of different sizes.

COTE, COTTE *O.E., O.F. Masc.* Outer garment. *Fem.* Long dress or petticoat, 12th-15th Cents. Word remains in English language -COAT.

COTE-HARDIE *Masc.* Tunic of varying length between waist and knee. *Fem.* Full-length waisted garment worn over kirtle. Both close-fitting and with sleeves. 1350. Until mid-15th Cent., flap from elbow was lengthened into a band called a 'tippet' or *Fr.* 'coudicre'. Sometimes with buttoned front fastening and often 'dagged' for decoration.

COTHURN, COTHURNUS (See BOOT)

COTILLION *Fem.* Underskirt. Name given to country dance because the garment was revealed during performance. 18th Cent.

COTTA *Masc.* White linen vestment with square yoke worn in churches. 12th-14th Cents. Sleeved, short form still worn by robed church choirs.

COTTAGE BONNET *Fem.* Straw bonnet with brim projecting beyond cheeks. From 1808. Style modified and by 1870 the brim was lined and rolled backwards.

COTTAGE FRONT *Fem.* A day bodice, with centre gap laced across over a linen or muslin fill-in. Early 19th Cent.

COTTON Cloth, fabric, yarn made from downy cotton seed.

COUDIÈRES *Fr. Coude - elbow.* Long narrow hanging band from elbow-length sleeve of COTE-HARDIE. Mid-14th Cent.

COUNTENANCES, COUNTENANCE *Fr. Fem.* Small muff, also tiny mirror, needlework accessories, scissors, suspended by ribbons attached to waist. 16th and 17th Cents.

COUPS DE VENT *Masc. Fr.* Hair style, cut with loose strands across brow. Seen in portrait by Ingres. Early 19th Cent.

COUREUR *Fem. Fr.* Short, tight-fitting upper garment, or blouse, worn during French Revolution. Late 18th Cent.

COURRÈGES *Fr.* Couturier, a Basque, created sensational styles after learning his trade as a cutter with Balenciaga. He became independent with a salon in Paris, 1961. He raised hem-lines, gained recognition in couture circles for fem. trouser-suits, plastic, long open-toed white boots and squared-off Egyptian-looking coiffures. The Begum Aga Khan, Princess Lee Radziwill and the Duchess of Windsor became his clients. His accessories, known internationally, include luggage and men's sportswear.

COURT PLASTER Beauty patch, patches. 18th Cent.

COURTEPYE *Masc. Fem.* An overgarment similar to SURCOAT. Usually short. Medieval.

COUTURE *Fr. - sewing.* Maison de Haute Couture - high quality dressmaking establishment.

COUTURIER *Fr.* Male dressmaker. *Fem.* COUTURIERE. For noted names and influences, see special listing of Couturiers in Addenda.

COUVRECHEF *Fr. Fem.* Head-dress, veil or head-cloth. Old Norman F., A.S.

COVERCHIEF *Fem.* Norman term for the Saxon head-dress. Worn from Medieval to 16th Cent.

COVERT A woven cloth, diagonally twilled, usually waterproof. Late 19th Cent. on.

COWBOY *Masc.* Cattle herder or horseman on a ranch in the Americas. Items worn include:-

Boots: Calf; high, Cuban heels, decorated tops.

Leggings: Deerskin chaps worn over trousers.

Hat: Quality, large sombrero called Stetson.

From 1870s.

COWHIDE Heavy leather from cowhide, used for boots and soles. Also for whips and thongs.

COUTURE   Yellow gabardine suit for spring, 1970 by Hardy Amies, with skirt worn above the knee.

COWICHAN KNITWEAR   Speciality knitted garments made by Indian women in Vancouver, Canada, from natural coloured sheep wool. The dark emphasis of designs is knitted with the wool of black sheep. 20th Cent.

COWL   *Masc.* Hood of monk's robe. From 14th Cent. Female term applied to draped folds around neck. Modern.

COWPUNK   *Texas, U.S.* Modern style of wearing traditional Texan riding garments with fashion 'flair'. Stetson hats are made from rabbit and beaver fur, some in colours to match low-heeled work boots. *Fem.* Fringes of ermine tails, sequins and feathers decorate black and coloured suede jackets; panels of snakeskin with animal designs are also incorporated. Bright-coloured, skin-tight trousers, fringed supple suede dresses, flounced skirts in denim or suede of distinctive style, are all worn at various times for events, at the many stock shows, and parades. 1980s.

COXCOMB   Notched red strip of cloth worn on head-dress of court jester. From Medieval times until 17th Cent.

CRACKOWES   *Masc. Fem.* Long pointed shoes worn by dandies. Sometimes held up by chains from knees or ankles. Late 15th Cent. (See also POULAINEO

CRAMIGNOLE   *Masc.* Velvet cap-like hat with turned-up brim and feather decoration. Late 15th Cent. -early 16th Cent.

CRAN   *Masc.* V-shaped gap between the collar and lapel of a coat. 1830s.

CRANT   *Fem.* Symbolic garland. Of decorated gold work, or flowers. Funeral crants were hung over seat of deceased in church. Medieval to 18th Cent.

CRAPAND   Bow of ribbon tying man's hair at back in a pouch or bag-shape. 1745.

CRAPE   Transparent black silk gauze, used for mourning. 17th Cent. on.

CRAQUELÉ   *Fr. Crackled.* Treatment given to silk materials, lace or net to form a broken interesting surface. Modern.

CRAVAT   *Masc.* Linen or lace neckcloth, from 16th Cent. Many varied styles in 19th Cent.

CRAVATE COCODES   *Fem.* Large cravat forming a big bow knot, worn with habit shirt for riding. 1863.

CRAVAT STRINGS   *Masc.* A piece of coloured ribbon tied around the two ends of the cravat forming a bow under the chin. It later took the form of a 'made-up' stiffened bow with many loops. Fastened from behind the cravat, the ends of which fell over the ribbon construction. 1665-1680s.

CREASE-RESISTANT   Term or label applied to chemical treatment given to materials and textiles to eliminate creasing. 20th Cent.

CREPE   Thin fabric with crinkly surface woven originally in the Orient. In the West, Italians made it in 13th Cent. The French produced some at Lyons in the 16th Cent. It was later introduced in England.

CREPE DE CHINE   Crepe of fine silk.

CREPE GEORGETTE   Beautiful, highly creped fabric in all silk, silk and rayon, or silk and cotton. Named for its designer, Mme. Georgette de la Plante.

CREPE MAROCAIN   Crepe material combining silk and wool, giving a weight more suitable for cooler conditions.

CREPE RUBBER   Durable rubber with crimped surface used for shoe soles.

CREPIDA   *Masc. usually.* Ancient Roman sandal, worn for long marches and travelling. Simplest version was a stiff leather sole with thong between first and second toes attached to ankle strap. Other types had leather tongues, or criss-cross thonging. All similar to Greek KREPIS.

CRÉPINE   *Fr. - fringe; créper - to crisp.* Pleated frill or edging to French hood. Early 17th Cent. Not to be identified with CAUL.

CRESPINE   *Fem.* Wide-meshed net allowing hair to be visible. Worn with barbette and fillet. 13th and 14th Cents.

CRETE   Mountainous island of Greece, where a civilization developed around Knossos, 3000-1400 B.C. Clay figures discovered there have revealed love of luxury and refinement. Their costume was characterised by extremely tight waists. *Masc.* Loincloths, wide leather belts, decorative knee-high boots and a kind of turban. *Fem.* Full skirts, bell-shaped with series of flounces, and skin-tight corsage bodices which exposed the breasts. Elaborate head-dresses and long hair dressed in spirals.

Jewellery, such as collars, necklaces, bracelets and hairpins has been discovered in tombs. Love of bright colour - red, yellow, blue, purple, can be seen on the well-preserved frescoes. In contrast to the 'draped' clothes of the Greeks worn on the mainland, garments worn by the islanders of Crete were cut and shaped to the body.

CRETE LACE Lace of coloured flax in geometric patterns now made on the island.

CRETONNE Twilled, unglazed cotton, or linen, which lends itself to printing in bright colours. From Creton in Normandy originally. Used for light furnishings and informal dresses and jackets. From 1867.

CRÈVE-COEUR *Fr. - heart-breaker. Fem.* Style of dressing curls at the back of the neck. Late 17th Cent.

CREWCUT *Masc.* Close cropped hair-style originating from North American colleges. Similar to an earlier European Prussian haircut and the G.I. style worn in World War II later.

CREW NECK Round, flat neckline close to throat. Similar to sweaters worn by boat crews. 20th Cent.

CREWEL Thin two-ply worsted woollen yarn used for tapestry and embroidery; on clothing, screens, bedspreads, curtains. Crule - 15th Cent.

CRIADES *Fr. Criard - clamorous, squealing. Fem.* Petticoats of gummed and hooped canvas, worn under fashionable panniered gowns, 17th Cent. The garment emitted squeaks as the wearer moved but were tolerated as they were cheaper than those made with whalebone stiffening.

CRINOLETTE *Fem.* A half-cage crinoline with hoops of horsehair or crinoline placed under the back portion of the garment. The front of garment was left flat and unpadded. 1868-1873.

CRINOLINE *Fr. crin -horsehair.* 1) A stiffening braid made from crin. 2) Hooped petticoat - reinforced with this braid in early 19th Cent. 3) Artificial or Cage, invented in 1856 to replace number of petticoats but retaining name of CRINOLINE. Some forms were strengthened by steel hoops and varied in shape from oval to pyramidal. The fashion of voluminous skirts needing such support lasted fifteen years and was at its greatest extent in 1860. In mid-1860s, the material of the skirt was pushed backwards, leaving the front of the garment flat and straight. This resulted in the formation of the bustle and was supported by smaller forms of padding or by the crinolette in the 1870s. 4) There has only been one attempt to revive the large crinoline skirt since that time. In 1938, when the King and Queen of Great Britain made a State visit to Paris, the Queen wore romantic gowns with full skirts, but the attempt by couturiers to popularise them was unrealistic. 5) After World War II, full stiff petticoats were worn under Christian Dior's 'New Look' designs but they were of far smaller size than those worn in 19th Cent. and only lasted as long as the fashion.

CRISP 1) Fine lawn material, 14th and 15th Cents. 2) *Fem.* A veil to cover the hair, 16th Cent. A curl of hair, 17th Cent.

CRISPIN *Masc.* Cloak worn for evening with large sleeves. Always lined, sometimes with quilting, 1839. *Fem.* Short, with high neck, caped. Of velvet or cashmere, sometimes with wadded lining. 1842.

CRISPINE *Fem.* Hair ornament. 13th and 14th Cents.

CRISS *Masc.* Girdle to support trousers. 15th Cent.

CROCHET A hook. From 14th Cent. Many uses. *Fem.* Sometimes suspended from waist for scented pomander.

CROCUS, CROKERS Yellowish-brown linen, dyed yellow with saffron. 18th Cent.

CROMWELL COLLAR *Fem.* Turnover flat collar, with front edges nearly touching edge to edge. Neat finish for morning dress. 1879-80s.

CROMWELL SHOES *Fem.* Comfortable leather, tongue and buckle footwear. Worn for croquet, 1868. Similar cut shoe revived with large bow instead of buckle. 1888.

CROP *Masc.* Short hair-style worn by Duke of Bedford and political friends as a protest against the tax on hair powder. Late 18th Cent.

CROQUET BOOTS *Fem.* Leather boots, laced with ribbons, decoratd with fancy toe-caps and tassels front and back. 1865.

CROQUIS *Fr. - sketch.* Drawing made rapidly, usually with reference to fashion.

CROWN Royal head-dress indicating sovereignty.

CROSS-GARTERING *Masc.* A long sash garter was placed below the knee with the ends crossed behind, then brought forward to be tied either to side or centrally. Used when stockings were worn over canions. Late 16th and early 17th Cents.

CRUCHES *Fem.* Small curls arranged on forehead. Late 17th Cent.

CRUSADERS Men from England, Scotland and Europe, who went to fight in the Holy Land, 11th-13th Cents. Each nation had a special colour: Red - France; White - England; Green - Flanders; Blue - Italy; Gules (Red) - Spain; St. Andrew's Cross - Scotland; Red on white - Knights Templar. These warriors brought back exotic styles, such as pointed shoes from Turkey, the turban of the Saracens, the steeple head-dress of Jewish origin and also the hitherto unknown colours of azure and lilac from Persia.

CUARAN *Masc. Scot.* Highlander's knee-high boot kept up with thongs. 16th-17th Cents.

CUCULLUS *Masc. Roman.* Hooded cloak, previously called SAGUM, worn by soldiers from Gaul. With long ends to wrap and secure at neck.

CUE *Masc. Fr. Queue - tail.* The hanging end of a wig. Early 18th Cent.

CUFF Turned-up fold on end of sleeve or trouser.

CUFF-LINKS Pairs of metal pieces, or buttons, linked to pass through sewn holes of cuffs for fastening. From 1840.

CUFF STRINGS *Masc.* Pair of thin ties for holding cuffs in place. 17th Cent.

CUIRASSE *Fr. -Breastplate. Masc.* Protective body armour made of leather, or metal. From 16th Cent.

Wide 1840.

Wider 1850.

Widest 1860.

CUIRASSE BODICE *Fem.* Long tight-fitting bodice giving new appearance to figure, after wide silhouette of Crinoline, and later bustle. Dipping front and back, it served to reduce the size of the tie-back skirt. 1874-1875.

CUIRASSE TUNIC *Fem.* Plain and influenced by current style of masc. jackets, was worn with bodice. 1874-1878.

CUIR-BOUILLI *Fr. Cuire - to cook, boil.* Leather treated with soaking and boiling, for moulding to shape, used especially for armour and corsetry. Medieval.

CUKAR *Fem.* Side piece of horned head-dress. 15th Cent.

CUL DE CRIN *Fem. Fr. Cul -bottom.* Bustle for gowns of 1788.

CUL DE PARIS *Fem.* Bustle for gowns of 1680s.

CULGEE Heavy East Indian silk fabric. Late 17th and 18th Cents.

CULOTTES *Masc.* Knee breeches formed by joining the tops of waist-high stockings, 17th Cent. *Fem.* Divided skirt designed for activities such as bicycling. LIDO pyjamas were introduced in 1920s; 'hostess' culottes and knee-length shorts followed in 1930s; but not until 1950s did trousers become recognised and acceptable for everyday fem. wear. In 1960s, Courrèges was one of the major designers in Paris, showing many styles in his collections.

CUMMERBUND *Masc.* Waistband or sash of Persian/Hindu origin. Adopted by Europeans in pleated black silk, replacing waistcoat in warm weather, late 19th Cent.

CUP-HILT RAPIER Light sword fashionable in Spain and S. Italy, 17th Cent. The guard was formed by circular bowl with straight cross and knuckle pieces. Until 18th Cent.

CUPOLA COAT *Fem.* Hooped petticoat in bell shape. Early to mid-18th Cent.

CURRICLE Two-wheeled open carriage drawn by two horses abreast.

CURRICLE COAT *Fem.* Long coat with lapels with one fastening. Very long sleeves. Also GIG COAT. 1820s. *Masc.* Box or driving coat with capes. 1840s. Other 'curricle' styles: *Fem.* DRESS with half-robe or tunic, 1794-1803; CLOAK usually three-quarter-length, trimmed with fur or lace, 1801-1806; PELISSE caped, 1820s.

CUSHIONET *Fem.* Form of bustle worn to give tilt at the back to the farthingale. Late 16th - early 17th Cents. Also QUISSIONET.

CUSTOM MADE U.S. term for 'Made to Measure' tailoring. British term - BESPOKE, as opposed to ready-made.

CUTAWAY COAT *Masc.* Single-breasted tailcoat with fronts curving to the bend of the knee at the back. From 1830s. Worn with contrasting trousers. Accepted style for formal morning wear in 20th Cent., with striped trousers. Its use and appearance has declined since World War II, except for certain social occasions.

CUIRASSE BODICE 1880
The Emergence of Conventional Tailoring. Both the female dress with the new CUIRASSE bodice and the masculine suit show a new interest in garments more closely shaped to the lines of the human form.

CUT-FINGERED GLOVES *Masc. Fem,* Fashion which allowed display of jewelled rings. Late 16th to early 17th Cents. *Fem.* Tips of glove fingers were cut. 1700-1750.

CUT-FINGERED PUMPS *Masc.* Footwear with decorative slashing. 16th Cent.

CUTPURSE Name given to thieves, who cut leather thongs, which attached a pouch purse to girdle. 15th Cent.

CUT-WORK 1) Decorative cutting of edges of garments, mid-14th Cent.-15th Cent. Also known as DAGGING. 2) Cut out, embroidery filled, work. Italy, England. 16th and 17th Cents.

CYCLAS *Masc. Fem.* Silken short tunic, or cloak, from Cyclades, Greek Islands. Worn over armour from 13th Cent.

CYPRUS Black crepe material used for mourning. Made in Cyprus.

CZAPKA *Masc. Fem.* Polish for cap or caul. Also KALL, KELLE.

CZECHOSLOVAKIAN EMBROIDERY Outstanding attractive geometric designs worked on linen in brilliant colours.

CZÓLKA *Fem. Pol.* Tall stiff tiara with side decoration of ribbons, flowers and feathers. Traditional.

The winner of the annual DOGGETT Coat and Badge race, held on August 1st for six Thames watermen, received an orange livery coat with silver buttons and a big silver arm badge. The race was instituted by Thomas Doggett, an actor manager of Drury Lane, to signal the accession of George 1 in 1715. It is rowed between Old Swan Pier, London Bridge, and the site of the White Swan Inn, at Chelsea Bridge.

DACCA   Capital of East Pakistan. Embroidery silk of untwisted thread, used for embroidery.

DACCA MUSLIN   Fine gauzy cotton cloth.

DADA, DADAISM   *Fr. Hobby-horse.* Art movement of rebellion stemming from Zurich, 1916, advocating spontaneity and rejecting traditional values at the end of the first World War, 1918. Influence upon fem. fashions of the '20s; dresses became simple, narrow sheaths; hair styles were short, expressive of a struggle for emancipation. Coco Chanel in France was one of the outstanding couturiers of that period whose creations are still admired and elegant today.

DAG, DAGGES   Decorative borders of deep indentations cut into edges of garments, inc. hats, 13th and 14th Cent. Types -castellated, flamboyant, foliated, leaf-shapes, tongues, V-shapes. Applied to hems, hoods, capes.

DAGSWAIN, DAGSWAYNES   Rough, coarse cloth woven for hardwearing simple clothes. 15th and 16th Cents.

DALK   Pin, clasp or brooch used for fastening. 10th-15th Cent.

DALMATIC   Wide-sleeved, long tunic of simple style originally from Dalmatia (now Yugoslavia, 1918). Adopted by Romans. Over the centuries used for State and religious ceremonies. Examples seen in Ravenna mosaics. One of robes worn by British Sovereign at the Coronation. When shortened, with embroidery and lace, is part of liturgical apparel, made in one piece, symbolizing the seamless robe of Christ.

DAMASIN   Silk brocade with metal threads. 17th and 18th Cent.

DAMASK   Rich linen or silk fabric made originally in Damascus, having woven designs, shown by reflection of light, with combination of flat and satin surface. Since 13th Cent.

DANDY   *Masc.* In Scotland, name stands for 'Andrew' - a valet or manservant, as 'Abigail' is for a waiting woman. In early 19th Cent., a fop, who considered dress and demeanour a fine art and was largely responsible for establishing the English reputation for good tailoring. Fashionable appearance included a moustache, a tight waist, much decorative braiding on the coat, peculiar hats and wellington boots with, until about 1815, an insolence of behaviour. The Frenchman, Count Alfred d'Orsay, was the last famous dandy and after 1839, masc. apparel became generally more moderate in appearance. *Fem. Dandizetta* - English Regency period, 1811-1820, remembered for stance called 'Grecian Bend', adopted when wearing dresses inspired by Grecian, Roman and Pompeian works of art.

DAGGING   Headdress of Louis of Anjou, 1415- , showing fine dagging of chaperon-hood, twisted and wound round the head. From a French painting.

DANISH OPENBOTTOM TROUSERS   *Masc.* Worn by young boys. The open-ended legs reached to just below the knees, uncuffed. 1870s.

DANNOCKS   Countryman's strong gauntleted gloves used for hedging. Recorded since late 18th Cent.

DÉCOLLETAGE   *Fem.* Low neckline of dress, usually in formal evening dress.

DEERSTALKER CAP   *Masc.* Tweed hat for country wear with peak fore and aft and adjustable earflaps fastened on sides of crown. Fashionable 1870-1890; supposedly worn by famous fictional hero - Sherlock Holmes, created by Sir Arthur Conan Doyle. 1887-1927.

DEL   *Masc. Fem.* Simple coat used for riding, Inner Mongolia; usually of dark reds or blues with hem and neck braided in contrasting colour. Wool used for cold weather, but for special occasions of brightly coloured silk or cotton. A contrasting sash tied round the waist. Worn over trousers.

DEMI-GOWN   *Masc.* Short gown worn when riding. 1500-1550.

DEMI-SURTOUT   *Mas. Br.* Lightweight fitted overcoat with low collar. 1818.

DEMI-TUNIQUE   *Fr. Fem.* Three-quarter length summer jacket or coat with short sleeves. End of 18th Cent.

DENIER   Measurement of fibre strand applied to thickness of yarns, particularly those used for hosiery and underwear.

DENIM   Stout, washable, twilled cotton material, previously used only for work overalls, etc. Today used for sports clothing, summer suits, dresses. *Fr. 'de Nîmes'*, a textile-producing town of S. France.

DENMARK COCK   *Masc.* Three-cornered hat, higher at the back than the front. 1750-1800.

DENTELLE   *Fr. dent -tooth, notch.* Lace with tooth-edge or pattern of small points.

DENTES DE LOUP   Pointed, serrated trimming used on dresses. Early 19th Cent.

DERBY   *Masc.* 1) Bowler hat as worn first by Earl of Derby, 1780. 2) Term used in U.S. from 1860s for bowler hat. 3) Necktie called 'Four-in-hand', long with narrow centre, tied in a knot.

DERRARA   *Masc.* Long, loose, blue shirt worn in Southern Sahara region. On the front is a large pocket embroidered with design associated with particular area. A long scarf, usually blue or white, is worn round the neck and head for protection against sandstorms or sun.

DERVISH   *Masc. Turk.* Follower of esoteric school of Sufism of Islamic Persia, from 13th Cent., featuring the partaking in mystic dance with alternate prayer and acting. A long dark robe, removed during action, reveals a costume consisting of white high-necked shirt, and open jacket, with floor length, flaring, white skirt, which billows out in a great circle when dance is in progress, hiding legs and feet. A high-topped cone-shaped hat completes the outfit.

DERVISH DANCERS

DESIGN   Early man painted his body with red, blue, yellow, white, representing earth, air, fire and water. Superstitions led to symbols placed wherever there was an opening in a garment. Decoration, fringing, embroidery used at neck, openings, cuffs, hems, tops of stockings and around the head. Some of these features persist in apparel of simple communities, with a wealth of meaning, still conveyed by man's oldest symbols such as circle, triangle, spiral and so on.

DETTINGEN COCK *Masc.* High, large hat with equal sized cocks. Named from battle of 1743. Discarded 1750. Compare DENMARK COCK.

DEVONSHIRE HAT *Fem.* Very large hat, wide-brimmed with deep crown, most fashionable with broad band and front buckle; sometimes trimmed with large bow in front and back, or with feathers. Known as 'picture hats' from the portrayal by Gainsborough of Georgiana, Duchess of Devonshire. 1783.

DHOTI *Mas. Ind.* Traditional wrapped garment, consisting of a single length of material. Worn long, or placed around the waist and through the legs.

DIADEM Plain or jewelled fillet, wreath, worn round head to represent status.

DIAMANTÉ *Fr.* Ornamented with diamonds. Scintillating paste used in brooches, buckles, neckwear, ornaments.

DIAPHANOUS *Gk. - showing through.* Applied to transparent materials.

DICKY, DICKEY *Masc.* False shirt front. Innovated England, early 19th Cent., developed for less well-off. In 1830, became separate shirt front for evening wear.

DILDO *Masc.* Sausage-shaped curl of a wig. 18th Cent.

DIMITY *Gk. Dimitos - double thread. M.E.Fr. di - twice. It. dimito.* Strong cotton fabric woven with stripes taking two threads or more to obtain raised or corded surfaces. Originally from Egypt in 18th Cent.

DINNER JACKET *Masc.* Informal evening short coat without tails, usually black, introduced in 1880s. In summer, made of white or light materials. Mid-20th Cent. in colours, velvets, etc.

DIRECTOIRE *Fr.* Term used of a style in women's clothes and furnishings which emerged during the Directoire, 1795-1799 in France, the body of executive power formed during the French Revolution, in reaction to previous extravagance. In fem. wear, simple, classic lines of ancient Greece and Rome were admired and imitated, usually made up in semi-transparent cotton or muslin materials, worn over narrow clinging underslips. Records reveal that dresses were sometimes damped to cling to the figure. 1803.

DIRECTOIRE KNICKERS *Fem.* Slim close-fitting knickers with elastic at waist and knees, worn from 1910 for many years. So called because of uncluttered simple style previously unusual.

DIRECTOIRE STYLES *Fem.* The re-emergence of Directoire styles was inspired by Sarah Bernhardt acting in the drama of *La Tosca*, 1887. Designs for her clothes included long, trailing, flared skirts, high-brimmed bonnets and hats, coats with tight sleeves, all reminiscent of attire worn at the end of the 18th Cent.

DIRNDL *Fem.* Skirt style from Austrian Tyrol. Full-gathered at waist. Became fashionable 1930s. Revived 1960s.

DISH DASHA *Masc. Baghdad, Iraq.* Long white shirt reaching to ankles, buttoned from neck to waist.

DISHABILLÉ *Fem. as Fr. deshabillé.* Term applied to loose, flowing wear on informal occasions. Late 19th Cent.

DIVIDED SKIRT *Fem.* Introduced for ease of movement when cycling, 1880s. Garment was cut to conceal the division of the two legs. By 1920s onwards, full, but shorter, divided skirts were designed, later being called 'shorts' or 'culottes'. Ankle-length culottes have been accepted also as evening wear by today's pundits.

DJELLABA *Masc. Fem.* Caftan-like robe of Moroccan origin with loose sleeves and calf or full length. Style copied for modern leisure wear.

DOESKIN 1) Inner side of doeskin, lambskin or sheepskin used for fine quality gloves and leather goods. 2) Soft, fine, superior West of England cloth with smooth, level surface from. From 1850s.

DOGALINE *Masc., Fem. It.* Rich-looking brocade or velvet robe with knee-length, full flaring sleeves, which were contrast-lined, sometimes with fur. Ankle or mid-calf length 14th Cent.

DOGGET UNIFORM *Masc. E.* Traditional costume worn by Thames watermen in the annual rowing race, inaugurated in 1715 by Thomas Dogget, a Drury Lane actor-manager, to celebrate the accession of George I. The winner received an orange-coloured livery coat, closed in the front with silver buttons, and with a large oval-shaped silver arm badge. The usual costume was dark blue coat, upturned peaked hat, matching buttoned knee breeches, with stockings to below the knees and buckled shoes.

DOILY 1) Cheap woollen textile mostly used for warm petticoats, named after the London linen-drapers, Doyleys, in the Strand, from late 17th Cent. to 1850. 2) Small napkin placed under finger-bowl on dining-table.

DOLLS Small figures, known also as 'moppets', were used to show current modes and sent from Paris to England, 1740-1800s. Probably the first recorded mannequins.

'DOLLY VARDEN' *Br.* Feminine popular fashion was influenced by this character from 'Barnaby Rudge' by Charles Dickens 1) Cap - of lace, with small, gathered crown, ribbon-trimmed, worn with tea gown, 1888. 2) Hat - of straw, with very wide brim and low crown, tipped forward and tied under chignon at back of neck and having decoration of small flowers or ribbon only. 1871-1875. 3) Polonaise dress wih overskirt bunched up at the back, of printed chintz showing a bright ankle-length silk skirt, plain or quilted. In winter, a printed cashmere or flannel was used. A popular rather than stylish fashion.

DOLMAN *Turk.* Originally an outer masc. coat but adopted in E. Europe, 16th-19th Cent. The ample sleeves are cut in one piece with main front and back of the garment, obviating set-in shoulder seams. When shortened and more fitted to the body, it became the jacket of the Hussar's uniform, 18th Cent. A fem. version in W. Europe was cut to fit over the long bustled gown, having loose open sleeves and with two hanging pieces in front, 1870s-1880s. By the 1890s, another version, long but less full, was made of rich, warm materials such as heavy plush, velvet, cashmere, for winter wear. In 1912 and 1920, a dolman wrap coat cut with very wide armholes, with sleeves tapering to the wrist; sometimes worn with large fur collar and matching muff also became fashionable. To date, the cut of similar style of sleeve in fem. wear is referred to as 'Batwing', but is used chiefly in blouses, loose shirts and dresses.

DOLMANETTE *Fem.* European 'comforter', or comfortable warm cape-jacket, made from crochet and tied with ribbon at neck. 1890s.

DOMINO Hooded woollen cloak originating from winter garments worn by medieval clergy.

Masc., Fem. A loose cloak with half-mask worn at carnivals, masquerades first held in Venice to conceal identity. Usually black silk and voluminous. Early 18th Cent.

DONARIÈRE *Fem.* Quilted satin short cape and hood, with sleeves. 1869.

DONEGAL TWEED Homespun material, hand-scoured, made in Donegal, Ireland. Most suitable for suits, coats and sportswear. Copies by machine, with slubs woven in, are made today but some weaving by hand-looms in the original way continues.

DONNA MARIA SLEEVE *Fem.* Extremely full sleeve from shoulder to wrist but looped on the inner side below the elbow. 1830s.

DOPATTA *Masc., Fem. Ind.* Lightweight shawl, or scarf, woven with gold or silver threads, worn by Hindus.

DORELET *Fem.* Hairnet of gilt threads interwoven with embroidered beads or jewels. Medieval.

DORINA *Fem.* Enveloping and concealing cloak in Bosnia. Made of check cloth, covering figure from head to foot, the face being hidden by a black gauze yashmak.

DORMEUSE *Fem.* Indoor or night-time cap of white muslin, lawn or fine linen, fitting loosely over coiffure. Full, high, puffed crown trimmed with ribbon. The side-wings called 'cheek wrappers' were downwards-facing, pleated frills of fine matching material or lace and the cap sometimes tied under the chin from a ribbon attached at the back. The Dormeuse became much enlarged and with a high gablelike shape to cover the elaborated hairstyles of the 1770s. (See also MIGNONNE)

DORNECK Linen material made in Norfolk. It was used for clothes worn by servants and hired helpers. 16th Cent. Originally from Doornik/Tournai in Belguim.

D'ORSAY Frenchman, Count Guillaume Gabriel, gained renown as leader of fashion in Paris and London. He was also a painter and sculptor. 1801-1852.

D'ORSAY COAT *Masc.* Fitted knee-length overcoat, with shallow collar. No pleats, plain sleeves. 1838.

D'ORSAY PUMP *Masc.* Classic shoe introduced by Count d'Orsay, with cutaway sides and low, broad heel. 1830s.

D'ORSAY ROLL *Masc.* Black silk top-hat with slightly curved high crown and a narrow rolled brim, higher and wider at sides. Usually worn at jaunty angle.1850s.

DOUBLET *Masc.* Padded, close-fitting body garment with or without sleeves, worn originally under a breastplate. Later worn over the shirt, 14th-16th Cent. Sometimes slashed. Became shorter after 17th Cent., evolving into the waistcoat. (See GAMBESON)

Fem. Garment adapted by women for horse-riding, late 17th Cent.

DOUBLET *An Elizabethan example from 1583, with peascod belly and narrow skirt worn over Venetian breeches. By 1603-1625 the doublet was less rigid with padding omitted.*

DOUILLETTE *Fem. Fr. douillet(te) - downy, soft.* Padded quilted outdoor pelisse or coat, for winter wear over flimsy gowns fashionable in early 19th Cent.

DOWLAS A rough linen cloth originally from Daoulas in Brittany. Used for smocks, shirts, working clothes in Scotland and England. 17th and 18th Cents.

DOWNY CALVES *Masc.* False padded calves shaped into stockings to give appearance of manly-looking legs. Late 18th Cent.

DRAB, DRABBET Strong, twilled cloth of dull brownish colour used for working smocks. 18th and 19th Cents.

DRAPER, DRAPERY TRADE From early 18th Cent., tailors, dressmakers, silk mercers, are recorded as having shops where materials and trimmings could be purchased and garments made to order. In 1809, a large house in Pall Mall, London, England, was fitted with departments selling furs, fans, silks, muslins, gloves, jewelry, gowns, millinery and perfumery. By the first quarter of the 19th Cent., warehouses were stocking not only manufacturers' own products but other items, such as parasols and ready-made clothing. The introduction of railway transport made the availability of many different goods possible. A farmer and weaver, John Watts, set up one of the earliest department stores, Kendal Milne and Faulkner, in Manchester, 1796. This was later owned by Harrods of Knightsbridge after the first World War and purchased by the House of Fraser

DRAWERS *Masc.* Two-legged undergarments for body and legs suspended from waist. Worn since 9th Cent.
Fem. In England, from early 19th Cent., both muslin and woollen drawers were worn. By 1840s, broderie anglaise was added as trimming and when crinolines were accepted as fashionable, scarlet flannel was used. After 1870s, much trimming such as lace, frilling, embroidery, was added to wider, fuller legs.

DRAWSTRING Cord or string drawn through slot along the bound edge of neck, wrist or waist, to secure loose fabric.

DRESS CLOTHES *Masc.* Costume for formal day and evening social occasions. From 19th Cent.

DRESS IMPROVER *Fem.* Name of small structure or device used for supporting the bustle in 1880s.

DRILL Coarse, twilled cotton or linen, washable, used for shirts, linings, summer hard-wearing outfits and uniforms.

DRUIDS *Welsh.* Costume worn at Bardic gatherings in Wales, United Kingdom. Based on that worn by priests of old pre-Christian religion. Long robes and head coverings, green for ovates, healers; blue for bards; white for priests and philosophers. The chief Druid wears white and a gold chest pectoral and a chaplet of oak leaves.

DRUM RUFFLE *Fem.* Graduated and filled ruff or ruffles, worn slightly below and around waist, usually more narrow in front than at the back, worn over the horizontal section of the wheel or drum farthingale. Early 17th Cent.

DU BARRY Jeanne Bécu, Comtesse du (1743-1793). Favourite of Louis XV. Her taste in clothes and furnishings influenced what came to be called the Rococo Period. Elaborate ornamentation in her dress included panniers, ribbon bow knots, feathers, ruching and flounces and was much imitated.

In England, a large fem. sleeve with 'bouffante' puffing above and below the elbow was called the DuBarry sleeve. 1835. In 1850, a fashionable front piece to fem. evening dress, ruched and tapering from the shoulders in a curve to the waist was named the DuBarry Corsage.

DUCK Canvas-like fabric, washable, used for sportswear and overalls, work clothes. 20th Cent.

DUCK BILLS Modern reference term for comfortable broad-toed shoes generally worn 1490-1540.

DUCK-HUNTER *Masc.* Striped linen jacket worn by waiters. 1840s on.

DUFFLE Heavy, woollen material used for warm coats from the Belgian town, Duffel. Since 17th Cent.

DUFFLE COAT Short, hooded warm overcoat fastened by toggles, worn by Armed Services in World War II, especially as protection from severe weather conditions. Government stocks were sold off after the War and the garment became immensely popular as a casual outdoor coat.

DUNDREARY *Masc.* Long combed-out side-whiskers (worn without beard); also known as 'Piccadilly Weepers'. 1870-1880.

DUNGAREE Coarse calico from India. (pl.) Overalls.

DUST COAT, DUSTER *Masc. Fem.* Lightweight summer covering coat worn as protection from road dust when travelling in new open motorcars. 1890-1910. *Fem.* Material usually alpaca, tussore.

DUST GOWN *Fem.* An overgarment, called a safeguard, worn when riding. 1600s.

DUSTMAN'S HAT *Masc. Br.* Working hat in fantail shape; also wide-brimmed turned up at one side and attached to crown. Late 19th Cent., early 20th Cent.

DUTCH CLOAK *Masc.* Wide-sleeved short cloak decorated with bands. 1590s-early 1600s.

DUTCH COAT *Fem.* Jacket, usually short, of velvet, trimmed with fur. 16th Cent.

DUTCH COIFFURE *Fem.* The front hair was dressed back from the forehead with a slight parting. The ears were usually uncovered. Powder was not always used. At the back, wavy tresses or curls fell to the nape of the neck. A cap was not worn, even for important occasions but ribbon knots and jewels were artfully placed to attract attention at such times. 1730-1750.

DUTCH WAIST *Fem.* Square-set front bodice attached above the wheel-farthingale. Early 17th Cent.

DUVETYN Smooth material resembling velvet, used for millinery and garments.

DUVILLIER WIG *Masc.* Very elaborate high and long dress-wig, named after a famous French wigmaker, 1700.

DYES Prior to the introduction of aniline dyes produced from indigo, most colouring was obtained from vegetable sources. The aniline dyes were of great strength and brilliance. Magenta was utilised first in textiles in 1859, and Solferino in 1860, both named after the Austrian-Franco battles.

DANISH INVASIONS OF BRITAIN, 797-900 and 977A.D.   The Dane was a terrifying pirate who stole, ravaged and plundered the sea-board of Western Europe. The havoc, pain and waste caused badly damaged the development of civilization in the regions concerned.

ÉCHELLES *Ribbon trimming resembling a ladder. From a portrait of Madame Pompadour by François Boucher. 1721-1764.*

EARCLIP Ornament affixed by spring clip-fastening to earlobe, replacing earrings in 1920s. Invented for women reluctant to have ears pierced.

EARED SHOE Square-toed style, with corners at the toes extended to resemble ears or horns. Middle 16th Cent.

EARMUFFS Adjustable earpads attached to headband, usually for protection from severe cold weather.

EARRING Ear ornaments inserted through hole pierced in lobe of ear. Worn by primitive communities and as symbol of rank in ancient Middle East. Fashionable in Spain from 16th Cent. In court life of 17th Cent., masc. fashion of wearing single pearl from one ear prevailed; fem. wore rings in both ears.

EAR STRING *Masc. Fem.* One or more strands of ribbon worn and tied over one ear only. A possible imitation of the then prevailing masc. fashion of wearing only one earring. Late 16th Cent.

EARTHQUAKE GOWN *Fem.* Warm covering gown made for outdoor night protection after the occurrence of two earthquakes experienced in London in the Spring of 1740.

EASTER BONNET *Fem.* Popular name given to a new hat or headpiece worn on Easter Sunday, from late 19th Cent.

ECCELIDE Striped, slightly shiny, silk and cashmere material produced in 1830s.

ÉCHARPE CLOAK *Fem.* Wide, long scarf with ends hanging low in front. Some with high collar attached and extending in two flat strips to just above ground. Late 18th Cent. and early 19th Cent.

ÉCHELLE *Fem. Fr. - ladder.* Decorative front panel or stomacher of dress, strengthened by whale bone, with graduated ribbon bows arranged like a ladder and usually diminishing in size from bosom to waist. An alternative was the use of cross-lacing to replace bows. Late 17th Cent. to early 18th Cent.

ÉCOSSAISE HAT *Fem.* Style of Scottish headwear cut higher in front than back. Decorated with hanging ribbon at back. Fashionable in 1860s.

EDGE, EGGE, OEGGE Decorated metal border, usually gold, for headdress. Late 15th Cent.

EDWARDIAN Period of reign of British King, Edward VII, 1901-1910. The stately 'hour-glass' silhouette for women and elegant narrow tailored suits for men, were popularized in the drawings of the well-known American artist, Charles Dana Gibson.

EEL SKIRT   *Fem.* Long, tight skirt worn for day; cut on the cross, with only centre panel having straight hem. Four other panels to cover sides and back, flaring from below knee level. 1899.

EELSKIN SLEEVE   *Fem.* Close fitting, tight sleeve. Fashionable early 17th Cent. and re-appeared for a short time 1880 and 1881.

EELSKIN TROUSERS   *Masc.* Extremely tight trousers favoured by young dandies called 'Mashers'. 1880-1890s.

EGHAM, STAINES AND WINDSOR   *Masc.* British local name for triangular, tricorne hat called after the geographical situation of those places. Early 19th Cent.

EGRET   Plumage of white heron birds, much used before protected, for head, hair and hat decoration.

EGYPTIAN CLOTH   Fine silk and woollen material. 1860s.

EGYPTIAN COSTUME   Clothing for the poor, children and slaves was simple and scanty. The oldest male garment recorded was a simple strip of linen called 'schenti', worn wrapped around the hips below a bare torso. Later, from 1425-1405 B.C., a skirt was adopted. An elaborate version worn by the highborn was gathered at the waist with a series of pleats and held in place by a decorated belt and suspended apron. Later, princes wore a tunic of transparent fine linen known as the 'haik'. Fem. costume was similar veiling the body rather than concealing it. A simple night tunic 'kalasiris' was worn loose or belted and often decorated by an apron. Another garment only worn by women was a long tight skirt from below the bust to ankles, supported by two broad shoulder straps, almost a predecessor of 20th Cent. pinafore dresses. Footwear consisted of simple open leather sandals. Jewellery, often in form of broad collars and pectorals set with precious stones, was an important part of the costume for the wealthy and were also linked with superstition and religion. Wigs were worn on ceremonial occasions.

N.B. After Napoleon's expedition to Egypt and later the Battle of the Nile, 1798, in many places there was much interest taken in Egyptian ornament and Egyptian motifs and decoration influenced dress ornament and furnishing.

EIGHTEENTH CENTURY   In spite of wars, there was continuous exchange of fashions across the English Channel, both by newspaper reports and by the model dolls used called 'moppets'. Flanders lace, Indian chintz and satins, Dutch calicoes, found their way into England; and in Italy silks of English manufacture were much prized.

A fashion of being painted in the dress of one's ancestors started in this Century. Although class distinction in dress prevailed earlier, there was an insidious change by the 1750s. Rational garments for informal and working wear were adopted. The frock coat for men was worn generally and in the country about 1730. By the end of the Century, the use and approval of woollen cloth was established in place of brocades. In England, when George III came to the throne in 1760, with his sympathy for outdoor activities, riding dress particularly affected the appearance of day clothes. Distinctions of occupation were displayed in garments worn by the learned professions, the Forces, merchants and squires. In fem. dress the outline of the hooped skirt became flatter and formed an ellipse by the middle of the Century and it remained as a symbol of rank in Court-dress after it was discarded for ordinary wear in the 1790s. Facial decoration was heavily applied and fem. hairdressing with the added use of false hair remained customary until the last decade.

The great social upheaval of the French Revolution, 1789, had a marked effect on masc. and fem. wear. Embroidered coats, brocaded gowns, wigs, powdered hair, face painting, disappeared. There was a quest for simplicity, apart from exaggerated movements from the 'Macaronis' in England and 'Les Incroyables' in France. The resulting version of the 'Empire' gown for women and a 'John Bull' costume for men prevailed and was worn all over Europe with little variation by the end of the Century.

ELASTIC   Cord, thread or string woven with india-rubber, invented by an Englishman, T. Hancock, 1820.

ELASTICIZED   Fabric, cloth or webbing woven with vulcanized rubber thread enabling it to be stretched. Used from 1836.

ELASTIC ROUND HAT   *Masc.* Tall dress-hat, with spring fitted in crown allowing it to be flattened and carried under the arm. Patented 1812 but improved in 1824. (See also GIBUS HAT)

ELASTIC-SIDED BOOTS   *Masc. Fem.* Comfortable footwear with inserted gussets of elasticized material on each side. Patented by J. Dowie, 1837.

ELATCHA   Indian striped silk material. 17th Cent.

ELBOW CLOAK   *Masc.* Short cloak fashionable from 1570s to early 17th Cent.

ELBOW CUFF   *Fem.* Turned back cuff of elbow-length sleeve. 1700-1750.

ELEPHANT CLOTH   Material woven with mesh pattern of twisted flax thread. 1869.

ELEPHANT SLEEVE   *Fem.* Extremely large sleeve in light material, with hanging fullness gathered into the wrist. 1830s.

ELEVEN GORE RIPPLE SKIRT   *Fem.* Fluted skirt made with eleven gores, narrow at waist and widening to the hem. Always lined and stiffened with horsehair at the hem, which usually measured twenty feet round.

ELIZABETHAN COSTUME   Garments worn during the reign of Elizabeth I, of England, 1558-1603. The main characteristic of this period was the rigidity of outline introduced by padding and stiffening of garments, replacing the easy, flowing lines of clothes worn in the early part of the Century. Men wore the peasecod doublet; and the chief feature of feminine dress was the wheel farthingale. The starched ruff appeared, a development from previous use of a drawstring at the upper

SCHENTI *or loin cloth*
and beaded collarette

Embroidered
KALASIRIS
with shoulder straps

KING'S HEADDRESS

of striped linen
and worn with gold pastiche.

ANCIENT EGYPTIAN COSTUME

OLD KINGDOM before 1500B.C.
schenti worn.
NEW KINGDOM 1500-332B.C.
Pharoahs wore kalasiris.

Fem.

KING 1200B.C. Wearing SCHENTI,
KALASIRIS and
royal apron and belt.

KALASIRIS
OVER DRAPE
worn with collar
and belt.

Overdrape ROBE of semi-transparent, fine
linen, which was pulled to front at waist,
forming a cape-like bodice.

50

edge of the shirt. Women wore the ruff open in front allowing it to rise at the back of the head. Flat caps were abandoned (except by apprentices) and high bonnets and hats favoured. Magistrates and professional men wore wide-brimmed hats with low crowns. Masc. breeches took many forms - galligaskins, gasgoynes, slops, venetians. Stockings made from cloth were worn until around 1590, when knitted hose took their place. Textiles and fabrics were handsome. Lace-edged handkerchieves, together with fringed, embroidered gauntlet gloves, often completed the outfits.

ELL Old European measurement of cloth. English 'ell' was formerly 45″, now obsolete. (See ALNAGE)

ELLEMENTES Worsted material. 17th Cent.

ELLIPTIC COLLAR *Masc.* Detachable patent collar with high fronts. 1850s.

ELMINETTA Thin cotton fabric. 18th Cent.

ELYSIAN Woollen cloth suitable for overcoats with rippled diagonal nap finish. 19th Cent.

ELIZABETHAN DRESS Jewelled dress worn by Queen Elizabeth 1, for a ceremony in St Paul's Cathedral. After an engraving made by C. de Passe.

EMBOSSED Raised pattern in relief obtained by pressing or shearing back part of design. Used on fabrics, leather and metalwork.

EMPIRE Period during which Napoleon I ruled as Emperor of the French, 1804-1815. He prohibited import of Indian muslin, gave his support to silk industry at Lyons. He took active interest in France's influence upon fashion but English tailoring continued to influence masc. dress both at home and in Europe.

Fem. Styles influenced by clothes worn by Empress Josephine of France, 1804-1810. Long, clinging gowns of silk, sheer fabrics, or velvet, belted under bosom, were worn over a straight fitted slip. Long or short sleeves. Very short jackets, shawls, a long high-waisted redingote or top-coat accompanied these slender dresses. Turbans and bonnets were high fashion. Small coiffured hair with short front fringe became a distinctive part of the style.

EMPIRE BODICE *Fem.* A 'revived' style. The bodice was made to appear short-waisted by drapery crossing the front. This was tied at side or back. 1889-1890.

EMPIRE CAP *Fem.* Small, close bonnet, usually trimmed with ribbon and tied under chin, resembling child's headwear. 1860.

EMPIRE JUPON *Fem.* Wide petticoat wired in rows near the hem, which took the place of the 'cage' crinoline. 1867.

EMPRESS CLOTH Woollen cloth, or wool and cotton resembling merino. Popular in Second French Empire 1852-1870.

EMPRESS ÉUGENIE Wife of Napoleon III and Empress of the French, 1853-1870. Leader of fashion during Second Empire and the period characterized by the wide crinoline. Examples of styles portrayed in paintings by Winterhalter. Fem. hair coiffure altered from classical look to a more romantic look, with the bulk of the hair puffed out at sides and back of head. Worth 'created' a town-dress for her, the fore-runner of the 'tailor-made' suit.

EN DOS D'ÂNE *Masc.* Hair style with side pieces and long pigtail. 1780.

EN TOUT CAS *Fem.* Small sunshade or umbrella. 1850s.

ENGAGEANTES *Fem.* Series of two or three ruffles in lace or muslin on elbow length sleeve, falling from elbow to wrist. Late 17th-mid 18th Cent. The fashion was revived from 1840s-1860 as detachable white undersleeves with the edges trimmed with lace or embroidery.

ENGLISH CHAIN *Fem.* English invention. Early form of chatelaine for suspending watch and small useful cases from the waist. Early 19th Cent.

ENGLISH FARTHINGALE *Fem.* Rolled structure producing rounded hang of skirt. 1580-1620.

ENGLISH GOWN *Fem.* Devised, long, simple gown, usually of rich, plain material, favoured by sitters portrayed by famous English painters such as Gainsborough, Romney, Reynolds. A flimsy kerchief, or fichu, usually was placed around the neck. 1780s.

ENGLISH HOOD *Fem.* Wired hood forming a pointed arch above the forehead. Worn over an under-cap and after 1525, two long, wide pieces of material at the back which hung down or were pinned in place. 1500-1540.

ENGLISH WORK Anglo-Saxon embroidery of outstanding quality and excellence. Medieval.

ENGLISH WRAP *Masc.* Overcoat, double-breasted, similar to loose-fitting Chesterfield. 1840.

EPAULET *Fr. épaule* -shoulder. *Masc.* Shoulder tabs or decoration on uniform. These held shoulder belt for supporting a weapon in 17th Cent.; later retained as decoration and indication of wearer's rank. *Fem.* Epaulette. Decorative shoulder pieces very fashionable in 1860s.

EQUIPAGE See ÉTUI

ERMINE White fur of small weasel. Used for legal and royal robes. Also called 'miniver'.

ESCARPIN *Fem.* Black satin slipper with ribbon ties. Early 19th Cent.

ESCLAVAGE *Fr. -slavery. Fem.* Jewellery, necklets, bracelets, which were made of rows of fine chains. Fashionable at various periods.

ESCOFFION *Fem.* Head-dress in which hair was rolled inwards and held in a net caul, 14th and 15th Cents. It became enlarged with a horn shape over each ear and was followed by the tall steeple head-dress, known as the 'hennin'.

ESKIMO WEAR The clothing of people in Arctic coasts of Greenland, N. Canada and Alaska includes:-

KAMIKS *Masc., fem.* High boots of skin, with seal-skin socks worn inside. (Greenland - women embroider them with handsome leather motifs and beadwork).

KOOLETAH Coat of caribou skin from Labrador.

PARKA *Masc.* **AMOUT** *Fem.* Hip-length, hooded, outer garment of skin. Fem. amout has an extra hood for carrying a small child.

TIMIAK Shirt worn in Greenland, made of bird skins sewn together with downy plumage, worn next to the body. Cuffs at the end of long sleeves and neck-line are edged with dog fur.

ESKIMO WOMAN AND CHILD, ALASKA Child is carried in Parka and the mother wears shirt, tunic and breeches of sealskin, with fur turned to the inside. She wears Kamik boots.

ESKIMO DRESS CANADIAN ESKIMO wearing cloth Parka and fur-lined breeches.

ALASKAN ESKIMO His outfit consists of wolf or fox fur and is edged with a leather fringe.

ESMERALDA Gauzy material in white, with black and gold embroidery. 1830s.

ESPADRILLE Rope-soled canvas shoe in the coastal regions of the Mediterranean.

ESPRIT *Fem.* Small plume or mounted feather decorating turban or bonnet. Early 19th Cent.

ESTACHES *Fr. Masc.* Strings which attached hose to under-garment, 14th Cent. Forerunner of points of 15th Cent. onwards, which were tipped with aglets.

ESTAMINE Loosely woven woollen fabric, 17th-18th Cent. Became firmer in texture, a kind of serge in Late 19th Cent.

ESTRICH Felted material made from soft down of ostrich feathers and used in hat making. 16th Cent.

ETON Eton College, England, famous public school for boys founded by Henry VI, 1440.

ETON SUIT Suit worn by scholars at Eton, comprising morning-coat and silk top hat. The previous uniform style had been retained since 1798 and was worn at the funeral of George III, who had taken a great interest in the school. Junior schoolboys wear Eton collar and short jacket.

ETRUSCAN CLOTH Rough surfaced cloth similar to towelling.1873.

ETRUSCAN COSTUME Worn by people of the ancient country, Etruria, in Central Italy, 8th-7th Cent. B.C. The clothes, mainly tunics and cloaks, were all covered in unusual bold designs showing Greek and Asiatic influence. The blunt-headed cone shape of headdresses seen on sculptures on tombs was characteristic. The intricate and skilful gold work showed craftsmanship of unique quality.

ÉTUI *Fr. Fem.* Small case attached to waist band. Used to hold sewing implements or small toilet articles. 17th-19th Cent. Also called - equipage.

EUGENIE'S WIGS *Masc.* Round fur caps given by Empress Eugénie to an Arctic Exploration group, 1875. Back flap and side-pieces could be turned down for protection from bad weather. Made of wool and fur.

EVENING HAT *Fem.* Early 19th Cent. brimmed silk hat worn at an angle and away from the face. Trimmed with large ostrich plumes against and from the brim. Fashionable 1829-1832.

EVZONE *Masc.* Guard soldier of the select Greek army. (See FUSTANELLA)

EXHIBITION CHECKS Cloth with large checks woven especially for masc. trousers, worn in the year of the Great Exhibition of 1851.

EYEBROWS *Fem.* Strips of mouse skin, which were advertised and sold in perfume warehouses and cosmetic shops. 1780s.

EYE GLASSES Lens reputed to be in use in 13th Cent. By 15th Cent., spectacles could be bought in Nuremberg. An eyeglass was worn singly by Dandies, 1822. From 18th Cent. the lorgnette was seen in aristocratic circles. Pince-nez appeared in 1840, but were generally discarded after the First World War.

Today light plastic or similarly light treated metal frames are available. Contact lenses appeared in the 1950s.

EYELETS Embroidered or bound holes through which cords or tapes could be passed for lacing purposes, until 19th Cent. Metal rings were invented and came into use, 1830 onwards.

ETHNIC FASHIONS   In the 1970s many colourful and decorated styles from several nations were adopted. Long cotton lace-trimmed dresses were popular. Both sexes wore Mongolian fringed, embroidered and fur-trimmed coats.

FUSTANELLA *Full pleated kilt of the EVZONE, Greek soldier.*

FACE PAINTING Cosmetics were used in Egypt, Mesopotamia and in Ancient Rome, B.C. Later it was practised during the High Renaissance and in the reign of Elizabeth I, of England. In 18th Cent., dangerous materials were used, including white lead, quick-silver boiled in water, bismuth, mixtures of rice and flour, causing skin complaints and poisoning. By mid-19th Cent., cosmetics were considered vulgar and complexions were guarded by use of parasols and sunshades. In 1920s, after World War I, most women began to use lipstick and powder. The American Hollywood film industry had made 'glamorous' appearance seem desirable and possible for all women.

FACING False hem or backing to the underside of edges of garments.

FAGGOTTING Criss-cross openwork embroidery stitch usually joining two edges.

FAILLE Silky, lustrous material with horizontal ribbing.

FAIR ISLE Scottish Island, famous for use of knitting patterns originally brought from Norway.

FALBALA (See FURBELOW)

FALDETTA *Fem.* Waist-length taffeta mantle, edged with lace, usually wide-sleeved. 1850.

FALL *Masc.* Turned down collar, 16th Cent. Later, worn with ruff, and then replacing ruff, mid-17th Cent. Buttoned flap to front of breeches, 18th Cent.

Fem. Black silk or velvet piece worn over hood, 16th Cent.

FALLING BANDS *Masc.* Collar divided into two and elongated. From mid-17th Cent. and still adopted by Protestant ministers. A wider version called 'rabatine' is shown in many portraits by the Flemish painter, Sir Anthony Van Dyck, 1599-1641.

FALSE (See CALVES, HIPS, SLEEVES)

FAN Folding or section-shaped object for agitating air. Used as dress accessory throughout history. In common use in Europe from 16th-19th Cent. and shaped according to fashion of the period.

FANCHON *Fem.* Small lace-edged kerchief used as head-dressing or trimming over the ears of a day-bonnet. 1830s.

FANCHON CAP *Fem.* Lace or tulle bonnet with deep ruffle at the back of the head. 1840-1850.

FANCIES *Masc.* Ribbon trimmings arranged to decorate suits, with petticoat breeches, mid-17th Cent. As much as seventy to two hundred yards were used when such decoration was fashionable.

FANHOOP *Fem.* Hooped petticoat forming a fan-like structure which allowed the skirt to fall with a curve on each side. Fashionable in first half of the 18th Cent.

FANTAIL HAT *Masc. Fem.* Tricorne hat with vertical semi-circular brim at the back. Much worn with riding-dress. Late 18th Cent. A similar shape in hard-wearing weather-proof felt adopted by coalmen and dustmen as protective headwear in early days of 19th Cent. industry.

FANTAIL WIG *Masc.* The tail or queue of a wig fanned out in row of small curls. Early 18th Cent.

FARTHINGALE *Fem. Fr. - verdugale. Sp. -verdugo.* This skirt was made of diminishing sized hoops, forming an upward truncated cone over which material was tightly stretched. Fashion originated from Spain but was also worn in France under Louis XIII and in England at the Courts of James I and Charles I. 16th-17th Cent.

FARTHINGALE BREECHES *Masc.* Breeches with inner padded hoop placed on hip as protection from sword thrusts. Worn by Charles I, of England, 1625-1649.

FARTHINGALE SLEEVES *Mas. Fem.* Full sleeves distended and supported by whalebone or wires. Late 16th Cent. - early 17th Cent.

FAUSSE MONTRE *Masc. Fr.* The sham of two watches, a fashion worn by men, one of which often disguised a snuff box. Late 18th Cent.

FAVOURITES *Fem.* Curls or locks of hair carefully arranged on the forehead. Late 17th Cent. -early 18th Cent.

FEARNOTHING *Masc.* Thick woollen jacket worn by seafaring men and those who worked out-of-doors. Made of a coarse, stout, cloth with shaggy nap, called 'Dreadnought' or 'Fearnought'. 18th Cent.

FEATHERBRUSH SKIRT *Fem.* Long day-skirt with overlapping frills below the knees. Late 19th Cent.

FEATHERS Used by mankind throughout history for decoration or display. In 16th Cent., plumage attached to skin was used on robes in place of fur; also for

FARTHINGALE   The French Farthingale or Vertugal(l)e used an underskirt made rigid with hoops of whalebone or iron sewn into the petticoat. Here it is shown worn with an ermine-lined cloak. From a painting of Anne of Austria in Versailles Museum, 17th Century.

The Italian silhouette and style of the Spanish Farthingale was less rigid, allowing the folds of the skirt to fall softly. The costume was often accompanied by gauze hood and veiling. From a contempoary engraving.

FESTIVAL DRESS   Modern interpretations of old style local costumes abound and are very popular for folk dancing. This is an example of a festival dress from Finistere, France. The feminine headdress is called a CORNETTE.

masculine military and ceremonial headwear. With the innovation of hats for women, feathers were used as trimming and as fashion of period dictated; also as head-dresses at Court functions. In 18th Cent., fans made of feathers were attached to waist-chains. During Directoire period in France, Madame Tallien, a leader of fashion, wore a head-dress of coloured feathers above a Grecian hair style. Feather boas - long scarves of dressed feathers from six to eight feet long - were fashionable in the late 19th Cent., with revivals in 1930 and 1960s. In the early part of the 20th Cent., wide-brimmed, low-crowned hats for women were loaded with feathers but in 1941 a law was passed in the United States forbidding use of rare wild bird plumage for such purposes.

FEDORA *Masc.* Soft, felt hat with crease or dentation from front to back. Named after Sardou's heroine in the drama 'Fédora' shown in Paris, 1883. Known also as Tyrolean or Homburg. *Fem.* Usually of brown felt with feather mount and veil; was much worn for cycling. 1890s.

FENÊTRES D'ENFER *Fem. Fr.* Large armholes of sleeveless surcoat, late 14th Cent.

FERRONNIÈRE *Fr.* A tiara with a single, precious stone, named after the favourite of Francis I, 1515-1547. It is shown in the painting by Leonardo da Vinci called 'La belle Ferronnière. The jewel is suspended from a fine metal band, chain or ribbon, in the middle of the forehead. The fashion re-emerged and was worn in early 19th Cent. in France and England.

FEZ *Masc.* Brimless felt hat in shape of truncated cone, worn in Turkey and Arabian states from early 19th Cent., usually dark red or black. If tasselled, in blue or black. It was made official dress from 1808-1839 and remained the national head-dress until 1923. It was named after the sacred city, Fez, in French Morocco and is still worn in other eastern countries.

FIBULA, FIBULAE Metal long pin or brooch used in Ancient Greece, Etruria, Rome. The predecessor of the modern safety-pin.

FICHU *Fem.* Small triangular shawl or neckcloth of fine cambric, silk or lace; usually draped to conceal decolletage. Fashionable in latter half of 18th Cent. until early 19th Cent.

FILLEADH BEG *Scot.* Small plaid worn as separate kilt. From 18th Cent. Known also as 'PHILABEG'

FILLEADH MORE *Scot.* Great plaid made from two lengths of homespun woollen cloth, used both as clothing and bedding prior to 18th Cent.

FILLET *Fem.* Narrow head band worn to keep hair in place. From 13th Cent.

FILIGREE Ornamental lacy work of delicate or fragile openwork. Usually of gold, silver or copper wire.

FINNESKO *Masc. Fem.* Boot of treated reindeer skin with fur on outside. Lapland.

FIREMEN'S HELMETS *Masc.* Of hardened leather with back neck flaps for protection, 19th Cent. Brass helmets were introduced in London, 1866.

FITCH Cream-coloured, hard-wearing European fur.

FITCHET *Fem. Fr.* Vertical slit or placket-hole in outer dress, enabling wearer to reach for purse hanging from inside belt or girdle. 13th-16th Cent.

FITZHERBERT HAT *Fem.* Hat with wide brim and crown of puffed, raised material. Smaller than the fashionable Balloon or Lunardi hat. 1786.

FLAMMEUM *Fem.* Deep yellow veil of Roman brides. Worn fastened to back of head with floating, long ends. c. 1st-3rd Cent. A.D.

FLANDAN *Fem.* Indoor cap usually with lace-edged lappet, joined to a day-cap. Late 17th Cent.

FLANNEL Woven woollen fabric usually without nap. Much used in late 18th Cent., early 19th Cent. for bathing robes. Later for dresses, sleep-wear and quilts and in red for winter underwear. White flannel was adopted as correct wear for cricketing, boating and tennis, late 19th Cent. to 1930s.

FLANNELETTE Mixed material of wool and cotton made originally in America to imitate flannel, particularly for night-wear. 1876.

FLAPPER *Fem.* Name given to young girl in British Isles and later in America, who had not yet reached marriageable status. As hair was worn long in the early years of the 20th Cent., it was plaited and tied back with large ribbon bows, thus possibly suggesting the term.

FLAT CAP *Masc. Fem.* Head-wear made with flat crown over narrow brim. 16th Cent. It was worn by citizens, merchants and most professional and elderly men. Queen Elizabeth I passed a law compelling all persons of the middle class to wear the cap on Sundays and festival days. Made of wool or felt in black and worn mostly in the city until 17th Cent. The portrait of Sir Thomas Fleming, 1596, in National Gallery shows such a cap.

FLEA *Fr.* Puce colour made fashionable by Queen Marie Antoinette. Late 18th Cent.

FLESHINGS Close-fitting, flesh-coloured body garment worn on stage to represent natural skin. Usually of silk.

FLOCONNÉ *Fr.* Small, white, embroidered or attached white flakes on coloured ground of fabrics.

FLORENTINE HAT Large hat made from straw grown in Tuscany, Italy. Also called 'Leghorn'.

FLORENTINE NECKLINE *Fem.* Broad, open neckline stretching from shoulder to shoulder.

FLORINETTE Glazed brocade, striped and flowered. Made in Norwich in late 18th Cent.

FLORADORA Popular musical play, the costumes of which epitomized the then contemporary fashion and in particular the appearance of the American 'Gibson Girl'. 1899.

FLOUNCES *Fem.* Strips of material, gathered or pleatd, used as trimming to women's garments, the lower edge being left free to flare. Notably fashionable 18th Cent., Empire, Early Victorian and late 19th Cent. periods.

FLOWER-BOTTLE *Masc.* Small glass bottle made for boutonnière or single flower. It was placed behind the left-hand lapel where a broad piece of ribbon supported it. Worn with a morning-coat. 1865.

FLOWER-POT HAT *Masc.* Hat with low crown, shaped like an inverted flower-pot. Large rolled brim. 1830s. Similar to the countryman's hat called the 'wide-awake'.

FLOW-FLOW *Fem.* Arrangement of ribbon loops in a sequence used to decorate an otherwise simple afternoon or evening dress. 1885.

FLUTING Narrow pleating made by heated goffering iron on fine material. Used for ruffles and ruches. 18th and 19th Cents.

FLY FRINGE A dress trimming of silk fringe with small tassels or ruffs. 18th and 19th Cents.

FLY FRONT FASTENING Row of buttons concealed by overlap of material. Not used until 19th Cent.

FOB POCKET *Masc.* Small pocket in front waistband of breeches for watch, etc. 17th Cent. on.

FOCAL *Masc.* Square piece of linen worn by Roman soldier around the neck, which served as towel, etc.

FOGLE Slang term for large silk handkerchief. 19th Cent.

FONTANGE *Fem.* Indoors cap with very high frontal decoration of firm frills or lace pleats. Inspired by the Duchess de Fontanges who, when her hat was blown off at a royal riding party, tied up her curls with a frilled lace garter, placing a bow-knot at the front. 1680. The fashion of wearing high bonnets named 'à la Fontanges' lasted until 1710. Ribbon ruching used to edge a dress bodice was termed 'fontange' in 1850s.

FOOT MANTLE, FOTE MANTEL *Fem.* A garment mentioned by Chaucer, 1386. Long skirt worn by women when travelling on horseback, probably to prevent soiling of gowns. Name also given to long mantle worn in Colonial days.

FOOTWEAR Covering for feet. Early forms covered sole. Legs in cold weather were bound like puttees. Sandals were in general use, also socks of leather or felt. These often reached the knees and wooden sandals were worn with them. An English clergyman, Lee, built the first stocking frame, 1589. Heels on shoes appeared in 17th Cent. and red heels and soles were privilege of courtiers. At this time enormous boots with funnel-shaped tops were worn over boothose. After this, more moderate sized boots developed. After early 19th Cent., more variety emerged, with the use in the 20th Cent. of some manufactured materials other than natural skins. The introduction of ladies' tights in 1950s was a revival of the medieval all-in-one-hose.

See also: Balmoral, Batts, Blüchner, Boot, Bottines, Chopines, Chukka, Cockers, Caliga, Escarpin, Espadrille, Gaiter, Galosh, Jackboot, Kamik, Krepis, Larrigan, Moccasin, Oxford, Pattens, Poulaines, Sandal, Shoes, Sollenet, Stockings, Tsaruchia.

FORAGE CAP *Masc.* 1) A cap worn by small boys, circular with vizor, and a tassel hanging from the crown. 19th Cent. 2) Infantry undress cap. 20th Cent.

FOREPART *Fem.* Decorative panel mounted on long underskirt, filling in front of a split farthingale overskirt. 17th Cent.

FORESLEEVE *Masc. Fem.* Sleeve covering lower arm, when over-garment sleeve finished at elbow. Often of contrasting colour and material. 16th Cent.

FORKED BEARD *Masc.* Beard trimmed with two points. Mentioned by Chaucer. 14th Cent. Occasionally seen in 17th Cent.

FORTUNY GOWNS *Fem.* Beautiful garments originally creatd by the Italian, Mario Fortuny, in 1910 for the dancer, Isadora Duncan. Made as tea-gowns in clinging, pleated silk but were much admired and also worn for evening. Now prized as collector's items and examples can be seen in some museums.

FOULARD Twill-woven, light-weight silk material, plain or printed.

FOUNDLING BONNET *Fem.* Headwear for young girls, made with small, stiff brim. With soft crown and tied under the chin. Late 19th Cent.

FOURIAUX *Fem.* Silk covering, forming sheathes to cover the two plaits of hair worn by high born ladies. A.N.

FOUR IN HAND *Masc. Fem.* Necktie or scarf knotted in front. Late 19th and early 20th Cent.

FOURREAU *Fem. Fr. - sheath.* Princess-style dress with no waist seam. Usually buttoned down front. Often worn with overskirt or a peplum fastened around the waist. 1860s.

FRAC *Masc. Fr. -dress-coat.* Mid-calf length coat, usually of pale colours such as green or yellow. Early 19th Cent., of decorative appearance in Paris, but more sober style in London. Replaced at the end of 19th Cent. by 'cutaway' coat, in more sombre colours.

FRAISE *Fr. - ruff.* 1) Linen band encircling neck from collar to chin. Predecessor of ruff. 17th Cent. 2) Neck scarf of ruched, embroidered muslin folded and secured with ornamental brooch. 1836.

FRANGIPANI Perfumed gloves. Introduced into European Court life by discovery by Count Frangipani, an Italian, of process of liquidizing solid perfume with alcohol. 16th Cent.

FRÄSE *Masc.* Beard style introduced into Babylon by the Semites. The lips were clean-shaven but sideburns framed the face.

FRENCH BOA Serpent. *Fem.* Long scarf of feathers, swansdown or light-weight fur. Fashionable in 1829, 1890s.

FRENCH CLOAK *Masc.* Long cloak of circular or semi-circular cut, usually with flat collar or small shoulder cape. 16th and 17th Cents.

FRENCH FALLS *Masc.* Lace cuffs on boothose, worn to save expensive silk stockings. 16th and 17th Cents.

FRENCH FROCK *Masc.* Full dress coat finished with gold buttons. Late 18th Cent.

FRENCH GIGOT SLEEVE *Fem.* Large topped sleeve tapering to wrist but with cuff extended over the back of the hand. A fashion introduced by Sarah Bernhardt. 1890-1897.

FRENCH HOOD · *Fem.* 1) Head-dress built on firm framework based on the bonnet shape and worn to the back of the head, with the front edge curving forward on each side to cover the ears. This edge was trimmed with ruching and sometimes gold ornamentation. A raised curved piece at the back was called a 'Billiment'; below this hung material in pleats or as a flap. The whole was secured by a chin band. 16th Cent.

Fem. 2) Headcovering of same material and attached to a cape, sometimes called a 'Capuchin' after the hooded order of Capuchin monks. Often quilted, fur-lined or fur-edged and usually in red colours. Worn by women on both sides of the Atlantic and known as a 'red robin hood' or cardinal. 18th Cent.

FRENCH POCKET *Masc.* Horizontal slit pocket covered by a flap. Late 17th Cent.

FRENCH RUFF *Masc.* Cartwheel ruff of exaggerated size. Late 16th Cent. - 1610.

FRET, FRETTE *O.F. Fem.* Trellis-work cap or coif made of golden wire, to hold and conceal hair. Mentioned by Chaucer, *Legend of Good Women.* c. 1385.

FRILEUSE *Fem.* A short-waisted cape-wrap worn for social occasions and at home. Of quilted satin or velvet, with long, loose sleeves. Mid-19th Cent.

FRIPERER *Fr. Friperie - old clothes.* Seller of discarded and old clothes. 16th Cent.

FRIPPERY The shop where the old clothes and odds and ends connected with garments were sold. Mentioned by Ben Jonson, 1572-1637.

FRISETTE *Fr. Little curl. Fem.* 1) Hairdressing style with crimped fringe over the forehead. 2) Also, a hairpad over which back hair was rolled. 3) Name given to padding used in underskirts. 19th Cent.

FRIZZ *Masc.* Wig crimped all over. 17th-19th Cent.

FROCK *Masc.* Monastic habit, medieval. Later, outer garment worn by workers. *Fem.* Informal dress or garment. 16th and 17th Cents.

FROCK COAT *Masc.* Emerged as style from 1816 or when Royalty is present.

FROGS Looped fastenings made of silk braid or cord, adapted from decorated uniforms worn by Prussian troops of 1674.

FROK *Masc.* Garment worn for protection by chandlers and butchers, usually accompanied by wide-brimmed felt hats. 17th and 18th Cents.

FRONTLET *Fem.* 1) Small fine chain, or loop of silk or velvet, hanging from the edge of a small cap worn under a large head-dress or hennin. Worn when fashionable plucked high brows were much admired, 15th Cent. (See ESCOFFION, HENNIN). 2) A decorative band worn across the forehead with a coif. 16th and early 17th Cent.

FROU-FROU DRESS *Fem. 1870. Fr. Rustling.* A day-dress with low-necked bodice, covered with muslin tunic. The matching muslin skirt was worn over a long silk petticoat or underskirt and showed rows and rows of small, pink flounces. Designed for the comedy, by Meilhac and Ludovic Halevy, called 'Frou-Frou' and worn by Sarah Bernhardt in London in 1869.

FROUNCE Meaning frown or wrinkle. 14th, 15th and 16th Cents. A gathered or pleated frill, or arrangement of small folds or pleats over a projecting understructure, such as a farthingale, giving a softer outline.

FROUTING Early method of freshening garments by rubbing prepared scented oil on to the material. 17th Cent.

FULL BOTTOMED WIG *Masc.* A very large wig favoured by professional, important, elderly men. The modern term 'big-wig' arises from the custom of judges and persons in authority in the past wearing them. Late 17th Cent.

FULL DRESS The clothes worn on occasions of ceremony; when Court dress, academic robes, evening dress, uniforms, etc. are requested.

FULLER Man who cleaned new cloth with fuller's earth; also cleansing soiled garments. From Biblical times, Malachi, 3,2; Mk., 9,3.

FULLER'S EARTH Powder used for cleaning. Hydrous silicate of alumina.

FUR COAT The female fashionable coat made with the fur on the outside, to show the type of animal used, was introduced by a Frenchman, Doucet, in the late 19th Cent. Before that time, furs had been used mostly as costly linings or trimming.

FUR FAKES Imitation, synthetic furs of quality were introduced in 1950s.

FURBELOWS Descriptive word for decorations on Court costume of the past, such as flounces, fringes, lace, braid, heavy embroideries, tassels. Also FALBALA.

FÜRTUCHSKLEMMER *Fem.* Large brooch worn on Austrian blouse.

FUSTANELLA *Masc.* Stiffly pleated short kilt, part of the uniform worn by men in Albania and of the modern Greek guard called 'Evzone'.

FUSTIAN Hard-wearing cloth of flax or cotton used by Norman clergy and others of that period. Made and used from the time of the Crusades. Reputed to have been dyed in solid, strong colours, also tufted and striped. A twilled cloth with velvety pile was originally made in Fustat, outside Cairo.

The *GIBSON GIRL* style immortalized by the American artist, Charles Dana Gibson.

GABARDINE *Sp. gabardina - a woollen cloak.* A quality material, with diagonal weave. Used for hard-wearing garments, uniforms, sportswear, raincoats.

Name of Jewish gown worn in Middle Ages. Buttoned to waist in front, ankle length. Also - loose overcoat, worn with or without girdle, from early 16th Cent. - 17th Cent., for 'raynie weather'.

GABLE HOOD *Fem.* Head-dress of Tudor period, 1500-1550 A.D., entirely covering the hair. Severe but attractive, consisting of gable, or diamond-shaped, upper piece, worn with wimple and gorget.

GABRIELLE GOWN *Fem.* Day dress, princess-style, fitted and gored from shoulders to hem. 1860-1910.

GABRIELLE SLEEVE *Fem.* Puffed from shoulder to wrist. 1860s.

GADROON *Fem.* Trimming of inverted fluting or pleating. Used on caps, cuffs and skirts. 1870s.

GAITER Cloth, linen or leather covering for ankle and leg, usually buttoned at side and with strap under instep. First recorded in France in 17th Cent. Used with uniform, 18th Cent. *Fem.* Discontinued when rubber galoshes invented in 1842; but shorter versions and masculine spats, have been periodically fashionable.

GAITER BOTTOMS, GAITER TROUSERS *Masc.* Breeches cut neatly around the ankle with strap passing under boot. 1840-1850.

GAITER CONGRESS SHOE *Masc. N. Amer.* Short boot of leather, with firm silk uppers and side pieces of elastic webbing, needing no fastenings. 1850s.

GALANTS Knots and clusters of coloured ribbon loops decorating masc. and fem. dress. 17th Cent.

GALATEA Name of legendary sea-nymph and given to H.M.S. *Galatea.* 1) Quality striped cotton dress material, used originally for children's sailor suits. 19th Cent. 2) *Masc. Fem.* Hat. Straw with sailor crown and turned-up brim, worn with children's sailor suits. Late 19th and early 20th Cents.

GALEA *L.* Helmet.

GALILLA, GOLILLA *Sp., Fr. collier.* Upstanding circular collar of mounted wired lawn. Worn by Philip IV of Spain, 1621-1665. In England and America it was called WHISK.

GALLIGASKINS *German - pumphose. Masc.* 1) Wide knee-breeches, similar to Venetian 'gallicascoynes'. Padded or smooth at the hips. 16th Cent., early 17th Cent. 2) Name given to sportsman's leggings made of leather, 19th Cent. Also: GREGS, GASCON HOSE.

GALLIOCHIOS Protective overshoes with wooden soles and strapping. Style of footwear worn since the time of Ancient Rome and similar kinds appeared in Europe and in American colonial life until 18th Cent. (See PATTENS)

GALLOON, GALON Narrow braid or trimming. 17th-19th Cent.

GALLOSHOES, GALOSSES Wooden-soled, low overboots. Late 16th, early 17th Cent. By 18th Cent., reduced in size and known as CLOGS.

GALLOWSES, GALLUSES Masc. Braces made of cloth bands, with hooks and eyes, worn over shoulders to keep breeches in position. From early 18th Cent. -19th Cent.

GALOSHES Overshoes made in rubber, invented in 1842. Modern types of waterpoof canvas with heavy rubber sole. 20th Cent.

GALUCHAT Fr. Treatment for polishing unusually grained leather or sharkskin, introduced by a Frenchman, Galuchat, 18th Cent.

GAMASHES Long protective leggings of cloth or velvet, worn with overshoes. Late 16th - 17th Cent. Linen leg coverings, worn by country people, were called 'spatter dashes'. Soles were added later in 17th Cent.

GAMBADOES Masc. Extremly large, heavy, boot shapes for wearing on horseback, attached to the saddle, strengthened with iron bands and used instead of stirrups. Turn of 17th Cent.

GAMBESON Masc. Padded bodice of leather or cloth, worn under armour of Middle Ages. Later in 16th Cent., worn by civil population.

GAMBETO Masc. Sp. Short, woollen, warm topcoat worn in Catalonia, Spain, instead of a cloak.

GAMBROON Plain, twilled, worsted or cotton cloth, sometimes with mohair. Used for masc. waistcoats, breeches, trousers. Early 19th Cent.

GAMP Name for umbrella derived from Dickens' character of Mrs. Gamp. Late 19th and 20th Cents.

GAMURRA Fem. Simple undergown with long sleeves, worn in the Renaissance. Over this was added a brightly coloured garment called 'cioppa', which was waisted, long, with decorated, loose hanging sleeves and a train.

GANDOORA Masc. Loose, flowing, sleeveless, circular mantle or burnous. Worn in Algeria, Arabia.

GANSEY or GUERNSEY (See JERSEY)

GARDE-CORPS Masc. Fem. Large, hooded overtunic, with hanging, long, wide sleeves and in those sleeves vertical slits for armholes. 13th and 14th Cents. Similar to HERIGAUT.

GARIBALDI BLOUSE Fem. Popular garment worn with skirt in 1860s. Inspired by the tailored red shirt worn by the Italian patriot and soldier, Garibaldi. Of scarlet merino and trimmed with black braid; with simple, full sleeves gathered into a wristband; small shoulder epaulets; turned down collar and front button fastening. Usually worn with ZOUAVE or GARIBALDI JACKET, also of scarlet, with military braiding and over a black skirt. 1860s.

GARIBALDI HAT Masc. Fem. A braided pill-box hat worn 1850s and 1860s.

GARNACHE Masc. Long, loose over-tunic. With cape-like sleeves cut in one piece over shoulders with the body. Sides sometimes left open. 13th and 14th Cents. Later, a lapel was added either side of neck opening; sometimes faced with fur. A shorter version or TABARD is associated with ceremonial and heraldic occasions.

GARNITURE Fr. garnir - to adorn. Term used for decoration or trimming with precious stones or ribbons; also sets of matching jewellery. 18th Cent.

GARTER Band or tie to support leg-hose, worn above or below knee.

GARTERING Cross-gartering mentioned in Anglo-Saxon writing. Bands of cloth, wool and leather worn over stockings (chausses). Linen used by monks. Gilded straps worn by those of higher rank.

GASCON HOSE As GALLIGASKINS

GATYA, GATYAK Masc. Long, full, white linen trousers, edged by fringe or peasant-made lace, worn by Hungarian cowherds. 20th Cent.

GAUNTLET Steel glove of mail worn with armour from the 14th Cent. to the 17th Cent. Subsequently, a strong glove with covering for the wrist or deep cuff.

GAUZE Transparent material first made in Gaza, Palestine. 13th Cent.

GAUZE HATS Fem. Large, fashionable hats of soft gauze, worn over high dressed hair. Late 18th Cent.

GAZELINE BAREGE Semi-transparent textile of llama wool. 1877.

GEFRENS Fem. Fringe decoration worn at back of head. 15th Cent.

GEGENDAS Fem. New style of corset made with steel stays. 1890s.

GENAPPE CLOTH Smooth, striped fabric of two colours, in wool and cotton. 1863. The yarn was used also in braid and fringes.

GENET Arab. jarnait. O.F. genete, genette. The pelt of a civet cat, small European and Old World mammal; grey, spotted with black. Used for trimming in Europe from Sixth Century, A.D.

GENEVA City at Western end of Lake Geneva, Switzerland. Home of Calvin, 1536-1564; became centre of the Reformation.

GENEVA GOWN Masc. Long, loose gown with wide sleeves, worn by clergymen, of black wool or silk, buttoned down front with white lawn bands at neck. 16th Cent. originally.

GENEVA HAT Masc. Severe, untrimmed, broadbrimmed, high-crowned hat worn by ministers. 16th Cent.

GENEVA RUFF *Masc. Fem.* Small, neat ruff made in the style worn by Genevan Calvinists. 17th Cent.

GENOA CLOAK *Masc.* Short, hooded cloak. 16th and 17th Cents. As SPANISH CLOAK.

GENOESE LACE The Italian city of Genoa was famous for bobbin, needlepoint, gold and silver laces in the 17th Cent.

'GENRE CANAILLE' Scornful description of female gaudily coloured costumes of 1860s, when coloured petticoats and cloth-booted feet were discreetly allowed to show.

GERMAN GOWN *Fem.* Straight-bodied, front-buttoned gown with sack-back and long sleeves. 1760-1780. Known also as BRUNSWICK.

GERTRUDE *Masc. Fem.* Long tunic worn from the time of the Holy Roman Empire to the 13th Cent. The simple shape was retained in a flannel garment for infants and named after St. Gertrude.

GETA A Japanese clog worn out-of-doors for many centuries. The height of the wooden sole varies and the clog is worn over the TABI, the white cotton foot-glove. The clog is not permitted indoors and is always removed on entering a house or temple but the tabi is allowed to remain.

GIBSON GIRL Type of young woman as portrayed in the magazine drawings of the American artist, Charles Dana Gibson, 1867-1944. Her costume usually consisted of a shirt-blouse with a tie scarf, worn above a neatly belted, long, tailored back-slung skirt. Her abundant, glossy hair was dressed in high 'pompadour' style and the pronounced forward stance of the figure was much imitated and called the 'Gibson bend'. End of 19th Cent.

GIBOUN *Masc.* Loose shoulder cape with straight fronts and wide sleeves. 1840s.

GIBUS *Masc.* Top hat for evening wear with folding crown, named after the Parisian hatmaker, Gibus, who was its inventor. 1823-1840.

GIG COAT *Fem.* Long coat with wrist-length sleeves, single front fastening and worn for carriage riding. 1800s. *Masc.* Long coat, with capes for driving or riding. 1840s.

GIGOT SLEEVE Full-shouldered sleeve tapering towards elbow, becoming tight at wrist. Seen in masc. sleeves 1820s and 1860s. *Fem.* Large and supported with hoops in 1827; used for summer dresses, 1862. Became prevalent and much enlarged from 1890-1897.

GILET *Fr.* waistcoat, vest. *Masc.* Short waistcoat worn by 'Incroyables' in France, late 18th Cent. and by young men of fashion in England called 'Macaronis' in 1770s.

   Fem. Sleeveless blouse, or bodice front, worn under a suit or to fill in low neckline of dress. Contemporary.

GILLIE Thonged rawhide Anglo-Saxon shoe. Also 'ghillie' in Scotland today. Laced through attached loops.

GILLS *Masc.* Term for upstanding points of stiffened collar. 19th Cent.

GIGOT SLEEVE This early 19th Cent. Durner Dress shows the main changes which occurred in feminine dress after the Directoire or Empire period. Women decided to resume the normal waistline after 1812, emphasizing it by the use of corsets.

Sleeves, expanded at the shoulders horizontally, and sometimes supported by flat undersleeves giving the strange leg-of-mutton shape, became very fashionable at this time.

The earlier large evening berets and turbans were superceded by elaborate hair decoration. Much jewellery, such as chains, cameobrooches and bracelets were worn. Fans and reticules were carried as accessories. Coloured silk boots, often with black toe-caps, completed the ensemble.

GIMP Trimming or braid made by interwoven threads of cotton, silk or wool upon a coarse silk mesh or wire. From 17th Cent.

GINGHAM   Cotton fabric first made in Glasgow, 1786, from dyed yarn. The name was given to a stout check cloth, of linen, and later of cotton. 19th Cent. Also used in the making of cheap umbrellas. (See GAMP)

GINGLERS   *Masc.* Rattling, 'jingling', metal drops hung on spurs, thus attracting attention when the wearer was walking. Very fashionable, late 16th Cent. and early 17th Cent.

GIPON   *Masc.* Padded bodice of 14th Cent. Forerunner of the doublet. (See GYPON)

GIPSER   Purse or belt pouch. Mentioned in Chaucer's 'Canterbury Tales'. 1381.

GIPSY HAT   *Fem.* Wide-brimmed, flat-crowned hat with ribbon stretching across crown to tie under chin. Early 19th Cent.

GIRAFFE COMB   *Fem.* Decorative high haircomb worn with long curls which fell smoothly downwards at the back of the head. 1870s.

GIRANDOLE   *Fem.* Ear-ring with suspended pendant stones or smaller ones set around a larger jewel.

GIRDLE   Cord or belt encircling the waist.

GIRDLE GLASS   *Fem.* Small mirror suspended from the waist girdle. 17th Cent.

GITE   *Masc. Fem.* 15th Cent. term for gown.

GLACÉ KID   Smooth, highly polished glove leather.

GLADSTONE OVERCOAT   *Masc. British.* Short double-breasted overcoat with cape, sometimes trimmed with astrakhan. 1870s.

GLASS FIBRE   Invention using threads made of molten glass. Suits of such lightweight material protect from heat and fire in industrial wear. 20th Cent.

GLEN CHECK, GLEN PLAID   Twilled, woollen cloth made in Scotland with chequered or tartan patterns.

GLENGARRY   Scottish cap or bonnet, high in front, lower at back, with hanging ribbons behind and small side feather.

GLOCKE   *Ger. bell. Masc.* Circular cloak with central hole for head. M.E.

GLOF   A.S. Glove.

GLOVE   Covering for the hand, usually with separated fingers, worn for protection, warmth or as a symbol of power. Rarely seen before 13th Cent.

GLOVE BAND   *Fem.* A band of plaited horsehair or ribbon, tied at elbow over the top of long glove to keep it in place. 16th Cent.

GLOVE LENGTHS   *Fem.* Wrist one-button; mid-forearm four or five-button; elbow eight-button; above elbow twelve-button; shoulder sixteen button. Late 19th and 20th Cents.

GLOVE-STRING   *Fem.* Purpose as glove band, often decorated and buckled. 18th Cent.

GOATEE   *Masc.* Chin beard trimmed into long point similar to the beard of a male goat. Fashionable U.S., Europe and British Isles in 1890s.

GOB CAP   White cotton twill cap worn by men in the U.S. Navy. Round crown and upturned stitched brim. 'Shall be worn squarely on the head and shall not be crushed or bent in the middle'. Modern.

GODET   Tapering, triangular piece of cloth inserted into garment for widening, flare or fluting; also GORE, GUSSET.

GOFFERING   Pleating, usually of fine muslin, made by heated goffering iron, used for ruffs and frills.

GOLE   *Masc.* Cape of hood or chaperon, 14th Cent. Called GOLET later in 15th Cent.

GOLILLA   (See GALILLA)

GOLLER   *Masc. Fem. Swiss.* Collar.

GONDOLIER NET   *Fem.* Wide-meshed hair-net; fashionable for supporting long hair; of black ribbon or braid, held by flat, black bows at back and on top of the head. 1870s. Also SNOOD.

GONDOURA   (See GANDOORA)

GONELLE   *Masc.* Knee-length tunic worn by Franks and Teutons, embroidered and belted. 481-752 A.D.

GONFANON   Norman lance with flag.

GOOSEBELLY   *Masc.* Padding of doublet worn with French hose. Early 17th Cent. (See PEASCOD)

GORGET   *Masc.* Piece of armour to protect throat. After 1600, only a small steel or silver tablet suspended from chain remained, usually engraved with officer's grade. Worn with full dress uniform, 18th Cent.

   Fem. Fr. GORGETTE. Soft cape-like collar covering neck and throat. 12th, 13th and early 16th Cents. (See WIMPLE)

GORRO   *Masc. Sp.* Knitted stocking-cap with tassels. Worn in Catalonia.

GORSEDD   Welsh gathering of Druids. Ceremony restored late 18th Cent. (See DRUIDS)

GOSSAMER   Silk gauze material of quality used for veiling. 19th Cent.

GOURGANDINE   *Fem. Fr.* Corselette of silk or velvet, laced in front, late Louis XIV period. Worn en negligée with silk petticoat in hours when not in attendance at Court functions. On those occasions tight, upright corsets were donned and helped to support during long hours of standing.

GOWN   *Sax. gunna. Masc.* A long, loose garment worn mostly on formal occasions, from 14th-17th Cents. Circular in cut, open in front, cape-like, of varying lengths. Relegated to the professions after 1600; used today to denote academic or clerical distinction. *Fem.* A term denoting a woman's dress.

GRANNY BONNET   *Fem. Br.* Worn at same time as GRANNY SKIRT. A large creation with high crown, wide brim and feathers. 1893. Seen in illustrations of works by Charles Dickens.

GRANNY SKIRT   *Fem. Br.* Voluminous, long skirt, made in circular shape, with tucks from knee level downwards, usually with pocket behind a placket hole and a velvet facing around the hem. Shape influenced by apparel worn by Queen Victoria at the end of her reign. 1893.

GREAT COAT *Masc. Fem.* An outdoor coat in style of period. So called from 18th Cent.

GREAVES *Masc.* Early Mediterranean leggings of leather, brass or bronze, worn with sandals, by military men. Also CNEMIS.

GRECIAN BEND *Fem.* Name given to stance adopted by women in early 19th Cent. and again in 1860s. (See FRISK, NELSON)

GRECQUE *Masc.* Style of dressing wigs. Late 18th Cent.

GREEK COSTUME During the period 500 B.C. to 323 B.C. (death of Alexander the Great). Shown on sculpture and vases with variations to the beginning of the Sixth Century, B.C.

CHITON The main garment worn short by men and long by women was made from a length of material. The earlier DORIC CHITON was a length of woollen cloth, folded over the top with double thickness over chest and back (see illustrations), fastened at shoulders with small clasps, pins or fibulae; a girdle round the waist gathered in the fullness and one side was left unfastened. The IONIC CHITON which followed was of silk or fine linen, often pleated and the edges of the breadth of a much wider piece of material used than the Doric were sewn together. The opening shoulder edges were clasped at intervals by small brooches because there was no overfall as in the Doric. Sometimes only one shoulder was covered.

Arranging the
1) Doric Chiton   *2) Ionic Chiton*
A girdle gathered in the fullness at the waist.

THE IONIC CHITON was of fine pleated linen. The edges of the material were fastened by a series of small buttons on the shoulders.

HIMATION. A wrap for the female figure.

HIMATION. *Masc. Fem.* An enveloping cloak.

CHLAMYS. *Masc.* Shorter outer cape or cloak.

Geometric or figurative decoration was used for bordering materials, the Greek key, wave, floral, being the basis of the motifs used. Homer mentions the use of gold and silver threads. Female garments included CHAMOIS, which was a bosom band of linen or wool; CAMISIA, a short tunic for nightwear; STROPHIUM, very brief trunks worn for dancing and running.

PETASOS. *Masc. Fem.* Hat, often of straw.

Indoors people went barefoot but sandals were usual outside, some of complex style and strapping. Much jewellery, of intricate workmanship, was worn, such as pins, necklaces, pendants, ear-rings, brooches, bracelets and rings.

THE DORIC CHITON

THE DORIC CHITON was a length of woollen cloth folded over at the top and fastened on the shoulders with pins.

GREEK COSTUME CHLAMYS *A short cloak worn by men, it is clasped on the right shoulder and worn over a short girdled Chiton. In the left figure the hat can be seen carried at the back.*

GREEK ARMOUR

with modelled crest of horsehair fastened to the back.
BREAST PLATE *with shoulder plate on cuirass.*

ATTIC HELMET *with hinged cheek pieces.*

Illustrations based on Hellenistic sculptures.

A soldier's equipment included helmet; body armour with leather cuirass covered with metal plates; shoulder plates; and greaves from knee to ankle moulded to the shape of the leg.

GREENAWAY, KATE An English artist and illustrator. 1846-1901. The style of clothes worn by the children she portrayed have a lasting charm and is still often copied in the dress worn by young attendants at weddings.

GREGS *Masc.* Galligaskins. Sportsman's leggings. 19th Cent.

GRELOT *Fem.* Ball fringe trimming, much used on the elaborate dresses of the 1860s.

GRENADINE A popular silk lightweight material with open mesh, for blouses, neckwear and summer dresses. Late 19th Cent. An all-wool grenadine was used for shawls.

GRISE *Fr. Grey.* Grey fur of squirrel. Medieval.

GRISETTE Grey, hard-wearing material of wool worn by French working women. During reign of Louis XIV, the name was given to young women, especially those working in the needlework trades.

GROSGRAIN Hard-wearing, corded silk fabric or ribbon.

GROSPOINT Venetian lace with raised work and large motifs; also embroidery.

GUÊPIÈRE *Fr. Guêpe - wasp. Fem.* Small, light corset creating the appearance of tiny waist. It was worn separately under the dress or sewn in to the clothes of the dramatic collection, called the 'New Look', by Dior, created after the Second World War in 1945.

GUERNSEY Heavy duty, navy-blue, woollen jersey originating from the Channel Islands. Often made of oiled wool. (See also JERSEY)

GUILD Medieval associations of merchants or craftsmen. The first tailors' guilds were formed in the 11th Cent. and well-established by the 13th Cent. Craftsmen contributed towards initiating variety and diversity of medieval clothes and aiding development of fashion. London craft guilds still survive in ceremonial and charitable companies. (See LIVERY COMPANIES)

GUIMPE Thin, white high-necked blouse or 'fill-in'. Usually worn with an open-necked type of dress. In 16th Cent., both sexes are shown in portraits wearing it above a square neckline.

Fem. A chemisette, worn in neckline with low decolletage. Late 19th Cent.

GUIPURE Heavy lace distinguished by raised motifs connected by bars.

GUISER *M.E. Mummer.* A local man who dressed up as play-actor.

GUNNA *Sax. Fem.* Garment worn over kirtle. Forerunner of gown.

GUSSET *O.F. Gousset.* Light piece of chain inserted in joints of mail-coat, armour. Triangular piece let into garment to strengthen or reinforce.

GYPON *Masc.* Well-tailored, fitting garment worn over shirt, later called DOUBLET. 14th-17th Cent. (Also GIPON)

Fem. Garment worn on horseback. 14th and 15th Cents.

HORNED HEADDRESS *'She is hornyed like a kowe . . . for syn.' - The Townley Mysteries, C1460.*

HABERDASHER *Possibly O.F. hapertas - fabric,* The Haberdashers is one of the twelve London Livery Companies, founded in the 15th Cent. The Hall was built by Christopher Wren but destroyed by enemy action, 1940.

HABERDASHERY Shop where small articles and materials used in sewing are sold. U.S.A. - store for men's clothing.

HABERGEON, HAUBERGEON *Masc.* Tunic of chain or ring mail with high neck, worn over a cloth undergarment to protect chest, neck and back. A leather belt at the waist held the sword. (See HAUBERK)

HABIT *Masc. Fem. Med.* Dress of certain religious Orders, rank or professions. *Fem.* Tailored dress for riding side-saddle. Late 19th Cent.

HABIT-BACK SKIRT *Fem.* Ankle-length skirt of hard-wearing material fitting over the hips and flaring to hem. Inverted pleat at centre back, partially stitched from waist but allowing material to spread and open towards hem. Late 19th Cent.

HAIK *Masc. Fem.* Full covering garment made of white wool or wool and silk. Arabian. (See HUKE)

HAINCELIN *Masc. Fem.* Short tunic or houppelande, worn in France. Early 15th Cent.

HAIR DYES Bleaching and dyeing of hair was practised in ancient times. Fashionable Roman, Medieval and Renaissance women, as well as those from Germania and Gaul, knew of such methods. By the 16th Cent. in Europe, resource was made to wigs and the powdering of hair. After the French Revolution, wigs and powder vanished. The Empress Eugenie, with reddish blonde hair aided by a secret herbal recipe, started a new fashion colour in 1853 and until the end of the 19th Cent. hair dyeing became more widespread. In the 20th Cent. the chemists have succeeded in reproducing natural shades, with the advantage of these being less harmful to the head than the previous more historic methods.

HAIR NET First made by the Chinese of silk many centuries ago. Copied in later periods in Europe with braided silk, gold and metallic threads, velvet ribbon. Nets of human hair - to keep the coiffure in place - were made later and today are of nylon. (See also CAUL)

66

HANOVERIAN BRITAIN *George I, 1714-27*
and **REGENCY FRANCE**, *1715-30.*

George II, 1727-60
ROCOCO IN EUROPE, *1730-89*
French styles appearing in Venice, Rome, Berlin.

CONTONCHE. *Comfortable female dress with fulness at the back. Male coat, collarless, was worn with knee breeches. A large hat, or a folded CHAPEAU CLAQUE was held under the arm. A wide hat completes the central lady's summer dress.*

Man's coat of rich brocade with deep cuffs and pockets, embroidered waistcoat, hose and shoes neater than in earlier part of the century. Hair combed backwards. The central figure wears a light house dress, the French Sac, showing two box pleats falling loosely from the shoulders. The second woman has a gown with 'dome' shaped skirt, the front open to display the sumptuousness of the fabric. Both ladies are wearing small head-dresses of 'dwarf' bonnets.

George III, 1760-1820

FRANCE Louis XVI, 1774-92 and the Revolution 1789

Simplified versions of dress worn in England, France and Germany. Gown with hooped skirt and low neck, covered with lace scarf or fichu. Clerical gentleman wears the predecessor of tailcoats or frac, having turned down collar and less ornamentation. Under the simpler coat he still wore a waistcoat with breeches, hose to the knees and lower shoes.

George III

Simple chemise evening gown of muslin or tulle, with bosom laced high. Worn with long gloves. The shape, which was a reaction against the full, hooped skirts of the late 18th Century, remained fashionable until the 1820s. 1804.

After the Congress of Vienna, 1814-15, English tailoring for men, with fine leather boots and high quality hats, was placed in the forefront of men's fashions. The lady's dress of 1819 shows a longer skirt and a higher neckline with the Betsy ruff.

HAIR PINS The earliest known are from the Bronze Age. They were used by women of Egypt, Greece, Rome, Germania. Some were beautifully decorated and made of precious metal and set with gems. The 20th Cent. manufacturers make wire grips and clips in a variety of styles for women of today.

HALBERD *O.F. haldebarde. M.G. helmbarte.* Combined spear and battle-axe, with 5 ft. -7 ft. long haft. Used 15th-16th Cents. (See PARTISAN)

HALBERDIER Soldier armed with a halberd.

HALF GOWN, HALF ROBE *Fem.* Low-necked, short-sleeved, thigh-length tunic, worn over a one-piece or 'round' gown. It was worn with a narrow ribbon band or belt. Late 18th Cent. - 19th Cent.

HALSHEMD *Ger.* Material used to fill in neckline and shoulders of garment. Late 15th Cent.

HALTER NECKLINE *Fem.* New neckline introduced in 1930 for beach wear. High front, tied at the back of the neck and leaving a bare back. The style was adopted for evening wear and remains in fashion.

HAMILTON LACE A coarse lace made with a diamond pattern at Hamilton, named after the Duchess of Hamilton. 18th Cent.

HAMMERCUT BEARD Combined men's face dressing of waxed moustache and twisted tuft beard under the lower lip. First half of 17th Cent. Also called 'Roman T'.

HANDBAG *Fem.* Accessory developed in the 20th Cent. With long gowns of earlier generations, pockets had been provided in skirt folds; or embroidered, knitted or netted drawstring bags used for small possessions. Today, the fittings of bags as well as exterior appearance are carefully considered, allowing space for travel and business papers, toilet necessities, money and so on. (See SHOULDER BAG)

HAND FALL *Masc. Fem.* Deep, turned-back widening cuff, sometimes starched, double or trimmed with lace edge. 17th Cent.

HANGING SLEEVE *Masc. Fem.* Long, wide sleeves with a cut in upper half through which arm emerged, leaving the long part of the sleeve hanging. c. 1400-1650. *Masc.* From 1600-1630, hanging ribbons were attahed ornamentally to back of the arm-hole of jerkins, a fashion also copied in fem. wear.

HANSELINE, HENSE LYNES *Masc.* Very short doublet fashionable in late 14th Cent. to early 15th Cent.

HAORI *Jap.* Black silk coat worn over the kimono. *Masc.* Knee-length and plain with centre fastening of small silk cords. *Fem.* Long or knee-length, sometimes embroidered.

HARDANGER EMBROIDERY *Norw.* Colourful cutaway embroidery based mostly on squares and diamond shapes. Used for the edging of aprons, dresses, blouses.

HAREM SKIRT *Fem.* Divided full skirt of silk gathered to the ankles imitating Turkish trousers. A fashion briefly introduced in Paris about 1910, it did not become popular.

HARLOT *Masc.* The introduction of this garment resembling modern tights and consisting of hoselegs and breeches all combined in one, was considered not decent. 14th Cent. Reference is made in 'The Parson's Tale', Chaucer. Also HERLOT.

HARRIS TWEED *Scot.* Soft, homespun, loosely woven woollen cloth, hand spun in the Hebrides. Became recognisd for its quality from the late 19th Cent.

HASP *Masc.* Decorative hook-and-eye fastening used for coats in place of buttons. Early 18th Cent.

HAT PIN *Fem.* Long steel pin finished with ornamental top, used for securing the large hats to the full coiffures of late Victorian and early Twentieth Century time.

HATTE *Fem. Sri Lanka.* Short-sleeved, tightly fitting jacket or blouse worn above midriff.

HAUBERK *Masc. M.E., O.F., W. Germ.* Hooded, long-sleeved, knee-length coat of ringed mail or mesh. Longer than Habergeon or Haubergeon. Accompaniments were a leather belt, leg and foot mail and steel helmet. Worn by nobility, 12th and 13th Cents.

HAVELOCK *Masc.* White cloth covering worn with military cap for protection of neck and head from sun. Worn in ancient times by Persians. Was also used by the British in the Sepoy Mutiny and named after the General, Sir Henry Havelock. 1857. A similar head-dressing was worn by soldiers in the American Civil War, 1861-1865.

HEADRAIL *Fem.* Linen, cotton piece of material of circular or oblong shape used as head-dess. Anglo-Saxon women wrapped it around the neck and it was held in place on the head by a narrow filet or crown. In later 16th-17th Cent. it became a veil or kerchief and was worn hanging behind the head, sometimes wired or starched and with a lace edge.

HEARTBREAKERS *Fr. Crève-Coeur. Fem.* Tight small curls, sometimes wired to stand away from forehead and nape of neck. 17th Cent.

HEAUME *Masc.* Helmet designed as head-dress for partaking in pageants and games. A long scarf or cointoise with dagged edges was attached to it, so that it spread out with movement or in the wind. Medieval.

HECTOREAN *Masc.* Ancient Greek style of hairdressing. Short with hair combed backwards into curls.

HEEL The idea of support under the heel came from flat pattens and clogs. In Europe, the first modern heel as we know it, was worn in the Spanish and Italian Courts in 15th Cent. In Venice, red heels were worn by retainers of Royal households in 16th Cent. In the 18th Cent. French Court, a gently inward curved heel became known as a Louis XV heel and this style has returned periodically. Today, masc. use is universally restrained, with only personalities in the public eye who wish to appear tall wearing raised heels. *Fem.* Styles in the 20th Cent. include varieties known as cuban, stacked, stiletto; wedge and platform soles incorporate the heel with a raised sole.

69

HEERPAUKE *Masc. Ger.* Heavily padded, short, rotund breeches. Influenced by Sp. fashion. 1550-1600. Also ROUND HOSE.

HELMET Defensive covering for the head.

HELMET Taken from the ship-graves discovered in Vendel, north of Stockholm, Sweden, it is decorated with bronze plates. The Vendel period, 500-800 A.D. preceded the Viking Age.

HEMLINE Women's dress became shorter in the second decade of the 20th Cent. during the reign of George V in England. It reached knee length in 1925 and after the 1930s two lengths became acceptable, shorter for day and long for evening and formal wear. A short dinner dress was introduced during World War II and been approved for less important evening wear since that time. The more casual attitude of the 1980s has welcomed an attitude that allows wearers to choose a length and style suitable to themselves.

HENKE Short Norman cloak.

HENLEY BOATER *Masc.* A felt hat in the shape of a straw boater, coloured blue or fawn. 1894.

HENNIN *Fem.* Originally an Eastern head-dress brought to France by Isabeau of Bavaria, Consort of Charles VI, 1392-1422. Usually referred to as a steeple head-dress. It was attached to an unseen velvet cap from which was suspended a black velvet frontlet across the forehead. This frontlet was worn only by the rich but all head-dresses were accompanied by a long hanging veil or kerchief, often wired at the edge. The fashion lasted for nearly a hundred years.

HERIGAUT *Masc.* Comfortable, simple-shaped over-gown, either three-quarter or full length, with hanging sleeves, sometimes with hood attached to shoulders. 1250-1300s.

HESSIAN *Masc.* Of Hesse in Germany. A high boot with tassel, first worn by Hessian troops. Became fashionable in the early 19th Cent.

HEUKE *Masc.* Sleeveless, bell-shaped cloak worn in Flanders, France and Italy; later adopted by women. 14th Cent. *Arabic - HAIK.* Some traditional forms persisted until 18th Cent. Also HUKE.

HEUSE, HUSEAU Long protective riding-boot reaching to mid-thigh. Fitted to the leg by buckles and straps or buttons on the outside of the leg. 13th-15th Cents.

HIGHLOWS *Masc.* Sturdy leather calf-length laced boots for country and working men. Late 18th Cent. Became more refined in style by end of 19th Cent.

HIMATION (See Greek Costume)

HIP BOOT A boot, usually made of rubber or water-proof material, reaching to the hips; used for fishing, work with boats and so on. Also known as WADERS.

HIPSTERS *Masc. Fem.* Term used since 1960s for well-fitting, straight pants, copied from cowboy's jeans; reaching as high as the hip-line and then secured by leather or self-belt. Worn mostly by young people and originally made popular by North American film actors.

HIVE *Fem.* High-crowned straw hat shaped like a bee-hive or cloche. Extremely popular over high hair styles. 1779-1781.

HIZAAM *Masc. Ar.* White silk cummerbund or waist-sash. Worn around the caftan and folded so that a dagger could be hidden.

HOBBLE SKIRT *Fem.* Long, tapered skirt so narrow that walking was difficult. Fashionable 1910-1914.

HODDEN Ancient Scottish word describing a woven mixture of undyed fleeces. The words of the song *D'ye ken John Peel in his coat so grey* are understood to refer to a garment made from such cloth.

HOGGERS *Masc.* Ploughman's boots. Also OKERS.

HOMBURG *Usually Masc.* Felt hat with a dent from back to front in the crown. The brim was curved up at the sides and braided. Worn by Edward VII when Prince of Wales and who visited Homburg for the waters - the town where the style was manufactured originally. 1870 on.

HOOD *Masc. Fem.* Loose covering to fit over the head. Worn separately or attached to garment or cloak. A variety of forms includes Academic, French, 14th and 18th Cent., Gable 16th Cent.

HOOP PETTICOAT *Fem.* Revival of the farthingale support of the 16th Cent. An under-petticoat supported and enlarged by cane or wire hoops. Worn for Court appearance in mid-18th Cent. and early 19th Cent.

HORNED HEAD-DRESS *Fem.* Head-dress, having a wide boss over each ear, a fillet over the temple and a stuffed wired horn shape on either side. A veil was suspended over this, hiding the back of the head. 1410-1440.

HOOD ENGLISH, 1520S. A wired hood formed a pointed arch or Gable above the forehead. An under cap was worn and front hair concealed. The two pendant flaps shown in the back view were often pinned upwards.

HORSE-HAIR PETTICOAT *Fem.* The original Spanish farthingale was a linen petticoat stiffened with horse-hair, 16th Cent. Crinoline, a material made first in 1829 with horse-hair warp and wool weft, was used in 1840s and 1850s for an underskirt, sometimes as much aa six feet round. It was replaced by the 'Cage Crinoline', but revived when the large skirts were going out of fashion, 1868-1870.

HORTENSE MANTEL *Fem.* Fingertip-length mantle with flat collar and lapels, having a square-cut cape edged with fringe to the waist. Named after the mother of Napoleon III, Queen Hortense. 1849.

HOUPPELANDE *Masc. Fem.* Long, full-skirted gown with high collar. First noted from the Low Countries in mid-14th Cent. Later forms were padded or lined with fur and had wide, extravagant sleeves and the garment was worn with or without a belt. Until late 16th Cent.

HOUR-GLASS SILHOUETTE *Fem.* Description of woman's figure when a long ·heavily-boned corset was worn in an attempt to gain a slim elegant posture with an 18 inch waist. 1890s.

HOUSECOAT *Fem. 1930s.* Loose, usually long coat in buttoned or zipped, of attractive material, not necessarily extravagant, worn for casual at-home wear. Another garment, appearing at the same time, was a HOSTESS GOWN, for informal evening entertaining, sometimes with floor-length skirt or with easy flowing culotte trouser legs.

HUARACHES *Mex.* Leather sandals trimmed with braid and leather lacings. Wooden soles.

HUGUE *Fem.* Short sleeveless tunic, as worn by Joan of Arc; a woman's wrap. Worn since 11th Cent.

Survives in the Kerry cloak of Ireland. English version, 1590. A development - (See HUKE).

HUGUENOT LACE A simple lace formed by muslin cut-out applique motifs on net mesh.

HUIPIL *Fem. Mex.* Handwoven, white cotton shirt or blouse, used and worn by some Mexican tribes as head-dress. Of varying length, sometimes plain or embroidered with floral or geometric patterns. Sleeveless, made of two pieces of material and even used as a shawl. It represents, and is named after, some beautiful clothes belonging to a baby rescued from the sea long ago. This child is reputed to bring good fortune to its rescuers. (See ZAPOTEC)

Festival dress - Tehuantepec with Huipil headdress.

HUKE *Fem. Dut.* Long black woollen mantle covering the body, with material extended to wear hood-like over the head and above a white linen coif and head-dress. 1550.

HUKE, HEWKE, HEUQUE *Fem. Eur. Veil.* Black square of woollen cloth sufficient to cover whole figure. Worn in Spain and N. Africa since 11th Cent., the period of Saracen domination. Unknown in British Isles excepting small part of Ireland.

HULA SKIRT *Masc. Fem.* Skirt worn by Hawaian dancer, of thick green leaves. A blouse and garland of flowers - lei - completes the costume.

HUNT DRESS With some regional differences, contemporary male hunting clothes consist of scarlet coats, white breeches, black boots with tan tops, black visored velvet caps; formal wear - top hats, black or grey coats, fawn or yellow breeches. A white shirt and stock always worn. *Fem.* Black, grey or dark blue coat. Green habits are worn by harriers and beaglers.

HURLUBERLU, À LAS HURLUBERLU, HURLUPEE *Fem. Coiffure.* A wind-blown hairstyle much worn around 1671. It was short with small tight ringlets around the face. Some versions were dressed in a bunch on either side of the face. Fashionable until end of 17th Cent.

HUVET, HOWVE, HOUVE *Masc. Fem.* Hood. 14th Cent.

HYDROTOBOLIC HAT *Masc.* Hat with a small hole in the crown centre allowing some ventilation. The opening was protected by a fine wire gauze. 1850-1860.

LES INCROYABLES *Based on a caricature by Antoine-Charles Vernet, 1758-1835, this drawing shows the exaggerated fashions adopted after the Revolution by some dandies. The men were proud of their large jabots arranged to cover the face. A French style. Female counterpart - Merveilleuses.*

ICHELLA *Fem. S. Amer.* Long woollen shawl with fringe. Bordered in brilliant colours with geometric designs. Worn by Indian women of Chile.

IHENGA *Fem. Ind.* Skirt; short but not tight; worn with abbreviated cotton V-necked blouse called 'choli' or 'cholee'. N. and Central India.

IHRAM *Ar.* Two pieces of white cotton forming the garment worn by pilgrims to Mecca. One piece is worn on the upper part of the body, leaving right shoulder and arm free; the other piece is wrapped around the loins.

IHS *fr. Gk.* 'Jesus'. A monogram often embroidered on church vestments.

ILLUSION Name for silk tulle used for veils, dresses and trimming. This light material was sometimes sewn with small spangles, beads or lace. 19th Cent.

IMBECILE *Fem.* One of the many names given to huge sleeves fashionable from 1825. Very full down to the wrist, then gathered into neat small cuff. 1829.

IMPERIAL *Masc.* (1) Overcoat, similar to paletot, which was without a seam at the waist; loose and fly-fronted. 1840s. *Masc.* (2) Small neat beard trimmed to

a tuft on chin, worn with elegantly cut moustache. After Napoleon III. 1852-1873.

INAR *Masc. Fem. Ir.* Close-fitting, sleeveless jacket worn with brooch. pre-1170. Ref. Book of Kells.

INCROYABLES *Fr. Unbelievable. Masc.* Name given to peculiar manner of dressing by young dandies in France, 1795-1799, when they exaggerated English fashions, which had been worn some years earlier mainly by members of the Macaroni Club in London. (See MACARONI). Sir Horace Walpole had written, in 1764, that this London Club was made up of 'all the travelled young men who wear long curls and spying-glasses'. 'Les Incroyables' favoured large cravats which covered the neck and chin; high shouldered clumsy tail-coats, very ill-fitting, with broad flapping lapels; chest-high pale yellow pantaloons; and military boots with decorative tops. Completing the untidy picture of a young fop was a large brimmed hat worn at a rakish angle over long flowing hair; a cane, and quizzing-glass. *Fem.* Counterpart. (See 'Les MERVEILLEUSES')

INDIAN GOWN, INDIAN NIGHTGOWN (1) *Fem.* Dishabille or negligée usually in bright materials. Late 17th Cent. (2) *Masc. Fem.* Originally a comfortable garment worn at home informally and sometimes lined so as to be worn either side. Wrapped over in front, or fastened with clasping or hooks. 1735. The comfortable but discreet appearance of the garment allowed it in time to be worn by gentlemen occasionally out-of-doors. By 1780 the shape was universally accepted by men for day wear. A slit was made at the rear to allow a sword, if worn, to protrude. The Dutch imported many robes for house wear from the Orient. (See BANYAN)

INDIAN LAWN (MUSLIN) *Ind.* Light cotton material introduced at the end of the 18th Cent.*Fem.* 'Les Merveilleuses' in France wore slender, low-cut muslin gowns in eccentric ways. They abandoned petticoats and the muslin being transparent, wore white or pink tights beneath. In an effort to resemble Greek sculpture, the material was often dampened to cling to the figure. Public reaction set in. The neckline was raised and rational underclothing worn, which made a version of the so-called 'classical' dress acceptable. Mme. Recamier was seen walking in such a dress in Kensington Gardens, 1802. Such charming garments, usually in white, had a disadvantage - the climate. The material also crushed easily, which spoiled a fresh appearance. Light-weight pelisses or cloaks were not warm nor protective enough. The fashion, however, persisted for at least eight years. By 1809, stronger colours became popular and in 1816 the wider skirt appeared and the 'classical' silhouette disappeared.

INDIAN NECKTIE *Masc.* A muslin cravat, the ends of which were placed in front and kept in place after being passed through a ring. 1815-1830.

INDIENNE Printed or painted muslin imported from India and which became popular in France and England, 17th and 18th Cents. The demand became so great that workshops were introduced in Europe for the production of hand-block printing of cotton, cambric and linen. White or pastel coloured Indienne was worn during last years of Marie Antoinette's reign in France. Later, fichus of white Indian muslin were worn 'à la citoyenne' in the revolution. Late 18th Cent.

INDISPENSABLE *Fem.* Small hand-bag which replaced hidden pockets and knitting bags. Became fashionable by end of the 18th Cent. Of handsome materials, such as velvet or brocade and closed with drawstrings. Edged with tassels or fringe. They were carried suspended from the arms by long ribbon ties.

INDUSTRIAL REVOLUTION Advances in clothing manufacture were made possible by the achievement and use of inventions such as James Hargreaves' 'Spinning Jenny', 1764; and John Kay's 'Flying Shuttle', 1773. Cheap cotton from America and India was imported to England and wash-proof dyeing was developed. The invention of the sewing machine enabled prices in the textile industry to be lowered.

INEXPRESSIBLES Prudish name for men's trousers, 1800. Others - 'Bags', 'Don't Mentions', 'Unmentionables', 'Kicksies', 'Unwhisperables'; all of which referred to leg-wear of three kinds - breeches, pantaloons and trousers.

INFANTA *Fem.* Daughter of King and Queen of Spain. The name given to style of dress worn by the Royal daughters of Philip IV, 1605-1665, and recorded in portraits of them by Velasquez, Court Painter. The finest painting showing the costume of the period was 'Las Meninas', 1656, now in The Prado. General style characterised by the flattened back and front farthingale, along with front-pointed corset or bodice. The coiffure was severely dressed and wide on each side of the face.

INFULA, INFULAE *Masc. L.* Sacred band, fillet. The hanging bands from the back of liturgical head-dress, the Mitre. Usually of silk and embroidered.

INSIGNIA Motif, design or mark used as a distinguishing feature or badge of honour.

INSURGEANT *Fem.* Simplified form of dress worn by French women prior to the French Revolution of 1789. Trimmings and frills were abjured as a form of sympathy with the American Revolutionists. 1778-1781.

INVERNESS *Masc.* Large loose overcoat. Close-fitting, turned down high collar and deep arm-length cape, made of woollen Scottish cloth, from Inverness. From 1859. Peaked hats of similar material were worn for winter in the country or bad weather.

IONIC (See Greek costume)

IPSIBOE A yellow crepe material favoured in 1821.

IRIDESCENT *adj. L. iridis, iris -rainbow.* Of shifting rainbow-like colours appearing to change and shine on certain fabrics, sequins, beads, when in movement.

IRISH CROCHET LACE Inspired and copied from Spanish and Venetian needlepoint. Hard-wearing, attractive motifs of shamrock and other designs on stitched mesh. Lacy picot edging is added.

IRISH LINEN Fine, bleached, plain woven linen cloth of Irish flax. Admired and used for quality shirts, blouses, handkerchiefs.

ISABEAU CORSAGE *Fem.* Bodice resembling a short-shaped jacket, although part of dress. The corners of the false front were open above hip level and the inverted V-shape was trimmed with crossing bands and button-studs. The high neckline was collared. The mancheron, predecessor of the epaulet, below the shoulder on the sleeve, and the sleeve edge at wrist, were both cut with a 'V' and trimmed with matching bands across the openings. 1846.

ISABELLA Creamy yellow colour named after Isabel of Austria. 16th Cent.

ISABEY, JEAN BAPTISTE The Court Painter commissioned by Napoleon to design the costumes for his Coronation, 1804. The Couturier, Leroy, was responsible for the making of the clothes.

ITALIAN HEEL *Fem.* Peg-topped slender heel on a shoe which had a wedge-like extension under the instep. This allowed the heel to be placed forward along the wedge, giving the appearance of a smaller foot than normal. The wooden heel was usually covered with white or cream kid leather. 1770s.

IZAR *Fem. - Arabic - veil* Large sheet of white calico used as covering garment by poorer Moslem women.

JUSTAUCORPS - 1786-1788. A coat which clung loosely to the body - juste au corps. Knee-length, made of heavy material, trimmed with facings and brandenburgs. Forerunner of lighter weight - Frac -

JABOT *Masc. Fem.* Ruffled or pleated frill of lace or cloth worn down the centre front of shirt or blouse. *Masc.* In France, during reign of Louis XIV after 1690, the concealment of shirt closure was by lace-trimmed scarf at shirt neck. In England, during the Georges, lace was replaced by black silk and then later by a white muslin scarf. *Fem.* In next century, real lace jabots much worn to soften the fashionable masculine-looking dinner jackets of the 1920s.

JABUL *Fem.* Large wrap or shawl worn as a dress. Philippine Islands.

JACK *Masc.* Tunic or jerkin of mail, quilted with stout leather. Often sleeveless. 14th-16th Cent.

JACK BOOT *Masc.* Heavy, hard leather boots worn for riding and outdoors. 17th-18th Cent. Heavy boots had bucket-tops to enclose knees, and square heels and toes. Later lighter boots were sometimes buttoned on outside, with the back of the knee scooped to allow for bending. 18th Cent.

JACK CHAIN *Masc.* Chain worn as decoration. The links were formed in figure eight shape but the wearing of such adornments was thought 'showy'.

JACK LEATHER Waxed leather coated with tar or pitch which was used for boots; also for tankards holding ale and beer. 17th-18th Cent.

JACKANAPES *Masc.* Very short jacket with short sleeves, worn with 'petticoat' breeches. Some were made entirely of ribbons. The brevity of the garment displayed the beautifully embroidered shirts worn at this time, 17th Cent. Not unlike the short coat worn by Austrian, Bavarian and Swiss countrymen. 'Jack' is a term for monkey and monkeys were sent to England from Italy in 15th Cent. The use of small, dressed-up monkeys with organ-grinders possibly led to the term 'monkey-jacket', the short coat worn by seamen.

JACKET *Masc.* Short S.B. or D.B. coat. In its earliest forms, (15th and 16th Cents.), it was worn by country folk as a jerkin and later by sportsmen. The short jacket gradually replaced the tailcoat during the latter part of the 19th Cent.

JACK-SNIP Old English term for tailor who worked clumsily.

JACKTAR SUIT Children's 'sailor suit' worn with

trousers by boys and with pleated skirt by girls. 1880-1915.

JACOB'S STAFF *L. Jacobus.* Reference - Apostle James, patron saint of Spain. A pilgrim's staff. The emblem of St. James and pilgrims was the scallop shell and this was also worn in some form on the clothing.

JACQUARD LOOM A machine for weaving figures and motifs upon silk and muslins, invented by Frenchman, Joseph Marie Jacquard, 1752-1834, of Lyons. This, and another remarkable machine for producing machine lace, were patented by him and gained recognition from the French Government.

JACQUERIE, LA Insurrection of French peasants, 1358. (see JAQUE)

JADE Semi-transparent silicate of magnesia and lime, capable of high polish ranging from green to white and also some shades of pink, lavender and yellow. Used in jewellery and in medieval times as a protection against colic. Some North American Indians still wear it as an amulet against snake bites.

JAEGER UNDERWEAR The introduction of natural wool underclothing for health and hygienic reasons by Dr. Jaeger in late 19th Cent.

JAMB, JAMBEAU *Fr.* Armour piece to protect the leg. Medieval.

JAMBEE CANE *Masc.* Knotty walking-stick made of bamboo, favoured by fashionable young men. Early 18th Cent.

JANUS CORD Black rep. material with corded appearance on either side. Much used for mourning, 1860s and 1870s.

JAPANESE COSTUME (See GETA, HAORI, KIMONO, TABI)

JAPANESE MINK Animal with short dark hair, some yellowish in colour requiring dyeing.

JAPANESE PONGEE Wild silk tussore material with crêpe finish. 1870.

JAPANESE SILK Close woven, springy silk material resembling alpaca. 1870s.

JAQUE *Masc. Fr.* Rough, long-sleeved waist-coat worn by poor artisan class called La Jacquerie. 1348.

JAQUETTE *Fem. Fr.* Short coat or 'waist-coat' ending at waist, 16th Cent. By 19th Cent., it evolved into an over-garment and by the end of the century was worn as part of a tailor-made costume and also worn for sportswear.

JARDINIÈRE Crimped, striped crêpe patterned with flowers, leaves and bowknots. 1840s.

JARRETELLE *Fr.* Stocking or sock-suspender.

JARRETIERE *Fr.* Garter.

JASERAN, JASERANT *Masc.* 1) Algerian tunic of very fine chain mesh worn for protection. 13th Cent. 2) Short coat of linen stitched with small metal plates. 3)*Fem.* Name adopted for high necklaces and collars made of rows of fine gold chains. 16th Cent.

JASEY Casual slang term for a wig made of yarn, Jersey flax, fine wool or artificial hair-like material.

JACK BOOTS Made of hard leather they were worn for riding. The details from a painting by an unknown artist include a frockcoat, waistcoat and tricorne hat, 1745.

Used of a judge's wig or contemptuously of an untidy head of hair. Late 18th and 19th Cents.

JEAN *It. Gene, Jene - for Genoa.* Twilled cotton material, since 16th Cent. Used for casual and work clothes since 18th Cent. Most used in blue colour.

JEANNETTE *Fem.* A necklace of velvet or narrow lock of hair supporting a small cross or heart. 1836.

JELLABA *Masc. Fem. N. Africa.* A woollen robe with long loose sleeves and hood. Often worn for protection with face protection made of litham when sand is blowing. Below knee-length. A garment style worn for many centuries. Also DJELLABA. (See LITHAM, HAIK, MANDEEL, YASHMAK, YASHMAC)

JELLY BAG *Masc.* Soft, washable nightcap in shape of a 'jelly-bag'. Often adorned with a tassel. 19th Cent.

JEMIMA *Fem.* British name for fabric boot with elastic insertions and leather toes. It was designed for Queen Victoria in 1836. The style was later worn by men and women and had cloth or leather uppers with elastic side gussets. Also BOTTINE.

JEMMY *Adj.* Spruce, dandified, smart, fashionable. 19th Cent.

JEMMY *Masc. Br.* Short shooting coat with many pockets, worn for outdoor pursuits and shooting. 19th Cent.

JEMMY BOOTS *Masc.* Smart riding boots, not heavy in style. 18th Cent.

JEMMY CANE A small switch carried under the arm, fashionable in mid-18th Cent., until early 19th Cent.

JERKIN *Masc.* Tight-fitting jacket which replaced the cotehardie in the late 15th Cent. Sometimes made of leather. Later with padded shoulders and sleeves. In 16th Cent., Henry VIII was in the habit of wearing a jerkin over his doublet and this was closed down front with laces or buttons. (An upper loose-fitting gown was worn over this.) In 17th Cent. the jerkin was often sleeveless. Fem. counterpart - JERKINET. In Northern England, the garment continued to be worn as a short, warm waist-coat until early 20th Cent.

JERSEY, GUERNSEY Hand-knitting has been known for over two thousand years but the first knitted tunics or shirts appeared in the Channel Islands in the 15th Cent. Jerseys, guernseys or ganseys were knitted for sailors and fishermen and the same styles have been worn for many years. Modern use of knitting includes cloth made not only of wool but of cotton, silk, artificial fibres and their combination. Chanel, the famous French couturier, used jersey for her world-wide known suit and plain chemise dress. Modern use includes athletics, sports and underwear.

JERSEY COSTUME *Fem.* So-called for a figure-fitting thigh-level knitted tunic worn, with a long pleated skirt, by Mrs. Langtry, the 'Jersey Lily' and friend of Edward VII. 1880s.

JESSAMY GLOVES *Masc. Fem.* Gloves which were scented with jasmine. They were given as wedding presents to the bride and groom. Other perfumes used were cloves, cinnamon, nutmeg, ambergris and floral scents. 17th Cent.

JESTER *Masc. usually* A person retained in Court households to amuse royalty or high-born people in the years following the Crusades. His dress consisted of a fool's cap with ass's ears and a scalloped shoulder cape. He held a mock sceptre, which was a rattle with a miniature head wearing cap and bells. The custom of using these persons disappeared by the 17th Cent. Also MOTLEY.

JET Black lignite mineral taking brilliant polish, found in England and Spain. *Fem.* Used as buttons on side of boots, early 19th Cent. Much used at the end of 19th Cent. for mourning jewellery.

JEWEL Precious stone; ornament containing valuable stones.

JEWELLERY IN BRITISH ISLES The Ancient Britons showed skill in the making of neck-rings and enormous torques. Unfortunately, much of finest later jewellery was sold to pay for the English Civil War, 1642-1652. Of the 17th Cent., we have only some pieces, mostly rock crystals, cut with facets and some worked with gold wire. With the Restoration, designs were copied from Europe. Bare shoulders and necks displayed large, spectacular necklets; ear-rings sparkled and were long. Plain paste was also used, mounted by the same jewellers as those who used better quality stones.

In the first half of the 18th Cent., gold work of exquisite workmanship was imported into England from Spain; stones came from Portugal; raised and sculptured settings from Italy. Designs were influenced by the Baroque and later Rococo styles. Many necklets took the form of a collar tied at back with velvet ribbon; brooches were often in the form of a bow with pendant drops and girandole ear-rings were fashionable. (See BRISTOL DIAMOND or STONE)

In second half of the 18th Cent., finds at Pompeii influenced gold and enamel designs. Diamond sprays were also made on bases of flower shapes.

Christopher Pinchbeck, a clock and watchmaker, invented in 1700 an alloy of copper and zinc, imitating gold in appearance. This metal, named after him, was used to simulate expensive items including beautiful buttons, now much prized, for the men's clothes of that period. In late 18th Cent., a Scotsman, James Tassie, produced paste replicas of cameos and intaglios, known as TASSIES. These were extremely popular. In 1830s, handsome bracelets, some with enamel miniatures, were worn below the enormous sleeves fashionable at that period.

With the Industrial Revolution, there was a demand from the growing Middle Classes for jewellery at reasonable prices. Machines were used to make settings and chains; designs in the mid-19th Cent. were mainly of classical and Renaissance styles. By the late 19th Cent., the South African diamond mines were producing quality stones but some of the machine setting was poorly fashioned. After the Great Exhibition, the Art Nouveau Movement began to dominate the emerging styles and among the great jewellery designers were René Lalique, C.R. Ashbee and Alphonse Mucha.

JEWELLERY, COSTUME Designed ornamental pieces, made from metals of not high value, such as plated silver or gold; jet with semi-precious or glass stones. Such imitation jewellery, providing a decorative smart effect and colour emphasis, was made to enhance special gowns in the 1920s and became popular again in the 1950s.

JEWELLERY, HISTORIC The earliest Sumerian graves in Mesopotamia revealed that gold was used in abundance, 3500 B.C. The culture merged with Babylonia, 2200 B.C., and beads, pendants, amulets, chains, have been excavated from that period. In Egypt, bracelets, diadems and pectorals have come from the wrappings of the dead, the finest from the tombs of XIIth Dynasty. The best general collection of ancient jewellery is housed in the British Museum; while the Hermitage in Russia has the finest examples of Greek jewellery in existence. Discoveries from the Royal Tombs at Ur are divided between the National Museum in Baghdad, the British Museum and the University Museum in Philadelphia, U.S.A. Cretans used and engraved gold; also stones such as agate, amethyst, jasper, porphyry.

Gold and silver Ionic work in archaic style has been found in S. Russia; made for the living, not for the dead as in Egypt. Thin sheet gold was cut in ornamental shapes and sewn on to dress; also used to make golden garlands, wreaths and diadems. Other items were necklaces, chains, pendants - made with great delicacy. Some granulation was used but not of the later Etruscan microscopic fineness.

In Europe, little jewellery was worn before 1100 A.D. but with men's tunics becoming longer, belts were worn and buckles and neck-ring fastenings became elaborate, some of copper gilt, and sculptured. Rome and Byzantine goldsmiths influenced the Germanic tribes.

The word JOUEL or JOYAU referred to a jewel worn on clothing in the last decade of the 14th Cent. 'Fashion' was born towards the end of the 15th Cent. A.D. in the Court of Burgundy and by the middle of the 16th Cent., the discovery of the New World had increased the availability of stones.

With the Renaissance, rich women braided pearls in their hair and wore diadems studded with gems. The wearing of ear-rings was a Byzantine habit and came to the West in the 16th Cent. Gold chains were popular in Spain and Italy but were replaced by ropes of pearls, 1628-1648.

Many artists began their careers as goldsmiths - Ghiberti, L. della Robbia, Botticelli, Andrea del Sarto -and Albrecht Dürer was the pupil of his goldsmith father.

By 1560, jewellery design changed and the pendant jewel was much admired. In England, the miniatures of Nicholas Hilliard, who was also a jeweller, provide much detail of the jewels his sitters wore; and towards the end of the century the watch was innovated; also cameos with the portrait of Queen Elizabeth were made, some small enough to be set in rings. The following years and period of the Civil War in England saw the development of medals.

JINGLE   (See GINGLER SPURS)

JINNAH CAP   *Masc.* Truncatted karakul cap worn in Pakistan, named after Muhammad Ali Jinnah, the first Govenor-General there, 1947-1948.

JIPIJAPA   Plant of Central and South America, whose leaves are used for making Panama hats.

JOCKEY BOOTS   *Masc.* Riding boot, which ended below knee, with turndown top of lighter soft leather. Pulled on by side leather loops. So-called from 1680-1780s. Later called 'Top Boots'.

JOCKEY CAP   *Masc.* Black velvet peaked cap. 17th-19th Cent. A silk coloured cap was worn for racing in 19th Cent. Today, great care is taken in precautions for safety by reinforcing the crown of the head-piece.

JOCKEY WAISTCOAT   *Masc.* Buttoned straight waistcoat with low collar, cut square below chin. 1806 and 1884.

JODHPURS   *Masc. Fem.* Trousers for horseback riding, the style taken from India; full to the knees and fitted tightly from knee to ankle. Worn with a low boot. In western world from 1920s.

JOINVILLE   *Masc.* Broad necktie with fringed ends. Worn in a wide bow. 1844-1855. It was named after the Prince de Joinville who visited Windsor in 1844.

JOSEPH   *Fem.* Full-length green riding coat. Buttoned down the front. Sometimes with slashed cape collar. Made of JOSETTE, a heavy twilled material. 1750s. Also known as JOSIE.

JOSEPHINE BODICE   *Fem.* Bodice of evening dress cut very low and draped with folds of satin or silk. 1879.

JOUY PRINTS   20th Cent. reproductions of 18th Cent. French prints on linen or cotton. Originally made in Jouy, France, of floral or pictorial landscape designs.

JUBBAH, JUBBA   *Masc. Fem. Ar.* Long loose coat worn by Moslems and Parsees. Made of camel hair or cloth. Occasionally fur-lined for winter wear.

JUBE   *Masc. Fem.* Traditional, and still worn, winter overcoat made of sheepskin, worn in the Balkans. Padded, with skin on the outside; decorated with embroidery and bright coloured appliqué. Usually long sleeves with mittens attached. *Masc. Eur.* Short sleeveless jacket. 17th Cent.

JUCHTEN   *Ger.* Russian leather.

JUIVE TUNIC   *Fem.* Tunic-garment designed to be worn over a dress for outdoor wear. Bodice with no waist seam and wide armholes and V-openings at front and back. The back skirt was cut to a point to form a train. 1875.

JULIET CAP   *Fem.* Small brimless head-dress worn at back of head. *It.* Of mesh sewn with jewels, Renaissance. Also modern.

JUMP   Connected with French jupe, jupon - a petticoat. *Masc.* Short coat of 17th Cent. Now obsolete.

JUMPER   *Masc.* Hip length shirt of hard-wearing material, originally worn by sailors and labourers. *Fem.* Loose pull-on blouse or jersey. Modern.

JUMPER COAT   *Masc.* Lounge jacket, high closure, four buttons. Narrow sleeves. Also known as BEAUFORT COAT. 1880.

JUMPS   *Fem.* Loose comfortable supporting under-bodice. Early 18th Cent.

JUMP SUIT   *Masc. Fem.* Work or play-suit similar to trousered overalls. Named SIREN SUIT during air attacks of World War II, when donned for night work, etc. Now made in many materials and styles.

JUPE *Fem. Fr.* Skirt. JUPE ENTRAVÉE - hobble-skirt. 1910-1914.

JUPON *Fem. Fr.* Petticoat. A riding-coat with protective overskirt. 16th and 17th Cents.

JUST-AU-CORPS, JUSTACORPS *Fr.* Close coat; body coat. *Masc.* Forerunner of jacket worn under a topcoat. 1650-1730s. *Fem.* Short neat riding-coat. 17th and 18th Cents.

JUTE *Sanskrit.* Juta -jata - braid of hair. Glossy fibre from East Indian plants used for sacking, mats, wrapping. Is also used combined with silk or wool in fabric making.

GREEK REPUBLICAN GUARD - off duty.

KRUSELER (Mid-High German - Kruiseler)
Woman with tightly frilled head veil. From the
Velislav Bible, c1340, University Library, Prague.

KABAYA *Fem.* Modern Indonesian jacket, in white or prints, worn with draped sarong skirt.

KAFFIYEH *Masc.* Arabian traditional head-dress worn over skull-cap; of varied pattern and colour. Triangular, with one point at back to protect neck and two over shoulders. The head portion is bound round with a band or hoop of thick cord called AGAL.

KAFTAN *Masc.* Traditional robe of Levant. (See CAFTAN)

KAIN *Masc. Fem. Indonesian.* Cloth of 9 ft. long by 4 ft. wide, wrapped and fastened around waist, reaching to feet. Also known as SARONG.

KALASIRIS *Masc. Fem.* Lightweight long thin tunic worn in Ancient Egypt. With short sleeves or shoulder straps; sometimes fringed. New Kingdom, 1500 - 332 B.C.

KALL *Fem.* 1) Untrimmed back part of head-dress. Medieval. 14th-16th Cent. 2) Net foundation for wig. 3) Soft top of cap or bonnet, 18th and 19th Cents. Also KELLE, FRET, CAUL.

KALPAK *Masc.* Three-cornered hat of Astrakhan fur worn by Tartars.

KAMAKA Silk fabric of Middle Ages. From Asia.

KAMBAL Rough woollen blanket or shawl used in India.

KAMELAUKION *Masc. Pers.* Tall cap of fur or felt, cone-shaped with no brim; worn by early religious fanatics in religious rites. (See DERVISH)

KAMIKS *Masc. Fem.* High skin boots worn by Eskimos. Some decorated and embroidered with leather and beads.

KAMIS *Ar.* Long under-garment, worn with sash and over full easy-fitting trousers. Usually white and embroidered at front and neck.

KAMISOL *Masc. Fem. Ger. From Latin Camisia - shirt.* Under-garment with sleeves, 16th and 17th Cents. Also sleeved jerkin, short coat or jacket made of leather.

KAMPSKATCHA *Fem.* Slipper lined with fur, pointed turned-up toe and shaped low heel. Usually black leather. Late 18th Cent. Also called CHINESE SLIPPER.

KANDYS *Masc. Fem.* Skirt of thin sheepskin; the garment worn by the early Sumerians, Assyrians, Babylonians and Persians. (See KAUNACE)

KAPTA *Masc. Lapland.* Tunic of suit made from carefully prepared and shorn reindeer skin. The upper part is belted but full-skirted. The complete outfit with cap, breeches, boots, is colourfully embroidered. Worn by all - men, women and children.

KARAKUL Hardy sheep bred originally in Karakul Valley, Russia, near Caspian Sea. Now mostly found in Asia Minor.

KAROSS Square rug made of animal skins worn by South African Hottentots, formerly of region near the Cape.

KARPASITIKO *Fem.* Festive costume worn in Cyprus. A white long-sleeved dress with high neck and calf-length full trousers, which are worn under dress. A long tight-fitting coat with loose sleeves and a draped, large head square completes the outfit. Low black shoes.

KASHA Trade name of twilled material of silky softness, produced in Twenties by Rodier, with wool from Himalayan sheep.

KASHMIR Area in Northern India, where the hair of goats is used for making fine material mixed with wool of sheep. Napoleon, during his Egyptian campaign, discovered some shawls made from this and sent several to Josephine. Similar were later manufactured in France.

KATE GREENAWAY (See GREENAWAY)

KAUNACE *Masc. Fem.* Mesopotamian skirt, which was evolved from earlier ancient KANDYS. Of fine dressed leather, felt or later wool, it was worn over linen tunic. Full length, except for soldiers and commoners.

KAUNAKES Sumerian fur-like fabric used to make ankle-length pagne-skirt, a form of loincloth worn by warriors. 2800 - 1600 B.C.

KAY, JOHN 1704-1788. British inventor of the flying shuttle, 1733; and of a power loom 1745; thus advancing textile manufacture.

KEBAYA *Fem.* Indonesian long-sleeved jacket worn with the KAIN and a twelve foot long sash around the waist.

KEILHOSE *Masc. Fem.* Trousers with gusset which became popular for skiing at end of 1930s. With the manufacture of modern elasticised fabrics, they have become more form-fitting and are accepted wear for skiing and 'apres-ski'.

KELLE Alternative name for CAUL, a woman's head-dress. 16th Cent.

KEMES, KEMSE *Masc. Fem. Late L.* From Medieval times, undermost garment. A simple shape with short sleeves or shoulder straps.

KENDAL GREEN A woollen green cloth made originally in Kendal, Westmoreland, for foresters. Reputed to be the livery of Robin Hood and his followers. John Kempe, of Flanders, established cloth-weaving in the borough, 1331.

KÉPI *Masc. Fr.* Stiff peaked round cap worn by Parisian police until 1982.

KERCHIEF *Fem., usually.* Cloth used for head-covering or as a collar or informal neck cloth similar to FICHU. (See also CURCH, CURCHEF). Medieval to late 16th Cent.

KERRY CLOAK *Masc. Fem. Ir.* Long cloak with hood. Type worn in Europe for generations but originated from Spain during Saracen invasions. 700 - 1500 A.D.

KERSEY Rough ribbed pliable cloth made in Kersey, Suffolk, from Medieval times. Used, when cut on the cross, for making stockings before the introduction of knitting. 'Russet yeas and honest kersey noes' Shakespeare writes in *Love's Labour's Lost*, V, ii. Medieval to early 19th Cent. KERSEYMERE Fine woollen cloth, a variation of CASHMERE, and made from hair of goats of KASHMIR. 18th and 19th Cents.

KERSEYMERES *Masc.* Trousers made of quality kerseymere.

KÉTHONETH *Masc.* Sleeved, white linen tunic, three-quarter length, worn by Hebrew high priest.

KETTLE HAT Irreverent name for the iron hat worn by a knight in the Middle Ages.

KEVENHÜLLER *Masc. Swiss.* Large military felt cocked hat, with the front brim cocked high into a peak. Named after famous Field Marshal 1740-1762. Adopted by American high army officers, with addition of felt cockade, 1780. Known in France as ANDROSMANE.

KEVENHÜLLER Hat à la Suisse, 18th Cent.

KHAKI *Urdu -khäk - dust.* Dust-coloured dull yellow used for uniforms of soldiers. First used by irregular corps at time of Indian Mutiny, 1857-1858; and as general service British army uniform since South African War, 1899-1902.

KHIRKA *Masc.* Mantle or large shawl worn by Moslem dervishes.

KHURKEH *Fem.* Traditional gown still worn in near East. Long, straight, but full, usually in dark blue or red linen, with short embroidered jacket having flared sleeves. Also called BETHLEHEM DRESS.

KIBR *Masc.* Arabian striped cotton or silk robe with hood. Worn over long white cotton dress called TOBE.

KICK *Masc.* Dandy. In Italy - a chic. In France, chic - the ability to do things with style.

KILMARNOCK Flat brushed wool tam-o-shanter of plaid, with a soft pompom on top. Named after Scottish town in Ayrshire and of the hero in Burns's poem *Tam-o'-Shanter*.

KILT *Masc. Scot.* Skirt of vertical pleats usually of tartan cloth, from waist to knee; also worn by women and children. Also worn by Scottish, Irish and Canadian regiments.

KIMONO *Masc. Fem. Jap.* Long loose gown with short sleeves, held together by sash caled OBO and fastening from left to right. For formal wear, the women's sash - KAKU-OBO - is tied back in a double knot. For daily wear a sash called HEKO-OBI is wound round the waist two or three times and tied with loose bow. The French couturier, Paul Poiret, introduced Japanese costume into Europe using exotic oriental fabrics and bright colours from the palette of the Art movement called the Fauves. 1910-1914.

KIMONO SLEEVES These are cut in one with the rest of the kimono garment and have kept their place and name in the modern fashion world of the 20th Century.

KINCOB *Urdu - kimkhab. Ind.* Rich brocaded silk with gold and silver embellishment. Used for Hindu turbans.

KING KLIPPER *Masc.* Name for extravagant five inch wide necktie of the 1960s. Usually Paisley or polka-dotted material, long enough to reach belt.

KIRTLE *O.E. cyrtel; O.N. kyrtill; L. curtus -short.* 1)*Masc.* Knee-length tunic, 9th-14th Cent. 2)*Fem.* Sleeved long garment, 10th-15th Cent. 3)*Fem.* For about 100 years from 1545 - a separate skirt; the name giving way to 'petticoat'. 4)*Fem.* A short jacket, early 18th Cent. 5) A protective outer skirt for horseback riding, early 19th Cent.

KISSING STRINGS *Fem.* Side lappets, or ties, from mob-cap which fastened under the chin. Mid-18th Cent. to early 19th Cent.

KLOMPEN Work shoe shaped from a solid block of wood, worn by Dutch peasants.

KNEBELBART *Masc.* Twisted moustache worn with a small beard. A fashion much favoured in Spain, 16th and 17th Cents. Revived by Napoleon III (1808-1873); he was in exile in England, 1871.

KNEE BREECHES *Masc.* Short trousers fastened below the knee. From 1570s on. Accepted leg wear of the 18th Cent.

KNEE FRINGE *Masc.* Decorative ribbon fringe which hung around the edge of breeches. Late 17th Cent.

KNICKERBOCKERS *Masc.* Loose-fitting breeches gathered in below the knee. Sports trousers which evolved from SLOPS or GALLIGASKINS. Fastened at knee with buckle and band. Used for cycling during early part of the 20th Century. Name originated from Cruikshank's illustrations of *Knickerbocker's History of New York*, a parody by Washington Irving showing worthy Dutch inhabitants wearing very full knee breeches. 1809. Today, if worn, they are considered correct cut if they extend about a hand's width below the knee.

KNICKERS *Fem.* Evolved as an undergarment in Britain, similar in shape to knickerbockers, in early 19th Cent. as a result of the revealing crinoline styles. They were tighter fitting than drawers and by the end of the 19th Century were worn with tailormades and sportswear. (See PANTALETTES). Prior to Renaissance, the wearing of feminine knicker-like underwear was considered indecent and respectable women did not wear them until Catherine de Medici, 1519-1589, launched the fashion.

KNIGHTLY GIRDLE *Masc. Fem.* Decorated belt or girdle worn at hip-level over tunic, gipon or long cotehardie. Fastened with clasp or buckle and worn only by nobility. 13th-14th Cent.

KNITTING Method of looping threads to form fabric. Evidence of knowledge of the craft in form of socks found in Egyptian tombs. The art was lost for many centuries and not until the first centuries A.D. was the knowledge brought to Europe. Paris and Florence became the centres for excellent work. The first hand-knitted silk stockings appeared in Spain in 16th Cent. and Henry VIII of England was presented with a pair. Queen Elizabeth I was the first English woman to wear a pair. After 1560, knitting became an important craft; and in 1589, an English clergyman, William Lee, built the first stocking frame.

KNOP A button, as mentioned in Chaucer's translation of the *Romance of the Rose* - 'Knoppis fyne of gold enameled'. 14th Cent. Also, a decorative tassel.

KNOT The tying of string, ribbon, cord etc., to make a knot. Used by Chinese and Japanese for fastening as button. Other uses - as shoulder or bosom ornament when arranged in a loose rosette of loops. A SUIT OF KNOTS - was a set of matching ribbon bows and hair ornament. TOP KNOT - a bunch of ribbon bows worn on top of the hair dressing. 17th and 18th Cents.

KOHL, KOHOL Finely powdered antimony used by women in Persia and the East to blacken the rims of the eyelids.

KOLAH Traditional brimless Persian hat made of black lamb or cloth in simple turban shape.

KOLBE *Masc.* Hairstyle worn by European men in late 16th Cent. The hair was cut to medium length all round and horizontally across the forehead above the ears and at back of the neck. A short beard was worn sometimes with it, cut horizontally across the chin.

KOLINSKY MINK Fine quality animal found in Siberia, China and Japan, with long silky top hair and short under-fur. When dyed dark, the fur resembles sable.

KOLPOS *Anc. Gk.* Draping of upper portion of chiton above the girdle, thus creating a bloused appearance. This over-fold was used as a pocket.

KOO *Masc. Fem. Chin.* Dark blue everyday dress.

KOOLETAH *Masc. Fem.* Protective coat of caribou skins worn by Eskimos.

KOTENY *Masc. Fem.* Traditional apron worn for festivals and dancing in Hungary. Valued in families because of fine embroidery and appliqué work decoration.

KOTHORNOS *Anc. Gk.* Boot with thick sole of three or four inches, worn by actors to give illusion of height. Of coloured leather and decorated. Also COTHURNUS.

KREPIS *Gk. Rom.* Light sandal with thin sole. Held to the leg and foot by a leather strap laced over the instep and around the ankle.

KRIMMER *Rus. Krim.* Curled fur of grey mixture appearance, from lambskins.

KRUSELER *Fem. Mid. High Ger.* Typical headgear of bonnet and head scarf trimmed with tight frilling, 1340-1430 A.D.

KULAH *Masc.* Felt or lambskin head wear, in cone shape, worn by monks, religious men, dervishes and so on, in Middle East.

KUMYA *Masc.* Shirt. Front is fastened with loops and buttons. Worn by North African Moor; over long cotton full trousers.

KUSAK *Masc.* Very long wide silk sash worn by Turks.

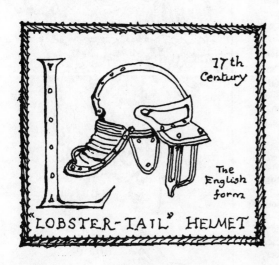

LOBSTER-TAIL HELMET   *The English form from the 17th Century.*

LABEL *Masc.* Turned back and folded lapel of 15th Cent. Tabard.

LACE 1) Thread or tie for fastening; of cord or tape, etc. 2) Network woven with interlaced cords or threads. When made with use of needle - called needlepoint; when worked with bobbins or pins on cushion - called pillow lace. 3) Openwork trimming of many designs, hand-made and machine-made.* 4) Gold or silver braid applied as trimming for uniforms. 5) Other feminine uses including covering for sunshades, lace pantalettes under crinolines, lace caps, 19th Cent.

  * Machine-made: Nottingham, England, became the centre of the industry when John invented the bobbin-net machine and John Leavers the first patterned lace-making machine in 1809. Until then, France was justly famous for hand-made laces such as Alençon, Chantilly, Valenciennes but there was a great demand for English machine-made lace in the early 19th Cent. The secrets of its manufacture were carefully protected but a strange saga unfolded. At the time when smugglers were bringing hand-made lace from the Continent to England, others were risking huge penalties from transporting parts of English weaving machines acrosss the Channel to be reassembled at a secret place near Calais. An Englishman, Robert Webster from Nottingham, set up machinery and lace-making was in production in France by the end of 1816. He and two other Nottingham weavers, Clark and Bonnington, are credited with pioneering Calais' lace industry. In 1824, repealing of export laws on machinery, together with an influx of British weavers to Calais, established that area as a great world centre for machine-made lace and today does so with co-operation of Britain. The modern lace produced is supplied largely to Italy but also to many firms working in the lingerie trade elsewhere.

LACED BOOTS *Masc.* 1) START-UP or START UPPES - Country shoes of rough leather, loose fitting, fastened with lacing. 1569-1570. 2) Also used for sports and hawking, with knee-high leggings of leather or wool. 16th and 17th Cents. *Fem.* Best quality were sometimes of velvet and ornamented. 16th Cent.

LACERNA *Masc.* Roman mantle, counterpart of Greek chlamys but with hood. Worn over toga in inclement weather.

83

LATTICE   Ermine fur - see LETTICE.

LAMB   Skin of young animals with wool-like fur.
Types - astrakan, broadtail, karakul, krimmer (from
Krim, in Crimea), merino, mouflon (from Russia,
Corsica, Sardinia), swakara (from S.W. Africa).

LAMB, PERSIAN   Best quality tightly curled furs
from Persia, Afghanistan, Russia.

LAMBA   *Fem.* Brilliantly coloured mantle or shawl
worn in Madagascar. Traditional.

LAMBALLE   *Fem.* Straw bonnet, made like an
inverted small saucer to lie flat on the head but
curving down on each side and tied with a large
ribbon bow under the chin. Variations - lace lappets
or short frilling falling at the back. 1865.

LAMBREQUIN   *Masc. Fr. lamper - scallop, also
veil.* 1) Medieval, decorative scarf which hung from
the helmet of a knight, often with scalloped edging.
2) Contemporary term also used for drapery over
door or window.

LAMÉ   Luxury fabric with flat threads of silver
and/or gold.

LAMINATED FABRIC   A fabric invented in 1960s,
of material as thick and thin, or wool and silk,
together. The thinner side of material acts as a lining.

LANCE   Weapon with pointed steel head on wooden
shaft.

LANDSKNECHT   *Swiss, Ger.* LANSQUENET -
a mercenary soldier. Cutting of material to reveal
under-lining material of contrasting colour and texture.
This strange development came from the practice of
the Swiss troops, the victors at Battle of Grandson,
1476, using booty of rich clothing to patch their own
ragged clothes. The German mercenaries copied them
and SLASHING became fashionable first in France
and later in England. Many articles, even shoes,
stockings and gloves, were decorated in this manner.
The fashion reached its height from 1520-1535,
although it persisted until the mid-17th Cent. It was
used mostly upon masculine garments. Feminine
dress, in comparison, was modest and restrained.

LANGET   *Masc.* Feathered plume decoration on
helmet of knight. Also a thin strap, lace or thong for
securing, through loops, any part of dress. 15th Cent.

LANGUETTE   *Fem. usually.* String of beads. 16th
Cent.

LANGTRY HOOD   *Fem.* Hood with coloured lining
similar to that worn with academic gown but easily
unclasped to wear with outdoor garments. It was
fastened by ends crossing in front or with hooks.
1880-1890.

LANSQUENET   *Masc.* Swiss and South German
mercenaries. Reputed to be the initiators of SLA-
SHING or of cutting their uncomfortable clothes,
revealing the shirts beneath and later with lighter
material to simulate fresh linen. This eccentricity
became a fashion and the long slits through which
decorative under-garments could be drawn out to
view were called PANES. Short slashes were called

84

LANSQUENET   *Example of slashing, 16th Cent. After
a woodcut by Flötner.*

'pinking'. This method of decoration lasted from
1530-1630. (See also LANDSKNECHT)

LAPEL   Part of coat-breast folded back, combining
collar turn-over and rever, back-edge.

LAPIN   *Fr.* Rabbit fur. Treated and blocked and
sheared by professional handlers; used for inexpensive
fur coats.

LAPLAND BONNET   *Biagga gallas.* A traditional
head-piece once worn by Lapland people, now only
rarely. A bonnet with four points, three of which
were stuffed with down and could be used as a
pillow; the fourth point served as a purse. Today,
peaked caps are usually worn.

LAPPETS *Fem.* Pieces of fabric or pair of pendant strips made of ribbon, fabric or lace hanging at back over shoulders from head-covering, bonnet or gable-hood. Term used since 16th Cent. Much worn as adornment, 18th and 19th Cents.

LAPPRA (See NIGERIA)

LAPLAND BONNET   called the Four Winds.

LARRIGAN Boot worn by Indians of North America. Leather moccasins reaching to knee. Worn by trappers and lumber men.

LATCHET Thong or strap used for shoe-fastening. Sometimes with clog. Medieval.

LATICLAVE *Masc.* A broad purple stripe on the front of an Ancient Roman toga. A person of high rank wore a garment decorated with two such stripes.

LATIN LOOK Before World War I, the American film industry encouraged the craze for Latin American dancing. The Tango, as danced by film stars, originated women's fashions such as slit tango-skirts, revealing slippers laced up the leg, Latin American hair styles with dark, shining hair and flat side curls on the cheeks all the rage. Men's hair styles also were brushed back and sleek-looking with sideburns. 1910-1914. An accompanying women's fashion was for long skirts and small head-dresses topped by osprey plumes.

LATTICE BREECHES *Masc.* Breeches made of wide strips of material separated from each other, reaching from hip to knee. This garment was launched by German troops but a similar costume was worn until recently by the Papal Swiss Guard in Vatican City. It is reputed that Michelangelo designed this uniform, which included the unusually designed breeches. 16th Cent.

LAVALLIÈRE, LAVALIER, LAVALIERE 1)*Fem.* A jewelled locket named after a favourite of Louis

XIV, Louise de la Vallière, 1660. Worn suspended from a neck chain. 2)*Masc.* Long, wide scarf tied in a loose knot, worn during Third French Republic. 1871.

LAVEUSE *Fem. Fr. washerwoman.* Day dress with overskirt which was drawn up at sides and towards the back and sometimes fastened by button closure. 1876. In spite of mocking name, the style contributed to evolution of the tie-back dress.

LAVINIA HAT *Fem.* Large straw hat, decorated by a ribbon which went around brim and crown and was tied under the chin. Fashionable early 19th Cent.

LAWN Delicate, fine, white linen or cotton material. Used since 16th Cent. in France and England for ruffles, ruffs, wimples and sleeves etc., of religious robes.

LEADING STRINGS *Children.* Two long straps or tapes attached to the back of arm-holes of child's clothes. Used when learning to walk. Early 18th Cent.

LEATHER Tanned or preserved skin or hide of animal or reptile.

LEATHER Various. *Fr.* CUIR BOUILLI - skins boiled in oil or wax, moulded into shape when soft and then steamed. Used in making of armour throughout the centuries until medieval period. JACK - waxed, coated with pitch or tar. Used for boots; also for large jugs and tankards. 17th Cent. PATENT - lacquered; introduced in early 19th Cent. for harness use but later became fashionable when utilised in light slippers. Continues to be fashionable in shoes and handbags. RUSSIAN - a lightweight skin treated with willow bark, sandalwood and cochineal; is moisture-resistant and has a fragrant odour. SADDLE - cowhide, hard-wearing; used for belts, saddles, bags and sports shoes.

LEDERHOSEN *Masc. Ger.* Leather breeches supported by leather braces. Worn in Bavaria, Black Forest, Italy. Most usual form - knee breeches.

LEDERSEN *Masc. Ger.* Simple, comfortable combination of leather breeches and shoes. Worn by travellers, peasants. 1500 A.D.

LEEK BUTTON Button invented with metal shell and rim allowing upper portion to hold matching or contrasting material to garment. With wired flexible shank. Invented at Leek, England. 1842.

LEGGINGS *Mod.* British term for leg-coverings from knee to ankle. In various forms.

LEGHORN HAT *Fem.* Also FLORENTINE HAT. Made from fine straw grown in Tuscany, cut green and bleached. Especially fashionable when crinoline skirts were worn. 19th Cent. The straw is still cultivated and used today for fine millinery.

LEG OF MUTTON *Fem.* Sleeve, very full at shoulder, tapering in size to the elbow and gradually tighter to the wrist. 1824-1836. Became even larger in 1862 and in late 1890s. (See GIGOT)

LEG WARMERS *Masc., mostly Fem.* Colourful

knitted footless socks, allowed to ruche. A fashion worn for extra warmth in cold winters, 1979-1980s, by young people and at spectator sports.

LEI A colourful garland of fresh, fragrant flowers worn by Hawaiians and given in welcome to visitors.

LEIBI *Fem. Ger.* Fitting bodice to dress worn in Black Forest area, Germany.

LEICESTER JACKET *Masc.* British lounge jacket, tailored, with raglan sleeves. 1857.

LEOTARD *Masc. Fem.* Close-fitting practice costume designed by Jules Leotard, a famous trapeze artist, 19th Cent. Adapted for professional dancers, acrobats and gymnasts and now made in modern stretch materials. Also known as BODY STOCKING.

LETTICE BONNET or CAP *Fem.* Warm bonnet covering the ears, made of laitice, a fur similar to ermine. 16th Cent.

LETTICE RUFF *Masc.* A ruff with flattened fluted pleating resembling the leaves of a lettuce. Early 17th Cent. A larger and similar ruff was called a CABBAGE RUFF.

LEVANTINE Early twilled silk made in Levant. Used for sashes, robes. Early 19th Cent.

LEVIS *Masc., later Fem.* Strong pants made of cotton denim, created by Levi Strauss in California, U.S.A. Now worn by men, women and children for work and play.

LEVITE GOWN *Fem.* An open day gown, with bodice closed in front by cross-straps. Of light weight, worn over petticoat skirt, with or without apron. 1780s.

LIBAS *Masc. Fem. Egyptian.* Long full cotton pantaloons. Worn with the GALLABIYA, a long-sleeved, collarless, cotton robe or with the GANDOURA, a cotton chemise.

LIBERTY The trade name for beautiful materials of high quality from the famous firm of LIBERTY of London.

LIBERTY BONNET or CAP So-named from the ancient Greek and Roman custom of placing the Phrygian bonnet on the head of a freed slave, as an emblem of liberty. It was adopted, in red - 'le bonnet rouge', by French Revolutionists in 18th Cent.

LILY LANGTRY COIFFURE *Fem.* Hair style worn by the beautiful English woman, a friend of Edward VII; it was dressed with curls across and above the forehead and with a low chignon. 1852-1929.

LIMOUSINE *Fem.* Fashionable evening cloak. Circular, with material gathered around throat and falling over shoulders and arms. 1889-1890.

LINEN The stem of flax plant produces strong fibres, from which are made durable fabrics, both coarse and fine, for many needs. It has been cultivated in Egypt for at least 5000 years.

LINGE *Fr. Linen.* White fabric used for underclothes and vestments until 20th Cent.

LINGERIE *Fr. for fem. undergarments.* A term

used as an English word in Godey's Lady's Book, 1850s. From 13th Cent., a form of shift or chemise, sometimes embroidered, was worn. By the 19th Cent., this simple garment was worn under a corset, with pantalets or drawers, and also several petticoats. These were always white and of soft material, with lace and embroidery when affordable. By the 20th Cent., underclothes became simplified. Synthetic materials, in a range of colours and needing no ironing, are now much used. Form-fitting supporting brassières and girdles are made of lastex, delicate silk and sheer fabrics.

The 'layered' look - with ethnic jewellery. 1974.

LINSEY-WOOLSEY A material of linen and wool, originally believed to have been made at Linsey, Suffolk. 16th Cent. It was much used in American Colonies.

LIRIPIPE Long pendant or tail from the chaperon hood. 14th Cent.*Masc.* Suspended, worn over one shoulder or wound round the head-piece like a turban. 15th Cent.*Fem.* Hanging from head-dress as a decoration. 15th Cent. Worn by liveried servants, folded or wrapped scarf-like around the neck. Only nobility were allowed to wear hats with liripipe. English name - TIPPET.

LISLE   Strong, fine thread of cotton used in making of hosiery, gloves and other items. Named after Flemish town where it originated.

LISSE   Smooth silk gauze or chiffon. 1894.

LIST   Closely-woven edge of material or selvage. Pieces were joined together to make slippers. 18th and 19th Cents. Of Jane Eyre - 'Her quiet tread muffled in a list slipper'. Charlotte Brontë, 1847.

LITHAM   *Masc. Fem. Arab.* Face covering or square folded diagonally to protect face against sand and sun, worn by Moslem Tuareg.

LITTLE LORD FAUNTLEROY   *Masc.* A costume for boys originating from the young hero of the novel by Mrs. Hodgson Burnett, 1866. It consisted of velvet tunic and knickerbockers, with large white lace collar. A wide sash was worn at the waist. It was reminiscent of Cavalier dress, which was admired by Oscar Wilde at that time.

LITURGICAL VESTMENTS   The chief components were defined in 9th Century Rome. The sacramental vesture has undergone no significant change since that time:

ALB   A narrow-sleeved, long linen garment tied at the hip with a CINCTURE or girdle.

AMICE   Square shoulder-piece of white linen with tapes and worn under the alb.

BIRETTA   Head-covering of the priesthood. Circular with rectangular edge surmounted by three or four curved ridges. Cardinal - red. Bishop - purple. Others -black.

CASSOCK   The clerical uniform. Long gown to ankles, buttoned at front and with close-fitting top. Often tied with cincture. Pope - white. Cardinals - red. Bishops - purple. Ordinary - black. A clerical frock-coat, similar but reaching only to the knees, is also worn in some countries and by certain academic judges and dignitaries.

CHASUBLE   Coloured vestment worn over the alb at Mass.

CINCTURE   Girdle.

COPE or PLUVIAL   Wide richly-embroidered long ceremonial cloak. Originated from hooded cloaks worn by monks in 9th Cent. processions.

DALMATIC   Robe worn by assisting deacons at High Mass. Of same colour as officiating priest's vestments.

MANIPLE   Band of material, 3 ft long and of same colour as Chasuble.

MITRE   Head-dress of Popes, cardinals and bishops. A stiff peaked hat of silk and often richly decorated. Ribbons hang from the back.

PILOS   Small round cap, removed only during Mass. White - Pope. Red - cardinal. Purple - bishop. Black -Abbot.

STOLE   Long narrow vestment worn around priest's neck, similar to Maniple but twice as long.

SURPLICE   Clerical wide-sleeved knee-length robe of white linen or lawn.

TIARA   The triple crown worn by the Pope on public occasions.

TUNICLE   Upper vestment of a sub-deacon.

LIVERY   *Br.* Dress worn by members of a livery company. Costume worn by servants of noble or rich Court or household. In Middle Ages, it was customary for nobleman of a feudal estate to give to his retainers an annual gift called livrée, the origin of the word 'livery'.

LIVERY COMPANIES   *Br.* Representatives in City of London today of the old City Guilds, who formerly wore distinctive liveries or costumes for special occasions. The twelve great companies, in order of date, are:- Skinners, 1319; Merchant Taylors, 1326; Goldsmiths, 1327; Grocers, 1345; Drapers, 1364; Fishmongers, 1384; Mercers, 1393; Salters, 1394; Vintners, 1437; Haberdashers, 1448; Ironmongers, 1463; Clothworkers, 1527; of which latter Guild Samuel Pepys was Master in 1677. There are about 90 City Companies of old standing, supporting charity and education from their funds.

LOAFER   *Norw.* Comfortable slip-on leather shoe introduced in 1940s.

LOBSTER HELMET   Open helmet worn by troopers in English Civil War, 1648. With laminated tail, hinged cheek-pieces and a peak, with bars from it over the face. A form of Burgonet.

LOCK STITCH   Machine sewing in which two threads are interwoven. Came into use 1860. The chain-stitch machine used only one thread.

LOCKRAM   Coarse linen used for making of smocks and shirts. 15th-17th Cent.

LOCKET   1) Upper part of the scabbard of a sword. 2)*Fem.* Ornament hanging from chain or cord around the neck.

LOCK'S   The famous hat shop in St. James' Street, London, which made the first bowler with a rounded crown, invented by William Coke of Norfolk. Early 19th Cent.

LODEN   Waterproof cloth woven from the wool of Tyrolean sheep. Dyed in several shades but most well-known is the blue-ish green called LODEN GREEN.

LONG CLOTH   Fine, plain weave, cotton cloth used for infants' wear. One of the first materials to be woven in a long piece.

LONG CLOTHES   The garments worn by a baby in arms which replaced former swaddling clothes, 1650 onwards. Some were 3 ft. in length and richly decorated and used as Christening Robes.

LONG MELFORD   *Fem.* Long stocking-purse formerly carried by country folk.

LONGYI   *Masc. Fem.* Burmese sarong-like draped skirt. Placed around waist with a deep pleat which is tucked into the belt. Worn with white cotton blouse or jacket.

LOOKING GLASS   Small decorated mirrors were

worn hanging from ladies' girdles in the time of Elizabeth I and James I of England.

LOO MASK *Fem.* A half-mask, which became widespread in 16th and 17th Cents. Used to protect against the weather, later in carnivals, and for concealment in amorous and political intrigue. 18th Cent.

LOONGEE *Afghanistan.* Large square piece of cotton or silk folded and worn on one shoulder. Many uses - such as muffler, sash or for holding possessions.

LOOPING *Fem.* The looping-up towards the back of voluminous skirts worn in 1869, instigated a marked change in the silhouette. The back view gradually became the focus of designers and the outline taller and more tailored.

LORGNETTE *Fem.* Eye-glasses held on a long folding handle; used for examining objects at a distance or as a fashion accessory at social functions when spectacles would appear heavy. Fashionable from 1893 to early 20th Cent.

LORICA Roman armour-piece, plain or decorated, for upper portion of torso. Fastened at shoulders with buckles and usually worn over leather doublet. 5th Cent. B.C. - 3rd Cent. A.D.

LOUIS XIV *'The Great', 'le Roi-Soleil', 1638-1715. King of France, 1643-1715.* His persecution of Protestants ultimately led to a mass flight of Huguenots and their skills from France. His Court at Versailles was the most magnificent in Europe. From 1660s, this Court laid down laws of fashion which not only unified clothes worn in other European countries but influenced the dress of the ordinary people. Wigs were introduced and in the early part of the reign, men's fashions were elegant, somewhat effeminate and much adorned by ribbons and lace. By 1680s, the Baroque period passed and splendour replaced fantasy.

Masc. The coat, or justacorps, waistcoat and breeches appeared. Later, the cravat, of lace or lace-trimmed linen, became customary. Coloured silk stockings and low-cut shoes with coloured high heels completed the costume.

Fem. High decorated fontange cap became counterpart of the men's heavy wig; bodice of gowns was cut low with elbow-length sleeves and the use of much lace; the skirt was bell-shaped and fashionable slenderness achieved by the use of long tight corsets. At the end of the 17th Cent., beauty patches appeared, made of black silk and impregnated with adhesive, shaped like tiny hearts, stars, full or half moons.

LOUNGE SUIT *Masc.* Suit consisting of easy-fitting jacket with matching waistcoat and trousers. From 1860. Originally created for informal wear but has been worn universally since that time.

LOVAT Colour combination of blues, greens, natural browns and greys, giving a heather or heath-coloured appearance to tweeds. Made in Lovat, Inverness, Scotland.

LOVE LOCK *Masc.* Single long curl over the ear, tied with a ribbon knot. From France, the accompanying fashion of wearing an ear-ring in the exposed bare ear

was introduced to England by Charles I, 1625-1649.

LUMBERJACK 20th Cent. style jacket for men, women and children styled in imitation of short, or three-quarter-length, coat worn by North American lumbermen. Straight, usually back-belted and closed with zip-slide fastener in front, Usually of colourful warm water-repellent material, with large roomy pockets.

LUNARDI HAT *Fem.* Extravagantly large hat of gauze with full high ballooned crown and wide brim. It was fashionable at the time when Vincenzo Lunardi flew in his famous balloon. 1780s. (See BALLOON HAT)

LUNGI *Masc.* Long cotton cloth used by East Indians for various purposes - scarf, turban, loincloth.

LUNULA Bronze Age, crescent shaped gold ornament, forming part of a necklace.

LUREX Sparkling synthetic material or threads used in many ways for decorative purposes - knitwear, scarves, dresses and so on. 1947.

LYCRA Modern man-made fibre with 'stretching' quality. Used for women's supporting undergarments.

LUSTRING, LUTESTRING 1) Lustrous fine taffeta. 16th-19th Cent. Also in late 19th Cent. corded, with glossy surface. 2) Narrow ribbon, used for monocle or eye-glasses suspension. 19th Cent.

LYON *Lyons -Eng.* Third largest city of France. Europe's chief silk and rayon producer.

LYONS LOOPS *Fem.* Velvet straps and/or ties used to loop up the overskirt of gowns when double skirts were worn. 1865.

LYONS VELVET Stiff rich velvet backed with silk, linen or cotton. With short erect pile, it is used for dresses and jackets but mostly for millinery.

Lapps, the herders of reindeer, live north of the Arctic Circle and keep alive traditions which reach back to 7,000B.C. Red stocking caps, embroidered coats, moccasins and boots with curled toes form part of their costume.

1837

MENTONIÈRE Chin Ruffle

MAB CAP, MOBCAP *Fem. Old verb - mab- to dress untidily.* A cap worn indoors for concealing hair not properly dressed. From early 18th Cent.

MACABRE Fabric of lightweight silk and wool with small designs and patterned border. 1832.

MACARONI *Masc. Ital. Maccherone -coxcomb.* Name given to foppish young Englishmen who had travelled in Italy. Characteristic garments worn were tight-sleeved coats with fullness directed to back pleats, resembling beetles' wings; tight trousers to four or five inches below the knee and fastened with a buckle; lace-edged cravats. Minute tricorne hats were perched above very high wigs. Coloured stockings were usual, wth light high-heeled buckled slippers. Female counterparts were called by the same name. Records suggest that with their taste for gambling, duelling and drinking, they were known for their insolence and in the pleasure ground of Vauxhall Gardens regarded with dread. The style had disappeared by 1780.

MACARONI CLUB Founded in London in 1764 by a set of extravagantly dressed young men who had travelled in Italy and introduced the Italian food of macaroni which had hitherto been unknown in England.

MACE A club once used in war. Used originally in battles and tournaments. Generally made of iron with a wood handle. A leather thong or chain was passed through a hole in the handle so that it could be suspended from the saddle and thus secured from falling out of the hand. It was often carried by ecclesiastics who were forbidden to wield a sword. Now used as a staff of office, a symbol of dignitaries.

MACFARLANE CLOAK *Masc. Scots.* Heavy wool topcoat with cape-covered sleeves. Late 19th Cent.

MACHINERY, MECHANIZATION The use of sewing machines and bootmaking machinery in 1870s, brought down the prices of clothing and footwear. As a result, more comfort was established for the working class.

MACINTOSH Cloth processed and waterproofed with rubber. Patented by Charles Macintosh, 1766-1843. He designed the first weatherproof coat made from this material.

MACKINAW *Masc.* Short outdoor coat worn in North America and Canada by lumbermen and hunters. Usually of heavy woollen tough material and often in bright plaids and colours. 19th and 20th Cents.

"MACARONIS" England
1770s

MACARONIS' TOWN WEAR   *Eccentric fashions worn by a group of travelled young men, who formed the Macaroni Club in the 18th Century, which led to the development of the tailcoat and the high buttoned waistcoat.*

90

MACKINTOSH Short loose overcoat made from Macintosh's patent india-rubber cloth, 1836. It was not popular at first because of the unpleasant odour.

MACRAMÉ LACE A knotted lace made mostly in Genoa, Italy. Often fringed with many of the ends tied together. Silk macramé is used for scarves and shawls.

MADRAS Fine muslin with raised soft patterning from India. 1825.

MAGENTA Brilliant bright bluish-red aniline dye discovered by British chemist, Sir W.H. Perkin, 1856. This first synthetic colouring was later named after the Battle of Magenta, 1859.

MAGYARS Ural-Altaic people who settled in Hungary in 9th Cent. Their historic dress is notable for colourful and elaborate embroidery on shirts, blouses, skirts and aprons. Men's greatcoat, or SZUR, is of felt or leather with much decoration. Garments are treasured and pass from generation to generation.

MAHARMAH Head and face covering of muslin worn in earlier times in Asia Minor. Only occasionally in present use. Similar to Moslem MANDEEL.

MAHOÎTRE *Masc. Fem. Fr.* Padded shoulder trimming late 14th Cent. Fashionable, 15th and 16th Cents.

MAID MARION Originally female character portraying Queen of the May; later portrayed in Robin Hood plays and Morris dances. The part was frequently played by a man dressed as a woman. 15th and 16th Cents. (See MORRIS DANCE)

MAIL Protective armour of interlocking chains or rings; also of overlapping plates.

MAILCOACH NECKTIE *Masc.* Usually white and worn by established drivers and dandies. A large long cashmere neckcloth, wound around the neck and tied in front to allow the ends to 'fall' in front. Early 19th Cent. Also called WATERFALL necktie.

MAILLOT *Fr. Tights, jersey.* Name adopted for close-fitting brief swimsuits which gradually appeared in 1920s, after earlier more cumbersome bathing suits. Also, French swaddling clothes.

MAINTENON, MARQUISE DE second wife of Louis XIV, 1635-1719. She persuaded the King to allow fashion design to be handled by women. Previously, the world of women's fashion had been dominated by men.

MAINTENON CLOAK *Fem.* Large flowing black velvet cloak with sleeves trimmed with pleated flounces. Sometimes with additions of black lace and embroidery. 1860s.

MAINTENON CORSAGE *Fem.* Front ribbon trimming of ribbon bows and lace above waist of evening bodice. 1839-1840.

MAJOR WIG *Masc.* A military wig with two corkscrew curls tied together at the back of the neck. Also worn by civilians on certain special occasions. 1750-1790. Called BRIGADIER in France.

MAKE-UP Term applying originally to use of theatrical cosmetics when transforming an actor's appearance to suit a character on stage. *Fr. MAQUILLAGE.*

MAKILA Wooden cane on a thong found in the Basque country. Used as a cudgel or a walking stick.

MALACCA CANE A cane made from the mottled stem of the Asiatic Malacca palm. Fashionable from 1700.

MALKIN *Fem.* Old form of Matilda, used for untidy kitchen wench; also for scarecrow or grotesque puppet.

MALO *Masc.* Hawaiian loin-cloth or girdle.

MALTESE LACE Heavy bobbin lace with Maltese Cross motifs, made in silk. Other designs include wheatear and simple geometric shapes. 19th Cent. to date.

MAMELUKE Fem. sleeve, fashionable and named after a squadron of Mameluke soldiers created by Napoleon I, 1799-1815. Long, full, tied with ribbons at intervals to form a series of puffs, large at the top and lessening in size to the wrist. Usually finished with a frill.

MAMELUKE TURBAN *Fem.* A head covering of white satin with a domed crown, trimmed with large curled ostrich feather. 1804.

MANCHERON *Fem.* Short plain epaulette on shoulder falling over upper sleeve, on day dresses or outdoor garments. Later named EPAULETTE. 1803, 1815, 1830s.

MANCHETTE *Fem.* Wrist ruffles of lace worn on afternoon dresses. 1830-1850. Also a cuff-bracelet.

MANCHU Member of Mongolian people from Manchuria which conquered China in 17th Cent. Reverted eventually to China, 1945.

MANCHU HEAD-DRESS *Fem.* Delicate decorative cap worn only by imperial princesses. Black satin bands supported by gold wire were ornamented with many tiny butterflies, flowers, birds, made of precious materials and stones such as jade, rose-quartz, pearls.

MANDARIN Chinese public official before the Republic of 1912.

MANDARIN HAT *Fem.* British and European millinery fashion, named after Franco-British war with China, which ended in 1860. Usually of black velvet in 'pork-pie' shape. Trimmed with feathers over the flat crown. 1861.

MANDARIN ROBE Chinese official's beautiful long silk gown with wide long sleeves and rich embroidery. Two large decorated squares, one at back and one in front, denoted the particular rank and office the mandarin held. He wore also a hat with jewelled button on top; also a long string of beads, such as coral, amber or jade. Prior to 1912.

MANDEEL *Fem.* Moslem veil covering the face and chest.

MANDIL *Masc.* Turkish or Persian draped turban. 16th and 17th Cents.

MANDILION *Masc.* Loose hip-length jacket with open side seams. 1570-1620. Later, shape was adapted for livery. (See COLLEY-WESTONWARD)

MANGA *Masc.* Mexican type of poncho with sleeves, worn for riding.

MANIAKIS *Fem.* Embroidered band set with precious stones and pearls draped across the shoulders of Theodora, wife of the Emperor Justinian. 527-548 A.D. Portrayed in the mosaics of San Vitale, Ravenna.

MANIPLE *Masc.* Narrow band over left forearm worn by priest celebrating Mass. Of similar colour and material as chasuble.

MANNEQUIN *Masc. Fem.* Person who models clothes in shop or stores or for couturiers. Also, dummy figures used for display by tailors, dressmakers, etc.

MANON ROBE *Fem.* Day-dress of silk with double box-pleat falling loosely at the back from collar to hem. The hem trimmed with flouncing. 1860.

MANTA *Sp. Shawl, blanket.* 1) *Masc.* Short cape worn over a bolero. 2) *Fem.* Large piece of black material, worn draped overhead and falling to ground length, thus concealing figure. Usually of simple cotton but of lace when worn by women of standing or affluence.

MANTEAU 1) *Masc.* Circular or semi-circular cloak. 16th Cent. 2) *Fem.* Important outer satin or velvet garment with train worn in the French Court of Louis XIV, from 1680 until 1700.

MANTEE *Fem. Fr.* Full-length cloak or cape with short frilled sleeves, often of very thin sheer material, open in front revealing bodice and attractive petticoat. Until 1770s.

MANTEEL *Fem. Eng.* Hooded cape with long scarf-like front pieces. 1730-1750.

MANTES *Fem. Ital.* Ruffled capes of gold and silver tissue from Mantua. Fashionable in European Courts and copied in simpler material by lower classes. One style with hood in black was worn for mourning; a similar kind of garment is still seen occasionally in Europe. 18th and 19th Cents.

MANTILLA *Fem. Sp. and S. Am., dim. of manta.* Traditional lace scarf or veil covering high hair-dressing and shoulders. In white, it is worn on Easter Monday, for important occasions and to bullfights. The black Chantilly lace version was made in France from 18th Cent.

MANTLE *F. mantle; O.F. fem. mantel; L. mantellum - cloak.* Loose everyday sleeveless gown or outer cloak. 12th Cent. until 14th Cent. Later became more formal. *Masc.* Fastened on right shoulder with three buttons. *Fem.* Tied in front. When lined, called a DOUBLE MANTLE. 16th Cent.

MANTLET, MANTELET *Masc. Fem.* 1) Short outdoor cape or cloak in varied forms. 14th-18th Cent. 2) *Fem.* Shoulder-cape for outdoor wear, sometimes hooded and with wide sleeves. 19th Cent. Also PELISSE.

MANTUA *Fem. Ital.* 1) Loose gown of good quality unboned bodice. The floor-length overskirt had a train and the front was left open to show an embellished, decorative petticoat. 17th to mid-18th Cent. 2) Name of silk material made in Mantua.

MANTUA MAKER Before the late 17th Cent., it was customary for men tailors to make women's clothes.

MANTEE French transparent coat or cloak worn with a large Thérèse bonnet to protect the elaborate hair style of the period, 1770s.

From that period on, female mantua-makers or dressmakers were accepted to the profession of not only making, but creating, women's garments. They became recognised as couturiers, mantua-makers, high-class dressmakers and milliners and no longer were relegated to the humbler tasks of sewing women.

MAQUILLAGE Collective word for complexion cosmetics applied to the face, including covering creams, foundation, colourings and powder; for cheeks, lips and eye make-up.

MARABOU Soft downy feathers from under the wings and tail of large West African stork. Used for women's dress and hat trimming since 1800.

MARBRINUS Thick cloth of unevenly coloured worsted. In use by the Normans. By using pale warp and coloured wefts, it was woven to represent the veins of marble.

MARCASITE Glittering form of white iron pyrites used ornamentally for jewellery, buckles and dress accessories.

MARCEL WAVE A Parisian hairdresser, late 19th Cent., named Marcel, was responsible for the method of styling hair with hot irons into deep waves. This method was used until the first World War, 1914-1918, when women cut their hair short. After the War, a method called 'Permanent Waving' was introduced. (See PERMANENT WAVE).

MARDI GRAS *Fr. - 'fat Tuesday'.* The last day of the Lent Carnival in France, on Shrove Tuesday. An imitation of a Roman sacrificial procession accompanied by mock priests and festivities' parades through the streets of Paris.

MARIE-ANTOINETTE 1755-1793. Queen of France 1774-1792, wife of Louis XVI. This ill-fated woman was the most elegant lady of the 18th Cent. She disliked the corset and introduced a new romantic style of dressing. Hoops were gradually abandoned by skirts falling in soft pleats and held at the waist by a wide belt tied at the back. High, puffed-up hair styles gave way to soft curls falling on the shoulders. A handkerchief knotted like a fichu was worn around the neck. Large straw hats were worn tied with pastel ribbons.

MARIE SLEEVE *Fem.* Full sleeve, tied into sections by a series of ribbons, 1813-1824, 1829 and reintroduced as 'Marie-Antoinette' sleeve, 1872.

MARIE STUART BONNET *Fem.* Small brimmed head covering, having a dip in the centre over the forehead. Often worn by widows in 19th Cent. 1820-1870.

MARIE STUART HAT *Fem.* Dress hat for evening occasions. Of tulle with stiffened up-turned trim and a centre dip over the forehead. 1849.

MARINO FALIERO SLEEVE *Fem.* Large hanging sleeve caught by a decorated band at the elbow. Named after Byron's tragedy of the forty-ninth Doge of Venice. Fashionable 1830-1835.

MARLBOROUGH HAT *Fem.* Large brimmed hat trimmed with ribbons and ostrich feathers. Named by French after the Duchess of Marlborough but known also in Britain as the GAINSBOROUGH because sitters for that English painter were often portrayed wearing one. 1727-1788. The style reappeared in 1882.

MARLOTTE *Fem.* Handsome, full-length robe with stand-up collar and short puffed sleeves. Fastened only at the neck, usually of brocade, flared with centre open to display the hooped skirt of gown. Late 16th Cent.

MARMOTTE *Fem.* Small bonnet with tiny brim briefly fashionable, 1832.

MARQUISE *Fem.* 1) Three-cornered riding hat, c. 1735. 2) Silk and lace parasol which possessed a folding handle. 19th Cent. 3) A finger ring set with long narrow cut stone or oval-pointed cluster of gems. 19th and 20th Cents. 4) Brief mantle with short sleeves, shaped to the waist at the back, with flounces and lace. 1846. 5) Evening bodice with frilled edge and heart-shaped neckline. 1874.

MARQUISETTO *Masc.* Close-cut beard style much worn, late 16th Cent.

MARRY-MUFF, MARAMUFFE Plain woollen cheap cloth. 17th Cent.

MARTEL DE FER Weapon which had at one end a hammer or axe-blade or other termination and at the other a pick.

MARTEN CHAYNE Cheap counterfeit jewellery chains sold on site of St. Martin's-le-Grand, 16th Cent. (See ST. MARTIN'S BEADS).

MARTINGALE A belt or strap to hold folds in place. Named after piece of harness which holds a horse's head down to prevent rearing.

MARY CAP, QUEEN OF SCOTS CAP *Fem.* Indoor cap in black and edged with beads. Curved above the forehead with a central V-shaped dip. Not stylish. 1762.

MASHER *Masc.* Ostentatiously dressed dandy of 1880s and 1890s.

MASHER COLLAR *Masc.* Very high starched standing collar worn by a 'Masher'. Late 19th Cent.

MASK Any of several coverings for the face, worn as a protection or disguise. 1) Hollow model of a head used by Greek and Roman actors. 2) Used for protection in 16th Cent.; half-masks or loo-masks, of velvet or taffeta, were worn for travelling. 17th Cent. 3) A full mask, the Vizard, was worn by women who wished to appear incognito in public. Later masks were held in place by a glass or silver button, held between the teeth; these were used by ladies when riding and were attached by a string to the side of the robe. 18th Cent.

MASKEL A spotted lace. 15th Cent.

MASSUELLE, MASNELL, MASNEL Early form of mace or club used for dealing heavy blows on the helmet. 12th Cent.

MASTIC A gum with which velvet or silk patches were applied to the face. 18th Cent.

MATADOR *Masc. Sp.* The man whose role is to kill the bull with his sword. Also TORERO. The standard dress: usually of black velvet with gold and silver brocade, red cape lined with yellow, pink stockings, black shoes and a large flattened black cap. Only the Maestro wears a white costume. (See TRAJE DE LUCES).

MATARA The finest dark brown fur from Alaskan seals. Only a limited quantity is permitted by U.S. and Canadian authorities.

MATELASSÉ *Fr. -mattress.* Name given to firm crepey fabric resembling quilting. 1839. In later years, when material net-backed, it was hand or machine-stitched, to give an embossed surface or blistered look. Used for warm wraps. Early 20th Cent.

MATILDAS *Fem.* Velvet applique or ornamentation sewn around or above the hem of a gown. Late 1890s.

MAUD *Fem.* Plaid shawl or wrapper with fringe. 1855.

MAUVE, MAUVEINE Pale purple dye made from

crude aniline, the first synthetic colour. Discovered by William Perkins, 1856.

MAXI-COAT *Fem.* The fashion world of 1968 saw the introduction of a very long coat with high collar in contrast to the mini-skirt of 1967. It was often worn with a huge Cossack hat. Such fur hats often spoiled the bouffant hair styles of that time and the wearing of wigs became quite fashionable for a period.

MATADOR

MAZARIN Jules, 1602-1661, Italian-born French cardinal and statesman. He passed an edict in 1656, forbidding the use of gold and silver on clothes and brought upon himself the protests of the makers of braids, embroideries, buttons and buckles. *Fem.* A hood, 1675-1690. Named after a female relative of the Cardinal.

MAZZOCCHIO *Ital.* 1) *Masc.* Head covering with long back piece to wind round the neck for warmth. Late 14th Cent. 2) *Masc. Fem.* A padded circle covering the head on which the metal crown, worn by some high-born persons, was placed.

MECHLIN LACE Fine bobbin lace with floral motifs made originally in Malines, Belgium.

94

MECKLENBURG CAP *Fem.* Indoor cap formed by a rolled or twisted scarf swathed around a turban, with the ends left hanging at the back. 1760s.

MEDALLION FANS Fashionable silk fans upon which were painted three medallion subjects by expert miniature decorators. Supported on narrow sticks of mother-of-pearl and occasionally with tiny Wedgwood jasper cameo decoration. 1770s-1790s.

MEDICI COLLAR *Fem.* High-standing collar, pleated and wired, rising from low décolletage. Worn by ladies of the Italian Medici family, 1573-1642. Developed from early linen frill and the later ruff of 1525.

MEDIAEVAL, MEDIEVAL, MIDDLE AGES Period of European history from the fall of the Roman Empire, A.D. 476, to the fall of Constantinople in late 15th Cent. Some scholars consider the flowering of the Gothic period occurred between the Tenth and Fifteenth Centuries. Throughout this time, religious orders and opinions governed the appearance of clothing.

MEDUSA WIG *Fem.* Wig dressed with snake-like curls falling downwards. 1800-1802.

MELON HOSE *Masc.* Padded short breeches with hose worn in 17th Cent. Mentioned by Samuel Pepys. Fell into disuse in Europe by 1630.

MELON SLEEVE *Fem.* Evening dress sleeve style shaped like a melon, placed around the shoulder or over the elbow, often finished with a transparent long sleeve to wrist. Early 19th Cent. Re-emerged in long sleeve style in 1890s.

MELOTE *Masc. Med.* Garment made from sheepskins. A cloak of rough fur worn by monks pursuing outdoor work.

MELTON Close-woven, heavy woollen fabric with even nap. Made for overcoats, uniforms, livery. Originally woven in England. From 1850.

MENNONITE Sect of German origin who settled in Pennsylvania, U.S.A., late 17th Cent. Characterised by strict rules and extremely simple clothing.

MENTONNIÈRES *Fem.* Chin stays. A ruffle of lace or tulle attached to the top of bonnet strings forming a frill around the chin. Early 19th Cent. (Example seen in portrait of the Duchess of Kent, 1837, by A.E.Chalon).

MERCERIZING Treatment of cotton fabrics with lustrous finish. Discovered by Englishman, John Mercer, a chemist and calico printer. 1791-1866.

MERINO Soft fine wool from sheep originally bred in Spain.

MERKINS *Fem.* False hair pieces dressed to hang down in curls on each side of the face. Late 17th Cent. (See portraits by Sir Peter Lely).

MEROVINGIAN A dynasty of Frankish Kings in France which developed significant changes in European costume. *Masc.* Gonelle - knee-length tunic, belted and embroidered, worn with banded breeches. *Fem.* Long tunic-robe, also belted and embroidered. 448-751 A.D.

MERRY WIDOW HAT *Fem.* Wide-brimmed straw hat style. Worn by actresses in the popular 'The Merry Widow' by Franz Lehar. Much copied and worn during 1908.

MERSEY PATTEN *Fem.* Small wooden platforms supported on little stilts. Worn for foot protection on muddy roads. 19th Cent.

MERVEILLEUSE *Fem. Fr.* Counterpart of the masculine INCROYABLE fashion worn by dandies, 1795-1799. The dress was long and full, with very tight short-sleeved bodice. Exaggerated high-brimmed bonnets were worn over unkempt flowing hair styles; and small sandals or slippers on the feet.

MESH BAG *Fem.* Bag of flexible link mesh in gold, silver or plated metal. Fashionable accessory for social occasions in the first half of the 20th Cent.

MESOPOTAMIA Region of S.W. Asia between Tigris and Euphrates Rivers. From 2800-1600 B.C., occupied by highly sophisticated peoples - The Sumerians in the south and Akkadians in the north, who were characterised by simplicity of dress. The chief garment was a wrap-around skirt, worn with the torso left bare. Hair styles were complex and wigs have been found in tombs at Ur. The Babylonians ruled from 2200 B.C., and towards the end of this time sculpture of this period shows that drapery was introduced. Ankle-length tunics with decorated shawls also appeared. Fitted garments, such as jackets and trousers, made with great skill from skins were introduced by the Persians, before Alexander the Great conquered Babylon in 331 B.C.

MESS JACKET *Masc.* Short uniform jacket worn by officers of the Armed Services for semi-formal evening occasions.

METAL EYELETS Small metal rings patented in 1823. Used for lacing in boots, corsets, etc., in place of stitched holes.

METAL LACE Motifs of gold, silver or copper threads supported or woven on a net foundation. 16th-18th Cent. Bobbin laces were often decorated with small metal spangles. 16th and 17th Cents.

MEXICO *Masc. Fem.* Costume consists of colourful combination of ancient Aztec and Spanish features. (See - HUIPIL, MANTILLA, REBOZO, SOMBRERO)

MEZZERO *Fem.* Italian head-covering worn particularly in Genoa, made from an embroidered shawl. 18th Cent.

MIGNONNE *Fem.* 'Dwarf' bonnet designed for theatre wear by a Parisian milliner, 1779. Also called DORMEUSES RACCOURCIES

MILAN *Ital. - Milano.* Capital city of Lombardy. Famous in Middle Ages for steel used in making chain-armour and swords. Today, an important World trading centre, where chief industries include silk and man-made textiles, leather and fashion goods.

MILAN BONNET *Masc.* Cap with soft beret-shaped crown and rolled brim. Usually in black. Occasionally slit, with contrasting colour or gold showing through

cuts. 1542. Examples seen in paintings by Holbein, the Younger, 1497-1543.

MILAN COAT *Masc.* Light armour. Normal defence during early Middle Ages. Remaining in common use until 17th Cent., although relegated to subordinate role in the 14th Cent. with the adoption of plate armour.

MILANESE Silk or rayon textile woven on the cross. Used for women's underwear, light gloves. From 1880.

MILAYA *Fem. Egyptian.* Long cotton covering mantle. (See HAIK, HUKE)

MILITARY FROCKCOAT *Masc.* Neat military-looking coat worn by civilians. Seamed at the waist with a roll collar, without lapels or flapped pockets. From 1820-1900s.

MILITARY STOCK *Masc.* Stiffened made-up neck-cloth. Tied or buckled at back of neck. Usually of corded white silk for civilians, black for military men. 1750-1850.

MILIUM Modern trade name for applied milium coating on back of lining material; resulting in warmth but not weight.

MILLINERY Straw, fabric and felt hats were made in the Duchy of Milan in 15th and 16th Cents. Known as 'Millayne bonnets'. English word 'MILAINER' used for maker of women's caps and bonnets.

MINARET *Fem.* A stiffened overskirt created by famous Frenchman, Paul Poiret, and inspired by Bakst's designs for the ballet 'Scheherezade'. From high natural waist, it flared outwards sometimes with fur edging to knee-length. Worn over a long slim straight skirt.

MINI-CORSET *Fr. - Guêpière.* Small under-supporting waistband incorporated into 'New Look' silhouette garments, presented by Dior in 1947.

MINI-DRESS, MINISKIRT *Fem.* Introduced by Courrèges in 1966-67 collection, with hem well above the knees. Worn often with thigh-length and mid-shin boots, above nylon tights. Coloured and white were favoured contrasts.

MINIVER *Fr. - Menu-vair.* Grey and white squirrel fur used in Middle Ages. Also white - used for British State robes. (See ERMINE).

MINK *Sw. - Maük, menk.* Valuable fur of semi-aquatic animal of the weasel family. North America, Russia, Northern Europe, China, Japan.

MINK STOLE *Fem.* In 1950s, a fur shoulder wrap became high fashion for informal evening wear. New methods of ranch breeding permitted mink skins to become less costly; an appearance of luxury was gained less expensively than before.

MINO Cape of straw or dried rushes worn by working Japanese peasants.

MINOAN (See CRETE)

MINTAN *Masc. Turk.* White linen shirt with embroidered collar. Buttoned in front. Traditional.

MI-PARTI English and European fashion only worn by nobility, of garment divided into two dissimilar portions by vertical, diagonal or horizontal stripes. From late 12th Cent. to early 16th Cent.

MIRRORS Mirrors were first made commercially in Venice in the 14th Cent. Until 17th Cent., fashionable men and women carried small mirrors in silk or ivory cases. *Fem.* When suspended from waist, named 'Countenances'.

MISERICORDA Small pointed dagger. Knights used it on unhorsed antagonists, inflicting the 'mercy stroke', depriving the wounded of life. 15th Cent.

MITRE, MITER *Gk. L. - mitra.* Crown, headband, turban. Original form - a round cap with depression. *Masc.* A head-dress symbolic of episcopal office with deep cleft at top. *Fem.* 19th Cent. term given by authors to women's heart-shaped head-dress of 15th Cent.

MITTEN Hand-covering of wool, cloth or leather worn from early times, in varying styles. *Masc.* Countryman's - worn for warmth, 14th-16th Cent. *Fem.* From mid-17th Cent., elbow-length fingerless gloves with opening for thumb, in silk, kid, worsted, lace, often embroidered. From early 19th Cent., of net and openwork. Short black ones for morning and long with evening wear. Revived for evening wear, late 19th Cent.

MOAB *Fem.* Turban of inverted bowl-like shape. 1865-1870. Ref.: 'Moab is my wash pot'. Ps. 60:8.

MOAT COLLAR Upstanding collar band on low round neckline usual on English garments of 13th Cent.

MOBCAP *Fem.* Frilled indoor bonnet of gauze, linen, cambric or muslin, of varying size. Sometimes worn outdoors under a hat. Plain caps were worn in bed, called 'night-caps'. 18th Cent. (N.B.: The 'Ranelagh MOB' was based on a folded square piece of material and was quite different in appearance).

MOCCASIN Foot-gear worn by North American Indians, trappers. Made of deerskin in one piece, gathered to a U-shaped piece covering the instep.

MOCKADO Material imitating velvet, with twilled cotton, wool or silk back. 16th, 17th and 18th Cents.

MOCKADOR Handkerchief or bib for a child. 15th Cent.

'MOD' LOOK *Fem.* Style of dressing with neat cropped hair, trim blouses and slacks, or tight-fitting suits. Early 1960s.

MODE Prevailing custom or fashion.

MODEL Original design of costume from which copies can be made. Person or mannequin on whom the garment is displayed.

MODESTY PIECE *Fem.* Bib or strip of fine material or lace, worn to conceal low décolletage. 18th, 19th and 20th Cents.

MODISTE Dressmaker, milliner, of high standing.

MOGGAN *Scot.* Closely knitted stocking, tubular-shaped, without a foot or sleeve, worn for extra warmth by Highlanders.

MOHAIR Fine lustrous wool of Angora goat. Introduced by Moors into Spain. 17th Cent.

MOILES (See MULES)

MOIRÉ, WATERED SILK Watered or wavy pattern pressed on to silk and synthetic fabrics, by passing through engraved rollers. From 19th Cent.

MOIRETTE Slightly stiffened fabric with watered texture, used for petticoats and gown foundations. When wearer moved, a 'rustling' could be heard. Late 19th Cent.

MOKADOR (See MOCKADOR)

MOKKADOES Woollen cloth worn in time of Elizabeth I. 16th Cent.

MOLDAVIAN MANTLE *Fem.* Long covering mantle, for outdoor wear, with deep cape falling over the arms in full folds on each side, forming an appearance likened to 'elephant's ears'. 1854.

MONKEY JACKET *Masc.* Seaman's short jacket or Pilot Coat, suitable for rough weather, of heavy navy-blue material. Nickname possibly suggested by likeness to very short coat worn by the monkey which usually accompanied the Victorian barrel-organ grinder of that era. 1850s on.

MONK'S ROBE *Masc.* In temperate climes and for many religions, usually a full-length simple garment from neck, with standing collar, to hem. Tied with knotted cord or girdle.

MONMOUTH CAP *Masc.* Traditional knitted cap worn from time of Elizabeth I, 1570s-1630s. Tall crown and unbrimmed. Made in Monmouth and Bewdley.

MONMOUTH COCK *Masc.* Style worn by Duke of Monmouth, 1670. Large black brimmed beaver 'cocked' or turned-up at back. White ostrich feather decoration.

MONMOUTH STREET FINERY Goods obtained from a London street noted for its second-hand clothes shops. Named after an Earl of Monmouth who died in 1661. Expression used for tawdry pretentious clothes.

MONOCLE Single unframed lens used for one eye. Evolved from earlier quizzing glass. In general use, late 19th Cent. Still in modern use.

MONTAUBAN Peaked iron hat of 17th Cent. armour-suit, modelled on 14th Cent. CHAPEL DE FER, a helmet worn over a hood of chained mail.

MONTENEGRIN *Fem.* Sleeveless embroidered caftan. An outer garment worn in Montenegro, Yugoslavia.

MONTERO *Masc. Sp.* A traveller's peaked cap with ear-flaps which tied under the chin. First worn by mountaineer guards of Spanish King. Worn from 17th Cent. and in present time by trappers, hunters, farmers, both in Europe and America. Empress Eugénie presented such caps, but made of fur, to an Arctic Exploration group in 1875. These latter were called 'Eugénie's wigs'.

MONT-LA-HAUT *Fem.* A wire frame covered with silk to raise hair or head-dress. 1694. Also COMMODE, FONTANGE, PALISADE.

MONTMARTRE The area in Paris associated with theatre gaiety and artists of the late 1890s and turn of the century. It was here that women's underclothes - called 'drawers' - were first displayed in the popular can-can dance.

MOP FAIR A fair, dating from 17th Cent., at which farm hands and servants were hired. Tokens were fastened to head-gear - wool on shepherds; whipcord to the carters; sponges for grooms; whilst others held mops, brooms and so on. When a person was hired, a cockade of streamers triumphantly replaced the trade emblem.

MOPPET Dolls made in Europe, dressed in latest French styles, and sent by dressmakers to England from France to show the prevailing fashions. 18th Cent.

MORDANT Chemical for fixing the dyeing of cloth.

MORIAN, MORION *Sp. Morrion -skull.* Open helmet without visor introduced by Spanish, copied from Moors. Worn by foot soldiers in late 16th Cent. Two types: 1) CABASSET - with pear-shaped pointed skull and narrow flat brim. 2) COMB-MORION - high and with curved brim peaked before and behind and pointed apex.

MORNE Head of a tilting lance having its point turned back, to avoid giving injury to opponent in tournament.

MORNETTES The points of the CORONEL or upper part of a jousting lance. (See CORONEL)

MORNING COAT *Masc.* Formerly a riding coat. Fronts sloped away from bottom button at waist. The skirt at back with vent to waist level. Collar was turned down with short lapels. 1850. Gradually this coat replaced the more formal frockcoat in the second half of the 19th Cent. It is retained to date for social occasions, functions, weddings. *Fem.* For a short period, a tailor-made equivalent was worn as a day jacket. It was fitted and sleeves were usually full leg-of-mutton style, tapering to the wrists. 1895.

MORNING DRESS *Fem.* Simple dresses of material suitable for the season, worn in the early part of the day when women usually spent more time in the home. 1900-1920s.

MORNING GOWN *Fem.* Loose long coat tied with a girdle, worn indoors. Early 19th Cent.

MORNING STAR A Tudor weapon formed by a ball of wood encircled by a band of iron into which spikes were inserted. It was appended to a pole by an iron chain. 16th Cent.

MORRIS DANCE English Dance, in which dancers represent and were costumed as characters from Robin Hood stories, 15th Cent. These included Maid Marian, Friar Tuck, the fool, hobby-horse and Moors. Originally a military Moorish dance brought from Spain in the reign of Edward III, 1312-1377.

MORTAR *Masc.* Square cap. Worn in 17th Cent.

MORTAR BOARD Academic cap with square flat top attached to round cap, adorned with projecting long silk tassel. Still worn at educational functions.

MORTIER *Masc. Fr.* Medieval headcap, flat and round, usually of velvet with braid or fur band. Distinguished wear for dignitaries, academicians and law administrators.

MOSCHETTOS *Masc.* Type of pantaloons but fitting over boots; similar to gaiters. Early 19th Cent.

MOTHER HUBBARD *Fem.* Name from 18th Cent. nursery rhyme given to: 1) Three-quarter-length roomy cloak of warm material, usually velvet, wool, thick brocade or satin, lined and quilted. High collar and loose sleeves. 1880s. Later, when bustle was again fashionable, vents were introduced into side seams to allow fullness to be gathered with a bow, and draped over the back. 1882. 2) Wrapper or dressing-gown evolved for at-home wear. Materials used varied from silks to cottons, according to wearer's circumstances. Essentially a good-looking, but comfortable, garment. Late 19th Cent., early 20th Cent. In U.S.A., the MUU-MUU, a shortened Hawaian dress, was evolved in style from this wrapper and worn for a period in 1930s by college girls. These were in attractive flower prints and eventually led to the creation in 1950s of another popular easy-to-wear style - called the 'SHIFT'.

MOTHER-OF-PEARL Iridescent internal layer of certain shells used in making of buttons, buckles. Large buttons of this substance used from end of 18th Cent. Small buttons for men's shirts appeared from beginning of 19th Cent.

MOTLEY *Masc.* Costume worn by Court jester in Courts in the Middle Ages. Of varied colours, usually with fool's cap having long ears as of an ass and bells. Shoulder cape with scalloped edge. The jester held a sceptre, which was a rattle with miniature head, cap, cape and bells. Until 17th Cent.

MOTORING WEAR In early days of motoring in Britain and Europe, it was necessary to be protected from cold and dust in touring cars. Both men's and women's costume consisted of full warm outdoor coats; men's caps with earpieces; women's, long motoring veils worn over hats, tied under the chin. Early 20th Cent.

MOUCHE *Fr. - fly. Fem.* Very small beauty patches on face. 18th Cent. Applied with mastic as ornaments. *Masc.* Only worn occasionally by dandies.

MOUFLON Wool obtained from wild mountain sheep of Corsica and Sardinia, also in some parts of Russia.

MOULDS, MOWLDS *Masc.* Padded underdrawers worn under full ballooned breeches in 16th Cent.

MOURNING ATTIRE The wearing of certain colours by mourners in many nations expresses sorrow for loss:

BLACK: The prevailing colour in Europe, Ancient Greece and Roman Empire.

BLACK-AND-WHITE: South Sea Islanders.

GREYISH BROWN: Ethiopia.

PALE BROWN: Persia.

SKY BLUE: Armenia, Syria.

DEEP BLUE: Bokhara, Romans of the Republic.

PURPLE: For royalty in France. For Cardinals.

VIOLET: Turkey.

WHITE: Fem. wear Sparta and ancient Rome. Spain until 15th Cent. Henry VIII wore white for Anne Boleyn.

YELLOW: Egypt, Burma.

In Europe, from 14th Cent., black was worn by all classes. The exception was made for Court and Royal widows to wear white, in 16th Cent. By 17th Cent., variations such as mourning bands on hats were made, a custom surviving to end of 19th Cent. People came out of mourning gradually, wearing purple, mauve and then white, but as the pattern of life changed, a black left armband gradually became sufficiently correct wear and this custom continued well into the 20th Cent.

MOURNING COLLAR A black velvet collar on a light coat was worn by French refugee aristocrats when mourning for Louis XVI, 1792.

MOURNING FANS Fans painted in black and grey with overlay of white. The ivory sticks were burnished with a design in silver, which blended with grey overall look. 15th Cent. European (including English).

MOURNING GLOVES *European.* Black kid. 18th and 19th Cents.

MOURNING JEWELLERY Early 16th and 17th pieces were gloomy in character, portraying coffin-shaped pendants of gold and enamel, with skulls and cross-bones in the designs. Oval frames for pendants, rings, lockets, bracelets became fashionable in Europe and British Isles in the latter part of 18th Cent. These frames were set with enamels. Miniature paintings, often with a piece of the deceased's hair, were inserted. Black jet from England was much in vogue in the making of mourning jewellery in the second part of the 19th Cent.

MOUSQUETAIRES, MUSKETEERS *Fr. Mousquet - soldier armed with a musket. Ital. - moschetto.* Bodyguards of the Kings of France originating in 16th Cent. No defined uniform until 18th Cent., when a cocked hat, deep cuffs, large flat collar and gauntlet gloves became usual. These items were periodically adopted as fashionable in women's wear of 19th Cent.:

1) MOUSQUETAIRE MANTLE: Braided black velvet overmantle with short sleeves, pockets and quilted lining. 1847.

2) MOUSQUETAIRE SLEEVE: Full with turned-back pointed cuffs. 1853.

3) MOUSQUETAIRE HAT: Brown straw, brimmed with decorative black lace edging. 1857-1860.

4) MOUSQUETAIRE CUFF: Large turned-up cuff on day sleeve. 1873.

5) MOUSQUETAIRE GLOVES: Gloves with embroidered gauntlets. 1890.

MOUSSELINE Fine light textile of silk, wool or cotton. From 1830s.

MOUTON *Fr. - lamb.* Fleece of Merino lamb wich can be sheared, bleached and dyed to resemble expensive furs. Heavy, warm.

MOWLES, MOYLES (See MULES)

MOZETTA *Masc.* Short linen cape worn by bishop over an alb.

MUCKENDER (See MOCKADOR)

MUFF Covering for hands, tubular or flat, and open each end. Originated in France in 17th Cent. Used to carry little pet dogs. Popular, men and women, until 18th Cent. In 19th and early 20th Cents., used only by women. Matching tippets and stoles were worn. Before use of handbags, pockets for cardcases and purses were concealed in the muffs. 1880s.

MUFFETEES *Masc. Fem.* Small wrist muffs worn for warmth and protection. Late 18th Cent., early 19th Cent.

MUFFIN HAT *Masc.* Flat-crowned hat of cloth, with upright narrow brim. For country wear. 1860s.

MUFFLER Scarf or neckerchief worn for protection and warmth. Known as CHIN CLOUT. 16th and 17th Cents.

MUKLUK Hardwearing half-boot of walrus or seal skin, with fur on inside, made for Arctic wear. Canvas uppers and leather sole.

MULES, MOILES, MOWLES, MOYLES Footwear without heels until 17th Cent. Later, and in present use as boudoir slippers, with or without heels.

MULL MUSLIN Soft fine muslin, plain woven. Late 18th, early 19th Cents.

MUMMER *British.* An actor called Mummer or Guiser - disguised. Parties of mummers gave performances such as St. George and the Dragon in dumb-show at Christmas and festival times. Thought by some to have originated from ancient pagan rituals. A stained glass 16th Cent. window at Betley, Staffordshire, shows some of the costumes worn by such characters who portrayed St. George, who fights many fights, and is always brought to life again by the Doctor; Beelzebub; Little Johnny Jack and his family; and sometimes Father Christmas. All the characters are disguised except the Doctor who, after 18th Cent., wore a black top-hat and coat. Alexander Pope, 1688-1744, the English poet, wrote: *Peel'd, patch'd, and piebald, linsey-woolsey brothers, Grave mummers! Sleeveless some, and shirtless others.* Dunciad III, 115.

MUSCADINS *Masc. Fr.* Predecessors of 'Les Incroyables'. Elegant young dandies who rebelled against austere simplicity, which had been imposed by authority at the end of 18th Cent. in France. They adoptd the mid-calf length, buttoned coat - the FRAC. This had a front opening cut at an angle. *Ital. GOLDONIANA.* Breeches were usually striped, boots had coloured turned-down cuffs. Monocles were worn and knobbly walking sticks replaced the thinner cane previously used.

MUSCADINE Musk-scented pastille, solid perfume, used by young dandies of the French Late Revolutionary period. 18th Cent.

MUSHROOM HAT *Fem.* Simple, round-crowned, mushroom-shaped straw hat, often trimmed over the crown with flowers and ribbons. 1870-1880s.

MUSHRU Satin striped or plain, cotton-backed material from East India.

MUSKET Portable infantry firearm. 16th-19th Cent.

MUSKETEERS French bodyguards. (See MOUS-QUETAIRES)

MUSLIN Plain woven cotton, first made in Mesopotamia.

MUSQUASH American-Indian name given to hard-wearing fur of rodent muskrat found in Canada and U.S.A.

MUSTERDEVILLERS Woollen cloth. 15th and 16th Cents. Woven at Montivilliers in Normandy.

MUU MUU *Fem.* Comfortable loose cotton dress of Hawaiian women, a style originally introduced by American missionaries but extremely attractive when made in colourful flowered, exotic-looking light materials. Adopted by fashion world in 1930s.

MYLLION Coarse twilled fustian from Milan. 16th Cent.

SAILOR HATS A London street market showing the length of women's dress and the popular sailor hat shape of millinery worn above the long hair styles of this period. From a photograph, 1904.

NECKED BONNER   *As worn by Sir Thomas More, after Holbein 1527.*

NABCHET   Common term for hat or cap. 16th Cent.

NABMAN   Sheriff's officer, or police constable, from colloquial 'to seize'.

NACAVAT   *Sp. nacarado.* Bright orange-red colour.

NACRE   *Fr. Sp. - nacar* Mother-of-pearl.

NACRE VELVET   Velvet producing an iridescent effect. Made with the pile of one colour and the back of another. .

NAIL   An old measurement of length of cloth, 21/2 inches.

NAINSOOK   Soft fine cotton fabric. Originally from India.

NANKEEN   Yellow or pale buff coloured Chinese cotton, named for Nanking where it was originally made.

NAP   Surface given to cloth by cutting and smoothing short hairy fibres to lie smoothly in one direction and form a soft surface which is not a pile.

NAPA   Soft leather made from tanning sheepskin or calf-skin with oil and soap mixture. From Napa, California.

NAPKIN   Square piece of white material. Luke XIX, 20. Term used in 16th Cent. for pocket handkerchief; also when used on head as a Head Kerchief.

NAPKIN CAP   *Masc.* Used as nightcap to cover head on removal of wig. 18th Cent.

NAPKIN HOOK   *Fem.* Clasp or hook used to attach kerchief from the waist. 17th Cent.

NAPOLEON BOOT   *Masc.* Military officer's high boot, of black heavy leather, distinguished by square scoop cut away at the back of the knee. 1815. Worn by European officers; and later by horsemen in 1850s. So named as compliment to Napoleon III.

NAPOLEON COLLAR   *Masc.* High-standing folded-down collar with wide revers, worn with black satin cravat. Early 19th Cent.

NAPOLEON NECKTIE   *Masc.* Violet coloured narrow necktie worn around the back of the neck, with ends brought forward and crossed in front without tying, then carried under the arms and tied at the back. Sometimes tied to braces. Later called the 'Corsican tie'. 1818.

NAPPING Process used to produce furry soft surface on cloths, coats and blankets, also used on felt hats.

NAPRON *O.F. Nape or nappe -a tablecloth.* Small apron. Early 15th Cent. After 1460, called 'Apron'.

NATTIER, JEAN MARC Lived 1685-1766. French painter noted for his portrayals of Louis XV's daughters and his use of a beautiful dull turquoise blue -'Nattier blue' - which was much admired and seen in silk dresses. 18th Cent.

NECESSAIRE *Fr.* Small enamelled box used to contain one or two perfume bottles, watch key, tiny scissors, pen-knife, ivory plate and pencil for notes. 18th Cent.

NECKATEE Term used for a neckerchief. Mid-18th Cent.

NECK-CHAIN *Masc.* A chain, gold or gilded brass, worn as adornment, or even as token-money by medieval travellers. Medieval to 17th Cent. See also JACK CHAIN.

NECKCLOTH *Masc., Fem.* Cravat or neckwear swathed around the neck. 17th-19th Cent.

NECKED BONNET *Masc.* Lined or unlined cap with deep piece fitting round back of the neck. 1500-1550.

NECKERCHIEF, KERCHIEF *Masc., Fem.* Square or strip of linen folded round the neck. 14th-19th Cent.*Fem.* Large diaphanous handkerchief swathed round neck and shoulders, gathered into corsage in front. 1780s. See BUFFONT.

NECKSTOCK White linen or black satin cravat wrapped twice round the neck over a high stiff collar. The two ends were buckled at back or tied in front. Early 19th Cent.

NECKTIE *Masc.* This name gradually displaced the term 'cravat' of early 19th Cent.

NEEDLE Thin round pointed implement with eye for thread at other end. Large numbers found in Palaeolithic caves, made of mammoth ivory, bones and tusks, left there forty thousand years ago.

NEEDLE MONEY A pittance paid to seamstresses working in 1800s, often only three pence for each shirt made.

NEEDLEPOINT Embroidery worked over threads of canvas or linen with a needle.

NEEDLEPOINT LACE Lace made with sewing needle instead of bobbins, using buttonhole and blanket stitches.

NEGLIGÉE, NEGLIGÉ *Masc., Fem.* Informal wear worn for leisure. French term used from 18th Cent.

NEGLIGÉE CAP *Masc.* Full folded beret-like cap of rich material, worn at home or in warm weather when wigs were temporarily discarded. 18th Cent.

NEHRU TUNIC *Masc.* Tailored knee-length coat of handsome material, with standing collar, buttoned centre front. Of East Indian origin. See CHOGA.

NELSON *Fem.* Name given to bustle worn outside to achieve the stance known as 'Grecian Bend'. See FRISK. 1820.

NELSON HAT *Fem.* Straw hat with lifted front and back brim, trimmed with feather plumes in front and ribbon rosettes at each side. 1895.

NETCHA Eskimo word for sealskin coat.

NETHERSTOCKS *Masc.* Lower portion of stocking hose; the upper part called 'upperstocks', breech or trunk hose. 16th Cent. Later, name was given to women's stockings. 16th Cent-17th Cent.

NETSUKE Carved button-like ornament worn by Japanese.

NETTING Openwork fabrics with meshwork of material sized according to requirement.

NEW LOOK *Fem.* Fashion style launched in 1947 by Christian Dior, after the Second World War. Characterised by narrow shoulders and waist and longish skirt with wide hem. See also COUTURE.

THE NEW LOOK   Pale shantung jacket and black wool crêpe skirt with padded hips and petticoats. Gloves were important accessories.

The little black dress with three-quarter length sleeves, worn with long, soft gloves.

'NEWGATE' FRINGE *Masc.* Name given to fringe of beard under the chin. 19th Cent.

'NEWGATE' KNOCKER *Masc.* Lock of hair twisted in a curl worn by costermongers who lived near, or had been in, Newgate Prison.

NEWMARKET COAT *Masc.* Single-breasted or double-breasted tailcoat, the fronts sloping away from above the waist. Short skirts with rounded corners, narrow cuffed sleeves, sometimes with flapped hip-pockets. 1838. Later known as 'Cutaway'. By 1870, the style had evolved into the MORNING COAT.

NEWMARKET JACKET *Fem.* Single or double-breasted close-fitting jacket, hip-length. Cut in neat masculine style with turnover collar and silk-faced lapels. Flapped pockets on hips. Often part of a tailor-made costume. Day wear. 1891.

NEWMARKET OVERCOAT *Masc.* Single-breasted overcoat cut short in the waist, very long in the skirts. Velvet collar and cuffs. 1881. *Fem.* Tailormade single or double-breasted and closed to the waist, with long skirts. Flapped pockets on hips. Velvet collar, lapels and cuffs. Usually of heavy-weight cloth for winter. 1889.

NEWMARKET VEST *Masc.* Plaid or check material waistcoat. Sometimes with flapped pocket. For sports-wear. 1894.

NIFELS, NYEFLES *Fem.* Veil. Late 15th Cent.

NIGERIA The predominant linguistic group in the north are the Hausa. Their long ankle-length robe is called a BOU BOU. On the head is worn the distinctive and intricately embroidered LAPPRA. a cylindrical shaped cap of raffia or other light-weight material.

NIGHT CLOTHES Until 16th Cent., men and women slept naked or in simple shifts or shirts, the quality of material according to the station of the wearer. After this, garments called night-shirts for the men or night chemises for the women were developed. These were usually long-sleeved, of ankle length and with simple neck openings.

NIGHT COIF, COYF *Fem.* Linen embroidered cap worn with triangular forehead cloth, also often embroidered. The straight edge was set across the forehead and the point of cloth hung behind. The cloth was worn to prevent wrinkles. 16th and 17th Cents.

NIGHT MASKS *Fem.* Face-covering lined with plaster, worn at night to smooth the skin and prevent wrinkles. Early 17th Cent.

NIGHT RAIL *Fem.* Large handkerchief-shaped cape worn shawl-wise indoors or outdoors. 16th-18th Cent.

NIGHTCAP, SKULL CAP *Masc.* Cap worn for comfort in privacy, especially after removal of wigs. Late 16th Cent., 17th Cent., and until 1790. *Fem.* Washable neat cap worn from earliest times. 14th-19th Cent. With larger and more important hairdressing, it became a mobcap tied under the chin and was worn in bed. 18th and 19th Cents.

NIGHTGOWN *Masc., Fem.* A comfortable, often elaborate, dress, distinct from night clothes or sleeping garments. Worn, when fashionable, for morning visits. 17th and 18th Cents. *Fem.* A similar garment but worn at any part of the day, was called a 'Morning Gown'. See MANTUA. (Anne Boleyn, 1507-1536, is recorded as possessing one made in black satin.)

NIGHTSMOCKS *Masc., Fem.* Garments of fine linen, usually imported from Holland, worn by the upper classes in bed. Often made with cambric sleeves and lace edging. 17th Cent.

NINON Hard-wearing silk voile. Used for lightweight summery-type dresses and lingerie.

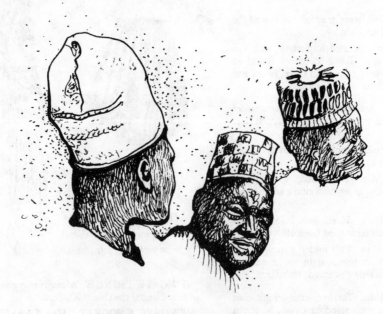

LAPPRA   The distinctive embroidered headwear of the Hausa group of Northern Nigeria.

NITHSDALE *Fem.* A long hooded red riding cloak. Named after the Countess Nithsdale, whose Jacobite husband, imprisoned in the Tower of London under sentence of death, escaped by wearing his wife's cloak. 1716.

NIVERNOIS HAT *Masc.* A three-cornered shaped hat with round crown and very wide brim rolled over into a broad triangle, with peak positioned in front. It formed some protection from wet weather. 1760s.

NORFOLK JACKET *Masc., Fem.* A sporting or lounge jacket made with side and back box pleats. Large hip pockets, with vertical slit pocket on left breast. Belted and sometimes yoked. Usually of tweed or homespun. 1890s.

NORMA CORSAGE *Fem.* A blouse style worn for evening, with a draped fold in the centre, to be pinned with a becoming brooch. 1844.

NORWICH CRAPE A fabric of worsted and silk. 18th Cent.

NORWICH SHAWL *Fem.* Small elegant wrap of silk or cotton, usually embroidered with flowers. End of 18th Cent. Sometimes worn under an echarpe-cloak. See ECHARPE.

NOSE JEWEL A ring of gold or silver worn by women from the east in the right nostril. In Egypt, this is confined to lower classes or ranks. See Isaiah 3: 20, 21.

20: The bonnets and the ornaments of the legs and the headbands and the tablets and the ear-rings.

21: The rings and the nose jewels.

NOSEGAY Small bunch of sweet-smelling herbs or flowers, used to counteract unhealthy atmospheres or even as an antidote to infectious disease. From 15th Cent. Later introduced as a decoration on head-gear at weddings. 16th Cent. Associated with weddings to the present day.

NOTCHED LAPEL *Masc.* Tailoring term for the gap cut out between the collar of a coat and the lapel. 19th Cent.

NOUCH or OUCH Jewelled clasp or buckle. 13th-15th Cent. Later called 'Pontifical'. 16th Cent.

NUB YARN A yarn of varying thicknesses and recurring twists used to achieve interesting raised surface in material.

NUN'S VEILINGS Lightweight woollen fabric in black, white and colours. Named after similar material used in clothing worn by nuns.

NUTRIA Name given to fur of rodent coypu found in South America.

NYCETTE *Fem.* Light wrap for the neck. 15th and 16th Cents.

NYLON STOCKINGS *Fem.* Hose made of synthetic plastic material possessing strength and elasticity, which became an essential part of every woman's wardrobe after the Second World War. 1946.

OILSKIN   Greatly favoured by sailors for Sou'wester hats, capes and overalls, 19th Century.

OAKAPPLE DAY   As celebration of rights, to collect firewood from Grovelly Forest, granted to the villagers of Wishford in 1603, a commemorative procession is held annually by women in historical costume. The men carry boughs and the women bear faggots. A band leads the procession and children in costume carry flowers.

OATLAND HAT   *Fem.* A summer straw or Leghorn hat, ribbon-trimmed round a dome-shaped crown, with the brim turned up in front and behind. Named after the Duchess of York who lived at Oatland. 1800.

OBI   *Fem.* The Japanese wide silk sash which is stiffened and worn over the kimono, the national dress.

OBI HAT   *Fem.* English high flat-crowned straw hat with a narrow front brim rolled backwards. Tied under the chin with ribbon streamers which also decorate the crown. 1804.

OBLONG HOOP   *Fem.* Under-garment to support dresses, especially for Court wear. It projected from the waist on each side but was flattened front and back. Some were hinged to allow wearer to compress the dress over skirt when passing through doorways or sitting in crowded assemblies. 1740-1760.

OCCIDENTAL INFLUENCE   Growing Western freedom and attitude towards comfortable costume with the use of machinery and better styling, permeated Asiatic life by the 20th Cent. The East responded and adapted with great expertise modern methods of manufacture and marketing.

OCELOT   Fur of the South American leopard. A well-marked flat fur accented by dots. Used by some couturiers in mid-20th Cent. for coats, jackets and trimming.

OCTAGON TIE   *Masc.* Made-up scarf tie arranged octagonally, worn with tiepin and suspended from a neck-band fastened at the back. 1860s onwards.

OES   Small eyelets sewn upon the material of a garment for decoration. Usually feminine. Late 16th Cent. Also OWES.

'OFF THE RACK'   Term for ready-made garments, as distinct from those 'made-to-measure'.

OFF-WHITE   Name for whites with a tinge of another colour, such as ivory, magnolia, cream, oyster.

OILETS   Name given to lacing holes or eyelets. 18th and 19th Cents.

OILSKIN Heavy waterproof cloth used for sailors' wear. Impregnated with oil and gum.

OKERS *Masc.* Ploughman's boots. Also called HOGGERS, HOKERS. 16th Cent.

OLD ROSE Colour name of deep soft greyish-pink.

OLDENBURG BONNET *Fem.* A large bonnet which received a great measure of criticism, referred to as a 'coal-scuttle'. Made of silk material on a firm base, the edge of the brim trimmed with frilled lace, artificial flowers or feathers. Ribbon ties under the chin. Occasionally with lace frill or flounce at back over neck. 1814-1820. The forerunner of the poke bonnet.

OLIVE BUTTON Long oval silk-covered button. 18th Cent.

OLIVE DRAB Deep olive-green colour used to dye military uniform fabrics. 19th and 20th Cents.

OLIVETTES Buttons of olive shape, used with frogs or loops on Brandenburg coats. 1674-1700. See BRANDENBURG.

OLLYET Woollen material made at Norwich, similar to bombazine. 17th Cent. See BOMBAZINE.

OMBRE French term for shading one colour into another, when applied to materials. Also a cloth or surface painted in graduated hues of one colour.

ONDINA CRINOLINE *Fem.* Crinoline cage with undulating hoops or wave-like bands. 1860.

ONDINE Soft very brightly coloured fabric of silk and wool mixture. 1871. Later, corded. 1893.

ONDULE Fabric with wavy appearance. 1865.

ONYX *Masc., Fem.* A kind of layered quartz. Much used for jewellery. 19th Cent.

OP ART Form of abstract art using contrasting colours to create an illusion of movement. Influence on youthful fashions of 1960s.

OPAL Stone composed of silica which shows changing irridescent colours.

OPALESCENT, OPALINE Descriptive term frequently given to exclusive and expensive materials, such as lamé tissues, which reflect varied colours and light.

OPANKY Laced sandal-like shoe with thin sole worn in the Balkans from Medieval times to present day.

OPEN ROBE *Fem.* Style of dress in which the skirt front, from the waist to the ground, is left open to reveal an ornamental or contrasting underskirt. The fashion appeared as early as the 16th Cent. but was not so named until the 19th Cent. Fashionable 1830-1849.

OPERA The combination of music and drama in the form of opera undoubtedly set the scene for the wearing of fashionable and high style clothes. The first opera house was opened in Venice in 1637 and thereafter opera became a recognised popular entertainment in Europe. In England it was also widely accepted, Henry Purcell writing some forty-two musical works. As a consequence, certain garments, worn when attending performances, became popular and some were named after operas, even after favourite singers, ballet dancers and musicians connected with such productions.

OPERA CLOAK *Masc.* A knee-length cape-like cloak for evening wear. Usually of fine or velvet cloth, the high collar was fastened with cords. 1850s. *Fem.* This cloak, sometimes hooded, was often of silk, brocade or velvet and trimmed with fur. Occasionally men's or women's garments would have a contrasting coloured lining of rich colour.

OPERA GLASSES Small binoculars for use at the performance, as were also Lorgnettes.

OPERA HAT *Masc.* 1) Small flat bicorne or three-cornered hat made for carrying under the arm. 1750-1800s. See CHAPEAU BRAS, BICORNE. 2) Crescent-shaped bicorne with soft brim still collapsible, named Military Folding Hat, Cocked Hat. 1800-1830. 3) Tall collapsible hat invented and made by Parisian hat-maker, Gibus. Worn with full evening dress until mid-20th Cent.

OPERA PUMP Low-cut, unlaced shoe with flat heels. Worn first in 16th Cent. See PUMPS.

OPIE, John English painter of portraits and figure groups. Portrayal of costume exact and informative. 1761-1807.

OPOSSUM A durable long-haired fur from North and South America. Used in natural shades of cream or pale brown but is also dyed to resemble stone marten or skunk, mostly in the United States.

OPUS ANGLICANUM Long outlining embroidery stitch used in Anglo-Saxon England. Sewn with jewels and gold thread, especially for religious and royal garments.

OPUS ARANEUM LACE Hand-made lace with pattern based on shape of a spider's web. 'Araneid.' -spider. This name was used in Middle Ages for most embroidery work.

ORANGE BLOSSOM In early 19th Cent., it was the custom to accept that in the Language of Flowers, orange blossom represented chastity. A wreath of these blossoms was worn by the bride to keep her veil in place. 1830s to 20th Cent.

ORANGE TAWNY Obsolete name given to colour allotted to clerks and persons of lower rank. Also worn by Jews. 16th Cent.

ORBY *Masc.* Single-breasted frock-coat with no waist seam. Designed and worn in the United States. Early 20th Cent.

ORFRAY, OFREY See ORPHREY.

ORGANDIE, ORGANDY A slightly stiffened white muslin fabric.

ORGANZA A stiff, almost transparent muslin, used for full bouffant dresses. Popular 1920s and 1930s.

ORGASIS Coarse cotton cloth from India. 18th Cent.

ORIENTAL INFLUENCES After the Crusades, many ideas and materials from the Middle East were carried back to Europe; also Venetian merchants brought trade and goods from their travels. Much later, in the

19th Cent., Napoleon's expedition to Egypt promoted a wave of interest in orientalism with resulting fashions of exotic appearance. Turbans were worn by women and the previous 'classical' style of dress worn at the beginning of the 18th Cent. was abandoned for an exotic extravagant look. In the 20th Cent., the Russian ballet with Eastern colourful designs by Leon Bakst, influenced the couture of the famed Paul Poiret in Paris and helped to promote an exotic trend in the fashion of the 'Twenties'.

ORLE   A wreath of two colours twisted together, worn on a knight's helmet or as a feminine head-dress. Heraldic. 14th-15th Cent.

ORLEANS CLOTH   Fabric of cotton and worsted. 1837.

ORLON   Trade name for scientifically-produced fabric which resembles fine wool and drapes well. 20th Cent.

ORPHREY, ORPHRIES   Gold thread embroidery applied to narrow bands and borders of garments, especially used on ecclesiastical or royal wear. From early 13th Cent.

ORRELET   *Fem.* Side pieces of woman's head-piece or coif, covering the ears. Late 16th Cent.

ORRICE   Braid trimming woven with gold or silver thread, much used in 18th Cent.

OSNABRUK, OSNABURN   Strong linen imported from Osnabruk, Lower Saxony, used for shirts, jackets and breeches. 16th Cent.

OSPREY   Fish-eating hawk whose beautiful plumage, until prohibited, was used for millinery decoration. Late 19th Cent., early 20th Cent.

OSTRICH   Soft curling feathers of flightless African bird, which have been used for decoration for centuries, especially upon head-dresses and millinery.

OTTOMAN   A ribbed heavy silk material, mixed with cotton or worsted. Used for coats and trimmings.

OUCH, NOUCH   Bejewelled clasp or buckle. Term also used for set of ornaments. 13th-15th Cent.

OUDAI   *Fem. Vietnamese.* Modern, high-collared, long dress, slit up one side, worn over silk or velvet trousers.

OURLE, ORLE   Border of fur. 13th and 14th Cents.

OVAL BEAVER HAT   *Masc.* Imposing hat made on an oval block, which was an improvement on earlier round hat which required stretching. 1817.

OVAL HOOPED DRESS   *Fem.* Garment made with extra material gathered over fan-shaped pleats upon hips. This allowed room for oval supporting hoops. 1750.

OVERALL   1) Garment worn as protection against wet, dirt, etc., over other clothes. 2) Term for military officer's full dress, worn with tight trousers.

OVER-ALL, BALANDRANA, SUPERTOTUS   A hooded coat with large enveloping sleeves, a protective garment. Europe. 16th and 17th Cents.

OVERCOAT   *Masc.* Top coat. Usually worn out-of-doors over clothes of lesser weight; sleeved upper garment. 17th Cent. Emergence of buttoned Frock

106

Coat and Dress Coat, 18th Cent.*Fem.* Of lighter, appropriate materials. From 1750. *Masc.* Paletot -morning, frock ,dress, with names such as: Ulster, Cambridge, Inverness, Chesterfield. Suitable materials were: Melton, Cheviot, Covert. Late 19th Cent.

OVERSHOE   Clog or patten worn on foot to raise the wearer above the dirt. Until early 17th Cent.

OVERSLOP   *Masc.* Cassock, gown, surplice. 10th-14th Cent.

OVERSTOCKS   Upper part of leg-hose or trunk hose. Worn prior to 1550.

OXFORD UNIVERSITY   Established as centre of learning, 1167. Since mid-19th Cent., many popular forms of clothing have been so named probably from adoption by students.

OXFORD   All. Modern type, usually a low shoe, laced, gillie-type, or buttoned, suitable and sensible for walking. Earliest type was a heavy half boot. 17th Cent.

OXFORD BAGS   *Masc.* A flared trouser fashion, characterised by extreme width of 24 inches at the ankles. 1920s.

OXFORD GLOVES   These were worn in period of Elizabeth I; so named because they were scented with the Earl of Oxford's favourite perfume.

OXFORD TIE   *Masc., Fem.* Narrow necktie of equal width from end to end. Men wore it with the new 'Lounge' suit of 1860 and onwards; and women with the then prevailing fashion of a morning blouse and long skirt.

OXONIAN JACKET   *Masc.* Informal for the period. Single-breasted, with pockets. 1850-1860s.

OYSTER WHITE   Couturier's and manufacturer's name for a pleasant off-white slightly greyish hue.

OZEENE, Jean   French designer who befriended and helped Christian Dior. 1945. He sold Dior's first designs.

OUDAI from Vietnam.

Feminine –

POST BOY HAT

POST BOY HAT   Tall, crowned, flower-pot hat which was a very popular feminine fashion around 1888.

Ps AND Qs   *Masc.* In France and other courts of Europe, when large heavy wigs were worn, great formality with bowing and bending was part of court etiquette. Care had to be taken that the wig remained in position on the head. Advice given by a French dancing master was to mind 'les Ps (pieds - feet) et les Qs (queues - wigs)'.

PAC, PACK   *Masc.* A heavy half-boot for winter wear, worn by foresters and logmen in North America. Also, a weather-proofed moccasin.

PACKSTAFF   The staff on which a pedlar carried his pack; pikestaff. 1550s.

PADDED CALVES   *Masc.* Pads worn inside stockings to improve the shape of the legs. 17th, 18th and 19th Cents. (See PARCHMENT CALVES)

PADDING   *Masc. Europe and British Isles.* Sleeves, shoulders, back and front of belted tunics or doublets were usually lined with padded material. 14th Cent. Sleeves often separate and attachable to many jackets. Shoulders were still padded in the 15th Cent. Breeches also were bolstered and stuffed. 16th Cent. The rigid Spanish type of men's doublet, particularly in the front

of the garment was popular, early 17th Cent. The doublet became looser and longer and by 1650 padding was no longer used.

PADDOCK COAT   *Masc.* Long overcoat with fly-front but without waist seam. Slightly fitted with deep side pleats. Pockets. 1890s.

PADUA SERGE   Used for lower class women's gowns. 18th Cent. Silk lining material. 1863.

PADUASOY   *Fem.* Strong silk material. Introduced in 17th Cent. Usually corded or black.

PAENULA   Hooded, circular cloak. Worn by ancient Etruscans and Romans as weather protection; of rough wool or pelts with opening for head. Later it replaced toga in 2nd Cent. A.D. In time, became a long sleeveless church vestment called chasuble. 17th Cent. Also ABOLLA, BYRRUS; *Medieval -PLANETA. Italian - PIANETA.*

PAFTI   *Hungarian.* Heavy silver belt buckle.

PAGEBOY BOB   *Fem.* Style of hairdressing based on medieval pageboy's straight shoulder length hair, with ends slightly turned under. Recurring 20th Cent. fashion from 1940s.

107

PADDING Masculine costume, in the first half of the 16th Century, gave an appearance of status and importance by the use of much padding. This resulted in the silhouette of the figure attaining a broad, squarish shape. Henry VIII is shown wearing a flat, wide cap. His long, skirted doublet shows a frilled shirt at the neck. The legwear of the period consisted of upper and nether stocks, forming one garment. These were attached to the doublet underneath by ties. The square toed shoes were a fashion which lasted until about 1540.

PAGODA PARASOL *Fem.* Sunshade with curved spokes under material which, when open, gave ogee shape, as in a pagoda. Known also as CHINESE. Early 19th Cent.

PAGODA SLEEVE *Fem.* Sleeve, with great width at the elbow, falling to the wrist on the outside. Some were slit on the inside to show ruffles or engageantes. 1849-1860s.

PAGRI *Masc.* Turban worn by Hindus. Made from a piece of cloth twenty-five yards long, wound round the head.

PAILETTES Small metal sparkling sequins or discs, with pierced holes for sewing on materials.

PAINT *Masc.* Used excessively by men of fashion. 18th Cent. Rouge, applied with Spanish carmine-

impregnated wool. *Fem.* Red and white paint - or white lead. The use of the latter proved in time to be very dangerous, giving skin complaints. 18th Cent.

PAIR OF RUFFLES *Fem.* Worn on sleeves for Court wear. In France called 'engageantes', a term later adopted in England. 1740-1750.

PAIS A BETGWN *Fem. Welsh.* Petticoat and bed-gown. Costume retained during 18th to late 19th Cent. Of strong Welsh flannel, in stripes, checks, dyed with local dyes. A gathered apron covered the divided skirt of gown, with front corners looped up to the back when the wearer was working. A neckerchief was tucked into the bodice. Shawls were worn and over-sleeves placed over the three-quarter sleeves on Sundays, also white aprons; black shoes with silver buckles completed the costume. A simple cap was worn under a tall-crowned hat.

PAISLEY SHAWL Soft woollen shawls woven in Paisley, Scotland, with richly coloured designs inspired by Indian and Persian pomegranate and cone patterns. They were worn first with the thin Neo-Grecian gowns at the beginning of the 19th Cent. Many shawls of fine workmanship and beautiful design were made in Lyons, France, and Norwich, Great Britain, and worn through-out the earlier part of the Victorian period.

PAJAMA See PYJAMAS.

PALATINE *Fem.* Cape-like tippet, covering shoulders, with long flat ends falling down some distance in front. 1840s. (See PALLATINE)

PALATINE ROYAL *Fem.* Hooded tippet with short ends in front made of fur. 1851. Worn by Elizabeth of Bavaria.

PALE Vertical stripe in middle of shield. Upright, coloured stripe, or one of a set of stripes of contrasting colours.

PALETOT Word adapted from Dutch 'paltrok', pals - palace, rok - garment, i.e. a palace cloak used for name of silk overcoat over armour. 17th Cent.*Masc.* Short overcoat with side seams. 1830-1900. *Fem.* Fingertip length pleated cape with short stiff cape. 1839-1843. In 19th Cent., the word described garments worn for town rather than country wear.

PALETOT CLOAK *Masc.* A lapelled short cloak, single-breasted or double-breasted, with armhole slits. 1850.

PALETOT-MANTLE *Fem.* A three-quarter caped cloak, with hanging PALETOT SLEEVES. 1867.

PALETOT REDINGOTE *Fem.* A long coat shaped to follow the figure, with revers, occasionally caped, with buttons down the front. No seam at waist. 1867.

PALISADE *Fem.* A wire frame for supporting a high coiffure. 1690-1710. (See also COMMODE, MONT LA HAUT)

PALL MALL Fine walk in London where formerly the fashionable game of Palle malle was played in the reign of Charles II. The thoroughfare was appropriated for the King and his Court. An area where personages wearing fine clothing were seen.

PALETOT-MANTLE The lady carrying a muff is wearing a three-quarter length PALETOT-MANTLE. She has on a SPOON bonnet edged at the back with a Barolet. The child wears an outfit similar to that worn by the adult. At this time , ready-to-wear garments in such styles reached Western Europe and the U.S.A., 1860s.

PALLA Rectangular wrap worn by general populace in ancient Rome.

PALLATINE *Fem.* Sable shoulder wrap of fine quality. 1694.

PALLETTAS Two circular saucer-like shapes of steel placed on armour to protect the armpits.

PALLIUM Large woollen cloak adopted from the Greeks by the Romans. Predecessor of church vestments.

PALMBEACH CLOTH A trade name for lightweight summer suiting. 20th Cent.

PALMERSTON WRAPPER *Masc.* Loose overcoat with very wide sleeves, collar and lapels, flapped pockets. Named after the British statesman. 1853-1855.

PALTOCK *Masc.* Doublet to which the combined stockings and thigh wear of that period were fastened. Worn by pages. 14th to mid-15th Cent.

PALUDAMENT Mantle worn by a Roman general. It was the 'scarlet robe' with which Jesus Christ was covered.

PAMELA BONNET *Fem.* Small open bonnet named after the heroine in Samuel Richardson's novel, Pamela, 1740. Of straw, trimmed with Spring flowers on sloping brim and tied with ribbons under the chin. 1845.

PAMPILION A felt material. Black lambskin from Navarre, France. 16th Cent.

PAMPOOTIE Simple leather moccasin. West coast of Ireland.

PANACHE *Fem.* Decorative feather or curled plume on hat or cap.

PANAMA HAT Finely woven straw hat made in Columbia, Ecuador and Peru for over 300 years. Marketed in Panama by American soldiers and so named. Ideal for tropical and summer wear.

PANES Decoration of garments formed by slashing material allowing coloured underlining to show. Often embroidered.

PANNE VELVET A velvet material woven with the pile pressed in one direction, giving a fine lustrous surface.

PANNIER *Fem.* Side hoops in 18th Cent. called 'hoopskirt' in England. Later, reappeared in the 1860s when the bustle was fashionable. (See CRIADES)

PANTALETTES *Fem.* Undergarment consisting of long straight drawers trimmed at the ankle with frilled edges, tucks or lace. Early 19th Cent. Also separate leglets tied by bands at knees or waist. 1812-1840s.

PANTALOONS *Masc.* Close-fitting trousers replacing 18th Cent. kneebreeches about 1790. By 1818, they were fastened by buckles or buttons at the ankle. By 1820, they were strapped under the instep.

PANTEEN COLLAR *Masc.* A white turned-down collar worn by clergy before 1870. *Fem.* A high collar style used in tailormade jackets and coats. 1880s.

PANTIHOSE, PANTYHOSE *Fem.* A 20th Cent. luxury hose reaching from waist to toe in nylon, silk and other fibres with perfect fit. 1960s on.

PANTILE *Masc., Fem.* Popular name for 'Sugar-Loaf' hat. Late 17th Cent.

PANTOFFLE, PANTOFLE *Masc., Fem.* Overshoe without back, slipped over other footwear. 16th Cent.

PANTS English term for underwear. American for trousers.

PANTS SUIT *Fem.* Adaptation of trousers and jacket for feminine wear. Variations include tailored as well as dressmaker handling for softer thinner materials.

PANTY HOSE *Fem.* Leg wear combining hose and pants. As PANTIHOSE 1970 onward.

PANUELO *Fem.* Starched gauze fichu worn by women in Philippines.

PANUNG Traditional straight length of silk or cotton worn in Thailand. *Masc.* Drawn between legs to form pantaloons. *Fem.* Wrapped around waist to form graceful skirt. Worn with jacket or blouse.

PAON Narrow hat with high crown protruding beyond the forehead. Often decorated with peacock feathers. 14th Cent.

GERMAN 1821

FRENCH 1814

A straw bonnet with sloping back. Trimmed with ribbons and flowers. Brim open to face.

ENGLISH 1846

Variations of the PAMELA BONNET

PAPER CAPS   *Masc.* Light disposable head gear. A square shape was used in 19th Cent., particularly by carpenters. Printers, spray-painters, glass-blowers and those working with foodstuffs are still often found wearing them.

PAPILOTTE   *Fr.* Small piece of paper used for curling hair. 18th Cent.

PAPILLOTE COMB   *Fem Fr.* Tortoiseshell side comb. Worn for decoration and to support hairstyling.

PAQUEBOT CAPOTE   *Fem. Fr.* Steamer, packet. Bonnet resembling Bibi or English Cottage bonnet. The inside of the brim was trimmed with lace and ribbon. 1830s. Suitable for summer travelling or visiting.

PAQUIN   One of the famous houses of couture in Paris founded at the end of the 19th Century by Madame Paquin. (See COUTURE)

PARACHUTE CLOTH   Synthetic plastic material of great tensile strength, originally perfected for the making of parachutes during World War II. After the War, before a variety of dress materials were again available, surplus stocks were used by home dressmakers for many domestic purposes. 1945-1950.

PARACHUTE HAT   *Fem.* Lunardi, balloon hat. Name given to a large hat with a crown of puffed gauze or silk sarcenet. This fashion created when Lunardi launched his famous balloon. 1783-1785. (See also LUNARDI, BALLOON HAT)

PARAGON   Strong popular silken material. 17th Cent. A combed woollen material from Turkey, 17th Cent., similar to Camlet which was made in 15th Cent. Used for hard wear and upholstery. Similar materials were PEROPUS, PHILISELLE.

PARAPES   Lighter weight material resembling paragon. Used for dresses. Early 17th Cent.

PARAPLUIE   *Fr.* Term for umbrella.

PARASOL   Decorative, light umbrella, carried as shield against the sun. Used in the 16th, 17th and 18th Cents. Up to this time, parasols were not closed but the newer umbrellas gradually developed folding frames. Tilting parasols with folding sticks appeared early in the 19th Cent., called ENTOUTCAS, MARQUISE. These gradually became more elegant, often constructed as a dome or the top of a pagoda. As the century progressed, the parasol became an important accessory of feminine fashion.

PARATROOPER   Uniform clothing worn by airborne troops landing by parachute.

PARATROOPER BOOT   Laced hard-wearing water-proof boot worn in World War II. Later adapted for hard general wear. From 1940s.

PARCHMENT CALVES   *Masc.* Padded shapes made of parchment, worn inside the stockings to improve the shape of the legs. 1750-1800.

PARCHMENT LACE   A lace of gold or silver wound on strips of fine cut old parchment and worked in a raised design. 16th Cent. Also called CARTISANE.

PARDESSUS   *Fem.* Descriptive term for outdoor garment of half or three-quarter length, with sleeves, usually trimmed. 1840-1900.

PARIS   After the brilliance of French Court in 17th Cent., Paris became the centre of haute couture, until mid-20th Cent. (See COUTURE)

PARIS DOLL   A dress-maker's lay figure used for displaying new models. Small figures were sent from France to other countries wearing miniature latest fashions. Early 19th Cent.

PARIS EMBROIDERY   Embroidery of white cord appliqué on piqué.

PARKA, ANORAK   Hooded outer garment of sealskin worn by Eskimos. The modern version is Scandinavian, made of lightweight weather-resistant material.

PARROCK   *Masc.* Full loose cloak with arm-holes. 15th Cent.

PARTA   *Fem.* Tall glittering head-dress worn by Hungarian bride. In white or pale colours, with artificial roses. Ribbons falling from the back.

PARTISAN   Longhandled spear. 16th Cent. (Spelt 'partizane' - Shakespeare). Similar to HALBERD.

PARTLET, PERTLETTE *Masc., Fem.* Separate 'fill-in' or chemisette for doublet or dress. Covering upper breast and neck. Some were finished with high collar or lace ruff. In late 16th Cent., outstanding for beauty of workmanship in embroidery. Of rich fabrics, often with added jewels. 16th and 17th Cents.

PARURE Selected, matching jewellery. Necklace, ear-rings, bracelets, brooches, tiara and so on, designed to wear together as a set.

PARVATI All-cotton cloth made in India. Usually hand-woven, absorbent, with graded colour and texture.

PASHM Underfleece wool from Tibetan goats, used for making fine shawls. Persian.

PASS Name given to front of hat. 17th Cent.

PASSAGERE A fashionable curl placed over the forehead, worn by fops and some ladies. 1690.

PASSE Thin wreath of flowers or trimming sewn under the bonnet brim. 1860s.

PASSEMENTERIE Ornamental trimming of braid, cording, gimp with beads, fringe, metallic thread, tassels. Used as decorative bordering for dresses. 19th Cent. Also applied to military, church wear and stage costumes.

PASTE Used for hands. 1710. One of many toilet accessories at this period.

PASTE A lead-glass of great brilliancy, produced by the German jeweller, Strasser. Used in the making of imitation gems. Paste jewellery was worn in the periods of Louis XV and XVI. It was of great delicacy, beautiful design and finish. Such work was valued in its own right and worn by the aristocracy. 18th Cent.

PASTE, FROSE PASTE Method of decorating head-dress. 16th Cent. An accessory to the French Hood. A jewelled border of lace, lawn or velvet mounted on thin pasteboard. Also used separately as head adornment for brides.

PASTEL Artist's crayon, made of dried paste with gum water. Name for soft delicate colours in fabrics.

PATCH POCKET Pocket sewn on outside of garment.

PATCHES Worn on the face in ancient Rome to simulate the mole, then considered a beauty mark. Worn in Europe and Britain; made of black velvet or silk, applied with mastic; fashionable 1590s until 1790. Those worn in Venice, by ladies at Court, were carried in exquisitely-made little boxes. 17th Cent. Also called MOUCHE (Fr. - fly). Made in many shapes - crescents, stars, flowers and so on.

PATENT LACE Lace made on machines. Early 19th Cent.

PATENT LEATHER A lacquered leather used for harness. Early 19th Cent. Later adopted for fashion wear in shoes. handbags, etc. To date.

PATENT LEATHERBOOTS *Masc.* Button boots of ankle height with patent leather uppers. 1870s. Shoes of patent leather worn with evening-dress became customary in 20th Cent.

PATROL JACKET *Masc.* Single-breasted fitting jacket with five buttons and high collar. Worn with knee breeches when cycling. 1878, late 19th Cent. *Fem.* Similar to men's but with decorative braiding. 1889-1890s.

PATTEN Overshoe with wooden sole on iron ring to lift wearer's shoes above the mud. Usually for country wear. 15th Cent. For fashionable wear in towns, they were often decorated to match the silk and satin embroidered shoes worn. 18th Cent.

PATTI JETS *Fem.* Jet ornament or faceted cut jet ball, suspended on a ribbon necklace and worn with matching ear-rings. Named after Madame Patti, the opera singer. 1870s.

PAUTENER *M.E.* Pouch or bag hanging from a girdle.

PAVÉ *Fr.* Setting of jewels placed close together, resembling stones on a pavement.

PEA JACKET Originally a rough short jacket worn by seamen. Chaucer's 'Clerk of Oxenford' wore a 'courtepy'.*Fr. court - short; Dutch piji - pig.* In dark blue, double-breasted with wide lapels, closed behind, worn by sailors 1830s on, known as PILOT JACKET. Adopted for civilian wear, 1850 onwards. Copied for small boys' coats. Also known as REEFER.

PEACOCK Bird native to Asia and India, introduced into Europe in 14th Cent. Nobles and even prelates used the feathers in head-dresses. Later ostrich feathers from Africa became more fashionable and supplanted them.

PEAKED SHOE Footwear with long points. 14th and 15th Cents. (See PIKED, CRACOWES).

PEARL Lustrous body formed within shell of oysters, prized as a gem. Pearls were worn in the hair, as eardrops. Seed pearls were sewn on dresses in 16th Cent. They ceased to be fashionable about 1630 but came into favour again towards the end of the 17th Cent., used for decorating muffs; and were worn in chains across dress until early 18th Cent.

PEARLIES London street-traders or costermongers, sellers of costers, or apples, who wear a traditional costume with mother-of-pearl buttons sewn on in floral and geometric patterns. In the early 19th Cent., these buttons were cheap but are now difficult to obtain and such costumes are prized and passed down the generations.

PEASANT COSTUME This term usually refers to the simple full white blouse, combined with full skirt or trousers, worn by people in Europe from early times. Such garments show regional differences in embroidery and ornament. Most are executed with great craftsmanship and skill.

PEASCOD-BELLY *Masc.* Padded doublet fashionable at the end of the 16th Cent. The stuffed frontal portion overhung the girdle.

PEAU D'ANGE *Fr.* 'Angel-skin' silk, a popular fabric much used for dress and lingerie wear. 1920s and 1930s.

PEAU DE SOIE Plain soft silk modern fabric with matt finish on both sides. Used in evening dresses. 1880.

111

PEBBLE GRAIN Grained surface given to imitation leather or waterproof fabrics. Became fashionable in 1930s with introduction of new plastic materials.

PECADILLY (See PICKADILL)

PECCARY Skin of small pig-like animal, native of Central Americas. Used for gloves and leather goods. Hard-wearing.

PECTOLL *Masc.* Name for breast of shirt. 16th Cent.

PECTORAL Jewelled breastplate. Worn by Hebrew high priests and Egyptian kings. The ancient Jewish pectoral consisted of two large plaques, one at the front and the other at the back, joined at the shoulders by gold chains. A pectoral cross is worn suspended on the breast by abbots and bishops.

PEDULE Medieval boot of untanned leather worn in Europe. Occasionally made in one piece with breeches.

PEDIMENT *Fem.* Gable head-dress or English hood, worn 1500-1540.

PEEK-A-BOO *Fem.* Shirtblouse of eyelet embroidery patterned lawn. 1890-1910.

PEEPER Spyglass or quizzing glass, worn on ribbon or chain. 1780-1800 onwards.

PEEP-TOE SHOE *Fem.* Footwear with front cut away to show toes. Fashionable 1950s.

PEG-TOP SKIRT *Fem.* Style with fullness over hips narrowing to the ankles. Innovated by Paquin. 1912.

PEG-TOP SLEEVES *Fem.* Sleeves with fullness at shoulder tapering to the wrists. 1850s to 1860s. Revival of Gigot sleeve of 1820s.

PEG-TOP TROUSERS *Masc.* Full cut and pleated into the waist and sloping inwards to the ankle. 1825-1840. Brief revival 1892.

PEIGNOIR *Fem. Fr. peigner - to comb, i.e. combing gown.* Loose long coat of light material for informal wear. From late 18th Cent.

PELERINE *Fem. Fr. pélerin - pilgrim, stranger.* Originally a sleeveless coat worn by pilgrims. In 18th Cent., name given to short cape with long ends which could be worn crossed in front and tied behind. By early 19th Cent., it became a large cape-like collar made in cambric or embroidered muslin. In severe weather, style was made in heavy silk or wool or fur.

PELISSE *Fem. Fr. pelice; It. pelliccia - fur, fur-coat.* An over-garment or coat, introduced in early 18th Cent. as a warm covering over hooped gowns. Made of rich brocade, velvet, heavy satin or silk, lined with fur, with two vertical slits for arms. Worn usually with muff. In early 19th Cent., became more fitted, often having shoulder capes. By late 19th Cent., although still a winter garment, often made of silk or velvet having loose large sleeves.

PELISSE-MANTLE *Fem.* Three-quarter or full-length cloak, cut with draping to form sleeves. 1840s.

PELISSE ROBE *Fem.* A day gown, similar in style to the pelisse. The front entirely fastened with bows or concealed fastenings. First half of 19th Cent. Later called a 'Redingote' dress.

PELISSON *Masc., Fem.* Furred overcape or gown of Middle Ages. 14th to early 16th Cent.

PELLUCE Early word used in 16th Cent. for plush.

PELLURE Early word used for furs.

PELURIN Medieval name describing fur edging on garment or hat.

PENCIL STRIPE Design of thin stripes on woven material, usually two or three warps wide, on contrasting solid colour ground.

PENDICLE *Masc.* Single drop ear-ring as worn by men. 17th Cent.

PENISTON, PENNISTON, PENNYSTONE Coarse woollen cloth, first made in Peniston, Yorkshire. 16th Cent. In use until 19th Cent.

PENNSYLVANIA HAT (See QUAKER HAT)

PEPLOS *Fem. Greek.* The rectangle of fabric hanging from shoulders, forming the bloused section worn over the chiton. It was weighed down by small weights to hang in folds.

PEPLUM In Ancient Greece, the peplum was a simple outer tunic. The modern usage of the word, from 19th Cent. to date, refers usually to decoration, flounce or skirt suspended from bodice or waist.

PEPPER AND SALT Material, usually tweed, designed with twisted black and white threads, giving a speckled effect of contrasting dark and light.

PERCALE Slightly glazed fine calico, often printed with small design. Late 19th Cent.

PERCALINE A printed light cotton. 1848.

PERDITA Mrs. Robinson, the famous actress and mistress of George IV, was noted for her playing of the part 'Perdita' in *A Winter's Tale*. A becoming day-dress was named the 'Perdita chemise'. It had a close-fitting bodice, with a falling collar around a V-neck. Ribbons or buttons were used to close the front and also the tight sleeves. A wide sash was tied at the waist and hung down the back. The 'Perdita Handkerchief' was a pleated collar made of three layers of very fine silk. 1783.

PERFUME A sweet-smelling odour for personal use made available in liquid, solid and powder form since early times. Containers have been in varying forms in Europe since the Renaissance. Scent balls or pomanders hung from women's girdles in 15th and 16th Cents. Henry VIII had a container hidden in the top of a cane. In 17th Cent., gloves worn by men and women were scented and women carried perfumed fans. Jessamine and perfumed pulvil powder was much used in 18th Cent. Eau de Cologne and lavender water have been used since this time. By the 20th Cent., the marketing of perfume has become a profitable and important part of the fashion world. (See also PO-MANDER).

PERIWIG Common name for a wig, derived through centuries from Middle Ages to 18th Cent. *Fr. perruque.*

E. peruke, then perwyke, later periwig and finally wig.
Worn in Restoration period over shaven or bald heads
after Roundheads had changed their allegiance. (See
WIG).

PERKALE *Fr. Cambric -muslin.* Early 19th Cent.

PERMANENT WAVING Expensive electrical method
of waving hair, perfected in 1906 by London hairdresser,
Nestlé. From 1920s it became available more cheaply.
After the Second World War, improved methods using
cold lotions were devised, which are less time-consuming
and safe.

PERO Roman patrician's shoe; also thonged leather
boot worn by peasants. 12th and 13th Cents.

PERPETUANA Glossy woollen material. Late 16th
Cent. Worn notably by Puritans in 17th and 18th
Cents. in American Colonies.

PERSIAN VEST *Masc.* Long simple black cassock
introduced by Charles II to restrict extravagance in
Court fashion. It is regarded as the forerunner of
simpler styles that followed. 1666.

PERUKE (See PERIWIG)

PETASUS *Masc.* Flat hat worn in Ancient Greece
for travelling, with brim and chin strap.

PETENLAIR *Fem.* Three-quarter, thigh or knee-
length jacket with sac-back; elbow length or three-
quarter sleeves and long decorated panel or stomacher
in front. A plain skirt or 'petticoat' of ground length
completed the total appearance. 1740s-1770.

PETER PAN COLLAR Flat round-ended collar of
tunic worn by character, Peter Pan, in J.M. Barrie's
play of that name. A simple pleasing finish to blouses
and children's wear; the name has been adopted for a
lasting style from the early 1900s.

PETERSHAM CLOTH A napped heavy woollen
cloth suitable for overcoating. 1904.

PETERSHAM RIBBON A slightly ribbed quality
ribbon. From 1840.

PETIT BORD *Fem.* Small brimmed decorated hat
for evening wear, worn at the back of the head. Early
19th Cent. In 1840, changed style becoming more like
a turban or toque. Until 1850.

PETIT POINT Fine embroidery worked decoratively
on canvas or linen with not less than sixteen stitches to
the inch.

PETTICOAT, PETTICOTE, PETTYCOTT An undercoat or gown worn by both sexes, shorter than top
garment. 14th-16th Cent. By 16th Cent., exclusively
female, sometimes tied by front lacing. By stages, it
developed from simple materials in 17th and 18th
Cents., until in 19th Cent. it became more elaborate;
much frilled and flounced by 1890s. In 20th Cent., the
form has become simpler and close-fitting.

PETTICOAT BREECHES *Masc.* A French fashion
introduced into England two years before the Restoration, 1658. Extremely wide and worn under a short
doublet. Decorated with many bunches of ribbon loops.
Worn above cannions of white linen and lace ruffles
which were tied around the knees. This style preceded

the simpler 'Persian Vest' or cassock, introduced later
by Charles II in 1666. It was worn with a jacket called
the JACK-A-NAPES.

PETTICOAT LANE Streets and alleys of this London
area were the centre for selling of old clothes, especially
in 19th Cent.

PEWTER BUTTONS Commonplace hollow buttons
worn in late 18th Cent.

PHRYGIUM, PHRYGIAN 1) Cap worn originally
by people of Asia Minor and Greece 12th Cent.
When Romans freed slaves they allowed them to wear
the Phrygian bonnet and this head-wear became a
symbol of liberty. Round in shape, with a point on top
which falls forwards, it was adopted by the French
Revolutionists as the Cap of Liberty.

2) The cap of white wool worn by Popes of the
Middle Ages which later became the papal tiara.

PHYSICAL WIG *Masc.* Worn by professional men,
doctors, lawyers and so on, in place of a full-bottomed
wig. Swept back from the forehead without a parting,
was frizzed or arranged in rolled curls and shaped like
a long bob. 1750-1800.

PICARDS *Fem.* A slipper made in the 'French'
current style of the 17th Cent.

PICCADILLY COLLAR *Masc.* Worn with formal
or evening-dress. High starched with pointed turned-
back tabs. 1880s to early 20th Cent.

PICCADILLY JOHNNY, MASHER *Masc.* Slang
description of dandyish men, who adopted the new
fashion of growing long hanging whiskers after the
Crimean War. 1850s.

PICCADILLY WEEPERS In 19th Cent. until beginning of 20th Cent., undertakers' attendants and
chief mourners at a funeral, wore long black streamers
from the hat, known as 'weepers'. Long side whiskers,
adopted by the fashionable young men in the 1860s,
were known popularly as 'Piccadilly Weepers' or
'Dundreary Whiskers' and worn as late as 1870 when a
smaller neater crop was adopted.

PICKADIL, PICKADILLY, PECADILLY Fashionable form of tabbed or scalloped decoration applied to
neck, shoulders, wrists and edges of doublets. Mid-
16th Cent. The name used also for stiffened frame at
the neck, which had outward protruding tabs on which
a decorative collar or ruff rested. Early 17th Cent.

PICTURE HAT *Fem.* Very large wide-brimmed hat,
usually lined, trimmed with broad band, bow, buckle
or feathers and worn with a tilt. Gainsborough painted
the Duchess of Devonshire, 1783, wearing such a hat.

PIECE DYED Fabrics dyed by the piece or roll
after weaving.

PIEDMONT SAC *Fem.* Back-pleated gown based
on Italian variation of sac. (See SAC, SAQUE).

PIERROT 1) Name of character, Fr. dim. of Pierre,
in Italian Commedia dell'Arte, 17th Cent., who wore a
white costume with large befrilled tunic and voluminous
trousers.

2) *Fem.* Fitting low-necked jacket, with three-quarter

or full-length sleeves, worn over a petticoat bordered or flounced to match the hem of the jacket. The jacket and skirt worn together was called the 'Caraco' day dress. Late 18th Cent. (See CARACO GOWN).

PIERROT CAPE *Fem.* Three-quarter length cloak, characterised by satin 'Pierrot' ruff over a small shoulder-cape. 1892.

PIERROT RUFF *Fem.* Fur-bordered ruff on outdoor capes. 1892.

PIFFERARO BONNET *Fem.* Bonnet with blunt high rounded crown and uptilted narrow brim. Feather trimming. 1877.

PIGEON'S WING *Masc. Fr. Aile de Pigeon.* Method of hair-dressing the sides of a wig or toupee, sometimes with rolled curls or puffs over the ears. The front at the top and upper sides were left smooth. A style worn with various queues. 1740-1760.

PIG-TAIL WIG *Masc.* Wig with hanging tail or queue, bound with black ribbon. Tied at top and bottom of tail with black ribbon bows. Late 18th Cent.

PIKED SHOE, PEAKED SHOE *Masc., Fem.* Extravagantly long, spear-pointed shoes, a fashion prevalent in the 14th Cent.; revived 1460-1480. Worn in England and Europe. Known as CRAKOW in Poland, POULAINE in France. Also COPPED.

PILCH *Masc., Fem.* Simple over-gown, close-fitting, lined with fur for warmth in winter. 14th and 15th Cents. Name of protective flannel garment for covering nether part of young children. 17th Cent.

PILEUS *Gk. Pilos.* Close small hat with chin-strap worn by athletes and militia in Greece, Etruria, Ancient Rome.

PILLION *Masc.* Hat worn by clergy. 14th Cent.

PILOT CLOTH Hard-wearing thick woollen cloth with nap on one side, of dark blue, used mainly for naval jackets and overcoats. 19th Cent.

PILOT JACKET (See PEA JACKET).

PINAFORE Originally a protective washable garment worn by children. 19th Cent. This developed into women's sleeveless garment, usually with low square, round or V-neck, worn over a blouse or sleeved top, or by itself in warm weather. 1960s on.

PIN MONEY Victorian name for rich woman's pocket money. (see NEEDLE MONEY).

PINCE-NEZ Spectacles or eyeglasses held in front of the eyes by a spring-clip on the nose.

PINCHBECK Copper and zinc alloy invented by London watchmaker, Christopher Pinchbeck, 1700. Used for making buttons and imitation jewellery. A brass or gold coloured wash applied to the metal giving an appearance of gold.

PINKING Decorative method of making a series of small holes or slits to form designs on clothes or even shoes. 15th, 16th and 17th Cents. In modern usage, serrated pinking shears are employed to neaten unhemmed seams or raw edges on inside of garments.

PINNER *Fem.* Small dainty and often beautifully worked apron pinned over the front of a gown. 17th and 18th Cents.

PINNERS *Fem.* Long side flaps of indoor cap which were pinned up on either side. 17th Cent. - 1750. Later, name given to actual cap, although the side lappets or flaps were later omitted and the head-dress became a frilled circular shape. 18th Cent.

PINSON *Masc., Fem.* Light indoor shoe or slipper. 14th, 15th and 16th Cents. (See PUMP).

PIPED SEAMS Narrow cord was first used as edging in seams of muslin dresses, early 19th Cent. Later copied by narrow edging of cord on coats and men's waistcoats.

PIPES Small pipeclay rolls used for heating and redressing the curls of wigs. 17th and 18th Cents.

PIPKIN *Fem.* Small flat-crowned hat with pleated sides and small brim, a narrow hatband, jewelled and sometimes trimmed with feather mount. Late 16th Cent.

PIQUÉ *Fr.* Stout ribbed fabric of silk, rayon or cotton. Used for women's dresses, men's shirts, waistcoats and articles requiring a stiff neat and crisp appearance. 20th Cent.

PIQUE DEVANT *Masc.* Short pointed beard, worn with brushed-up whiskers or moustache. (See paintings). Elizabethan period. 1570-1600.

PITH HELMET Hat of pith cork from India, covered with white cotton and lined with green. Light in weight and impervious to water and air. First worn by British army, 1860. Hindu - topee, topi.

PLACKARD, PLACARD *Masc.* Frontal piece of cloth, filling in the cut-away gap of a low-fronted jacket or doublet. End of 15th Cent. to mid-16th Cent. *Fem.* Embroidered inserted front panel of long loose overgown. 1350-early 1500s.

PLACKET *Fem.* Opening usually in skirt or trousers, on which buttons, snaps, hooks and eyes or zip are placed for ease of fit.

PLAID Travelling rug or shawl of tartan pattern. Scotland. 17th Cent.

PLASTIC Man-made material used in making of costume jewellery, i.e. bracelets, buckles, brooches, in Art Deco style of 1930s. Some of these have become collectors' items.

PLASTRON *Masc. Fr. Plastron - breast-plate.* Protective frontal breast-plate in suit of armour. Padded protective front of fencer's costume. *Fem.* Contrasting inserted front panel of dress. 19th Cent.

PLATED BUTTONS *Masc.* Silver-plated buttons used for men's coats, so named to distinguish these from gilt or pinchbeck. 1700s.

PLATFORM SOLE *Fem.* High raised cork sole to shoes fashionable for economic reasons at end of World War II; revived in 1970s for beach wear.

PLATOK *Fem. Russian.* Silk summer head scarf, worn by peasant women.

THE PLANTAGENET KINGS named after 'plante de genet'. 1154-1485.
THE NORMAN INFLUENCE, 1189-1199.

HENRY II, 1154-89 and RICHARD I, 1189-1199.

The gowns were well fitting and graceful. Some had back-lacing. Belts were worn to emphasize slim waists. A head covering or Barbette was introduced in 1170 and the Wimple in 1190. During the 12th Cent., new and costly materials were worn by noblemen. A full semi-circular cloak with cord fastening was worn on top of the under-tunic or robe.

PLANTAGENET DRESS AFTER THE NORMAN INFLUENCE

From Edward III, 1327. Drawing A. The woman wears a fluted Cap and Barbette. The sleeves of her Cote or Kirtle are tightly buttoned. Above this, she wears a Surcote or Suckeny, made of high quality fabric. In drawing B, the girl also has a sleeveless Surcote, but tucked into a belt for easy movement, 1329. Drawing C shows the female English head-dress, with wide Templers or Bosses enclosing the hair, and worn with a veil, 1423. Diagrams D and E show men wearing versions of the Cote-hardie, a knee-length over garment. The sleeves were sometimes open and wide to the elbow. Belts were worn low at hip level after 1360. Hats were made of beaver skins from early 14th. Cent. The figure in D wears his hat above a Chaperon or hood with a cape. Young persons were clad in clothes similar to those worn by adults.

HENRY V, 1413-1422. A lady of rank with a Horned head-dress and veil. The gown is trimmed and the cape lined with ermine. The male attendant has a long tunic with wide sleeves and a high neck. He wears a bowl-cropped hairstyle. In the 15th Cent. the long male robe was gradually laid aside for a shorter tunic.

HENRY VI, 1422-1471. Female gowns now have long Trains or Traynes. The left hand figure has a Horned head-dress with veil. The right hand figure shows the Butterfly head-dress - a wire frame with a gauze veil spread over it. These were fastened to a small cap worn to the back of the head. The drawings are based on brass-rubbings, early 15th Cent.

HENRY VI, 1422-1471. During this period the nobility and the rich used sumptuous materials. The man wears a fur-trimmed Jerkin with a Burlet, padded roll of a Chaperon, on his head. His shoes are pointed. The lady's dress is full and also fur-trimmed. She has a Butterfly head-dress. The guard has a simple helmet. His legs are protected by greaves.

PLEATED TROUSERS *Masc.* Baggy trousers, originally inspired by those worn by Russian Cossacks, 1814. Fullness was pleated into the waistband and at the ankles by a drawstring. By 1820, the garment was simplified with less material and drawstrings omitted. Straps used under the instep. 1840. Also COSSACKS.

PLEATING Pressed series of folds of material, used for decorative purpose or greater movement.

PLIMSOLL Canvas rubber-soled beach shoes worn first in 1870s. So named in 1876 with reference to the Plimsoll Line Act which required the loadline on ships to be so marked. The join of sole and upper on this new type of shoe was fastened all round with a line of rubber.

PLUME Until the reign of Elizabeth II, who discontinued the custom, young ladies 'presented' to the English sovereign wore a head-dress of three upstanding ostrich plumes with attached tulle veil.

PLUMPERS Small thin balls of cork held in the cheeks to fill out cavities in sunken cheeks. Late 17th to early 19th Cents.

PLUS FOURS *Masc.* Easy-fitting tweed or worsted knicker-bockers, worn for golf and walking. The material at the kneeband was four inches wider than usual measurement. Often worn with Prince of Wales' 'Fair Isle' sweater. 1920s-1930s.

PLUSH Fabric, silk or cotton, with high pile, longer and softer than velvet.

POACHER'S POCKET Pocket contained inside a countryman's smock.

POCKET 1) Small bag or pouch inserted into or upon a garment.

2) *Masc.* Before the Middle Ages, small bags or pouches were used for carrying money as there were no pockets in garments before that time. Later valuables were carried in a handkerchief, or in a small box concealed in the opening of trunk hose. By 16th Cent., a form of pocket was introduced into breeches and into coats and waistcoats by 18th Cent. Some were protected by flaps. Over centuries variety of types have provided decoration as well as use. Masc. names included - Bellows, Breast, Caddie, Cross, Fob, Hip, Pistole, In the Pleats, Poachers, Saddle Bag, Salt Box, Slashed.

3) *Fem.* Prior to 17th Cent., pockets were usually two bags sewn on to a band tied round the waist. After 1650, pouches were inserted into side seams of the gown.

POCKET HOOP *Fem.* The smallest size of hoops worn in 1720s and later in 1770s.

POCKETBOOK *Fem.* A reticule, or lady's decorative drawstring handbag, made in soft materials, had been used since early 19th Cent., due to the absence of pockets in women's dress. This was replaced by a small folding leather purse shaped like a book in 1890s. It was closed by a metal ornamental catch. By the early 20th Cent., the style of a leather pouch, used for carrying military orders, was copied and from this time the pocketbook shape developed into a more spacious

functional handbag. *Fr. PORTMONNAIE.* (See SABRETACHE).

POET'S COLLAR *Masc.* Romantic style of unstarched collar of shirt preferred by some notable artists and poets in early 19th Cent., including Lord Byron, 1788-1824; John Keats, 1795-1821; Percy Bysshe Shelley, 1792-1822.

POINT LACE Lace made entirely with a needle.

POINTS *Masc.* Ties with metal tips or tags, aglets, used for fastening hose or breeches to doublet. 16th and 17th Cents. Also used by men and women for adornment of sleeves in bunches and bows. 17th Cent.

POIRET PAUL 1880-1944. Famous French dress designer. Most remembered for his work in 1910, including the hobble-skirt and his tunics. (See COUTURE).

POKE *M.E. Poque - Bag, sack, pouch.* Name given to equivalent of pocket. 1590-1610.

POKE BONNET6 *Fem.* Bonnet with coal-scuttle shaped brim, protruding over face, first worn over cap and with ribbon ties. Late 18th Cent. - 19th Cent.

POKING STICKS Sticks of bone and/or wood which, when heated, were used for setting the pleats in ruffs. 16th Cent. Later steel was used.

POLO COAT *Masc.* Casual sports coat, usually camel colour, worn during non-participating periods of sport. 20th Cent.

POLO COLLAR *Masc.* Stiffly starched white shirt collar. End of 19th Cent.

POLO NECK Name used for soft high collar, turned over all round the neck of pullovers or shirts. Much favoured for comfortable casual knitwear. 20th Cent.

POLONAISE The word implies garments of Polish origin.

1) *Masc.* Man's overcoat of the late 18th Cent. was decorated with braid and tassels and called 'Brandenburg' after the Prussian military uniform of the Brandenburg troops. Ladies' jackets were also decorated with braid and tassels.

2) *Fem.* Polonaise gown consisted of a fitting bodice with three panniers below waist, looped at back and sides. 1770-1780. The bustle style, in 1870-1880, was similar, with the material gathered up behind over the bustle.

3) *Fem.* Boots had high heels with hanging side tassels. Early 19th Cent.

POLONIA *Masc., Fem.* Extremely high heel of boot or shoe, a fashion worn in 17th Cent.

POLVERINO *Fem.* Loose, unlined silk cloak, sometimes lined and hooded. 1846.

POMADE Scented paste or ointment made from apples and grease. Later used as a hair dressing.

POMANDER Spherical or circular flat container, usually of gold or silver, holding a ball of scented substances. Perforated, and suspended from the girdle or worn on a chain around the neck. Oranges pierced with cloves were also carried as additional protection against infection. 16th and 17th Cents. Gradually superseded by 'vinaigrettes' in 18th Cent.

POMPADOUR   Name given to fashions and features favoured by the Marquise de Pompadour, 1721-1764, mistress of Louis XV of France. Some of these styles re-emerge periodically. Favoured items were small dainty aprons; a square-necked bodice with tight elbow-length frilled sleeves; the colour of claret purple; a high-dressed hairstyle; high slender curving heel with small base; a brightly patterned polonaise worn with a plain skirt; laces, flowered taffeta and velvet ribbon bows. Mid-18th Cent.

POMPADOURS   Fine fans made during the reigns of the first two Georges. 1714-1760. They were gilded, set with jewels and decorated with fine paintings resembling the work of Watteau and later of Boucher.

POMPEY   *Masc.* Wig. (See PHYSICAL WIG).

POMPOM   *Fem.* Term given to 'Pompadour' hair or cap decoration. Made of feathers, twists of lace, tinsel, lace, even butterflies, etc. The ornament was worn centrally on cap or above high-dressed hair. 1740s.

PONCHO   Simple square of blanket cloth originally used by South American Indians as a garment by day and a covering at night. Usually brightly coloured, with hole in centre for the head. Name given to men's and women's cape-like cloaks with wide sleeves. 1860s. Adopted as an attractive cheap over-garment by young people and children, 1960s onwards.

PONGEE   Silk material from India, strong and of a natural light fawn colour. Resembling TUSSORE. Late 19th Cent.

PONTIFICIAL   A clasp. 15th Cent. (See OUCH).

PONY-SKIN   Hardwearing flat glossy fur from young animals. Introduced early 20th Cent. Black, dark brown, beige. Used for women's coats, jackets, waistcoats.

POODLE CLOTH   Fabric with looped textured surface, resembling coat of clipped French poodle dog. 20th Cent.

PORCELAIN BUTTONS   *Masc.* Decorative fastenings on silk coats and waistcoats. 18th Cent.

POPLIN   Fine corded material originally from Ireland, in silk and fine wool. 17th Cent. on.

PORK PIE HAT   *Fem.* Small round hat fashionable in 1850s. Usually decorated with single feather.

PORT CANNONS   (See CANNONS).

PORTE-MONNAIE   (See POCKETBOOK).

PORTE-JUPE POMPADOUR   *Fem.* Under-belt with eight hanging hooked strings for lifting hem of skirt above ground when walking out-of-doors. 1860s.

PORTMANTEAU   Bag for cloaks. Originally a large sac for carrying an important valuable cloak when travelling. 16th and 17th Cents.

PORTUGUESE FARTHINGALE   *Fem.* A style of hooped skirt which was brought to England by Catherine of Braganza, the wife of Charles II, which lasted only a few years. Flat at the front and back, with width at the side. It was not regarded as very fashionable. 1662-1668.

POT   Term designating any type of open helmet worn by pikemen. 17th Cent.

POT BOARD   The open shelf or board for helmets on the lower part of a court or livery cupboard. 17th Cent.

POSTICHE   Something added, artificial. Coil of hair, hair-piece, wig.

POULAINE   *Fr. peaked, piked.* Fashionable shoe-style with extended toe; worn in Poland, Italy and later Western Europe. Late 14th Cent. - early 15th Cent. In spite of laws curbing their flamboyant wear, there was a revival -1460-1480. Also called CRACOW after Polish city. (See CRACKOW).

POULT DE SOIE   Corded shiny silk fabric of high quality mixed with alpaca. 19th Cent.

POURPOINT   *Masc.* Close-fitting jerkin, padded. 14th Cent. Predecessor of doublet. (See GIPON).

POWDERING GOWN   *Masc.* Loose garment, or wrapper, worn for protection of clothes when wigs were powdered. 18th Cent.

POWER LACE   Light elasticised lace made on machine invented in 1960s. Used for foundation garments from 1966.

PRÊT-À-PORTER   *Fr.* Term for ready-to-wear clothes, an exciting market established after World War II.

PORTE-JUPE POMPADOUR BELT   The suspenders hooked up the voluminous skirt for walking or in bad weather.

PRÉTINTAILLES *Fr.* Appliqué motifs of lace and coloured fabric pieces attached to gowns as ornamentation and for enhancing decorative appearance. Late 17th Cent.

PRINCE ALBERT 19th Cent. (See ALBERT).

PRINCE OF WALES' JACKET *Masc.* As worn by Edward, son of Queen Victoria. Loose-fitting jacket resembling Reefer with three buttons.

PRINCE REGENT 1811-1820. Afterwards George IV until 1830.

PRINCESS DRESS *Fem.* Dress-style fashionable in late 1870s; without a waist seam, the bodice and skirt being made in one, flared towards the hem, giving a gentle flowing line over the waist and hips. The simplicity of this design has been used repeatedly in the 20th Cent.

PRODDS Crossbow gun used at time of Elizabeth I. 1533-1603.

PRUNELLA Black woollen material with twilled weave. 17th, 18th and 19th Cents. Used for legal, clerical and academic gowns.

PRUSSIAN COLLAR *Masc.* Shallow coat collar, stand-fall in cut, with ends not quite meeting in front. 19th Cent.

PUBLICATIONS The first fashion publication which appeared in Paris was *Le Cabinet des Modes,* in 1785. This included, fortnightly, male and female costume, hair-dressing, interior decoration and information on carriages! Within a year, the name was changed to *Le Magasin des Modes Françaises et Anglaises.* It continued, despite the Revolution, until 1790, when it became *Le Journal de la Mode et du Goût,* lasting for about seven years, then becoming *Le Journal des Dames et des Modes,* continuing for forty years more.

In England, *The Lady's Magazine* appeared in 1770, with engaging pocket-book engravings of the latest hats and dresses drawn by many good artists. The most outstanding, true fashion paper produced in England in 1794 was *The Gallery of Fashion,* which included four plates every fortnight. This luxurious periodical lasted until 1803.

By the early 19th century, magazines became more numerous in European capitals and America and sometimes issuing unacknowledged copies of Paris original engravings.

The Englishwoman's Domestic Magazine, 1853 and *The Queen,* 1861, were founded by S.O. Beeton, the husband of the famous Household Management authority, Mrs. Beeton; these two journals sustained an enviable reputation for many years.

Berlin established the international paper *Die Modenwelt* in 1860s with marked success and from Vienna in the 1880s emerged *Wiener Mode,* and *Chic Parisien.*

Among the important American fashion magazines produced in the 19th Cent., are *Harper's Bazaar* 1867, *The Delineator* 1879 and *Vogue* 1893.

Publications of the 20th Cent. enter a different era as at the beginning of the century experiments with photography commenced; and by 1910 soft focus and diffused lighting were both used to enhance a new portrayal of the fashion world.

Trade Publicity:

A trade periodical of great chic was published in France, 1912 until the 1920s, called *Gazette du Bon Ton,* with hand-coloured plates showing models of such designers as Paul Poiret. The artists included famous names such as Raoul Dufy, Georges Barbier and Pierre Brissaud. In Britain *The Ambassador,* 1946, was produced and sold to subscribers, whilst in the U.S.A. *Women's Wear Daily* is widely exported.

PUG HOOD, SHORT HOOD *Fem.* Soft hood, usually lined in contrasting colour. Pleated fullness from centre back. The edge of hood folded back to frame the face and tied under the chin by ribbons matching the lining. 17th-18th Cent.

PUGAREE, PUGGREE *Masc.* Hindu turban, using a length of material up to twenty-five yards long, wound round the head.

PULTNEY CAP *Fem.* Indoor wired cap, with two short hanging lappets at back. 1760.

PUMP Low-cut indoor shoe of soft leather in court style, with no heel or very low heel. Worn since 16th Cent., but very fashionable in 18th Cent. *Masc.* Black leather with bow or buckle. *Fem.* Heel-less, of satin or silk, fastened by cross-over ribbons over foot and at ankle. Until 1830.

PUNCH WORK Decoration made by embroidered holes in fabric.

PUNK LOOK A style of dress worn by a large number of unemployed young peope in the late 1970s. They favoured pale faces with excessive eye make-up and heavy lipstick. Black leather jackets and jeans pierced with metal studs and having many zippered pockets were worn as the prevailing uniform. Other clothing was artificially torn and held together with safety pins, the latter often used as necklaces and earrings. Bicycle chains were also carried. Fem. 'Chicks' wore very tight sweaters, with side slit skirts and spike-heeled sandals. The appearance implied a demand for attention.

PURFLE Border or trimmed hem of a gown. Early 16th Cent.

PURITAN DRESS In 17th Cent., adaptation of current styles to simple restrained garments, worn by those who emigrated to North America. Worsted and holland materials, plain felt hats with little trimming. Colours - sober - greys, browns, black, purple and white. Woollen hose. Plain shoes.

PURPLE *Latin - Purpura.* Colour formed from the shell-fish, purpura, that yielded the deep crimson colour which is the 'true' purple.

PURSE Before 14th Cent., a pouch. Later a small bag. By 18th Cent., a knitted stocking shape was used. In 19th Cent., metal fastenings were invented and various containers evolved.

PUSSY-CAT BONNET *Fem.* Fur bonnet made of catskin. Early 19th Cent.

PUSSY-CAT BOW *Fem.* Soft scarf tie of woman's shirt-blouse, which is part of the garment and provides a neat appearance at neck opening of jackets. 1970s-980s.

PUTTEE *Masc.* Strip of cloth wrapped spirally round the leg from ankle to knee. Worn by infantry in World War I. East Indian origin.

PYJAMAS, PAJAMA Coloured suit of light-weight material originating from India for informal leisure wear. 17th Cent. Adopted at end of 19th Cent. for men's sleeping wear in place of night-shirts. By mid-20th Cent., adaptations of style were being worn by women and children, both for casual and nightwear.

QUIZZING GLASS *Gold rimmed glass worn on a ribbon. Fashionable for military men and civilians in the late 18th and early 19th Centuries.*

QUADRILLE CAP *Fem.* Caps of light muslin or gauze, the lappets of which were embroidered with the aces of hearts, clubs, diamonds, spades. A brief light-hearted fashion called 'Quadrille Heads'. Late 18th Cent.

QUAIL-PIPE BOOT *Masc.* Tall boot of soft leather, which formed soft wrinkles and folds down the leg. 16th and 17th Cents.

QUAKER DRESS Quakers in Europe, as the Puritans in Colonial America, adopted no specific form of dress. Over-ornamentation was avoided, although good quality well-made garments were worn. In the 17th and 18th Cents., wigs, silver shoe-buckles, lace trimmed linen and even bright coloured cloaks in the current mode were allowed. *Masc.* 1) Quakers, or 'Pennsylvania' Hat, also named 'Wide Awake', 1780s. 2) Three-cornered hat. 3) All-round wide-brimmed variety with low crown, decorated with ribbon and small buckle. 4) A beaver hat with rolling brim, usually in grey or brown. 18th Cent. *Fem.* The 'Quaker Bonnet' or 'Joan' was a close-fitting indoor cap, shaped like a baby's bonnet. Often frilled and tied under the chin. 18th Cent. The 'Wagon Bonnet' large outdoor style, so-called because the large

enfolding brim resembled the shape of a covered wagon. The top of the crown was gathered; a cape was sometimes attached made of the same material. Late 18th, early 19th Cent.

QUARTER Name given to side of a shoe.

QUARTERED CAP *Masc.* Headwear, worn by boys, with flat circular crown divided into sections or quarters. Stiff headband, with or without peak or visor. Sometimes tasselled. Second half of 18th Cent.

QUATRE-FOIL SPUR LEATHERS *Fr.* Leather attachments worn on lower front of cavalier boots for concealment of the fastening of spurs. Shaped in quatre-foil design of four leaves. 17th Cent.

QUEEN ELIZABETH WIG Elizabeth I owned many wigs. She had fair hair as a young woman but preferred auburn, red and henna colouring. The wigs were dressed with ornaments of pearls, jewels and feathers. 16th Cent.

QUERPO *Masc.* Spanish word denoting a man in a state of casual 'undress' without an upper garment or cloak. 17th Cent.

QUERPO HOOD *Fem.* Plain soft hood or head covering for undressed hair. 17th Cent.

QUEUE *Masc. Fr. queue - tail.* Hanging tail of a wig. In the late 18th Cent., as the fashion for wearing wigs waned and natural hair was encouraged to grow, the 'ribbon tied' queue was adopted, particularly by military men as the hair was growing.

QUIFF *Masc.* Short lock of hair, dressed to hang over forehead. British. Sometimes worn by servants and general workers when hat-less - hence the saying of 'touching the forelock' to the gentry. Late 19th Cent.

QUILLING Type of frilling made by partially sewing down finely pleated tulle or lace, allowing the edge to remain in open folds. 19th Cent.

QUILLON DAGGER A type of blade made with a cross-guard.

QUILLONS The cross-guard of a sword or dagger.

QUILTED PETTICOAT *Fem.* Exposed skirt part of dress. 1710-1750.

QUILTING A padded surface made of three layers -the outer or right side of material, the middle padding or wadding and the inner lining. The three layers are stitched together often in fancy or geometrical patterns. Much used in the 18th Cent., in modern times for many purposes, i.e. jackets, waistcoats, dressing gowns, linings.

QUINTIN Delicate lawn made originally in Quintin, Brittany. 17th Cent.

QUINTISE *Fem.* Trailing scarf worn from lady's head-dress; also favour presented to knight who attached it to his helmet when jousting. Also CIMIER, COINTOISE, COINTISEC, LAMBREQUIN.

QUISSERS Armour worn on the thighs.

QUITASOL *Sp. parasol.* Large fan, later parasol, of oiled, coloured silk for hot climate, affording protection and mobility for making cooling breeze. Used in Americas. 18th Cent.

QUIVER *O.F., quivre.* Long case, suspended over one shoulder by strap, for holding arrows.

QUIZZING FANS Fans provided with peep-holes. Covered with transparent material, when open the fan showed only a pattern of perforations along the upper border. Behind such a fan, the holder would miss nothing of the risqué plays or behaviour of the mid-18th Cent. fashionable world, although appearing modest. Later, fans were made with a quizzing glass fitted above the pivot. 18th Cent.

QUIZZING GLASS *Masc., Fem.* A monocle suspended on a neck-chain. Late 18th and early 19th Cents. Canes fitted with similar glasses into the head, were in fashionable use by fops of the early 19th Cent.

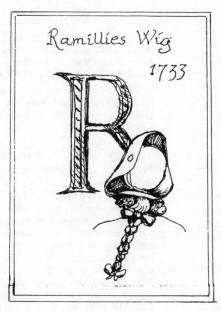

Ramillies Wig 1733

RAMILLIES WIG   *Worn by officers of the Guards, 1733. Made of plaited hair and tied with ribbon.*

RABAGAS BONNET   *Fem.* Small bonnet with narrow turned-up brim. High-crowned with various trimmings, feathers, flowers, ribbons, falling behind. Ties under chin with large bow.1871.

RABAT   Collar of white lawn edged with lace. Examples seen in paintings of Sir Anthony Van Dyck, 1599-1641. (See REBATO, FALLING BAND).

RABATINE   Wider version of RABAT; sometimes called a VAN DYCK. 17th Cent.

RACCOON   Long-haired fur from light-coloured mammal of North America. Bulky coats made from the skins were popular in the 1920s, for wearing in open cars and winter events in sports stadiums of the U.S. To date *now* used, with shearing and expert cutting, to imitate other furs.

RAFFIA   Treated smooth fibre from leaves of Madagascar raffia palm. Used for hats, baskets, bags.

RAGLAN   Fitzroy James Henry Somerset, 1st Baron, 1788-1855. British Field Marshal, commanded the British troops in Crimean War. Items of clothing were given his name as a compliment.

Boot: Mid-thigh length of soft black leather. 1850.

Cape: Loose, single-breasted over-garment distinguished by simple wide sleeve, reaching from underarm, front and back to neckline. Unflapped pockets. 1857 onwards.

Overcoat: Full long coat with Raglan sleeve. Fly-front fastening, of water-proof material. 1898.

Sleeve: Characterised by elimination of separate shoulder seam, being carried up the arm to join the collar at the neck. 1857.

RAIL   *Fem.* A piece of square material gathered or folded. Worn like a small shawl around the neck. 16th Cent. - late 17th Cent. Also RAYLE.

RAILROAD TROUSERS   *Masc.* Trousers made of material with vertical stripes. Popular name given at a time when the new railways were of great interest to all. 1837-1850.

RAILWAY POCKETS   *Fem.* As travel by rail became more usual and as yet handbags were not carried, women placed their light valuables and money in flat inner bags. These had a side opening, attached with tapes around the waist, and were worn under the crinoline dress as protection from pick-pockets. 1856 onwards.

RAMILLIES COCK *Masc.* Hat worn with Ramillies wig, both of which named after the Battle of Ramillies, 1706, an English victory won under the Duke of Marlborough. The brim of the hat was cocked into three. The deep back flap rose higher than the two side flaps which protruded forwards. 18th Cent.

RAMILLIES WIG *Masc.* Military style wig worn by Guards and admiring imitators. Distinguished by long queue tied at nape of neck and at base. Later, it was looped up and secured with comb or bow to the back of the wig. Early 18th Cent. -1780s.

RAMPOOR-CHUDDAR *Fem.* Fashionable shawl, imported from India, of fine twilled woollen material. Popular colours - red and white. 1850-1900.

RANELAGH MOB *Fem.* Fashionably informal style of wearing a large gauze handkerchief as head-dress. Folded diagonally over the head with the point hanging behind. The two side ends were then tied under the chin, taken to the back and hung down at the back. It was not a mob cap. 1760s.

RAPIER Light slender sword used for thrusting. Unknown origin.

RAPLOCH Homespun undyed woollen material made in Scotland. 16th Cent.

RAPPER Short sword used in traditional North of England sword dances.

RATEEN Thick twilled material of wool used for capes, coats, dresses. 17th Cent. Coarse woollen cloths of 18th Cent.

RATINET Thin twilled material, resembling thicker rateen. 18th Cent.

RATIONALS *Fem.* Sensible knickerbockers introduced for cycling and outdoor sports wear. 1890s.

RAYÉ *Fr. - striped.* Term, now obsolete, used for pin-striped materials.

RAYLE *Fem. Fr. - couvrechef.* Loose light-weight piece of material, worn over head and upper bodice, indoors or out. From Anglo-Saxon times.

RAYON Artificial silk made from cellulose. 20th Cent.

RAYONNE *Fem.* Hood worn in American Colonies, usually black, of corded silk. Lined with contrasting coloured silk, usually striped. The front edge of the hood was turned back to frame the face and tied under the chin with ribbons. Resembles Capuchin and Pug Hood of same period. Late 16th - early 17th Cent.

READY-MADE, READY-TO-WEAR Ready-made clothes, frocks and coats were available for the working classes by the end of the 18th Cent., but were of poor material. It was not until the 1830s, when better quality garments were produced, that the middle classes - mainly women - purchased these. Most professional men continued to have suits made to measure up to the mid-20th Cent.

Amongst early department stores supplying ready-made clothes were:-

Kendal Milne and Faulkner - Manchester. 1836.

Bainbridge's - Newcastle. 1845.

Swan & Edgar, Dickins & Jones, Peter Jones - Developed and expanded in London. 1855-1875.

Bon Marché - Paris. 1860.

Macy's - New York. 1860.

Wanamaker's - Philadelphia. 1876.

REBANINGES Embroideries, laces. 14th Cent.

REBATO *Fem.* Stiffened, semi-circular, white collar worn round back and sides. Used as a wired support for large ruff above a low-necked bodice. Pinned usually at the shoulders to keep it in place. 1580-1635.

REBOUX 'Maison Reboux'. Parisian milliner who created and made famous small cloche hat for women after World War I. Trimming restrained to single ribbon band or single clip. (See COUTURE).

REBOZO *Fem.* Long scarf or piece of material worn by Mexican and South American women for centuries. Used as a covering shawl, for marketing and carrying small children, etc.

RÉCAMIER, Mme. Leader of fashion with Mme. Tallien of the Parisien social set 'Les Merveilleuses'. From 1790, after the Revolution, their followers abandoned such accessories as panniers, bum-rolls, even corsets and petticoats. They introduced the style known as *robe en chemise*, which resembled a simple under-garment. These gowns, made of sheer muslin material, were worn over flesh-coloured close-fitting garments resembling modern tights. Open Grecian-style sandals complemented the costume. The material of the dress was gathered at neck and under the breasts falling from the very high waist to the ground in simple folds. The sleeves were short and puffed and excess material from the hem was draped over the forearm. This fashion, which lasted to the beginning of the 19th Cent., was later introduced to London by Rose Bertin, who had fled from Paris during the Terror.

REBOZA SHAWL used for many purposes, also seen in South America.

REEFER   The man wears a short double-breasted jacket or Reefer and a hard felt domed hat with a narrow brim -an early bowler.

The woman has her dress hitched up for walking (see Porte-Jupe). Her hat is an Empire Bonnet.

RED FEATHER   Worn on a knight's helmet. A red feather denoted that the wearer had performed an act of great courage or chivalry. Medieval.

RED RIDING HOOD   *Fem.* French hood. Worn in Europe and American Colonies by many women. Attached to a long or short cape, sometimes called 'Capuchin' because of resemblance to cloak worn by Capuchin monks. For winter wear, the garment was sometimes fur-lined, quilted or fur-edged. Usually scarlet, cherry-red or cardinal. 18th Cent. Also known as CARDINAL.

REDFERN   English house of fashion established in Paris in the Rue de Rivoli, 1881, and became famous in North America and London, designing for Sarah Bernhardt and Mary Garden. Redfern, whose real name was Charles Poynter, was the innovator of ladies' tailoring and numbered Queen Victoria amongst his clients. (See COUTURE).

REDINGOTE   *Fr. - Riding coat.* Overcoat worn by both sexes from 18th Cent., the style varying from the heavy masculine form worn about 1725, and sometimes

caped for travelling, to the more fitted single or double-breasted garment by the end of the 1780s. *Fem.* Until 1820, it was a high-waisted coat left open, unfastened. After that time until 1860, it was made of lighter material, becoming a gown rather than a coat and called a Pelisse-robe. By 1875 it was styled again as an outdoor coat, being tailored, with a collar, fitted waist and having a long flared skirt. In the 1890s, made of broadcloth, it developed as a lady's coat with full puffed sleeves, fastened with buttons.

REDINGOTE DRESS   *Fem.* Day dress in shaped Princess-style, worn with buttoned waistcoat. 1869.

REEFER   *Masc.* Short double-breasted buttoned jacket, with low collar, short lapels, having no back seam. Short side vents. After 1860. (See PEA JACKET, YACHTING JACKET).

REFORMATION   A 16th Cent. religious movement against the abuses existing in the Roman Catholic church in Western Europe. It strengthened the economic position of the mercantile class and brought about some reformation in dress. Finery and gay colours were condemned. Cheaper fabrics were used. By the 1650s, a new strange fashion emerged - that of slashing material at shoulders, knees and elbows, revealing shirts beneath. Later the openings were underlaid with contrasting light material. 17th Cent.

REGALIA   Symbols of royalty - crown, sceptre, decorations. Highly ornamental dress pertaining to some status.

REGATTA SHIRT   *Masc.* Shirt of striped blue and white material known as 'Oxford'. 19th Cent.

REGENCY   Period of time when a regent governs. In European history there were two which affected costume:-

   1) The French Regency; the Duc d'Orleans was Regent for Louis XV, 1715-1723.

   2) The English Regency; George, Prince of Wales, acting for George III, 1811-1820.

REISTER CLOK   *Masc.* Knee-length cloak, usually with square, flat or plain collar. Also known as FRENCH CLOAK. 16th and 17th Cents.

RENAISSANCE   The great revival of fine art and learning in Italy during the 15th Cent., which influenced all the important textile manufacturers and tailors. Display and adornment was enjoyed and encouraged. By the 16th Cent., much new and sumptuous material was used and the outlines of clothing became broader. Opulent sleeves, large jewellery, handkerchiefs, gloves and fans were features of High Renaissance costume for both men and women.

RETICULATED HEAD-DRESS   *Fem.* Head-dress of 14th and 15th Cents., the main feature consisting of a net or mesh made of metal threads, or silk, encasing the hair within its framework.

RETICULE   *Fem.* In the period at the turn of the 18th to 19th Cent., fashionable dresses in Europe were of light-weight material with no pockets. A small handbag came into use to hold such things as a fan, perfume bottle, handkerchief. Usually oval or circular

127

and drawn up by cords, they were made of soft material - velvet, silk or satin, often embroidered or beaded. Affectionately referred to as 'ridicules'.

RHASON *Masc.* Robe, made in shape of cassock, worn by Greek Orthodox clergy.

RHINEGRAVES *Masc.* Short-lived fashion of very wide, pleated or gathered breeches, made like a divided skirt, which were always trimmed with ribbon loops at the waist and occasionally down the outer sides of the legs. Named after Count Rhinegrafen Karl, who introduced the fashion to Louis XV in 1660s.

RHODES, ZANDRA Outstanding dress designer of great originality, who first gained attention in the '60s. She uses beautiful fabrics designed and painted by herself and fostered the vogue of dyeing hair in brilliant colours to accentuate the general appearance. (See COUTURE).

RIBBON Long narrow strip of silk, velvet or fine material woven into narrow band.

In 17th Cent., clusters or pom-poms of coloured ribbon loops decorated male and female costume, until the fashion was banned in France for its extravagant use, sometimes two or three hundred yards on one garment.

RICCI, NINA Parisian couturier who, with her son, inaugurated her salon in 1939. Her work is notable for its sculptural use of fine materials and beautiful handwork. A dress cut to the waist at the front caused a sensation. Her output extends across Europe and North Africa. (See COUTURE).

RICE POWDER Rice, ground to fine powder, was used as a facial cosmetic throughout the 19th Cent. In the 18th Cent., it was gradually realised by sensible people that earlier face powders made from ground alabaster and even lead, were extremely harmful to the skin. Face painting had been fashionable and much used in the French Court from 16th Cent., after it had been introduced by Catherine de Medici. In the 20th Cent., since the 1920s, wholesome preparations have been marketed and made available, with strict laws on their ingredients and manufacture to ensure they are harmless to the skin of the users.

RIDING HABIT Clothes evolved for wearing when travelling by horse. various coats and popular names:-

Masc. Riding Coat - short-skirted, with fronts slanting away from waist. 1825-1870.

Morning Walking Coat. 1830s.

Newmarket Coat, Cutaway Coat. 1850s.

Shooting Coat. 1890s.

Riding Dress-Coat, with cut-ins at waist, worn for riding in town.

Fem. Riding Coat Dress - A gown resembling a greatcoat with large collar and lapels, buttoned down entire front, tight sleeves. 1785-1800.

Habit - consisted of coat, waistcoat, similar in cut to men's style, with skirt for women riding side-saddle. From 18th Cent. By 1840, jacket and long trained skirt was usually worn.

In 20th Cent., simpler men's and women's forms of tailoring developed the jacket and breeches having tight-fitting calf-length legs, worn with accompaniment of appropriate stock and boots.

RIVIÈRE *Fem.* Many stranded necklace of diamonds appearing as a flowing river of the sparkling stones.

ROBE *Fem.* By 1700, France was acknowledged as the leading authority upon matters of feminine fashion, the French word 'robe' for gown was mostly used for describing a particular style. Examples:-

Robe à l'anglaise: Waisted gown, fitted bodice with softened décolleté neckline and long full skirt. 1780s.

Robe à la française: Style evolved from sack-gown, having fitted bodice, with open front over decorative under-garment or stomacher. The neckline was square and low. Double box pleats fell from the shoulders at the back, with material falling to the ground. Skirt open to front showing decorative or matching underskirt, 1745-1770s, when it was restricted to formal Court wear. (See PIEDMONT SAC, GOWN, ROBE - 1775; also POLONAISE -late 18th - mid-19th Cents.)

SCOTS GUARDSMAN in full REGALIA   with bearskin hat, sporran and tassels, tartan cloak and kilt.

ROBESPIERRE COLLAR *Masc.* High-standing, folded coat collar with broad revers, under which was worn a soft lawn jabot. 1794.

ROBIN HOOD HAT Style with pointed crown, turned-up back brim and long thin feather. From 12th Cent.

ROCCELO (See ROQUELAURE)

ROCHET *Masc.* Garment of white lawn with full sleeves, worn by Anglican bishop over the cassock.

ROCKET, ROKET, ROQUET *Masc., Fem.* Short, full, smock-like garment adapted from Middle Ages in various forms.

ROCOCO 18th Cent. period of decoration characterised by the shell design.

ROGUELO *Masc.* Lined ample cloak made of four pieces, shaped to neck with no collar, fastened with brass or gold buttons. 1794-1810. Also known as ROCULO, ROCKO.

ROLL Circular pad of the Chaperon, or hood. 14th Cent. (See also LIRIPIPE).

ROLL COLLAR The rolled curve of a waistcoat or coat collar without a notch. 19th Cent. The name remained later when the collar was laid flat.

ROLL UP BREECHES *Masc.* Breeches worn with roll-up stockings. Buttoned at the knee. Late 17th Cent. to mid-18th Cent.

ROLLER Small round hat with rolled brim, worn by boys and girls. Of straw or felt. Early 20th Cent.

ROLLERS, ROLL UP STOCKINGS or HOSE *Masc.* Long stockings worn over the knee of knee-breeches and turned over in flat, broad roll. Late 17th Cent.

ROMAINE Gauze-like fabric in basket-weave used by ladies as, or on, head wear.

ROQUELAURE, ROCULO, ROCCELO *Masc.* Knee-length cloak with cape collar, buttoned in front. Made popular by the Duc de Roquelaure in Europe and American Colonies. Fashioned with back slit for wearing on horseback. Late 18th Cent.

ROMAN INFLUENCE IN BRITAIN The dress of the Roman occupiers was made of finer material than that of their subjects. The man at the right is wearing a Roman toga. A married woman always wore a head-veil or scarf. An upper tunic was worn above the kirtle or long gown. The sculpture of a Roman soldier shows the Sagum draped over the left arm, the short tunic and protective Lorica. A.D. 43-410.

ROQUET, ROCKET Weather-cape made of heavy grey cloth called 'rocket'. Worn with or without sleeves. Early 18th Cent.

ROSEBERRY CLOTH Mercerized, lustrous cotton fabric, water-proofed, of fine quality. Used for raincoats, hunting and fishing garments. Also a heavier Cheviot cloth known as BURBERRY.

ROSEBERRY COLLAR *Masc.* High detachable white linen collar, 3 inches high, with rounded front points. As worn by the English Prime Minister, Lord Roseberry. Late 19th Cent.

ROTONDE *Fem.* Short circular cape, usually matching the material of the dress. Mid-19th Cent.

ROULEAUX *Fem.* Tubes of material, loosely puffed. Much used for trimming of skirts in early 19th Cent. Rolls of ribbon worn as hat trimming.

ROUND HOSE *Masc.* style of padded trunk-hose. 1550-1610.

ROUND-EARED CAP *Fem.* Also known as COIF. Indoor cap with sides curving round the face. Usually made of white cambric, lace or gauze, with front border of single or double frill and the back plain to show back hair. Lappets were optional and when worn by domestics, tied under the chin. 1730s-1760s.

ROUNDLET *Masc.* Turban-like hat made of padded round shape, worn with draped liripipe. 15th Cent.

ROWEL Spiked revolving disc at end of spur, such as that on boot of cavalier-mounted soldier. 17th Cent.

ROXALANE BODICE *Fem.* Low-necked, V-shaped bodice trimmed with pleats, meeting at an angle over the central stiffened support to waist. 1829.

ROXALANE SLEEVE *Fem.* Puffed-out sleeve from above to below the elbow, finished with fringed band, Style was much used in evening dress, sometimes with added white lace ruffle at wrist. 1829.

ROXBURGH MUFF *Fem.* Large swansdown muff decorated with series of white satin bands. Early 19th Cent.

ROYAL GEORGE STOCK *Masc.* Handsome high stock of black velvet and satin. The satin sloped across the velvet and was tied in neat frontal bow. 1820s-1830s.

RUFF *Masc., Fem.* Circular collar of cambric or lawn, etc.; a starched and goffered frill around the neck. At first this collar was attached to shirt collarband but became a separate piece in the later 16th Cent. Styles developed from large wire-supported stiff structures in 1580s, to the FALLING RUFF, for men and women, which was gathered and not pleated. 1615-1640. The OVAL RUFF, for women, was a larger ruff with tubular pleats, worn by women donning a wide-spreading brimmed hat. 1625-1650. These ruffs were tied with tasselled band-strings.

RULLIAN A Scottish brogue shoe.

RULLION A shoe made of undressed hide. 17th Cent.

RUMP *Fem.* Stuffed pad worn under gown; also made of cork, in form of crescent and called CORK RUMP. 1770s-1800.

RUBASHKA *Masc.* Russian smock blouse with high collar, full sleeves and narrow cuffs. Embroidered, worn belted or tucked inside trousers.

RUBENS BONNET and RUBENS HAT *Fem.* Both styles, large and small, influenced by famous paintings of Rubens and were worn with brim turned up on one side. Usually trimmed with side bow and feather. 1872.

RUCHE Pleated or goffered piece of linen, lawn or lace net, worn around the neck. In the early 16th Cent., the tiny frills finishing neck and cuffs of the shirts of Spanish men were copied in many parts of Europe and by the middle of the century the ruching developed into the larger RUFF.

RUNNING CLOTHES *Masc.* Apparel worn by running servants and footmen. E.g. 'Drawers, stockings, pumps, cap, sash and petticoat-breeches'. 1720. (Ref.: Gentleman's Mag. lxi).

RUSSIA Traditional, includes -*Masc.* Embroidered black sleeveless jacket; black felt hat; bolero; shuba, an embroidered white black-bordered, shaped, knee-length coat, often with black lamb collar; full breeches; high boots; fur hat. *Fem.* Blouses, loose, confined with belt; sleeved waistcoat; sleeveless jacket; caftan; velvet skirt; head scarf; smocks.

SAC, SACQUE

16th,
17th,
18th,
Cs.

SAC, SACQUE *Gown with two box-pleats at the back from neckline to shoulders, 16th, 17th and 18th Centuries.*

SABA   Fine-textured material produced from the fibre of banana grown in the Philippines.

SABLE   Fur from small carnivorous mammal related to weasel, native to Arctic and Sub-Arctic Europe, Asia, Alaska. The Russian or Siberian, of silky fine and lustrous quality, is most esteemed. Rich, glossy, dark brown or black in colour.

SABLE   Black as an heraldic colour.

SABOT   Shoe hollowed out from one piece of wood, worn in rural Belgium, France, The Netherlands, Germany. A leather work-shoe with wooden sole. (Named -Klompen, Dutch).

SABOT SLEEVE   *Fem.* Puffed-out bouffant expansion above the elbow of sleeve of evening dress. First worn 1827-1836. After Queen Victoria's accession, style used in day clothes and called 'Victoria Sleeve'.

SABRETACHE   The soldier's leather cavalry bag of late 18th Cent., Directoire period, was copied for female use and made in choice fabrics. Embroidered, fringed and tasselled. Predecessor of late 19th and 20th Cents. women's hand-bag, when pockets could no longer be concealed in the less bouffant styles of dress that later became fashionable.

SACHET   Small padded bag impregnated with perfume. For use in wardrobes, chests and garments.

SACK, SACQUE   *Fem.* Loose gown. 16th Cent. Later, with influence from France, became more elegant with its main feature consisting of two box pleats, stitched down on either side of the back seam, from the neck to the shoulders. The fullness below flowed into the skirt. 1720-1780. Seen in French paintings by Watteau and other artists of period.

SACK BACK JACKET   *Fem.* Loose short jacket sometimes edged with fur. Late 19th Cent.

SAFEGUARD   *Fem.* Protective skirt made usually of homespun stout material, worn when riding. Other names - Foot-Mantle, Weather Skirt, Riding Petticoat. 17th and 18th Cents.

SAGUM   Large rectangle of woollen cloth worn by men in Germany and Ancient Rome. It was fastened by a thorn instead of a brooch and used also as a military blanket.

SAILOR HAT   *Fem.* 'Merry Widow' style. Wide-brimmed crinoline straw hat as worn in the popular operetta *The Merry Widow*, by Franz Lehar, first performed in 1908.

131

SAILOR STYLE Naval outfits adapted for children of either sex. Influenced in style by clothes worn by the children of Queen Victoria and popular for many years from 1880s to early 20th Cent. Included were 'sailor' blouses as worn by schoolgirls; 'sailor' hats or boaters, often with embroidered name of an imaginary ship on ribbon round base of crown. For boys there were complete suits with long or short trousers. Accessories often included boatswain's whistle and a lanyard.

SAILOR'S TIE *Masc.* Also Reef Knot. Fashionable form of tying necktie with centre knot, leaving ends flowing loose but tidily with gap in between. 1880-1890s.

SAINT LAURENT, Yves Arrived in Paris from Algeria, 1954, as apprentice to Christian Dior. When Dior died in 1957 he became head of the Dior fashion house. In 1962 he established his own couture establishment. (See COUTURE).

SAINT MARTIN'S LACE Cheap, copper-braid lace made near St. Martin's Parish, London. 16th and 17th Cents.

SAKKOS *Gk. - bag, sack.* One-piece embroidered vestment as worn by bishops of the Eastern Orthodox Church. Symbolic of the seamless robe of Christ.

SALADE, SALLET *Masc.* Unadorned helmet extending over the back of the neck, with or without visor. 15th Cent.

SALISBURY FLANNEL Woollen flannels, druggets, manufactured in Salisbury, Wilts. Late 18th Cent.

SAM BROWNE *Masc.* Wide leather military belt worn by officers. Supported by narrow strap over right shoulder. Designed by General Sir Samuel Browne, 1824-1901.

SAMARRE *Fem.* Short loose jacket of rich material, velvet, silk or plush, sometimes fur-trimmed. Worn over full silk skirt. Depicted by Dutch Masters, e.g. Vermeer. 17th-18th Cent.

SAMITE Costly silk fabric interwoven with gold and silver threads. Middle Ages.

SAMPOT Length of cotton or silk material worn as part of Cambodian costume. Wrapped around waist and drawn up to give the effect of draped trousers.

SANDAL Sole attached to foot by thongs, straps, cut-out pieces or ties.

SANDAL SHOES *Fem.* Thin-soled low-cut slippers with flat or no heels; tied with crossing ribbons over and round the ankle. Indoor and evening wear. 1790-1890.

SANS CULOTTES *Masc.* Name given to French Revolutionaries or Jacobins distinguishing them from aristocracy. Meaning - 'without breeches'. The common men of the people wore trousers, often striped, not the fashionable knee breeches of the nobility at that time. Late 18th Cent.

SANTON, SAUTOIR *Fem.* Coloured silk cravat, sometimes worn with small ruff which it helped to support. 1820s.

SARAFAN *Fem.* Traditional dress of Russian peasants, consisting of long full skirt, a white blouse with ruffles

or cuffs at wrists. Worn with sleeveless, embroidered jacket or bolero.

SARAPE Shawl-like square wrap with opening slit at centre front, worn in Mexico and South America. Woven motifs in decoration are Aztec in origin.

SARCENET Fine thin silk woven by Saracens. Used for veilings, dresses, trimmings. Sometimes with 'shot' appearance. 15th-17th Cents.

SARDINIAN SAC *Masc.* Loose single-breast overcoat, square-cut collar, full sleeves, no lapels. Cord and tassel fastening. Mid-19th Cent.

SARI *Fem.* Length of material about 100 cm. wide and 550 cm. long, worn by Hindu women from the age of 13 years. Worn over a short blouse, it is folded into pleats and tucked into a drawstring, then wrapped around waist to form a skirt. The end is taken in front over the left shoulder and left to hang or draped over the head as a hood.

SARONG *Masc., Fem.* Coloured piece of silk or cotton worn in Malay Peninsula, Sri Lanka and parts of India. About five yards long, it is joined at both ends, placed round the hips and tucked into a sash forming a draped skirt.

SARPE *Masc.* Decorated flat collar lying on shoulders. 15th Cent.

SASH Long wide piece of fabric worn around hips or waist or over one shoulder.

SASHUNE *Masc.* Lengths of padded or quilted leather strapping for binding around lower leg, allowing the over-boot to 'sit' well and be unwrinkled. Late 17th Cent.

SASSOON, Vidal Famous London hairdresser. 1960s onwards.

SATIN Silk fabric with shiny surface on one side obtained by catching warp-threads only at intervals.

SATINESCO Inferior type of satin. A 'New Drapery' originating from Norwich. 17th Cent.

SATINET Thin striped satin used for women's nightwear. 17th-19th Cent. In early 18th Cent., sometimes mixed with wool and with a satin stripe.

SATTINET A worsted cloth in satin weave. Made in Norwich. Late 18th Cent.

SAUTOIR *Fem.* Long fine chain on which to suspend a watch, chain purse, any of which was tucked into a belt. Also called ENGLISH CHAIN. Late 19th, early 20th Cent.

SAXON EMBROIDERY, ANGLICUM OPUS Very fine Anglo-Saxon embroidery of excellent quality worked by ladies from 7th to 10th Cents. It was much prized abroad as well as in England. The design was outlined with long stitches and couched with metal or silk threads.

SAXONY CLOTH Name given to fabric made from fine Merino wool of Saxony. Late 18th Cent. Since 1820 the name has been given to a group of soft tweeds and fine whipcords.

SAY Thin woollen serge, sometimes twilled. Medieval period.

SAYA *Fem.* Long silk sarong skirt with train, worn as Philippino and Spanish-American formal evening wear.

SAYETTE Textile of wool and silk. From Norwich. Late 16th Cent.

SCABBARD Metal or leather sheath for sword, dagger or bayonet.

SCALLOP Ornamental edge cut into semi-circular curves.

SCANBENDAS As LEG BANDS.

SCANDERBEG BOLERO Black fur-trimmed bolero. Named after Albanian hero who led his country against Turkish domination, 1443-1468.

SCAPULAR *Masc. Lt. -scapulare; Fr. - scapula, shoulder.* Sleeveless coat with front and back panels, worn by certain monks. The badge of membership of some orders worn on back and chest, on two pieces of cloth joined by strips over the shoulders.

SCARBOROUGH HAT *Fem.* Fashionable hat with deep turned-up brim in front dipping to point at back. Considered by many as 'rather vulgar'. 1862.

SCARF *Masc., Fem.* Thin strip of material worn for ornament or warmth round neck or shoulders. From 16th Cent. Adapted by men as large cravat over shirt front, held in place by decorative pin. Early 19th Cent.

SCARPETTI Hempen-soled shoes used for climbing in some European mountain areas.

SCHENTI *Masc.* Loincloth of ancient Egyptians, worn by King and slave alike, leaving remainder of body bare. Prototype of modern shorts worn in warm climates.

SCHLAPPE *Fem.* Head-dress worn by Swiss women, Appenzell. Of lace, with pleated black and white gauze side wings.

SCLAVEYN, SCLAVIN Pilgrim's mantle. 14th and 15th Cents. (See SLAVIN).

SCRATCH BOB or SCRATCH WIG *Masc.* A half-wig for the back of the head, sometimes with one curl. The natural hair was brushed up and over it from the front. Late 18th Cent.

SCRIP Pouch or wallet. Medieval. SEERSUCKER Striped, crimped material of cotton or linen; originally an Indian cotton textile. 18th Cent.

SEINT A girdle. Medieval.

SENDAL Silk fabric from China used in Middle Ages for robes and banners. It could be painted and was of varying thicknesses according to need. Also CENDAL.

SERGE DU SOY Stout twilled silk or woollen cloth used for men's waistcoats and coats. 18th Cent.

SERPENT *Fem.* Lock of hair which hung down and was rolled back upon itself. 18th Cent. evening style.

SEVIGNE, Mme. de Marie de Rabutin-Chantal, Marquise, 1626-1696, French letter-writer. Able, witty descriptions of manners and modes in city, Court and country life. The hair-style with hanging curls on the cheeks seen in many European portraits was named after Mme. de Sévigné.

SGIAN DHU Small Scottish black dirk tucked into right-hand garter.

SHAG Long-napped shaggy cloth of wool or silk. 17th and 18th Cents.

SHAGREEN Untanned leather made from skin of horse, camel, ass, etc. with granulated surface. Usually dyed bright green to resemble sharkskin. Used for fashionable goods, shoes, bags, purses.

SHAG-RUFF *Fem.* Ruff with irregular or shagged outline. 17th Cent.

SHAKO *Masc.* Military head-dress with high crown and plume. Originally from Hungary, the style was adapted by American Congress in 1810. Still worn by cadets at West Point.

SHAKSHEER *Fem.* Long full pantaloons worn by women in Turkey working out-of-doors.

SHAM *Masc.* A short or half-shirt worn over a full-length or plain shirt. 17th and 18th Cents. *Fem. Eng.* Made of rough material worn by country women. Late 18th Cent.

SHAMEW *Masc.* Sleeved gown of rich material open at front, sometimes bordered with fur. Late 15th -early 17th Cent. Academical gown of 14th and 15th Cents. (See CHAMMER).

SHAMIYA *Fem.* Head shawl or kerchief (M.E. -curchef) of green, red or white silk worn by Bulgarian women working outside. The married woman wears hers tied under the chin; the young girl ties hers round the head with the ends at the back.

SHAN *Masc., Fem.* Every day dark blue, cotton jacket worn in China.

SHANTUNG Undyed Chinese silk woven from coarse silky yarn with rough surface.

SHARPKA *Masc.* Cossack cap of astrakan. (See also CALPAC).

SHAWL Square, oblong or triangular covering for the head or shoulders in various materials and sizes. Fashionable for women in French Empire period in cashmere, over thin dresses. Late 18th Cent. Used by men for extra warmth when travelling by coach. Originally made in Kashmir, they were imitated in France with similar designs in silk and wool from 1804 and later with floral patterns and deep borders. In Paisley, Scotland, from 1808, shawls were made of silk, or of silk and cotton warps, and woollen or cotton wefts. By 1830, Botany wool from Australia in rich colours was used. Paisley shawls were characterised by an abstract, elaborate pattern with characteristic teardrop-shaped motif. The size of the shawl increased with the expanding size of the crinoline skirt but Norwich shawls with all-over patterns of silk and wool, introduced in 1803, were smaller and usually a yard square. (See RAM-POOR-CHUDDAR).

SHAWL COLLAR *Masc.* Wide turn-over collar of a coat or waistcoat continuous with lapels. 1820s. Still in use from the latter half of 19th Cent., named the ROLL COLLAR.

SHAWL WAISTCOAT *Masc.* Name given to waistcoat with shawl collar and/or of material having a shawl design. 19th Cent.

SHEATH GOWN *Fem.* Straight, narrow, close-fitting gown. A style recurring throughout history.

SHEPHERD'S CHECK, PLAID Thick cloth with long pile impervious to weather, woven with checks in black and white or other contrasting colours. 18th Cent. Other names -DREADNOUGHT, FEARNO-THING, FEARNOUGHT.

SHERRYVALLIES *Masc. Sp. - Zaraguellas.* Large loose pantaloons worn over leather riding-breeches for protection from mud and dust. Laced to the belt.

SHIFT Under-garment worn next to the skin by men, women and children, with long sleeves. Of home-spun, linen or cotton, often smocked at shoulders for extra fullness. From 18th Cent. Known later as CHEMISE.

SHINGLE *Fem.* Hairstyle of 1920s; cut short and shaped to back of the head, covering the ears and pointed in the nape of the neck.

SHINTIYAN *Fem. Turkish.* Wide loose pantaloons worn by some Moslem women.

SHIP-TIRE *Fem.* Lifted high-style of hairdressing above the brow. Shakespeare used term in 'Merry Wives of Windsor'. 1598.

SHIRT *Masc.* Chemise with sleeves worn since Medieval times. In 14th Cent., Norman noblemen wore shirts with neckbands and cuffs. In 15th Cent., made of varied materials and by the 16th Cent., embroidery and separate frills, edged with lace, appeared. English law forbad the wearing of decoration, pleats, etc. by a man without social rank. In the 17th Cent., ruffles at the neck and down the front showed below the short doublet. The cravat and jabot were placed at the neck in the 18th Cent. and in the early part of the 19th Cent. a large neckcloth concealed the shirt front until Beau Brummell influenced male fashion by displaying the ruffled shirt with a high pointed collar around which was tied an elegant crisp cravat.

SHIRTWAIST Feminine adaptation of men's shirt. Late 19th Cent. Usually of white linen or muslin with starched high collar, finished with bow or necktie. Illustrated in drawings of U.S. artist, Charles Dana Gibson. 1867-1944.

SHIRTWAIST DRESS *Fem.* Simple neatly-styled dress, an extension of the shirt then fashionable to hemline. Usually buttoned to the waist, hip or hem. Sleeves of any length. From early 20th Cent.

SHOE Foot-covering of leather or material which does not extend above the ankle, with durable sole or base to protect the instep.

SHOE BUCKLE Ornamental rectangular or oval metal buckle extremely fashionable late 18th Cent. From 17th Cent. to 1790.

SHOE LACES *Masc.* Strings or laces for tying sides of uppers together. Ribbons used for women's shoes. 19th Cent.

SHOE-MAKING Manufacture of shoe-nails replaced wooden pegs. 1812. After sewing-machines were patented in 1846, machines were invented and patented for sewing uppers and soles together. 1858.

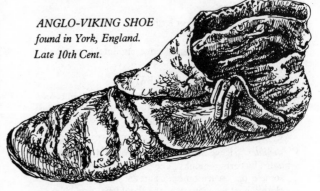

ANGLO-VIKING SHOE found in York, England. Late 10th Cent.

SHOE-TIE NECKTIE *Masc.* Very narrow necktie passed through a ring or tied with ends dangling. Sometimes known as BYRON TIE. 1850s.

SHOULDER BAG *Fem.* Handbag with long strap, worn either across or hanging straight from one shoulder. Included as part of the uniform of Women's Services in World War II, thus leaving the hands free. Its usefulness in daytime wear has made it popular since that time. 20th Cent.

SHOULDER KNOT *Masc.* Ornamental bunch of cords, ribbon loops or laces worn on right shoulder. Part of livery worn by footman. 18th Cent.

SHOVEL HAT *Masc.* Shallow black felt hat with broad brim turned up at sides, protruding back and front, resembling a shovel. Worn formerly by clergymen and Roman clerics.

SHRUG *Fem.* Very short jacket, usually to give warmth to shoulders and upper arms. Fashionable for evening wear. 1950s-1960s.

SHUBA *Masc.* Russian winter top coat made of sheepskin with the wool inside. Worn over warm shirt. (See RUBASHKA).

SICYONIA *Fem.* Intricately front-laced shoe of coloured or gilt leather worn by women in Ancient Rome.

SIDE BODY *Masc.* Tailoring term for insertion of separate panel of material below the armhole of a coat, thus giving a shapelier fit. *Fem.* Side pieces. Introduced 1840s.

SIDELESS SURCOAT *Fem.* Sleeveless, low-necked, long over-garment. It had a decorated front panel called the PLACKARD. From 14th-16th Cent. Used in State apparel until early 16th Cent. (See SUR-COAT).

SIKH North Indian monotheistic sect. In late 17th Cent., the practices of wearing a turban, carrying a dagger and never cutting the hair were introduced.

SILK HAT *Masc.* Invented and worn by London draper, John Hetherington, 1797. It became a rival to the beaver hat and the accepted head-gear of the 'Gentleman' from 1830.

SIMAR *Fem.* Short jacket for indoors wear of velvet, plush or brocade. Jacket edges and long sleeves fur-trimmed. Worn in The Netherlands and American Colonies. 17th and 18th Cents. (See also SAMARRE).

SIMARRE (Fr.), SIMARRA (Ital.) *Masc.* Long hand-some robe of brocade with wide-spreading sleeves. Originated in Venice in 16th Cent. Worn by professors and magistrates, with square, mortar-board cap. *Fem.* Venetian ladies adapted the opulent garment and added a long train.

SIREN SUIT *Masc., Fem.* Name given to easily donned matching buttoned shirt-and-trousers suit worn by wardens on duty in air raids during World War II. 1939-1942.

SKANE, SKENE, SKEAN Long dagger. 15th-17th Cent. Also shorter dirk worn in the knee-length stocking of Scottish highland dress called SKEAN DHU.

SKELETON SUIT *Masc.* Suit for young boys. Tight jacket had two rows of buttons to shoulders in front. The ankle-length trousers buttoned at and over the waist of the jacket. 1790-1830.

SKILTS *Masc.* Knee-length breeches worn by farm-hands in the American Colonies during late 18th Cent. and the War of Independence. Of Dutch style, full, fitting tightly at the waist with no braces or suspenders.

SKIMMER *Fem.* Attractive wide-brimmed leghorn hat lined with silk and tied with ribbons from above the brim to under the chin. Late 18th Cent. *Masc.* The straw hat or boater worn by Eton scholars was also so-named. Late 19th to early 20th Cent.

SKIRT Part of garment which hangs from the waist. It appeared first as a separate piece of apparel in Italian Court dress of the 14th Cent.

SKIVER Thin soft dressed leather from the side of a sheepskin.

SKULL-CAP *Masc.* Flat or round-topped cap fitting the top of the head. With no brim. From 17th Cent.

SLACKS *Masc., Fem.* Term for trousers adopted for winter sports and sailing. Accepted gradually for femi-nine wear after the end of World War II.

SLAMMERKIN *Fem.* Loose, unboned, morning gown with sack-back of the period and short underskirt. Worn without a hoop. From 1730-1770. (See also TROLLOPEE).

SLAP SHOE *Fem.* Term for high-heeled backless shoe. Predecessor of mule. Late 17th Cent.

SLASHING A fashion of making slits in a garment to show puffing of contrasting colour and material to form a decoration. Originating in Renaissance when the Swiss soldiers in 1477 mended their ragged uniforms with the banners and tents of the vanquished Burgun-dians. The style prevailed to the middle of the 16th Cent.

SLAVIN *Masc.* Pilgrim's robe of simple cut. 14th and 15th Cents.

SLEAVE Untwisted raw silk. 16th Cent.

SLICKER *Masc., Fem.* American term for weather-coat, in waterproof fabrics such as oilskin, rubber. 20th Cent.

SLING DUSTER *Fem.* Protective fitted dust cloak, buttoned in front, with sling sleeves. Sometimes of silk or lightweight material. 1886.

SLING SLEEVE *Fem.* Cape sleeve of dust coat. Attached also at waistline and thus supporting arm as in a sling. 1885. (See BERNHARDT MANTLE).

SLINGBACK *Fem.* Shoe with front but only a strap at back. From 1950s.

SLIP *Masc.* Narrow white piqué under-waistcoat with edge showing as a border, worn with MORNING COAT. Fashion introduced by Prince of Wales. 1888. *Fem.* Undergarment worn as foundation below dress. From 17th Cent. The slip cut on the bias became popular in 1920s, when fashionable Parisian dressmakers Chanel and Vionnet created their slim bias-cut dresses requiring smoothly fitting undergarments.

SLIPPER *Masc., Fem.* Anglo-Saxon -'Slypte-Shoe'. Comfortable light shoe for indoor wear. Easily slipped-on footwear.

SLIP-SHOE *Masc.* Mule with flat heel. Term 'slip-shod' derives from shuffling gait when wearing this footgear. From 16th Cent. SLOP, SLOPPES *O.E.* Loose-fitting garments, i.e. nightgowns, cassocks, smocks, knee-breeches, sailors' trousers issued from stores. Seamen were earliest working-men to wear trousers. Name retained until mid-19th Cent.

SLOPPY JOE *Fem.* Loose-fitting knitted woollen pull-on-jersey, made popular by college students in 1940s.

SLOUCH HAT *Masc., Fem.* High-crowned hat of comfortable shape with flopping brim. Early 19th Cent.

SMOCK *Masc. O.E.* - *smoc*. Loose-fitting outer gar-ment. Ornamented by self-coloured or coloured emb-roidery smocking stitches, used to gather cloth and make it hang in folds. Worn by waggoners, country folk, artists, children. Materials - linen, holland, cambric, cotton twill.

SMOCKING Needlework using a honeycomb pattern to divide and hold together tiny pleats, which give ease to the garment.

SMOKING JACKET *Masc.* Lounge jacket or casual short coat worn late 19th and early 20th Cents. for smoking at home, SB or DB, of plush, velvet, printed flannel, merino, usually frogged and corded with Brandenburgs or with large buttons.

SNEAKERS *Masc., Fem.* North American term for canvas shoes with rubber soles, used for sports. 20th Cent.

SNOOD *Fem.* Hair-net or bag to hold hair at the back of the neck.

SNOSKYN, SNOWSKIN *Fem.* Little furred muff for the hands. Late 16th and early 17th Cents.

SOLANA *Fem.* Crownless straw hat worn by Italian ladies to bleach their hair in the sun. 16th Cent.

SOLFERINO Purplish-red colour aniline dye dis-

ROLLER SKATING COSTUME, 1876. Note the variety of men's headwear – tophats, bowlers, a round pill-box. The lady is wearing day costume with the fashionable bustle of that period. Specifically designed sportswear had not yet appeared. The sketch is based on a contemporary drawing from the Illustrated Sporting and Dramatic News, *1876.*

covered in 1859, the year of the battle of Solferino. Also MAGENTA.

SOLITAIRE *Masc.* A black ribbon tied in a bow over a neckcloth; also a black ribbon used to tie the bag which held wig at the back of the neck. When the ribbon ends were brought to the front, these were tied in a bow-knot, becoming the predecessor of gentleman's black silk tie. 1730s-1770s. Also a single gem stone set in brooch, ring or tiepin.

SOLLERET *Masc.* Style of footwear resembling foot-covering made of steel plates in armour. It followed the fashion of the long-toed poulaine and when padded with dried moss its square shape resembled the paw of a bear. Seen in paintings during periods of Henry VIII, England and Francois I, France. Also worn by mercenary soldiers in Germany. 15th-17th Cent.

SOMBRERO Wide-brimmed felt or straw hat worn by horse riders. Originally Spanish but adopted in Mexico, Spanish America and S.W. United States.

SOOSEY Striped fabric of mixed cotton and silk from India. 18th Cent.

SORTIE *Fem.* Knot of small ribbons showing at side of bonnet. Late 17th Cent.

SORTIE DE BAL *Fem.* Hooded warm evening cloak of silk, satin or fine wool with quilted lining. 1850s to 1870s.

SOUFFLET SLEEVE *Fem.* Very short evening dress sleeve. Vertically pleated into puffs. 1832.

SOUTACHE Narrow flat braid used to finish edge on garment and decorative motifs.

SOUTANE *Masc.* Flaring knee-length or ankle-length garment buttoned from neck to hem, sometimes worn with sash, by soldiers, horsemen. 17th Cent. For clergy and choir wear covered by surplice. (See CASSOCK).

SOUTHWESTER, SOU'WESTER Sailor's water-proof hat with broad brim behind to protect neck. Oilskin. 19th Cent.

SPANGENHELM *Masc.* Spiked European helmet worn by feudal lords. 9th and 10th Cents.

SPANGLES Small pieces of glittering material used on dresses as ornament. From 15th Cent.

SPANISH BLACKWORK Distinctive embroidery worked in small geometric designs in black silk, combined with red or gold. Fine examples - 16th and 17th Cents.

SPANISH BREECHES *Masc.* Long-legged high-waisted breeches, full in the back and pleated into waistband, ending below the knees, to be closed by bows or rosettes, or sometimes left open to overhang stockings. Braid or a line of buttons trimmed the outer side of the legs. 17th Cent. Loose-fitting, sometimes referred to as SPANISH SLOPPES.

SPANISH CLOAK *Masc.* 1) Short cloak with hood. 16th and 17th Cents. 2) Shaped short cloak with bright coloured lining worn for evening wear. Second half of 19th Cent.

SPANISH HAT *Fem.* Large hat of velvet or silk with turned-down brim trimmed with large soft feathers. Worn for evening or promenades. Early 19th Cent.

SPANISH MODE Elegant style of 16th Cent. Included short cape, cloak, corset, farthingale, hoop, 'kettledrums', or padded hose, padded doublet, ruche and ruff. The Spanish toque, or hat, was characterised by a soft high crown, with narrow brim, having a jewelled band or decoration. It was worn by men and women.

SPARTERIE Straw fabric made from esparto grass grown in Spain and Algeria. Used for hats and shoes.

SPATTERDASHES *Masc.* Protective leggings made of leather, stout canvas or heavy cloth. From late 17th Cent. Later, there was an extension over front of foot and a fastening strap placed underneath to hold this foot-covering in place. 18th Cent.

SPATTS or SPATS *Masc.* Shortened ankle-high spatterdashes buttoned on the outside. By mid-19th Cent., they were worn with trousers and made of matching material. They were considered correct with the Morning Coat in white, fawn or grey until early 20th Cent.

SPENCER *Masc., Fem.* A very short jacket first worn by Lord Spencer in the late 18th Cent. The style was adopted by women and worn over the thin-textured high-bodiced slim French Empire fashions at the turn of the century. The masc. style is still to be seen in the military mess jackets worn by officers.

SPENCERETTE *Fem.* Tight-fitting spencer, closed or buttoned in front but with low neckline. Edged with a frilling. 1814.

SPIT BOOT *Masc.* Working-man's boot combining gaiter and shoe, closed by fastenings on outer side with an iron spike or 'spit'. 18th Cent. - mid-19th Cent.

SPLINTER HAT A straw hat made of flattened braided pieces of split straw. 16th Cent.

SPOON BACK *Fem.* Name given to back of circular draped skirt of woollen outdoor dress. 1880s.

SPOON BONNET *Fem.* Bonnet fashion, lasting about four years, which had a narrow brim at the sides but rose up high above the face in a spoon-shaped curve. It sloped downwards at the back and was edged with a neck-covering frill or barolet. 1860-1864.

SPORRAN Large purse, pouch or bag worn in front of the kilt by Scottish Highlander. Usually made of leather and fur and silver-mounted.

SPUR Pointed metal prong attached at heel of rider's footwear to urge speed by pressure.

SPUR LEATHERS Large cut-out quatrefoil shapes on the instep of leather boots to conceal spur fastenings. 17th Cent.

STAMBOULINE *Masc.* Impressive long robe worn by Turkish sultans. Made of velvet, brocade or satin, with elbow-length sleeves. Fastened in front with jewelled gold buttons from neck to hem. Over it was worn a matching loose robe or dolman. A decorated white silk turban draped over a tarboosh or fez completed the costume.

137

STUART - CHARLES 1 1625-1649   *The hairdressing style of the lady shows a knot at the back with the side pieces allowed to fall loose. The dress is less rigid than earlier years and the farthingale has disappeared. The low neckline has a large collar which matches the cuffs. The high waisted bodice has a tabbed basque with satin sash and rosette.*

The man is wearing a leather jerkin with fabric sleeves. He has a broad lace-edged falling band or collar. Breeches are widened and lengthened. For the first time leather boots with bucket tops appear. They have well blocked heels, and have 'butterfly' spurs attached. A large hat with feather, a tall cane and a sword carried on a decorated baldric, complete the costume. The armour is contemporary 17th Cent.

CIVIL WAR IN ENGLAND, 1642-49 (PURITAINS) The mounted soldier wears a Lobster-tail helmet. The standing man has a broad brimmed hat, a tunic with linen collar, breeches gathered at the knees and plain hose tops over cuffs of the boots. A similar wide brimmed hat is worn over a simple cap by the woman. Both she and her attendant wear simple dresses, with deep collars and long sleeves with cuffs. The Puritains took this simple style of dress to North America. It is interesting to note that Benjamin Franklin took these plain fashions to Paris in 1776, more than a century later. Dress-à-la Franklin became a sign of republican approval and freedom.

139

CHARLES II, 1660-1685.

The re-emergence of Decoration After the Commonwealth Regime.

The man, wearing a tall hat, has a large turn-down collar worn over his sleeved doublet and pouched shirt. Full breeches are worn above short stockings topped with flounced Cannons. The shoes have raised heels and decorative bows, sometimes rosettes. His hair is long. After 1660, wigs were worn at Court. The lady's gown has a long and tight waist with a deep collar, known as a Whist. The ballooned sleeves were called 'Virago'. The front of the dress is open to show the decorated underskirt.

STAND COLLAR *Masc.* Upright collar on waistcoat or coat, with no fall or turn-down. 19th Cent.

STAND-FALL COLLAR *Masc.* Stand collar with added turned-over part, sometimes called 'leaf'. 19th Cent.

STARCH White tasteless powder obtained from corn and potatoes, used for stiffening linen and lace. The method was perfected in The Netherlands in the 16th Cent. At that period, yellow, green or blue colouring was used for ruffs as well as white.

START-UP, STARTOP, STERTOP *Masc.* A high shoe reaching above the ankle, not a boot. Worn in the country and usually made of leather. *Fem.* Neater, sometimes of velvet, laced or buckled. Late 16th and early 17th Cents.

STATUTE CAP *Masc.* Knitted cap which all persons of low rank were ordered to wear on Sundays and Holy Days. Disobedience entailed a fine of 3 farthings. Act of 1571 was repealed 1597. Reference *Love's Labour's Lost*, W. Shakespeare.

STAY HOOK *Fem.* Metal, usually gold or silver, small hook attached to front of bodice. 18th Cent. By end of 19th Cent., a pin was added and an étui for containing useful small articles suspended from it.

STEEPLE HEAD-DRESS *Fem.* A style of high head-dress, brought to Europe in the 14th Cent. by Isabella of Bavaria, which lasted a hundred years. It was attached to a tiny skullcap with a velvet frontlet across the forehead and draped with a veil or loose kerchief. The height became so extreme that eventually it was necessary to regulate this according to the status of the wearer. (See HENNIN).

STEINKIRK *Masc., Fem.* A fashion of loosely tying a long cravat or scarf, sometimes edged with lace, under the chin, with the ends tucked into the shirt or threaded casually through a buttonhole or ring. Named after the victorious but disordered French Cavalry riders at Battle of Steinkirk in 1692. Worn with riding-habit and in other ways for over half a century.

STEPHANOS *Fem.* Diadem of precious stones with strings of pearls hanging down on each side. Worn by Theodora, Byzantine Empress (527-548), Consort of Justinian I. (See BYZANTINE).

STETSON *Usually Masc.* Broad-brimmed slouch hat or sombrero, made for the North American Western cowboy by John B. Stetson, of Philadelphia, in 1870s.

STICHARION *Masc.* Tunic of white linen worn by patriarchs of the Eastern Church.

STIRRUP HOSE *Masc.* Long protective over-stockings with a strap under instep. 17th Cent.

STOCK *Masc.* Made-up high stiff neckcloth buckled or tied at the back. Early 18th Cent. to end of 19th Cent. From 1820, the black military stock was worn at Court and often adopted by dandies.

STOCKINGS Leg coverings were worn from Saxon times, called hose, stocks, netherstocks, until late 16th Cent. From that time stockings were knitted or 'stuck' with sticking needles and the name 'stocken' or 'stucken' became 'stocking'. *Fem.* Coloured hose matched petticoats in the mid-19th Cent. and in the 1890s most women wore black lisle in the daytime and silk at night, a fashion which lasted to the 1920s. By the 1930s, artificial silk stockings became available prior to World War II. From 1945, nylon stockings and tights have been available in varied shades and textures as suitable for the occasion.

STOCKS *Masc.* Leg portion of hose, sometimes called 'nether stocks'. 1400-1610 c.

STOLA *Fem.* Long straight robe with short sleeves of linen or thin wool worn in Ancient Rome.

STOLE *Fem.* Warm shoulder wrap or shaped fur-piece to cover shoulders. Term used from 16th Cent.

STOMACHER Separate decorative front panel ending in a sharp or rounded point, a fashion which derived from Spain; worn by men and women over doublet or bodice. *Masc.* Usually very ornamental, covering gap of a low-cut doublet. Late 15th-early 16th Cent. *Fem.* Laced to the figure over tight bodice, it was decorated with ribbons, laces or jewels. A favoured French version with ribbon-bows arranged like a ladder was called *échelle - Fr. ladder.* (See ECHELLES, late 18th Cent.; PLASTRON, 19th Cent.)

STOVEPIPE *Masc.* Name given to a style of top hat 7 inches high. Late 19th Cent.

STRAPPED PANTALOONS *Masc.* Each trouser leg was strapped down under the instep. 1819-1840.

STRASS Imitation jewellery of considerable brilliance invented by Joseph Strasser, a jeweller in Germany. It was worn by the aristocracy and was remarkably fine in design and quality. The French 'strass' during Louis XV and XVI are considered to be unsurpassed in delicacy and more than a substitute for valuable jewels.

STRING TIE *Masc.* Narrow bowtie fashionable in 1896.

STROPHIUM *Fem. Ancient Greek.* Band of ornamented material worn over the chiton and below the bosom. Decorated with gem stones, it was also used as a filet for the hair.

STUD *Masc.* Two-headed button for use with two buttonholes in shirt. Used from 1830s in evening dress, gradually coming into fashion in day wear by 1860, together with cufflinks.

SUBA *Masc.* Hungarian sheepskin coat. Elaborate. 19th Cent.

SUBARMALE *Masc.* Sleeveless tunic with short pleated skirt worn by Ancient Roman foot-soldiers under metal cuirass.

SUCKENY *Masc.* Semi-circular cloak of same length as garment worn beneath it, had slits instead of sleeves. Worn 12th and 13th Cents.

SUGAR LOAF BONNET *Masc.* High cap worn with bobbed hair-style. Mid-15th Cent.

SUGAR LOAF HAT *Masc., Fem.* Hat with high conical crown and wider brim than the earlier fashionable COPOTAIN. 1650-1670.

SUIT Set of clothes made of one material. Term originally used for uniform, riding-habit or livery. From 17th Cent.

SULTANE *Fem.* Comfortable gown open at centre front. In late 17th Cent., trimmed with buttons and loops. Worn when travelling. 18th Cent. Named after Turkish Emperor's robe. Early 1700s.

SUMPTUARY LAWS Decrees forbidding the wearing of specific styles by certain classes of people.

SUNSHADE Used from 16th Cent. Called 'Umbrella' but did not close. By 18th Cent. umbrellas for rain closed and in early 1800s a parasol with hinged stick named the 'Pompadour' appeared.

SUPERTOTUS A traveller's weather cloak. Medieval. 16th and 17th Cents. (See BALANDRANA).

SURCOAT *Masc.* Loose garment worn over armour by Crusaders, to avoid the glare of the sun on the metal being seen by the enemy. Straight front and back of two rectangles worn knee-length. *Fem.* Overgarment of rich material, often with fur-linging, sleeveless with deep arm-openings, through which the tunic worn below could be seen. Similar to SUCKENY. 13th and 14th Cents.

SURPLICE A white clerical vestment of lawn or linen with flowing wide sleeves worn over a cassock. From 17th Cent.

SURAH Brilliant soft twilled Indian silk material.

SURCINGLE *Masc.* Girdle worn with a cassock.

SURTOUT *Masc.* Comfortable loose great-coat with wide cape-like collar. 18th Cent. After 1730 called WRAP-RASCAL. From early 19th Cent., called SURTOUT GREAT-COAT and often made with several broad capes. *Fem.* Caped style often in velvet and trimmed with fur. Late 18th Cent.

SUSPENDERS Pair or set of attachments to which tops of socks or stockings are hung. Also name for braces in United States.

SWADDLING BANDS Long strips of cloth used for wrapping a young baby, which were usually kept in place until it was weaned. Medieval. 'Long Clothes' replaced this method by the early 18th Cent.

SWANBILL CORSET *Fem.* Back-lacing corset with long supporting busk in front. 1876.

SUGAR LOAF HAT   Cone shaped crown over a bonnet covering the ears, 17th Century.

SWEATER *Masc., Fem.* Loose knitted garment usually reaching to hips, worn for sports. An American term. 20th Cent.

SWORD Long bladed weapon dating from Bronze Age. It became slimmer and was a ceremonial ornament

141

rather than a weapon of defense. Symbol today of judicial, legal or military authority.

SYKCHOS   Soft low leather boot worn in Ancient Greece.

SYRMA   Trailing robe worn by actors of tragedy in Ancient Greece.

SZUR *Masc.* Hungarian long great-coat with enormously wide and decorated sleeves. Worn with strap across chest to keep it in place and with the sleeves hanging.

MEN OF SEGOVIA, SPAIN   Jackets of appliqued leather worn by men of Segovia. The drawing is based on photographs by James Snowden from 'The Folk-dress of Europe'.

TIPPET 1354

TIPPET *Hanging streamers from the sleeves of the Cote-Hardie, 1354.*

TABARD *Masc. M.E., Fr., O.F. - tabart.* 1) Simple tunic worn by knight over his armour and decorated with his arms. 2) Cloak worn by heralds displaying arms of the sovereign or lord they served. 13th-14th Cent. Became heraldic and ceremonial.

TABARRO *Masc., Fem.* Italian tabard, tunic. Adapted with fullness as an ornamental cloak used in carnival and masquerade dress, particularly in Venice. Of rich fabrics, with much decoration. 18th Cent.

TABBY Watered or striped weave fabric made originally in Attab, Baghdad. Usually a silky poplin. 17th Cent.

TABI White Japanese cotton foot glove with separate shape for the large toe. Fastenings at back. Worn for indoors.

TABLIER SKIRT *Fem.* Skirt fashion with descending trimmings giving an apron-like appearance. Late 1860s, 1870s.

TABLION Semi-circular mantle, evolved from the Roman toga, worn by Byzantine emperors and Church dignitories. Named from embroidered, jewelled squares which decorated the front edges and centre back of garment.

TAENIA *Fem.* Thin girdle tied with knot, worn by Grecian maidens.

TAFFETA Thin glossy silk of plain, crisp texture. M.E., O.F.

TAGAL Straw braid made from hemp grown in Tagal, Java. Used for hat-making.

TAGALOG *Masc.* Light-weight decorated shirt worn in the Philippines, sometimes made of banana fibre material. Also called BARONG TAGALOG. 20th Cent.

TAGLIONI *Masc.* Distinctive double-breasted greatcoat, reaching usually to just below knee. Very large collar lying flat on the shoulders, the wide lapels spreading over the chest. Collar, lapels and cuffs of handsome material and texture resembling fur, satin or velvet. Coat slightly waisted but full, without pleats and having a three-cornered, decorated, central vent at the back. Slit or cross pockets at front, sleeves with turned-back cuffs, all bound with simple or twilled binding. Made fashionable by the celebrated Italian dancer, Filippo Taglioni, creator of the ballet, La Sylphide. 1838-1842.

TAGLIONI FROCK-COAT *Masc.* Single-breasted frock-coat, with skirts short and full. Back vent. Very

143

broad collar and single large cape; slashed or flapped pockets. 1840s.

TAIL COAT *Masc.* Appeared in 1790. Cut straight across at front waist level, descending to tails at the rear. Over the years details changed but fundamental style endures in modern evening dress. 20th Cent.

TAILOR-MADE *Fem.* Simple costume, with little ornament, of jacket and skirt, using one cloth. Made by tailor and not by a dressmaker, giving a trim neat appearance, often imitating fashionable male cut of the time. Charles Worth styled such clothes in Paris in 1858; Doucet, also of Paris, launched a costume, often

TAILORMADES   The male lounge suit of jacket, waistcoat and trousers, all made of the same material, evolved from the 1860s. In the drawing the man is wearing a suit with peg top trousers made to fit close at the ankles. His bowler hat was known as a Derby. The costume of the ladies for morning or country wear was made by tailors not dressmakers. Drapery after 1880 was

abandoned and both outfits show the new skirts of the 1890s. After 1877 two different materials were often combined. The lady on the left wears a feather trimmed hat and her hair is dressed with a curly fringe. Her companion's three-quarter length coat shows the fashionable Gigot sleeve, 1890-96.

in white, of English fabrics, for resort and sports wear in the 1880s. By early 20th Cent., the suit had become accepted smart street wear, often in navy or black.

TALAR Talaria - winged slippers. From Latin for ankles. In mythology, winged shoes worn by Greek god Hermes or Roman god Mercury.

TALLIEN REDINGOTE *Fem.* Attractive covering garment, created by Worth, with heart-shaped front opening and full back. Trimmed by bow with long sash ends which fell behind and terminated in bows. Made of same material as gown or of black silk. 1867.

TALLIS, TALLIT, TALLITH Prayer shawl worn by Jews. A tasselled white scarf bordered with blue.

TALMA *Masc.* Cape-like overcoat with wide sleeves. 1850s. Name also used for South American PONCHO.

TALMA CLOAK *Masc.* Cloak of knee-length, with quilted wide collar. Silk-lined, worn for evening. (Named after French tragic actor, François Talma, 1763-1826). 1853.

TALMA MANTLE Fem. Long cloak with hood or falling tasselled collar. 1850s. Made with sleeves, 1870. Became a loose-sleeved long overcoat with deep collar of velvet or with lace cape. 1890s.

TALMA OVERCOAT *Masc.* Overcoat in Raglan style with very wide armholes. 1899.

TAM-O'SHANTER Woollen cap with close-fitting headband and very full flat round crown. Of heavy brushed wool. Usually decorated with a pompom. (Named after the hero of Robert Burn's poem, 'Tam O'Shanter'). 1880s.

TAMEIN Thin cotton sari or sarong worn in Burma.

TAMINE Fine silk and wool material made in 16th Cent. Became a worsted fabric with smooth surface. 17th Cent.

TANK TOP *Fem.* Hip-length sleeveless jersey or sweater, with round neck. worn over mini-skirt or tailored straight skirt. 1960s.

TAPIS *Fem.* Black silk squares worn on the head by peasant women of the Philippines.

TARBOOSH *Usually masc.* Brimless red felt cap resembling a fez, worn in E. Mediterranean by Moslems. Worn as base for turban or alone. Arab -tarbush.

TARLATAN Heavily sized thin muslin used as stiffening in garments.

TASS, TASSES Piece of armour reaching from waist to mid-thigh, made of four to eight steel bands. Hinged on the left side and buckled on the right. 15th-17th Cent.

TASSEL Pendant knob of loosely-hanging cords used as ornament.

TASSETS *Masc.* Small skirts or basques attached below waistline of doublet. 1600-1660. *Fem.* Imitation of male fashion. 1628-1640.

TASSIES Glass paste impressions and replicas of intaglios, worn as jewellery. James Tassie innovated and made famous these cast gems in London from 1766.

TATER *Masc. Tetour - hood.* Long tail suspended from hood. 15th Cent. Also LIRIPIPE.

TATTERSALL Woollen check material used for sporting garments. 1890s.

TATTERSALL VEST *Masc.* Waistcoat of clear bright check. Single-breasted, four flapped pockets, six buttons. Late 1890s.

TCHARCHAT *Fem.* Casual style of dress worn in Turkey after 1925. Long sleeveless cotton upper garment covering the pantaloons (chalwar). A shawl is worn over a lace cap and held in front of the face.

TEAGOWN *Fem.* Comfortable loose dress of considerable elegance in Europe and America. Socially acceptable and worn without corsets, by married women only. From 1877. Usually with fitted yoke, full sleeves and made of silk, satin or lace. By the end of the century, the style also worn by 'young ladies' at afternoon tea.

TEBENNA *Masc.* Large semi-circular cloak worn by ancient Etruscans. 8th and 7th Cents., B.C.

TEDDY BOY FASHION *Mostly masc.* Ted - short for Edward. The main features were narrow trousers or 'drain-pipes'; high-heeled pointed shoes or 'winkle-pickers'; waisted long frocked coats often with velvet collars. 1940-1955.

TEGUA Mocassin shoe of buckskin worn by Pueblo Indians, New Mexico.

TEJA *Fem. Sp. teja -roof-tile.* A high comb worn in the hair to lift a shawl or mantilla above it.

TELESCOPE PARASOL *Fem.* The tube-like shaft of this parasol was elongated by pulling outwards like a telescope. Early 19th Cent.

TEMPLE JEWELLERY Fashionable artificial jewellery made on La Rue du Temple, Paris. 17th Cent. Jewelled buttons were especially in great demand in that period.

TEMPLERS *Fem.* Ornamental cauls of fine needle-work or gold net-work. Worn above the temple, enclosing hair arranged or plaited on each side of the face. These small box-like bosses were supported by the head-dress or a fillet across the forehead. 1400-1450 c.

TENNIS SHOES When the King of France sent Henry V of England a box of tennis balls, an item was recorded in the royal accounts of soft shoes, suitable for playing this game, made with 'feltys' - felt soles. 16th Cent.

TENT SILHOUETTTE *Fem.* Simple loose shape created by couturier, Balenciaga, Paris, in 1951. The outstanding example was a black coat that flared from the shoulders with a small mandarin collar. In 1960 Yves St. Laurent followed this style with his design called the 'A-line'. (See COUTURE).

TENTER A frame with hooks which held homespun material taut for bleaching. Usual in every home where cloth was woven.

TENTERHOOKS *L. tentus - stretched.* Stretching of wet cloth by hooks passed through selvedges, placed on ground to dry in open air.

TERAI HAT *Fem., occ. masc.* Riding-hat with brim worn in tropical countries. Formed by two felt hat shapes sewn together at the edge of the brim. Lined with a vent fitted in the crown. Late 19th Cent.

TERESA *Fem.* Light transparent silk or cotton gauze scarf, worn over the head or over the indoor cap. Late 18th Cent.

TERNO *Fem.* Long evening gown worn in Philippine Islands and characterised by outstanding stiffened short sleeves called 'butterfly wings'. Worn to date.

TERRIER OVERCOAT *Masc.* A form of Pilot coat, loose, knee-length and with large china buttons. Mid-19th Cent.

TÊTE DE MOUTON *Fem.* A head-dress of false curls, styled to cover back and sides. 1730-1755.

THAI SILK Beautiful silk fabrics of Thailand from silk-weaving villages where the people raise silkworms, tie the silk, dye and weave into interesting designs.

THEODORE HAT *Fem.* Large brimmed hat with very high crown, trimmed with gauze and net bordered with blue satin ribbon. A large bunch of scarlet flowers in front. Long waist-length lappets of gauze at sides. 1787.

THÉRÈSE *Fem. Fr.* Large bonnet of fine gauze worn over a high-dressed hair style. Supported by wire frame. 1780s.

THOLIA *Fem.* Straw hat worn in Ancient Greece. With round brim and pointed crown. Worn over a head veil. Examples can be seen on Tanagra terra-cotta figurines.

THREE STOREYS AND A BASEMENT *Fem.* Name given to a very high toque-like hat worn in Jubilee Year of 1887.

THRUMMED HAT *Masc., Fem.* Hats made of felt or silk with a nap or long pile. Mid-16th Cent.

TIARA *Masc.* Ancient Persian head-dress worn by kings. Adopted by Jewish and Christian prelates. The triple crown of the Pope. *Fem.* Brilliant head-piece for evening and State occasions. 19th and 20th Cents.

TIE or TYE WIG *Masc.* Wig with queue of hair taken straight back with black silk bow. 18th Cent.

TIE-BACK SKIRT *Fem.* Style of skirt with inner series of tapes placed so that when tied the back of the skirt hung full and the front was pulled smooth. Seen in day and evening wear. 1874-1882.

TIFFANY *Fem.* Transparent silk gauze material used for fichu or scarf. 17th Cent. on.

TIGHTS *Masc.* Name given to pantaloons worn in evening. 19th Cent. *Masc., Fem.* Close-fitting garments used by dancers, acrobats. Also women's leg-wear much worn since the fashion of the mini-skirt. 1960s.

TIKKA Red mark or spot worn on the centre of forehead by Hindu women.

TILBURY HAT *Masc.* Small hat with tapering crown, flat top and narrow brim. 1830s. At this period, the two-wheeled horse carriage designed by London coach-maker named Tilbury came into use.

TILE O.E. slang for hat, being a covering to the head as tiles are to a house.

TILSON (See TISSUE)

TILTER *Fem.* A type of bustle, worn under petticoat, which tilted as wearer moved. 1865-1875.

TIMIAK Eskimo shirt made of bird skins. The soft feathery down sides worn next to the body. Neck and sleeves of garment are edged with dog fur.

TINSEL Dress fabric adorned with glittering threads or strips to give sparkling effect.

TIPPET Pendant streamer from elbow-length sleeve of cote-hardie. 14th Cent. *Fem.* Muffler, deep shoulder wear from 1680. Also long black scarf, part of costume of judges and Anglican clergy. M.E. From 16th Cent.

TISSUE, TILSON, TYLSENT A fine gauze of open weave made of twisted metal threads. Also coloured silk with gold or silver. A sparkling material dating from 16th Cent.

TITIAN Tiziano Vecelli, 1487-1576. Greatest of the Venetian painters. He usually laid an underpainting on his picture of plain red earth colour. The reddish glow of this colour permeated most of his work and has become a term descriptive of auburn-coloured hair. Since late 15th Cent.

TITUS WIG *Masc.* A wig or hair style, closely cropped, adopted at the time of the French Revolution, reminiscent of Roman style of short hair, named Titus or Brutus. 1790-1810.

TJELD *Fem.* Striped shoulder shawl worn in Norway.

TOBE *Masc.* Arabian, ankle-length, loose garment, collared with buttoned opening on chest. Worn with an over-garment called ABA.

TOG *From L. Toga – a coat.* Naut. Togs - shore clothes, slang for finery.

TOGA Outer dress of Roman people. It consisted of a single piece of undyed woollen cloth, cut in a near semi-circle. 1-300 A.D.

TOGGLE 17th Cent. seaman's term for wooden pin passing through loop of rope or through link of chain. Term used for fastenings on travel clothes, duffle-coat and similar loose-style garments. Present Cent.

TOILE *Fr. - cloth, linen.* Term used for 20th Cent. couturier's sample patterns made up in temporary fabric.

TOILE *Fr.* Term used in lace-making, in preference to English 'mat' or 'cloth work', to describe the solid part of the design.

TOILE DE JOUY Printed cotton fabric made in Jouy, France, from 1760. Pastoral landscapes, flower designs were printed in a single tone of red, brown, blue, green, on a natural coloured ground. The name is now mainly given to modern imitations or fabrics with similar designs used for soft furnishings and summer dress materials.

TOM-BONS *Masc., Fem.* Full loose pantaloons tapering to ankles. Of white cotton, worn by Moslem Afghans.

TON *Fr.* Style, fashion. Bon ton - good manners. Donner le ton - to lead the fashion.

TONSURE *Masc.* Shaving of the crown of the head leaving a fringe of hair and symbolizing Christ's crown of thorns. From 5th Cent. A.D.

TOP BOOTS *Masc.* Boots to just below the knees, with turnover tops of different or lighter colour. Side loops for pulling on. From 1780s.

TOP COAT *Masc.* Garment of middle-weight material suitable for walking. Not a greatcoat. 19th Cent.

TOP FROCK *Masc.* Overcoat generally double-breasted, worn without an undercoat. Cut like a frock-coat. From 1830.

TOP HAT *Masc.* Tall high-crowned hat with narrow brim, usually black but occasionally grey and brown. In 1830-1840 was also made in white. The SILK HAT with 8″ high crown was worn in 1850 but height was reduced by the end of the century. The lower height has been retained for formal wear until present day. Lady riders also wore TOP HATS from 1830s.

TOPEE Insulated hat or helmet for protection from sun, first worn by British Army in India, 1860s. Made of pith of sola, a tropical swamp plant. Light in weight, covered with white cotton and lined with green cloth. Impervious to air and water.

TOQUE *Fem.* Cap or round full bonnet of soft material, originally gathered into a headband, worn out-of-doors. From 19th Cent., a close turban without a brim. The wife of George V, Queen Mary, was noted for appearing in a hat of this style until the end of her life.

TOQUE TURBAN *Fem.* Evening head-covering fashionable in 1840s.

TORC (See TORQUE)

TOREADOR *Masc., Sp.* Popular misnomer for mounted bullfighter.

TOREADOR HAT *Fem.* Fashionable hat inspired by opera 'Carmen'. Circular with flat shallow crown, made of felt or staw, worn tilted on one side. 1890s.

TORERO *Masc. Sp.* Bullfighter.

TORQUE Bracelet or neck-band of twisted valuable metal worn by Ancient Britons, Gauls and Northern Europeans, usually of high rank.

TORSADE *Masc.* Edging of gold or silver fringing, edging the shoulder pieces or epaulettes of military or commanding officers' uniforms. 19th Cent. *Fem.* Decorative plaited or twisted velvet coronet with long-falling lappets. Head-dress worn with evening dress. Late 1860s.

TOTE BAG Large shopping bag, which came into use in World War II, when shoppers began to carry their purchases home and deliveries were non-existent. Based on a paper carrier-bag shape with straight sides, roomy and with strong handles, these practical bags became popular and large stores provided some, often with colourful advertising on the sides.

TOUPEE *Masc. O.F. toup - tuft.* Front portion of wig that rolled back or curled back from the forehead. 1730-1799. Later, the name given to an artificial piece of false hair worn to cover a bald piece. *Fem.* Fringe or decorative frizzed piece of false hair worn above the forehead. 1890s.

TOURNURE *Fem. Fr.* Pad or bustle worn under polonaise or skirt just below the back of the waist. Replaced side hoops in 1770s. Created as a 'style' by Worth after crinoline skirt went out of fashion. 1871-1880s.

TOVAGLIO *Fem.* Italian name for peasant bonnet, having a deep frill or ruffle at back of the neck. Hat fashionable, 1855. (See FANCHON).

TOWER, TOUR, TORRE *Fem.* High hair-style built up with or without false hair. The indoor linen cap, with tall lace frills called 'fontange' was worn above this coiffure. Late 17th Cent. to early 18th Cent.

TRABEA *Masc.* Wide scarf crossed over chest, worn by Constantine, Emperor of Byzantium.

TRAFALGAR TURBAN *Fem.* Evening hat. Decorated and embroidered with the name of Nelson, after Trafalgar. 1806.

TRAIN Part of formal costume that trails behind the wearer. In 14th Cent., the length of train was regulated according to rank of wearer. In French Courts, until the regime of Napoleon, luxuriously embroidered trains were very long and fastened at shoulder or waist and could be removed at the end of a ceremony. Ermine-trimmed velvet robes persist for affairs of State.

TRAPEZE LINE *Fem.* Dress style inaugurated by Yves St. Laurent, successor to Dior, in Paris in 1958. It was the predecessor of the 'A-line' and the Tent Shape dress.

TRAPUNTO *It.* A type of padded quilting.

TRAWERBANDES Black ribbons or bands worn to denote mourning. 17th Cent.

TREMBLING CAP *Fem. It.* Picturesque, slightly stiffened conical cap of gold or silver net mesh with a long tail like that of a chaperon. The headband was usually decorated with a line of pearls. 16th Cent.

TRENCH COAT *Masc.* Protective coat of waterproofed gaberdine with extra lining, worn by officers in World War I. 1914-1918. It was copied for civilian use afterwards and again used in World War II. Since that time it has been worn by both sexes, having become a classic garment.

TRENCHER CAP (See TRENCHER HAT)

TRENCHER HAT *Masc., Fem.* Square college cap, the shape of which was based on the wooden platter called a trencher. Also known as 'mortar-board', with obvious likeness to board used for mixing mortar by builders. *Fem.* Triangular brimmed hat style. Early 19th Cent.

TRESSOUR, TRESSURE *Fem.* Term for netted head-dress or caul, of metal or cords. Also wreath or chaplet. 14th and 15th Cents.

TREWS *Scot. Gael. triubhas, Ir. trius.* Tartan trousers, as chosen by some Scottish Regiments.

'TRICKSIES' *Masc.* London coster name for trousers.

TRICOLINE Fine modern cotton, poplin material with silken finish.

TRICORN, TRICORNE HAT Name given to three-cornered hat. The brim, bound with braid, was turned up, 'cocked' on three sides to form a triangle and the hat was worn with the point in front. 19th Cent.

TRICOT Imitation or hand-knitted woollen fabric.

TRICOTEUSE *Fr.* Small work-table to contain sewing materials with movable gallery. 19th Cent. origin.

TRILBY *Masc.* Soft felt hat, the style of which was inspired by that worn in due Maurier's play, 'Trilby'. 1895 to date.

TROLLOPEE, TROLLOPPEE *Fem.* Loose-fitting morning gown or saque, with unboned bodice. The overskirt was trained but this could be looped up at sides and back. 1740-1770. A style worn without a hoop indoors was generally popular, from 1756-1760. Also called SLAMMERKIN.

TROLLY CAP *Fem.* Indoor cap trimmed with Trolley Lace. Late 18th Cent.

TROLLY or TROLLEY LACE A coarse Flanders bobbin pillow lace, also made in Devonshire. Patterns of flowers, sprays, squares and dots outlined with heavy thread with a border. 17th and 18th Cents.

TROTCOSY *Fem.* Scottish name for small warm cape with hood worn when walking.

'TROTTER CASES' *Masc.* London Cockney name for boots.

TROTTEUR *Fem. Fr.* Name given to stylish walking costume for town or country. 20th Cent.

TROUSERS *Masc.* Two-legged garment from waist to ankles. Many kinds and shapes after 1823, including Cossacks, Gaiter Bottoms, Straight, Zouave, Tight-Slacks. *Fem.* Long frilled drawers, worn by women-riders. 19th Cent. Long drawers worn by young women under skirts. 1830-1860.

TROUSES, TROWSES, TROUSSES *Masc.* Undergarment worn underneath trunk-hose. 17th Cent.

TROUSSEAU *Fem.* Clothes and outfit of a bride.

TROUSSOIRE *Fem.* As CHATELAINE.

TRUNCATE To cut top or end from cone. 'Truncated' is applied to hat with its crown flattened, as in M.E. fez.

TRUNCHEON Short cudgel or club as carried by authority.

TRUNK-HOSE *Masc.* Loose or padded breeches attached to long stockings. Varying in length and fitted with waist and thigh bands. 1550-1610. Covering strips of material called panes, often embroidered, allowed the hose of different colour and material underneath to be displayed. This deliberate form of decoration was called SLASHING.

TRUSS *M.E.* Verb - to tie or fasten. 14th-16th Cent. Fitted corset or waistcoat. 17th Cent.

TRUSSES *Masc.* Fashionable fitted knee-breeches. Usually tied below the knees. End of 16th Cent.

TRUSSING COFFERS Leather-covered travelling chests used for packing garments and small goods. Early 17th Cent.

TSARUCHIA *Masc.* Black leather shoes decorated with pompoms, worn by guardsmen in Greece. 20th Cent.

T-SHIRT *Masc., Fem.* Simple modern sports shirt of light-weight porous washable material. 20th Cent.

TUCKER *Fem.* A yoke of tucked fabric or lace, sometimes frilled, worn to fill a low-necked bodice. From 17th Cent.

TUDOR The English sovereigns from Henry VII to Elizabeth I. English Tudor style architecture - late Perpendicular, characterised by flattened arch; the Tudor rose - a five-lobed flower, was much used in ornament and design. The appearance of clothing gradually became broader and head-dresses echoed the flattened appearance, accentuating the horizontal line. Even shoes became broad-toed. The fashion of slashing, as a method of decoration from Europe, became prevalent in the early 1500s. Necklines used drawstring ties, leading to the beginnings of the ruff in the latter part of the century and these were allowed as a mark of privilege. In 1556, the Spanish Court style of Philip II influenced all Europe; rigid styles, mostly in black, were admired and followed. Knitting was introduced and elegance of accessories, such as beautifully crafted leather, perfume, embroidered gauntlet gloves, fine lace handkerchiefs and trimmings were much used. Other characteristic styles worn were masc. sleeveless cassocks, wider sleeves, fem. bum-rolls and stomachers, the latter made rigid with busks; also skirts with farthingales.

TUDOR BONNET *Masc.* Cap or hat, usually of black or dark-coloured velvet, with brim turned up nearly all the way round. Fine bonnets were decorated by large brooches and pins and many of high quality were made in Milan. 1495-1545.

TUDOR CAPE *Fem.* Fashionable name for circular cape with a Medici collar and pointed yoke front and back. Often of embroidered cloth. 1890s.

TUDOR PERIOD Henry VII, 1485-1509. The man wears a sleeved jerkin over a pleated shirt which has a frill at the neck, the first sign of the ruff. He has long hose and large square-toed shoes. His hat is soft and rounded. The lady has an English hood, the butterfly headdress is no longer worn. The low neck of her gown is filled with a Partlet, a kind of chemisette. The guard wears a voluminous belted form of Houppelande, hooded with a high bottleneck.

149

TUDOR PERIOD Henry VIII, 1509-1547. The man
has a flat cap with a feather. His doublet has a standing
collar open to show an embroidered shirt. The puffed
shoulders on the sleeves are slashed and the skirt is full.
There is a narrow belt for dagger and sword. 1540.

The lady wears an English hood. Her kirtle has a low
neck. The skirt is open in front and the oversleeves have
turned back cuffs. 1536.

Professional and elderly men wore long gowns, often lined
with fur. This man has a soft velvet cap with medium
length hair. He has a quilted waistcoat to which his hose
is attached. His shoes are square-toed. 1530.

150

TUDOR PERIOD   The Yeomen of the Guard, under Henry VIII, were becoming increasingly used for ceremonial purposes and their dress reflected this. The striking red and gold costumes are in use today by the warders of the Tower of London. The tunic is retained and worn above the modern trouser legs.

TUDOR PERIOD   Edward VI, 1547-1553. The woman wears the English version of the French hood. Her gown has a Medici collar, with over and under sleeves, and the Spanish farthingale skirt. 1545.

The man's costume comprises flat cap with a small brim, a long fur-trimmed gown over a doublet, which shows the frilled shirt collar. He wears hose and round-toed shoes.

MARY 1553-1558.
Dress of older, middle class women, mid 16th Century.

151

TUFT Bunch of threads held together as in a tassel. 15th Cent. Applied to pendant tassel from centre of University mortar-board head-dress. 18th Cent. onwards.

TUFT MOCKADO Woollen or silk material with design raised in a geometric arrangement of tufts. 16th and 17th Cents.

TUFTAFFATA, TUFTAFFATY, TUFTTAFFETA Heavy silk taffeta woven with velvet or raised pile stripes. 16th, 17th and early 18th Cents.

TUKE, TEWKE Buckram, canvas, used in 15th and 16th Cents.

TULLE *Tulle - a city in France.* Fine silk net.

TULY Silk fabric. 16th Cent.

TUNIC 1) *Masc., Fem.* Ancient Grecian or Roman short-sleeved body garment reaching to knees.

2) *Masc., Fem.* Loose slim garment as kirtle. 9th to late 13th Cents.

3) *Masc.* Loose coat or surcoat to above the knees, having large loose sleeves. Worn over a vest, this garment was distant forerunner of the shorter waistcoat. Late 17th Cent.

4) Jacket worn by young boys which had attached pleated skirt to above knees and was worn over trousers. 1840-1855.

5) Tunic Shirt. Garment opening from collar to hem. Patented 1855.

6) *Fem.* Hip-length blouse or a dress of shorter length than the skirt over which it is worn. Modern.

7) *Masc., Fem.* Close-fitting uniform coat such as that of policeman, service-man, bell-boy, etc. To date.

TUNICLE *Masc. L. - tunicula.* Eccl. short vestment of delicate white material. M.E.

TUPU *Fem.* Decorative silver jewellery consisting of chain work with pendant coins, attached to a small plate or shield fastening a cloak. Chile.

TUQUE *Masc., Fem.* Double thickness wool stocking-cap. Canada.

TURBAN Head-dress or hat. Persian word denoting veil material from which coiled head-gear was made. Later worn by Arabs and other oriental people; introduced to Europe after the Crusades. Variants seen in LIRIPIPES, 15th and 16th Cents. caps; women's head-dresses of early 19th Cent. and again in 20th Cent., particularly in World War II.

TURKIE BONNET, TURKEY BONNET or HAT *Masc.* Tall round hat, similar to Copatain hat. 15th and 16th Cents.

TURKEY GOWNE, GOWN *Masc.* Robe similar to long Hungarian coat with narrow, not full, sleeves. Front fastenings of loops or buckles and straps. Adopted by Puritan ministers who considered simplicity of appearance preferable to full and more ornate dress which savoured of Popery. From 1525. Henry VIII possessed one of black velvet, edged with lynx fur, fastened with gold and black enamel buttons.

TURKEY RED Cotton cloth and embroidery. The cotton was dyed a bright durable red, imported from Turkey in late 19th Cent. A material much used at this period.

TURKISH VELVET Silk velvet material, ribbed, with plain satin bars. Mid-19th Cent.

TURNOVER *Fem.* Piece of cloth or square kerchief used as head-covering. 17th Cent.

TURRET *Fem.* White linen head-dress, shaped like a toque but crownless, with chin-strap. Worn over loosely-flowing hair or wimple. 12th Cent.

TURRET BODICE *Fem.* Upper portion of dress which was decorated by hip basque cut into tabs resembling battlements on a turret. 1883, 1884.

TURTLE NECKLINE *Masc., Fem.* Wide knitted tube-like collar or neckline, rolled to level required. Comfortable, neat and warm, it became fashionable in 1960s.

TUSCAN STRAW Fine quality yellow wheat-straw from Tuscany. Woven into lacy patterns for making of hats.

TUSSORE Strong, natural-coloured silk woven from the tussah silkworm of India. Used for summer suitings and dresses.

TUTULUS Characteristic head-dress worn by Etruscan priests. The conical shape is built up of braids into a pointed cap.

TUXEDO *Masc.* North American comfortable adaptation of the Englishman's single-breasted dinner jacket. It was worn in the evening by wealthy financiers in Tuxedo Park, N.Y. In 1920s, it became double-breasted and the waistcoat became unnecessary.

TURBAN worn by a Sikh in ceremonial dress.

TWEED Material of twilled woollen or wool and cotton fabric with rough surface. Usually two colours combined. Named varieties include Homespun - both in Scotland and Ireland; Donegal, Harris, also West of England.

TWEEDSIDE *Masc.* A fashionable loose jacket developed from 1858 onwards. Buttoned high and single-breasted, mid-thigh length.

TWEEDSIDE OVERCOAT *Masc.* Knee-length form of the Tweedside jacket. 1859.

TWIN SET *Fem.* Matching set of knitwear, i.e. jersey and cardigan. Much favoured 1930s, 1940s.

TWINE *Masc.* Loose overcoat. Double-breasted similar to its later development called the 'Chesterfield'. 1840s.

TYLSENT (See TISSUE)

TYROLEAN DRESS Attractive costume still worn in the Tyrol, Western Austria. *Masc.* Jacket and short leather breeches held by embroidered braces. *Fem.* Full skirt and apron. Both wear white linen blouse, embroidered cloth waistcoats, white knitted stockings and black leather boots or shoes, often buckled. Hat styles vary from wide-brimmed to more typically recognised style which is worn with brim turned up at one side, decorated with feather quill and cord and having a slightly conical high crown.

TYUBETEVKA Embroidered cap of pillbox shape with flat or peaked crown. Worn throughout certain areas of Russia and Central Asia. Usually referred to as the Uzbek cap.

TZUTE Squares of woollen fabric, coloured red and black and orange, hand-woven in Guatemala. This handwork is worn in many ways - shoulder wraps, sashes, head-gear and so on.

EDWARDIAN HATS   Tea in the garden, 1908.

ULSTER from 1869

ULSTER   Overcoat of water proof material, with waist or half-belt and caped. Usually of a long length and with a ticket pocket in the sleeve, from 1869. A female version with two or three capes appeared from 1877.

UDO, UDONES   *Masc.* Stocking, stockings, of cut-out and sewn cloth worn by Roman citizens and early Christian clergy. Shaped over the foot and above knee length. 5th-11th Cent.

UGLY   *Fem.* Term for folding extra brim worn to the front of a bonnet, for protection from strong sunlight. Made of silk covered cane strips which folded flat when not needed. 1848-64.

UHLAN   Cavalryman in some European armies armed with lance, as in former German army.

ULSTER   *Masc.* Long, loose overcoat often belted, originally made of ulster frieze, a coarse napped woollen cloth and for travelling and weather protection. Early styles had detachable hoods, capes and a ticket pocket in the left sleeve above the cuff. From 1869. *Fem.* Similar to the masc. but occasionally with extra capes and long back train. These were of suitable water-proofed materials and worn for travelling.

UMBO   The boss of a shield.

UMBRELLA   Covering circle of material attached to frame and carried in the hand to protect from sun or rain, dating from antiquity. In some Asian and African countries was regarded, and later adopted by Catholic Church in Middle Ages, as a symbol of dignity. Used by women in 17th and 18th Cents., becoming very fashionable in France. By 1800, the frame was pagoda-shaped with metal supporting stretchers. In 1848, alpaca covers were general and U shaped metal ribs were patented by a Mr. S. Fox in 1852. From this time, considered correct for fashionable men to carry a closely rolled umbrella. In cities, particularly London, the habit still continues in inclement weather.

UMBRELLA HAT   *Masc.* Large broad-brimmed hat of felted beaver fur wool. In fashion 1800-1810.

UMBRELLA ROBE   *Masc.* Stout over-cloak for weather protection during out of doors functions, processions, funerals. Late 18th Cent.

UMBRIL   Browpiece of Burgundian bugonet helmet which shaded the eyes. 15th-17th Cent.

UNDER PINNINGS   Informal term for corsetry. Late 19th Cent.

UNDER PROPPER   Also Supportasse. Wire framework, usually semi-circular, placed at back of neck to support starched ruff or collar. Late 16th Cent.

UNDER WAISTCOAT *Masc.* Short sleeveless waist-coat which protruded above the edge of the over-waistcoat. Usually of bright, rich material. Fashionable early 19th Cent. Discarded 1850s but persisted in white for evening wear at end of century.

UNDERCAP *Masc.* Simple coif, or skull-cap, usually worn indoors, and by older men, or under hat or outdoor bonnet. Also a form of night-cap. 16th Cent. *Fem.* Indoor cap of soft muslin usually white, with or without ties. From 16th Cent. Worn under fashionable or rural 'milkmaid' hats. 1745-1760. Named 'undress' cap 1777 but discarded by 1790s.

UNDERSHIRT, SHIFT VEST *Masc., Fem.* Loosely cut under garment, which did not exist in classical age. Under-tunics of fine linen first worn in Byzantium and regarded as luxury until 16th Cent. *Masc.* Full, straight-cut with full, long sleeves of wool. 1890s. *Fem.* Chemise of fine material with low neck, embroidered. Late 19th Cent. - First World War. Pastel shaded silk or artificial fabrics from 1925.

UNDERSKIRT *Fem.* Skirt worn under the outer garment. The farthingale, Spanish, was a linen stiffened underskirt. Mid 16th Cent.

UNDERVEST *Masc., Fem.* Introduced as undergar-ment for hygienic reasons from 1840s.

UNDRESS *Masc., Fem.* Everyday attire, especially morning. 18th and early 19th Cents.

UNDRESS, MILITARY Prescribed uniform for ordinary or off-duty occasions.

UNIFORM Official dress, such as livery, worn by military units, sailors, organizations, schools, police, etc. Clothes characteristic of the wearer's occupation. The Industrial Revolution brought about production for more extensive use. From 19th Cent.

UNISEX Although trousers had been worn informally by women privately and during war activities, it was not until the mid 1960s that these garments found general acceptance. In 1966 Yves St. Laurent devised and showed skin-tight trousers. By 1967, the fashion 'Unisex', designed to be worn by both sexes, was launched. This included suits, trousers, jackets of wool cut in masculine style and represented an assertion of equality of choice with men. Developments for both sexes in late 1960s were of ethnic character - kaftans, kimonos, smocks, peasant garb, loose cotton trousers.

In 1969, important designers showed well-made silk

The emancipation of this period has led to a more relaxed attitude by both sexes to dress. Jeans remain popular and stretch fabric two-pieces, track suits, athletic clothing of unisex style are now worn generally apart from areas of sport.

UNIVERSITY GOWN Official robe of professional scholar or graduate. Loose flowing upper garment. Usually with appendage of hood denoting university or degree.

UP HELLY AA Midwinter torchlight festival held in Lerwick, Scotland, when the populace dress in costume as Vikings to commemorate the burning of Viking ships.

UPARNÁ *Masc., Fem. Indian*Long shawl of thin silk or muslin with metallic threads.

UPHOLSTERED *Fem.* The reappearance of the bustle in 1880s became known by this name in England due to the extravagant amount of drapery deemed fashionable to cover the skirt framework and which often resembled the padded furnishings in vogue at that period.

UPPER GARMENT *Masc.* Term for extra cassock, cloak or gown considered essentially correct by gentlemen of standing, when out-of-doors. 17th Cent.

UPPER STOCKS *Masc.* Seat part of trunk hose known also as 'overstocks'. 1400-1550.

UPPERHOSEN *Masc.* Upper leg wear or breeches varying in length and size. After 1510, a lower garment was added known as NETHER HOSEN.

URAEUS Egyptian symbol worn on royal head-dress above the centre of forehead. A representative of the sacred asp of ancient Egyptian divinities and rulers symbolizing supreme power.

UTILITY CLOTHES During World War I, simple tailormade garments were adopted for war-work. These had simple metal buckles for all-day wear. 1918. During and after World War II, the name was given to articles of wear sponsored by the Government. Top designers were encouraged to produce attractive, stylish clothes in spite of severe rstrictions. They were sold to the public at officially controlled prices.

shirts, leather tunics, fringed leather trousers, polo-necked jumpers, bush-shirts and jeans. Ready-to-wear shops followed, offering similar styles of conservative cut for both men and women.

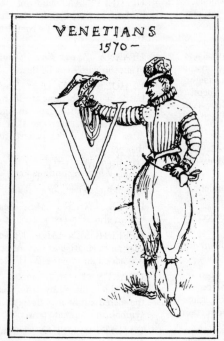

VENETIANS 1570—

VENETIANS *Pear shaped knee breeches, gartered below the knees. Also named SLOPS, 1570-* .

VAIR Squirrel fur from Northern Europe and Russia, worn by nobility. Med.

VALENCE *Masc.* Falling linen cover for helmet of medieval knight. Material of thin wool and silk. 14th Cent.

VALENCIA Strong material with carp of cotton and weft of worsted. Used for livery waistcoats. 1830-1840. Striped or figured.

VALENCIENNES Fine lace of cotton or linen thread made originally Valenciennes, France, 18th Cent; with wide net background and very clear pattern made from the same thread. Machine made imitations are now widely used.

VALLANCY *Masc.* A very large wig. 17th Cent.

VALONA *Masc.* Simple white starched upstanding collar worn by Philip IV of Spain. 1620-50.

VAMP Front upper portion of the shoe. Since 15th Cent.

VAMP *Fem.* The dramatic look exemplified in 1920s-1930s by film stars Theda Bara and Pola Negri. Look usually included - short hair with fringe or band covering forehead; heavy kohl-rimmed eye make-up; flowing, fluttering dresses with lowered waistline; long cigarette holders.

VAMPAYS Warm knitted socklike tubes of wool worn above footwear or stockings or on arms in Colonial America and in some parts of northern England. Known also as SCOGGER.

VAMPEY *Fr.* Upper portion of boot or shoe. 15th Cent.

VANDYKE Term applied to many decorative features and garments portrayed by the Flemish painter Sir Anthony Van Dyck.

VANDYKE BEARD Small pointed style as worn by Charles I of England and shown in portraits by Van Dyck. 17th Cent.

VANDYKE COLLAR Decorative lace-edged collar of lawn on falling band. Also called RABAT.

VANDYKED BORDER *Fem.* Used for decoration on hems, etc. long indoor gowns. 1790-1803.

VANITY CASE *Fem.* Small fitted bag or box usually for make-up articles.

VAREUSE *Masc.* Undervest worn by French sailors especially when on naval maintenance work.

VASQUINE *as Basquine Masc. and Fem.* Padded bolster shaped to tie around waist to give rounded silhouette seen in Spanish portraits 1620s-30s. A pad worn fastened at centre front. To achieve stylish appearance of the period, tightly laced corsets were also worn by both sexes.

VAST WINKER *Fem.* Cap with wide starched side frills wired to stand out from the face. 1745-1750.

VATERMORDER *Masc.* Biedermeier style tall collar attached to shirt with stiffly starched prominent points. Early 19th Cent., survived as wing collar worn for present day formal dress. Other names - A la Byron, Primo Tempo, Irlandaise, Orientale.

VEIL *Light material draped over face by many Eastern women for modesty and protection. Transparent material used as hat trimming. The head-dress of a nun. In early ancient times, it was not a general custom for women to wear a veil. Its scrupulous use in the Orient and Middle East dates from the decree of the Koran, which forbade women appearing unveiled except in the presence of their family. Otherwise, it was occasionally worn as additional ornament or for concealment.*

VELCRO Overlapping strips of fabric faced with tiny hooks which when pressed together act as fastening. To open, the strips are merely pulled apart. Invented by Swiss G. de Mestral. Early 1960s.

VELDTSCHOEN A South African shoe of Dutch origin made without nails of rawhide. The upper edges turned outwards and then stitched to sole. Similar to some N. American footwear.

VELOURS BEAU Treated calf skin which has been rubbed and brushed to a velvet-like finish.

VELOURS VELVET Luxurious fabric originally made in India and imported into Italy. In 16th Cent., velvet was manufactured in Florence, Genoa and Milan, later in Lyons, France. The French word 'velours' applies to velvet but English word is used for a heavier, thick, close-napped faced cloth.

VELVETEEN Cotton velvet with close, short pile. 1880s. An imitation of velvet.

VENETIAN BONNET *Fem.* Small straw bonnet trimmed with flowers, the long ribbon-strings coming from a back bow and tied across the breast. 1800.

VENETIAN CLOAK *Fem.* Satin, wide-sleeved cloak with cape. Usually black. 1829.

VENETIAN LACES Elaborate, raised needlelaces with flower-decorated and scrolling patterns. Punto in aria, Gros Point, Rose Point, Point de Neige. Flat lace - Point plat. 16th and 17th Cents. Densely patterned flat lace of beautiful quality. 18th Cent.

VENETIAN SLEEVE *Fem.* Style for a day dress. Fitting at the arm-hole, widening to mid-forearm. Split up the front to show puffed under-sleeve with tight cuff. 1858.

VENETIANS *Masc.* Fashionable knee breeches. Padded, full, narrowing downwards and fastened below the knee with fringed sash or a garter. Sometimes called Venetian slops. 1570-1620.

VENTOYE *Italian.* A fan, short stemmed with top vane. 17th Cent.

VERDINGALE *Fem.* Skirt-shaped petticoat with graduated hoops of cane or whalebone from waist to hem, introduced from Spain 1550, remaining popular until 1590. Worn with single-piece dress or separate bodice and skirt. The French style that followed in 1600 still pushed skirt away from legs but added a large hip-bolster, causing overlapping, covering material along flat top around the hips to resemble the spokes of a wheel. This dress was shorter than formerly and showed the ankles. Example - Tomb of Jane, Countess of Shrewsbury 1618 in Westminster Abbey. In 1616, James I issued an edict forbidding their appearance at court but they continued elsewhere for another four years. A revival was introduced in 1711 similar to the old Spanish form, flattened in front and behind. This oval shape was superseded by twin hoops tied to each side of the waist. 1750-1755. Also VERTUGADIN, VERTUGADO.

VERGETTE *Masc.* Style of wig with bag of rubberised silk at back and side curls. 1730.

VEST *Masc.* A continuation of the doublet of Middle Ages and a forerunner of the waistcoat. 1) Knee length, short sleeved, girdled and worn under tunic. 1660-1670. 2) Under garment or 'waist' coat worn for warmth. From 17th Cent. 3) When sleeveless, worn for evening dress. 1790-early 19th Cent. Name also given to French long corset. Early 19th Cent. Since 1850, name given to undervest in England.

VESTMENTS Accessories and robes of ecclesiastical dress; e.g. alb, amice, cassock, dalmatic, stole, surplice, etc.

VICTORIA Queen of Great Britain 1837-1901. Although she was not a leader of fashion, many changes of dress occurred during her long reign, worn also in Europe and N. America. She forbade the ladies of her court to wear the crinoline in 1856. In 1850s, the emergence of haute couture revolutionized dress and the fashion business. An Englishman, Charles Frederick Worth, with Otto Bubera, a Swede, became famous in 1858. Queen Victoria purchased some of his gowns from his salon in the Rue de la Paix, Paris and later some from Redfern, another Englishman also established in Paris. Her fondness for all things Scottish fostered the wearing of plaid trousers, kilts, Highland shawls and bonnets.

From 1864, Glengarry caps and 'pork-pie' hats were popular. Ribbon streamers hanging from behind such head-gear were fashionable and named 'follow-me-lads'. The influence of the Industrial Revolution was reflected in the changing appearance of clothes and there was great contrast between the wealthy and the poor. In men's dress, however, even Frenchmen accepted the skill of London tailors. By 1880s, the frock coat and top hat were established for masc. town wear, the cut-away coat with black silk facings was worn for evenings; other garments - short jackets, reefers, sports coats with belt, pockets and vertical pleats, knee breeches, gaiters and, accompanying the latter, a soft dented hat

VICTORIAN DRESS *The dress of the lady shows a jacket bodice, with the fullness of the Bustle pushed to the back. She has a small hat trimmed with the veiling fashionable at the period. Both men wear the prevailing top hats and frock coats. The right hand figure has a lapelled waistcoat and has a starched, pointed bow tie. Details of costumes based on contemporary paintings by Degas.*

was worn. *Masc.* Overcoats - Chesterfield, Gladstone. Capes - Inverness, Ulster. Quilted smoking jackets introduced for informal evening wear. With increasing prosperity, the clothes of those in domestic service also improved.

After 1850, in feminine dress, the fullness of material in the skirt was pushed to the back and looped into a kind of bustle. The newly available sewing machine and introduction of aniline dyes, contributed to the voluminous and garish coloured garments characteristic of this period. The coiffures of 1870 were elaborate but by the 1880s became more simple. Bonnets gave way to small hats, which were worn on top of highly piled chignons. As a protest against ugliness, a style called 'Aesthetic' dress was developed. A comfortable flowing gown was worn by a small section of the female community, corsets were discarded and the hair dressed more simply. Male Aesthetes wore velvet jackets, knee breeches, comfortable shirts and flowing ties with romantic-looking wideawake hats.

The 1890s saw another influence, that of 'Art Nouveau', characterised by decorative work using flat, naturalistic patterns of winding plant forms such as irises, orchids, poppies, wistaria, in applique work. At this time, fem. styles included lampshade capes, upstanding collars and velvet bonnets. The popularity of outdoor sporting pursuits at home and abroad after 1890 introduced a demand for more practical clothes. Tailormades and well-cut gored skirts were introduced but at the 'fin de siècle' the typical female day dress was still uncomfortable, with high-boned collar, tight waist and fitted hipline and a long, encumbering, full-length skirt still worn.

VICTORINE *Fem.* Narrow muffler or tippet, surrounding back of neck and shoulders, short ends in front, edged with fur and tied with ribbon at the throat. Mid 19th Cent. Name was also given at end of 19th Cent. to short or long cape with high collar.

VIENNA Capital of Austria with considerable influence on fashion in Europe and cultural institutions from 18th-19th Cent.

VIETNAM *Fem.* Simple Asiatic style of dress which became fashionable in 1960s. Features included straight tunic shape with standing collar, skirt length below the knees, often with tight pantalette trousers showing below. Materials - silks.

VIGONE *Masc.* Hat made from vicuna wool brought back from expeditions to South America. 17th Cent. Most European hats of this period made of beaver fur.

VIKING Scandinavian sea warriors who raided coasts of Europe and British Isles, Iceland and Greenland. 9th and 10th Cents. The main features of protective and warlike dress included horned helmet, round shields with metal boss, byrnies or coats of mail, large heavy swords, axes and spears, also leather thonged leg trousering and footwear. Fur cloaks worn over garments of good materials, fastened with massive brooches of silver and bronze. Necklaces, arm-rings of gold, glass and amber also worn.

VINYL Waterproofed fabric invented in U.S. in 1965 and used for protective garments and also for accessories. Manufactured in brilliant colours.

VIOLIN BODICE *Fem.* Form of decoration, in dark material on the back of bodice of a princess-shaped dress, like a violin. 1874.

VIRAGO SLEEVE *Fem.* Voluminous, padded and slashed sleeve tied with bands over elbow, to form two or more puffed portions. Usually finished with lace cuff. 1600-1650.

VISCOSE Solution of cellulose drawn into fibres and used in making of artificial silk. 20th Cent.

VISITE *Fem.* Name given to covering outdoor garment usually a cape or cloak. Styles changed from sleeveless to loose mantles with high collars but purpose of decorative outdoor protection remained. 1845-1890.

VISOR, VIZOR *Masc.* Movable upper piece of a helmet which could be lifted to show face. Med. Peak of cap, i.e. in sports wear to protect eyes from sun or wind. Contemporary.

VIYELLA Trade name for modern twill part-wool fabric made in England. Widely used and of high quality.

VIZARD Face covering or whole mask worn usually to conceal identity. 16th, 17th and 18th Cents.

VLIEGER *Fem.* Dutch name for surcoat or sleeveless ankle-length, high-necked outer garment, usually with short sleeves or shoulder roll. Made of rich materials. Late 16th Cent.-early 17th Cent.

VOGUE - the mode, the fashion. Also the title of a 20th Cent. magazine dealing with fashions.

VOIDED SHOE Low cut shoe style, leaving only covered toe-cap and instep strap. 16th Cent.

VOILE Thin, strong, semi-transparent dress material in cotton, wool, silk or rayon.

VOILETTE *Fem.* Tiny veil worn in 1840s.

VOLAN, VOLANT *Fr. Ruffle, flounce.* Trimming for sleeve. 19th Cent.

VOLET 1) Scalloped pennant decorating a helmet worn by knights in tournaments. 2) Short veil hanging from ladies head-dress. Both Middle Ages.

VOLUPERE *Masc., Fem.* Head-dress. Unidentified. 14th-15th Cent. *Fem.* Cap. 16th Cent.

VRAKI *Masc.* Very wide Turkish trousers with fullness between the legs. Also worn in Greece.

VULCANITE Rubber hardened by vulcanizing, a process increasing strength and elasticity. Used for making accessories. Late 19th Cent.

VULCANITE BUTTONS Manufactured in 1888.

VULTURE CAP Head-dress of Egyptian royalty. Worn by Queen Nefertari XIXth Dynasty.

159

ZIVKA *Masc.* Dark-coloured trouser worn by Turkish men. Full in upper part of garment but tight below the knee.

ZOCCOLO High platformed clog or wooden over-shoe worn to protect elegant shoe from mud. Used in Venice. 16th Cent.

ZONA *Masc.* Leather belt worn under armour by Greek soldiers. *Fem. Ancient Rome.* Band worn under or over breasts, made of cloth or soft leather.

ZONA BELT *Masc.* Obligatory outer belt worn by Christians and Jews in the Levant to distinguish them from Moslems.

ZONE *Fem.* Sewn-in decorative bib or 'fill-in' for low necked gown. Late 18th Cent.

ZOOT-SUIT *Masc., U.S.A.* Eccentric and exaggerated style of suit worn by followers of the swing music of the 1930s, consisting of long frock-coat, baggy trousers, a flowing tie, vast key-chain and broad brimmed hat. All in vivid colours.

ZORI *Japan.* Footwear designed to keep feet clean. Flat wooden sole supported by two cross slats and fastened by two thongs passing between first and second toes and divided across the foot. Also 'geta'. Worn with ceremonial kimonos.

ZORNEA *Masc., Ital.* Little cape with wide sleeves, fastened tightly into the waist by a belt. Worn by fashionable Venetians above close-fitting knitted tights.

ZOUAVE Member of French light infantry corps in Algeria. 1831. The uniform consisted of a collarless jacket made of Arabian blue cloth edged and decorated with red braid; red cloth pantaloons; red cap with blue tassel. Adopted by some companies in U.S. Civil War; also copied for feminine fashion in 1870s.

ZOUAVE COAT *Masc.* Fashionable cloak-like top-coat with velvet collar and cuffs, lined with quilted silk. Considered stylish for riding, walking or evening wear. 1845.

ZOUAVE JACKET *Fem.* Short coat of velvet or silk with many variations but all retaining the unfastened open front with collarless neckline and braid decoration. Fashionable 1859-1870 and re-emerging in 1890s.

ZOUAVE PALETOT *Masc.* Simple, straight, short overcoat made of waterproofed llama wool. 1840s.

ZOUNARI *Masc., Crete.* Long sash made of dark wool wound round and round the waist, allowing a dagger to be supported through the folds. Traditional.

ZUCCHETTO *Ital.* Small skull-cap worn by Roman Catholic priest; white for the pope, red for a cardinal, purple for a bishop and black for others.

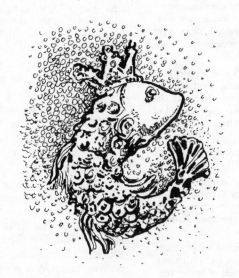

Crowned-fish pin, made of baroque pearl, gold and diamonds by the DUKE of VENTURA.

WHISK *from 1625*

WHISK *Wide, flat collar, plain or laced, covering the shoulders, from 1625 until 1680s.*

WABORNE LACE Braid lace made at Waborne, Norfolk. 16th Cent.

WADDED HEM *Fem.* Padded hem, fashionable for short period in Britain. Early 19th Cent.

WADERS Greased, high, leather boots which were not evolved until the 17th Cent. Used for angling or occupations which involved standing in water. Rubber was applied for proofing foot and leg wear in early 19th Cent., rubber boots became available for fishermen and agricultural labourers. Some thigh length wader boots were still made of leather until the early 20th Cent.

WADMAL, WADMOL Rough, hairy, woollen material used for jerkins and cold weather outer garments. Medieval.

WAFFEN *Ger.* Weapon.

WAFFENKAMMER *Ger.* Armoury.

WAFFENROCK *Masc., Ger.* Quilted doublet, tabard, tunic worn with armour. Also called WAMBAIS.

WAFFLE CLOTH Fabric with honeycomb weave used in children's and fem. fashion wear; also for masc. white waistcoats, ties for evening wear. 20th Cent.

WAGON BONNET *Fem.* Large simple bonnet worn in N. U.S.A. The wide projecting brim was rolled to surround the face; the hat was completed by material gathered into the crown; tied by a large bow under the chin. Usually of black material. Late 18th and early 19th Cent., and so named because of the semblance to covered wagons forming main transport of New World. Cp. Cabriole, Calash, large hats of same period worn in Europe, both resembling some kind of carriage and affording enlarged protection for fashionable, high, full hairdressing of the time.

WAISTCOAT *Masc., Fr. veste, gilet.* Development of the doublet from Middle Ages, extending over three hundred years. By the 17th Cent., worn for warmth or display, with or without sleeves, sometimes quilted. Also known as 'petticoat' or short coat. At the beginning of the 18th Cent., it was cut on similar lines to the coat but became shorter by 1775 and left unfastened at the top to show shirt underneath. Both the use of embroidery and brocade material had become fashionable by the 19th Cent. and either S.B. or D.B. styles were worn for day and evening wear until the end of the century but becoming more sombre in appearance after 1840. *Fem.* A tight jacket worn mainly for warmth. 17th

161

Cent. When worn for riding, it became masc. in appearance. Late 18th Cent. In early 19th Cent., the flannel waistcoat worn as a warm undergarment was gradually replaced by the under-vest. In 1850s, a fashion of incorporating elaborately decorative waistcoats with carriage dress became prevalent and late in the 80s and 90s, waistcoats of mannish cut were part of the tailor-made costumes of that period.

WAKEMAN'S HORN A costume of sobriety was worn by men who held the position of Wakeman or Watchman. This included a large horn on a baldric or shoulder-belt. The office was in existence five hundred years ago and the horn is still sounded in Ripon, England, daily.

WALE Raised ribs or ridges in twilled, corduroy or piqué fabrics.

WALKING STICK Not always a support or crude weapon, sometimes a personal decoration denoting rank or chic. Herodotus mentioned a Babylonian stick with decorated handle. 500 BC. In Middle Ages, some military leaders carried ornamental forerunners of the baton. In 17th Cent., fashionable women in France walked with little canes as accessories to their costume. In 18th Cent., men sported sticks, sometimes together with muffs. By the 19th Cent., masc. fashionable morning dress was completed with top hat and stick.

WALKING-OUT DRESS Smart uniform worn by British soldiers when leaving barracks and not on duty.

WALLABY Excellent shoe leather made from smaller kangaroo of Australia, the wallaby.

WAMMUS Masc. Jacket padded with flax, also heavy belted cardigan. Modern U.S.A.

WAMPUM Shell beads strung for currency and ornament by some North American Indians. Algonquin wompi - white.

WAMS, WAMBAIS Ger. Jacket, doublet.

WANAMAKER'S One of the first large stores opened in Philadelphia, U.S.A., to sell under one roof clothing from head to toe. Wares were displayed on stalls with prices clearly marked. In Paris, Le Bon Marché, La Samaritaine, Louvre and Printemps were launched. See also Whiteley's of London.

WARM Masc. Army overcoat worn in World War I. Referred to as 'British warm'. Usually camel coloured.

WASP WAIST Tight-lacing enhanced belt was much favoured by Cretan men and women. 17th Cent. B.C.

In France, late 17th Cent., women favoured slenderness. This was achieved by a tight corset from below breast to the end of the body. The corset also provided support when standing during long court ceremonial.

In 1890s, fashionable women in Europe and America achieved what was popularly known as a 'wasp-waist', or hourglass silhouette, by wearing a heavily boned corset. The desired measurement at waist was eighteen inches.

In 1949, after World War II, Christian Dior changed fem. dress outline by introducing into his New Look built-in belts or 'waspies' sewn in to the garment above

the post-war fuller skirts. This mini-corset was called a guêpière.

WATCH The first watch was made by Peter Henlein in Nuremburg, who invented the small mainspring at the end of the 15th Cent. In the 16th Cent., a watch was worn on a chain around the neck but one was presented to Queen Elizabeth I in the shape of a bracelet, or armlet, set with rubies and diamonds and containing a clock. James II of England possessed a gold watch with outer case of Cornelian made by Stringer c. 1687. Other beautiful enamelled and jewelled watches were made in this century, notably by David Bouquet 1628-65. Repeater watches in openwork cases were also made by Thomas Tompion and Edward Banfer about 1701. By the 18th Cent., watches became flatter and were kept in a fob-pocket. In 1838 watches made by machine appeared. At the turn of the 19th Cent., ladies' watches were worn on chains or tucked into a pocket at the belt. In the early 20th Cent., when the 'Gibson Girl' was popular, a watch was worn attached to the blouse or dress by a pin or brooch. The introduction of the watch attached to the wrist by a leather strap was developed in World War I for the use of military men. Since that time, as a useful but fashionable accessory, the watch has been made in many shapes and forms. The introduction of the modern quartz watch in streamlined, jewelled and attractive styles has proved useful and popular to many.

WATCHET Med. Name of pale greenish blue colour associated with the town of Watchet, Somerset, England. Also a cloth of that colour. To attend a wedding in 1623, the Duke of Bristol had more than thirty 'rich liveries made of Watchet velvet with silver lace up to the very capes of their cloaks'.

WATCHMAN Masc. In London, Bow Street Horse and Foot patrols were established as watch. 1760-1770. In 1805, a uniform was introduced consisting of long, blue great coat with cape, breeches, stockings and gaiters and red waistcoat. The watchman carried a rattle, lantern and long spear, stick or cudgel. A white nightcap was usually worn under a low crowned, wide-brimmed, dark slouch hat. The chief duty was to watch against fire.

WATER REPELLENT Garment or cloth allowing air to breathe through; water resisting and more comfortable to wear than a waterproof impregnated with a rubber solution.

WATERED SILK See MOIRÉ.

WATERFALL HAIRSTYLE Fem. Coiffeur arranged to allow hair to fall from a knot on the top of the head to the nape of the neck. 1860s.

WATERFALL NECKCLOTH Masc. As - Mail Coach Necktie; a large, long cashmere cloth folded round neck and tied loosely in front, the ends allowed to 'fall' and spread. Usually white, worn by high class drivers. 1818-1830.

WATERFALLBACK Fem. Name given to tablier or back piece of drapery, hanging straight down the dress in a fall, similar to water over a precipice. Late 1880s.

WATERMEN See DOGGETT.

WATERPROOF Garments made from material of which threads of fabric used are rendered waterproof before weaving. From 1880.

WATTEAU, JEAN ANTOINE French painter, 1684-1721, who considerably influenced fashion. His work was extensive, comprising scenes of military life, characters of Italian comedy and the fêtes galantes. His work was original, decorative and charming. The fem. dress named after him consisted of a pointed front bodice, stiffened with whale bones with pleats which hung from the shoulders at the back. Short sleeves had ruffles to the wrist. The skirt gave an impression of immense fullness and a gathered cape fell from the back of the neck to the ground.

WATTEAU PLEAT *Fem.* Style incorporating 18th Cent. Sack Back, for afternoon wear and Tea Gowns. 1890s.

WEDDING DRESS In Europe and parts of North America, it was customary for brides to wear white from about 1800 on, with variations according to style and custom. A notable historic collection of Royal wedding dresses can be seen in the Museum of London, including those of Princess Charlotte, Queen Victoria, Queen Mary and H.R.H. The Princess Margaret.

WEDDING SUIT *Masc.* For the affluent groom, previous to the 19th Cent., a ceremonial dress with white waistcoat and stockings was worn. In the British Isles, slowly, after 1820, a conventional blue dress-coat, black knee breeches and white waistcoat became standard or customary. Ten years later, white pantaloons succeeded knee breeches and the morning coat gradually replaced the dress coat. By the 1870s, the frock coat became 'de rigeur'. Accessories included white button-hole flower, silk top hat, light-coloured gloves.

WEDGE SOLE Wedge-shaped supporting piece of wood, cork, etc., placed under the arch of a shoe to make heel and sole of one piece flat on the ground. First recorded in Greek drama wear. See Cothurnus, Kothornus. *Fem.* Fashionable in 1940s, during World War II, when leather was difficult to procure by shoemakers because of wartime shortages.

WEEDS *O.E. Woede, a garment.* In 20th Cent., term refers usually to 'widow's weeds', mourning clothes.

WEEPERS *Masc.* Hired mourners at funerals. Late 18th-19th Cent. Black crepe or muslin hat sashes tied round hat with ends hanging at the back. Custom falling into disuse towards the end of the century.

WELDON'S LADIES JOURNAL An English middle class magazine that supplied paper patterns of high class but uncontroversial models. Early 20th Cent.

WELLINGTON, ARTHUR WELLESLEY, 1ST DUKE OF 1769-1852. As soldier, statesman and British Prime Minister, his name was given to many items of clothing.

WELLINGTON BOOT Leather knee-high top boot but without turnover, being cut straight across top. Early 19th Cent. A rubberized version was manufactured for general use from 1900 onwards. The name is still retained in the modern slang term 'Welly', a protective useful sporting or outdoor rubberized all-purpose boot worn by all.

WELLINGTON FROCK *Masc.* Single-breasted forerunner of Victorian frockcoat. Stand-fall collar but no lapels. No waist seam with full nearly knee-length skirt and buttoned to the waist. 1816-1820s.

WELLINGTON HAT *Masc.* Tall beaver hat, with slightly spreading crown eight inches deep, with brim. 1820-1830.

WELLINGTON PANTALOONS *Masc.* Pantaloons characterised by side splits from the calf down, closed by buttons and loops. 1820s.

WELSH COSTUME Until the end of the 18th Cent., dress worn in Wales was similar to that of English country people. Welsh women continued to wear a costume made of handwoven woollen and flannel cloth over the next hundred years. This consisted of 'pais a betgwn', petticoat and bedgown, the latter word anglicized, not meaning connected with bed. These garments were woven in stripes and check material dyed with local dyes and were warm and showerproof. The front divided skirt of the 'betgwn' was covered by an apron of similar material and the four corners were looped up by buttons to the back when required. Sleeves were elbow length with varied oversleeves to suit weather or Sunday wear. During 18th and 19th Cents., a white cap, plain or goffered, often worn under tall crowned hats until 19th Cent. Red flannel cloaks with large hoods also used in bad weather. In mid 19th Cent., an artist, Lady Llanover, encouraged interest in Welsh peasant costume and a so-called national costume was evolved encouraging tourism and more interest in Welsh life.

WELT Strengthening edging or border to garment. Piece of leather sewn round edge of boot or shoe uppers to aid attachment to sole.

WHALEBONE Pliable horny substance growing in thin plates in upper jaw of certain whales, used in many kinds of dress support. Used for long pointed toes of shoes and tall head-dress hennin. Bodices and stays were stiffened with strips from 16th Cent., and also in the peascod gentleman's doublet of 16th Cent.

WHANG *Scot.* Name given to leather straps, thongs and fastenings.

WHEEL FARTHINGALE *Fem.* Fashionable support for skirt of dress made in shape of a wire, silk-covered wheel worn round the waist and tilted slightly to the back. The material of the gown was placed over this and fell vertically to the ground. This style was worn in France and Italy from 1580-1620s.

WHIPCORD Durable corded fabric used for riding breeches, coats, etc., made from worsted yarns. From 1863.

WHISK *Masc., Fem.* Stiffened lace or lace-edged large collar. Also Wisk. 16th and early 17th Cents.

WHITE COCKADE Badge worn by the followers of Charles Edward, the Young Pretender.

WEDDING DRESS Both the bride and her attendant are wearing long dresses with fullness to the back of the skirts. The bodices are tight and slim waisted, having high collars and trimming at neck. Shoulders are made prominent with flounces. The attendant has a wide hat decorated with ribbon and stiffened plume. Late Victorian, 1899.

WHITE FRIARS *Masc.* Order of the Carmelites, who wore a white mantle over the brown habit. Their house, founded near Fleet Street, London in 1241, gives the name to that district.

WHITE TIE *Masc.* Term used on invitations to denote wearing of formal evening dress - black tailcoat, white waistcoat and white tie. (BLACK TIE implies informal wearing of dinner-jacket).

WHITECOLLAR WORKER Designation of the salaried working population whose duties call for the wearing of neat conventional clothing. 20th Cent.

WHITELEY, WILLIAM An Englishman who, influenced by the Great Exhibition in the Crystal Palace, Hyde Park, London in 1851, procured a whole street of shops and thus was able to build a large store with much success. He employed hundreds of assistants and sent goods all over the world.

WHITTLE *Fem.* Large white shawl, sometimes fringed, of good flannel. Recorded end of 17th and early 18th Cents.

WIDE-AWAKE *Masc.* Hat with low crown and rolling broad brim. From late 18th Cent. to mid-19th Cent. Sometimes banded with a centre buckle, as worn by American Quakers, but generally plain of soft felt. As earlier hats had been made of beaver fur and the felt used later had 'no nap', it is possible the name was in the nature of a joke.

WIDOW'S BANDORE *Fem.* Head-dress composed of a black band with a point or peak curving over the forehead. It was worn with a black veil hanging from the back. Early 18th Cent. Also, when called Widow's Peak, dated in France from 1572.

WIG Head covering of interwoven human hair or synthetic fibres shaped to decorate or to hide a lack of human hair. The ancient Egyptians wore them also as protection from the sun 2000 B.C., Cleopatra possessed wigs in many colours. In Greece, Aristophanes and Lucian refer to 'bags of har', 'helmets' and 'false heads'. Roman women wore wigs made from hair of captives and slaves, 1st Cent. A.D. Later, blonde hair was fashionable in Italy and yellow silk, fair or flaxen coloured wigs were worn by men and women. 16th Cent. Queen Elizabeth I in England is recorded as possessing at least eighty.

In France, wigs were introduced at court, c. 1640; Louis XIV granted licences to forty-eight Parisian wigmakers and the wig became a symbol of the aristocracy of that period. Colbert, the Chief Minister, imposed a tax on the wigmakers' trade; and by 1720s the size of wigs had decreased. In the early 18th Cent., much powder was used throughout Europe on the wigs but gradually this use of powder on wigs and hair was considered anti-social. By 1795, wigs were abolished, especially in France, as they were considered symbolic of the tyranny of fashion. It was not until 1950s and 60s that the wig became fashionable once more, in America and Europe chiefly as a stylish accessory for the flamboyant, youthful-looking outfits worn at that time.

In 18th Cent., men universally wore wigs in Britain and Europe. Names include Adonis, Artichoke, Bagwig, Barrister's, Bob, Brigadier, Buckled, Campaigne, Catogan, Cauliflower, Caxon, Chancellor's, Clerical, Club, Cue Peruke, Cut-Wig, Dalmatroy - a bob worn by tradesmen, Duvillier, Hedgehog, Pigeon's Wings, Pigtail, Ramillies, Scratch, Sollitaire, Toupee, Tye, Welsh, White Bob and many others. Women also wore wigs from 1795 to 1810.

Note: Bigwig. Term alluding to large wigs worn by aristocracy and by the Lord Chancellor, judges and barristers in 17th and 18th Cents. Such head wear encumbered the head and shoulders.

WIMPLE Development of Roman chincloth 'focalin' worn by public orators. *Fem.* Long piece of linen or silk, forming head covering which draped over the front of the neck and swathed round under the chin. Ladies of rank secured it by a crown or metal fillet. From 12th-14th Cent. Survives in nun's dress.

WINCEY, WINSEY A soft cloth made of cotton and wool mixture. 19th Cent.

WINDBREAKER, WINDCHEATER Outdoor jacket worn in 1930s of heavy lined material to resist sharp winds. Replaced to date by lighter anoraks of synthetic materials.

WING COLLAR *Masc.* Stiffened standing collar of shirt. Front with pointed turned-down corners. Late 19th and early 20th Cents., still worn with formal evening dress.

WIMPLE 12th-14th Century headdress which survives in nun's dress.

Side view of the wimple, copied from the 'Burial of Christ' by Dirk Bouts.

WINGED CUFFS *Fem.* Stiffened cuff falling away from sleeve on the outer side. 1700-1750s.

WINGS Decorative, stiffened bands of material projecting across the shoulder seam of doublets and jerkins. 16th and 17th Cents.

WINKERS *Masc.* Extremely high collar points of shirts worn by fashionable men. Early 19th Cent.

WINKLE-PICKER *Masc.* Shoes with excessively pointed toes, a fashion of the 1950s.

WINTERHALTER, FRANZ XAVIER German portrait painter. 1805-1873. Notable for his paintings of beautiful women in the age when crinolines were worn, particularly for those depicting the Empress Eugenie and her ladies-in-waiting. He was also court painter of portraits to Queen Victoria.

WISCIA *Fem.* Italian leather bodice embroidered with gems and pearls, worn on outside over a long under-tunic. Early Middle Ages. 14th Cent.

WISK *Masc., Fem.* Standing band or upright collar without a turnover but with framework or wire fixed at the back of the neck to support a starched ruff or large collar. Early 17th Cent. It was supplanted by the falling band. See WHISK.

WITNEY Heavy woollen cloth from Witney, Cotswold England. Since 18th Cent. Used for men's overcoats from mid-19th Cent.

WITZCHOURA, WITCHOURA *Fem.* Named from Polish coat named 'wilczura', wolfskin. Long, warm coat, fur-trimmed and fur-lined, it was designed to be worn over the lightweight dresses that were fashionable in the early 19th Cent.

WOODSTOCK GLOVES *Masc., Fem.* Fawn leather skin gloves made in Woodstock, England, by noted glovemakers. Late 18th Cent.

WOLVERINE Carniverous mammal about three feet long found in N. America, Russia, Siberia and Scandinavia. Possesses long, black, thick hair which does not frost. Used by Eskimos and as trimming and as fringe by Indians.

WOOL Fibrous growth forming fleece of sheep, mohair and angora goat, alpaca camel, llama, etc. When cleansed and spun into yarn, used for knitting or weaving into a soft warm fabric. The art of weaving was known in ancient times by many different peoples.

WORSTED Smooth yarn or thread made of wool; from Worsted (old Sp.) a village near Norwich, once the centre of a thriving woollen-weaving industry. The name existed as early as the 13th Cent.

WORTH, CHARLES FREDERICK. An Englishman who became a great dressmaker in France. Innovator of haute couture and founded the House of Worth in 1858. The Empress Eugenie and most European royalty were his patrons. He predicted successfully what would become fashionable and dictated Paris fashions for thirty years.

WRAPAROUND SKIRT *Fem.* 20th Cent. style, worn usually for leisure and of one piece, designed to be wrapped round the body and fastened at the waist with a deep overlap.

WRAPPER *Fem.* Negligee or informal robe. Since 18th Cent. *Masc.* Thigh-length loose overcoat, single breasted and double breasted but often held in place by hand. Deep shawl collar. Worn often with evening dress. 1840-1850s.

WRAPPING FRONT *Fem.* The bodice of a dress fastened by a front with cross-over folds. 1800-1830.

WRAPPING GOWN *Fem.* Dress with wrapover front continued down the skirt to the hem. Early 18th Cent.

WRAP-RASCAL *Masc.* Long, loose, travelling overcoat, usually of heavy material, fastened with metal buttons, often with multiple capes overlapping each other, to shed the rain. Used for coach travel. 18th to early 19th Cent.

XANTHUS *Gk.* Ancient name of the River Scamander. The colour of its gold-red water tinged the fleeces of the sheep washed in it. A reddish yellow.

XENOPHON Athenian historian, who described the expedition of Cyrus against Artaxerxes 401-399 B.C. He described gloves with separate finger shapes, worn by the Persians.

YACHTING COSTUME   Ladies wore a peaked hat, tailored jacket and a long skirt resembling naval uniform.

YACHTING JACKET   *Fem.* Short, hip-length jacket, square cut, with loose sleeves, large buttons. Late 19th Cent. Yachting became accepted as part of the extended life style of the wealthier and more leisured classes. It was made popular during the reign and influence of Edward VII of England.

Suitable costumes were evolved for those who could participate in this lifestyle. In the early 1900s women, largely in the role of spectators, wore 'naval' looking tailor-mades, usually of white, cream or navy material. The jackets were fitted, with neat revers, and the skirts smoothly flared and long. A neat high-necked blouse and a sailor hat or large beret-like peaked cap completed the outfit. Men's suits followed the well-fitting appearance of a ship's officer. Modern times and materials have, however, provided excellent suitable sea-going garments at reasonable prices, thus making the participation of water and naval sports of today available to many.

YAK LACE   English bobbin lace made in Northampton, England, from Yak wool. Heavy and slightly rough, it was used for fashionable warm shawls. 1870-1880.

YANKEE NECKCLOTH   *Masc.* High stock, pleated on each side of the front centre portion; the narrow ends of the tie are brought to the front and tied low in a knot. Also named American Neckcloth. Early 19th Cent.

YARD MEASURE   Linear measure established in the reign of Henry II, 1154-1189, by the length of the King's arm. Thirty-six inches long.

YARK   A buckled strap used by labourers for hitching up trousers, worn below the knee. 1880s.

YARMULKE   *Masc.* Skullcap worn by Orthodox Jews.

YARNFIBRES or FILAMENTS   Thread made suitable for knitting or weaving, after being laid or twisted into a continuous thread.

YASHMAK, YASHMAC   *Fem.* White or black veil worn by Moslem women covering the whole face or hanging below the eyes. Other names - litham, maharmah, mandeel.

YASDI   Silk tissue made in city of Yadz, Iran.

YATAGHAN   *Turkish.* Dagger, usually curved, without a handle or hilt.

YATSHMAGH   *Masc. Iraq.* Draped headscarf of black and white or red and white cotton.

YELLOW Colour of gold, a primary colour. In heraldry and in ecclesiastical symbolism, yellow is often used in place of gold. In some medieval countries, the law ordained that Jews must be clothed in yellow. The victims of a Spanish auto-de-fe were robed in yellow to denote heresy.

YEOMAN Man owning and farming his own land; officer of royal household; member of volunteer force of cavalry.

'YEOMAN' HAT *Fem.* A style of the early 19th Cent., made of soft material with the crown gathered into a broad band, sometimes with a close turned-up brim. Worn when walking or for mornings.

YEOMAN OF THE GUARD Men appointed by Henry VII, in 1485, to form part of retinue at banquets and grand occasions. Yeomen Extraordinary were appointed as warders of the Tower of London by Edward VI and still wear the Tudor-period costume as Yeomen of the Guard. The popular name 'Beefeater' bestowed on them refers to rations given to 'eater' - O.E. for servant. The uniform included a black, low-crowned, brimmed beaver hat trimmed with band of ruched red, white and black ribbon; a knee-length doublet or jerkin, with low belted waistline, ornamented royal decoration at front and a frilled ruffle at neck. Knitted hose was worn below matching breeches, with wide, round-toed shoes. From 15th Cent.

YOKE Separately cut piece of material fitted to the shoulders or hips. In 16th Cent., fem. bodice often had inserted a yoke of pleated linen, which formed the ruff as well. In the first quarter of the 19th Cent., the style of sloping shoulders forced an inset of a yoke with a high ruff about the neck. This was designed to hold up the heavy sleeves then fashionable.

YORK WRAPPER *Fem.* High-necked morning dress, which was buttoned down the back. Usually of muslin decorated in front with lace 'diamond' shapes or embroidery. 1813.

YORKSHIRE The area where the woollen cloth was made entirely in the home of the head or master weaver - every member of the family, every spare hand helped. 18th Cent.

YOUG Irish needle lace with flat open mesh and floral patterns. Late 19th Cent.

YOUNG ENGLISHWOMAN 19th Cent. fashion magazine, which printed work by French artists of renown, including that of Jules David.

YEOMAN WARDER of the Tower of London in state dress uniform.

YUKATA *Masc., Fem. Japan.* Short, summer kimono worn at home over an undergarment. Style worn since 12th Cent. and which remains practical and elegant today.

ZOUAVE JACKET *Inspired by the uniform jacket worn by Algerian Zouve troops, it was fashionable in the late 19th Century.*

ZAMARRA *Masc., Sp.* Shepherd's coat of goatskin or sheepskin, sleeved. Sometimes worn with protective cap of similar skin.

ZAPOTEC Tribe in Oaxaca, Mexico, whose women wear a spectacular costume for festive occasions consisting of long wrapped colourful skirt with an unusual pleated Spanish blouse or huipil worn as a head-dress. This is made of starched ruffed white lace worn framing the head, covering the shoulders or flowing down the back.

ZARAPE Fringed, colourful wrap worn by South American Indians and Mexicans. Larger than poncho, with slit in centre front for the head. Dated from the Aztecs and decorated with woven motifs and colours used originally by them. Also - sarape.

ZENDADO *Fem., Ital.* Black veil worn by Venetian women during High Renaissance; it was enlarged and developed into a cape and was worn as a shawl by 16th Cent.

ZEPHIRINA Lightweight coating material of mixed colours. 1841.

ZEPHYR Thin, silky gingham, with supporting warp and finer weft. 1880s.

170

ZEPHYR SHIRTING Fine, lightweight flannel mixed with silk used for wear in hot climates. 1880s.

ZEPHYR SILK BAREGE Lightweight, gauzy material of silk and wool. 1840s.

ZIBELLINE Lustrous woollen cloth or cotton or wool, with silky nap brushed in one direction. Used for fem. capes, cloaks. 1856.

ZIMARRA *Masc., Fem., Ital.* Renaissance gown of varying lengths with arm openings. Sometimes lined and faced with fur or false sleeves. An imposing similar costume called SIMARRE is still worn by French university professors and magistrates.

ZINGARI *Ital.* Gipsies, possibly from India, Sind (India) or from Ethiopia, or Egypt Zangi (Persian).

ZIPONE *Masc., Ital.* Buttoned Venetian tunic to just above knees, worn over close-fitting, knitted tights. A Renaissance style which was imitated by wealthy Europeans.

ZIPPER Slide fastener of interlocking teeth on tapes, used for garments. First made in 1920s and perfected in 1930s and now in general use.

ERRATUM
The continuation of this alphabetical list
is on page 160

Appendices

Couturiers, Designers, Couture Houses

BEFORE 20TH CENTURY

Prior to 1850, there were few individual dress designers of quality. The Courturier developed from the dress designer to high class fashion houses. During the 20th Century the Courturier became the most powerful creative figure in the world of fashion.

BERTIN, ROSE   Fr. Dressmaker to Queen Marie Antoinette. Fled to London at the time of the French Revolution. Late 18th Cent.

DAVID, JACQUES LOUIS   Notable Fr. artist commissioned with ISABEY, another court painter, to make designs for Napoleon's ceremonial robes. (1748-1825).

LEROY   Fr. dressmaker, who undertook the making of costumes for the coronation of Napoleon, 1804.

The Emergence of Haute Couture

In the 1850s, the emergence of 'Haute Couture' was brought about in Paris by the Englishman, CHARLES FREDERICK WORTH. He established premises in the Rue de la Paix, with a staff of twenty in 1858 and,

by 1865, he was dressing the nobility of Europe. With the French defeat in the Franco-Prussian War, the House of Worth was closed in 1870. The firm of REDFERN, an Englishman whose name was Charles Poynter, opened a branch in the Rue de Rivoli, 1881, which became famous for tailor-mades. The firm was originally founded in 1842. Queen Alexandra and the actress, Sarah Bernhardt, were among his notable clients. The firm of CREED, is still maintained in London and Paris, with a reputation of fine tailoring for over two hundred years. He became tailor for the Comte D'Orsay and was originally recommended by Queen Victoria to the Empress Eugénie, as a maker of riding-habits. It was founded in the Rue de la Paix. CHARLES CREED, the great grandson of the founder, opened a house in London after World War II. A tailored suit made for the Duchess of Alba by him was possibly the first step towards 'UNISEX' designs, which made fashion news in the 1960s. He took small collections to the American market most successfully and continued designing until his death in 1966.

20TH CENTURY

ADRIAN   Chief creator of U.S. film fashions, famous in 1930s and 40s. Noted for full-skirted flower-printed evening wear and also for the padded shoulders worn by filmstar Joan Crawford. He left films in 1939. Presented couture and ready-to-wear collections, 1942-1952.

AGNES, Mme.   Fr. milliner, Paris. Created elegant, small draped turbans, 1920s. Achieved a 'sculptured' look with use of crinkled silk and new synthetic materials. 1930s.

AISSA   Spanish branch of BALENCIAGA.

ALIX   See GRES.

AMIES, EDWIN HARDY   B. 1909. English. Began career with Digby Morton. One of the Society of London Fashion Designers, 1942. Established a saloon in Savile Row, 1946; also exported his collections to the Americas. He later promoted a boutique and ready-to-wear section. He has had international success and designed for Queen Elizabeth II.

ARMANI   Italian designer of unisex clothes. Noted for use of soft bright colours in men's wear. 1980s.

ASHLEY, LAURA   Welsh producer, with great success, of simple flowered textiles and dress designs. Immensely favoured by the young. Has received world

acclaim for simple attractive designs, quality and appeal. Her unfortunate death, in 1985, has not stopped production of merchandise bearing her name.

BALENCIAGA, CHRISTOBEL   Sp. A native of the Spanish-Basque area and the last of the 'pure courturiers; he retired in 1968. Famous early in his career for sophisticated toilettes in black. He was a master of sculptured shape, with tailored detail.

BALMAIN, PIERRE   Fr. Opened his first house and collections in 1945. Started originally with Molyneux, the Englishman, in 1934. After the war, he visited London and toured and lectured in U.S. and S.A. He dressed filmstars of a new generation, including Sophia Loren, Brigitte Bardot and the ageless Dietrich.

BIBA   A London boutique. See designer, Barbara HULANICKI.

BLASS, BILL   Leading New York designer and manufacturer. His career was interrupted by World War II service, but is now head of a successful ready-to-wear business. 1980s.

BOHAN, MARC   Outstanding Fr. designer, who worked with Molyneux and Paton. In 1958 he joined Christian Dior.

CALLOT SOEURS   The fashion house that led the social world from 1895 until World War I. Controlled by three sisters, their garments specialised in toilettes made of soft laces, chiffon and georgette.

CARDIN PIERRE   One of the young designers of the Sixties. He created futuristic clothes for both men and women and also directed his inventiveness to include other projects - furniture, glass and china. In 1970, he showed printed floral skirts with an ethnic look. These were worn with leotards and high boots.

CARVEN, MME., CARMEN MOLLET   Began her career before the occupation of France, World War II. After the war, she opened a new house successfully, becoming one of France's leading designers. Her perfume MA GRIFFE is much favoured by smart women.

CARNEGIE, HATTIE   U.S. successful designer of ready-to-wear neat suits, with trim jackets having slanted hip pockets, worn above pleated skirts. 1950s.

CASHIN, BONNIE   U.S. Famous award-winning couturiere. Leisure clothes, with oriental as well as Californian flare, are characteristic of her individual style. 1950s, 1960s. She has combined leather and knits in large coats, all having a simple good-looking natural appearance. 1980s.

CASSINI, OLEG   Russian, born in 1913, lived in Florence, opening a dress salon in Rome, 1933. In 1937 he went to U.S. and became an outstanding designer in New York.

CHANEL, GABRIELLE   Began a fabulous career in 1914 and her influence has remained powerful for more than fifty years. She interrupted this career from 1939-1954 but continued working later until her death in 1971. Her house still goes on and her initial style of extreme simplicity is maintained. The Chanel suit is more a way of life than a fashion. She innovated the sweater line, the pleated skirt, the triangular scarf; also originating the fashion chunky glass bead necklaces and strings of fake pearls as contrast to these subtle simple styles. Her perfume 'Chanel No. 5', 1925, has had lasting acclaim. Her re-opening in 1954 was based on her pre-war themes and led to a second reign of success.

CIERACH, LINDKA   A private dressmaker of unusual ability who came into fame with the celebrated wedding-dress she made for the Duchess of York, 1986.

CLARK, OSSIE   One of the new London designers for the young. 1960s onwards.

CONNOLLY, SYBIL   Of Dublin, Ireland. Produced beautiful knits, linens, tweeds and handmade laces, which she used to create elegant, wearable garments of outstanding quality.

CONRAN, JASPER   British designer with great style. 1960s on.

COSTELLOE, PAUL   Irish-born designer working in London, exporting tailored clothes in classic fabrics. 1960s on.

COURRÈGES   Native of the Spanish Basque area, who worked for Balenciaga for ten years. He became independent in 1961. His collections showed the first raising of the hemline to mid-thigh, named the MINI. 1963-1964. He introduced other innovations such as top-stitching, double rows of buttoning down suit-fronts, trouser-suits, masculine mid-shin boots and mannish hats, always retaining quality of cloth and good cut. He has been extensively copied; and has expanded his business with accessories, bearing his name, all over the world.

DIOR, CHRISTIAN   1905-1957. Formerly an art-dealer and later a designer with Lucien Lelong, he established himself as a couturier in 1946. His first Paris collection took the fashion world by storm and launched his famous 'New Look'. The new shape had unpadded, rounded shoulders, a shapely bust-line, small waist, slightly padded hips, with billowing skirts reaching to below the calves, often requiring petticoats to support them. Within six years, there were Dior companies all over the world. The 'New Look' was followed by the H-Line, 1954; the Y-line, 1955; the A-line and F-line, 1956. Even after his sudden death in 1957, the vast fashion complex named after him still operates around the world.

ERTÉ   Famous French artist and designer. He worked originally in Paris with Poiret before World War I. He came to U.S.A. in 1968. An exhibition of his dress and stage designs was held in the Metropolitan Museum of Art.

FARHI, NICOLE   Designed for d'ALBY. In 1984, joined Stephen Marks to form FRENCH CONNECTION. She also produces her collections under her own name.

FATH, JACQUES   A brilliant designer and painter who enjoyed success in United States. 1912-1954.

FÉRARD   Parisian designer using ethnic themes. 1970s.

FRATINI, GINA   Young designer in London, 1960s. Produced unconventional delightful dresses, using pretty cottons in Watteau-like dairymaid styles.

GALANOS, JAMES   Of Greek parentage, settling in Los Angeles, 1951. Specialised in sophisticated evening gowns and has shown collections annually in New York.

GALITZINE, PRINCESS IRENE   Born in Russia. Now of Rome, she shows collections of outstandingly beautiful lingerie and evening wear in Paris.

GIBB, BILL   British designer, worked for Baccarat, starting in 1972. Won prestige for his combined use of leather or fur with fabric; patterned knitwear and outstandingly simple elegant dramatic clothes. Died 1988.

GIVENCHY, HUBERT DE   Frenchman, who studied at L'Ecole des Beaux Arts, Paris; he trained with Schiaparelli and Balenciaga, opening his own house in 1957. His first collection, which was a triumph, was made in gingham, for economy's sake. He introduced the 'Sack' which, although simple, was a landmark in leading to the 'Shift'.

GRÈS, ALIX   French designer of great skill, who draped and manipulated fabrics. She was noted for her unusual bold colour schemes and the skilful cutting of material on the bias.

GRIFFE, JACQUES   Frenchman who worked with Vionnet until World War II. After war service, he came to U.S.A., becoming famous. His clientele includes Royalty and well-known American and English personages.

HARTNELL, NORMAN   Englishman, who initiated a new era of couture in Britain. He was 'discovered' in the 1920s, establishing premises in Bruton Street, London, in the early '30s. Thereafter, he also showed his collections in Paris and maintained a long association with Royalty. Died 1986.

HULANICKI, BARBARA   Famous for launching a boutique, BIBA, and later converting Derry & Toms, of Kensington, into an Art Deco store in the '60s. She now works in Brazil and provides expensive and extreme fashions in an international field.

KAMALI, NORMA   A designer of the '80s, who launched her own boutique and used her label OMO -'On My Own', popularising cotton jersey and quilted nylon. She created the RA-RA skirt, much favoured by younger women, in 1983.

KHANH, EMMANUELLE   French designer, who had originally modelled for Balenciaga and Givenchy, held her first collection in 1961. Produced simple high quality ready-to-wear clothing in the '70s.

LAPIDUS, TED   Designed in Paris, setting fashion in the unisex wear of conservative appearance, with crisp tailoring. Late 1968, 69.

LAGERFIELD, KARL   Fr. Designs furs, knitwear, shoes and fabrics, gowns and separates. Sells ready-to-wear clothes under the name of CHLOE. Appointed chief designer to House of CHANEL, 1980s.

LANVIN, JEANNE   Haute couturiere, famous for great style. She used colours from the works of artists and even from stained glass windows. Her house was founded in 1890 but still today is carried on and has much cachet. Her nephew Bernard is in charge of a boutique opened in 1968.

LELONG, LUCIEN   Internationally known Paris fashion house, established 1889, and the first one to open a boutique in 1933. During German occupation of World War II, he resisted plan to move French couture to Berlin and Vienna. He also was the first couturier to promote perfume as part of couture.

LUCILLE, LADY DUFF GORDON   Came into prominence with her opening parade in Paris in 1912. Developed business in New York during World War I. She dressed many of Florenz Ziegfield's productions and sold her London house in 1918. Her post-war designs were elegant and beautiful. Died 1937.

MAINBOCHER   Born in Chicago, U.S.A. Fashion editor to Vogue, opening a couture establishment in Paris, 1930. He returned to America, introducing many new fashions, including his evening sweaters of the '50s, which gained world acclaim, and other relaxed leisure wear.

MOLYNEAUX, CAPTAIN EDWARD   An Irishman, who worked with Lucille. He began a cycle of change in the '30s and after World War II presented full dirndl skirts. He was one of the TOP TEN members of the Incorporated Society of London Fashion Designers inaugurated in 1942. His own house was in Paris, where he designed for both society and the French and English stage.

MUIR, JEAN   A London designer in the '60s with Jaeger and in 1962 was backed by Courtaulds; later working independently under her own name. She sells throughout Britain, the U.S., Canada, Australia and Europe. Her clothes are elegant, distinctive, mannered; mostly manufactured in light-weight jersey, crepe or silk, in neutral tones or black.

PAQUIN, MADAME   French. The first woman to achieve recognition and eminence since Rose Bertin. Her house, founded in 1892, was particularly known for her 'tailleurs' and shimmering evening gowns. She introduced the use of fur as trimming.

PATOU, JEAN   French. Opened a salon in Paris, 1919, designing for American as well as French women. He claimed credit for the longer skirts which came in the late '20s. By 1967, his firm was showing young short bolero-topped suits.

PERTEGAZ, MANUEL   Leading Spanish designer, who creates beautiful austere and successful clothes. His house in Barcelona was opened in 1940s.

POIRET, PAUL   Fr. The first of the modern couturiers and the last of the traditionalists. He banished the elaborately curved and corseted 'S'-shaped figure and brought the natural line into fashion by loosening the constricted waist. He introduced strong startling vibrant colours, influenced by paintings of 'Les Fauves' in 1905 and by the exhibition of Russian art, 1906. By 1912, floating panels and panniers, tunics and tube-like skirts appeared. Poiret-inspired slinky dresses with slit hems were worn for the new TANGO teas and parties. Sadly, after World War I, after many years of poverty, he died in 1943.

PUCCI, MARCHESE EMILIO   His collections shown in Florence are renowned for simple beautifully-cut silk jersey gowns, elegant culottes and pants. 1960-1980.

QUANT, MARY   The English designer who, with her husband Alexander Plunket Green, initiated and led the new fashion movement in London in the '60s. Her startling inventiveness included crisp lively clothes, with short and shorter skirts. She launched a range of fashion goods named 'the GINGER GROUP'. By 1967, she had business with America and most other Western countries, receiving the O.B.E. for her services to fashion. About 65% of her output goes for export and includes clothes, boots, tights, foundation wear, cosmetics, household textiles, shoes.

REBOUX   Fr. milliner who caused a sensation after World War I with chic small cloche hats. They were head-hugging, of light-weight materials and extremely attractive with a minimum of trimming.

RHODES, ZANDRA   The most original British creator of the 20th Cent., for unconventional clothes. These are made in lovely fabrics, designed and many painted by herself. Her work caused a sensation in the '60s and she is still achieving beautiful creations today and has a world-wide reputation.

RICCI, NINA   Italian. She founded a most succesful house in Paris with her son in 1939.

RODRIGUEZ, PEDRO   Sp. A couturier with establishments in Barcelona, San Sebastian and Madrid.

SAINT LAURENT, YVES   Working at the house of Dior in 1958, he was acclaimed as the great couturier's successor when Dior died that year. He created the 'Trapeze silhouette' and in 1962 opened his own establishment. In 1966 he was showing 'Pop Art', featuring plain dresses in varied fabrics, including see-through chiffons. He adapted copies of the clothes worn by pop-culture idols, such as decorated studded leather jackets. Later he made a feature of geometric sheath dresses. In 1967 the maxi-coat was paraded and worn over the mini-skirt. He returned to simpler forms of sophistication in the '70s.

SCHIAPARELLI, ELSA   Italian. Settled in France in 1920s. She promoted the squared padded shoulders shown in *Vogue* in 1933. These were an outstanding feature of pre-war and wartime fashion, emphasising slenderness of waist and hips. She was always inventive, introducing unusual knitwear, embroideries, burnouses, using tweeds from Skye and designing material for Viyella. Her use of bright pink, which she called 'Shocking', was her hallmark. Salvador Dali created a window display for the boutique she opened in 1935.

SCOTT, KEN   An American, who uses beautifully printed silks and lives and works in Milan. He is acknowledged as a superb designer.

SIMONETTA-FABIANI   Established in Paris in 1962, showed satin and brocade pants, with lavishly decorated matching jackets. These were shown in Florence at the Palazzo Pitti, which had been made available as a salon by the Italian Government. Other couture houses showing here have included Emilio Pucci and Valentino of Rome.

TIFFEAU, JACQUES   A Frenchman who became eminently successful in New York from 1960s onwards.

TOP TEN   The Incorporated Society of London Fashion Designers was launched in 1942 to present a common front to the Board of Trade in face of wartime restrictions. Early members were Norman Hartnell, Peter Russell, Worth, Angele Delanghe, Digby Morton, Victor Stiebel, Hardy Amies, Molyneux, Creed and Michael Sherard.

UNGARO, EMMANUEL   Worked with Balenciaga and opened his own house in Paris in 1961. In 1965 he showed a collection of 'Space Age' designs, using primary colours and mannish cut.

VALENTINA   American couturiere, who created a short ballerina dinner dress in 1940s. This garment became extremely fashionable when business escorts did not wear evening dress.

VIONNET, MADELEINE   Fr. She worked in London as a young woman, returning to Paris. Opened an establishment in the Rue de Rivoli, after working for five years with Doucet. From 1918-1939 she had great influence upon the top couturiers of that period.

YUKI   Born in Japan. An acclaimed contemporary designer working in Britain. A master cutter of material and unusual drapery. 1970s on.

Bibliography

Adaptable Stage Costume for Women   Elizabeth Russell   (J.Garnet Miller, 1974)

A Concise History of Costume   James Laver   (Thames & Hudson, 1977)

Corsets and Crinolines   N. Waugh   (Batsford, 1970)

Costume   P. Cunningham   (A.& C. Black, 1966)

Costume   (Cassell, 1963)

Costume and Fashion in Colour   Jack Cassin-Scott   (Blandford Press, 1975)

Costume in England   F.W.Fairholt   (Chapman & Hall)

Costume in Pictures   R.Cunnington   (Dutton, 1964)

Costumes of Everyday Life   Margot Lister   (Barrie & Jenkins, 1968)

Costume in Antiquity   James Laver   (Thames & Hudson, 1964)

Costume in Detail, 1730-1930   Nancy Bradfield   (Harrap, 1968)

Costume of the Western World   Doreen Yarwood   (Lutterworth, 1980)

The Dictionary of Costume   R.Turner Wilcox   (Batsford, 1969)

A Dictionary of English Costume   C.W. and P.E.Cunnington   (A.& C.Black, 1966)

Dress   James Laver   (John Murray, 1950)

Dress and Undress   Iris Brook   (Methuen)

Dressed for the Job   C.Williams Mitchell   (Blandford Press, 1982)

English Costume   Dion C. Calthrop   (Black, 1907)

English Costume from the Second Century B.C. to 1972   Doreen Yarwood   (Batsford)

Everyday Life Series   M. & C.H.B.Quennell   (Batsford)

Fashion from Ancient Egypt to the Present Day   Mila Contini   (Paul Hamlyn, 1965)

Fashion through Fashion Plates   Doris Langley Moore   (Ward Lock Ltd, 1971)

The Fashionable Lady in the Nineteenth Century   C.H. Gibbs-Smith   (H.M.S.O., 1960

Five Centuries of American Costume   (A. & C.Black, 1966)

Folk Costume of the World   Robert Harrold and Phyllida Legg   (Blandford Press, 1978)

Handbook of English Costume in the Sixteenth Century   Willett and Cunnington   (Faber & Faber, 1970)

Handbook of English Costume in the Seventeenth Century   Willett and Cunnington   (Faber & Faber, 1973)

Handbook of English Costume in the Eighteenth Century   Willett and Cunnington   (Faber & Faber, 1973)

Handbook of English Costume in the Nineteenth Century   Willett and Cunnington   (Faber & Faber, 1970)

Handbook of English Costume in the Twentieth Century, 1900-1950   Mansfield   (Faber & Faber, 1973)

Historical Costumes of England, 1066-1968   (Harrap, 1970)

History of American Costume, 1607-1870   (Tudor, U.S.A., 1969)

History of Costume in the West   François Boucher   (Thames & Hudson, 1966)

History of English Costume   Iris Brooke   (Methuen Ltd, 1972)

History of Fashion   Anderson Black and Madge Garland   (Orbis, 1975)

History of World Costume   Carolyn Bradley   (Peter Owen Ltd, 1970)

The Mode in Costume   Turner Wilcox   (Charles Scribner & Sons, New York, 1969)

Modes and Manners of the XIXth Century (4 vols.)   Dr Oscar Fischel and Max von Boehn   (Dent)

The Pictorial Encyclopaedia of Fashion   L.Kybalová, O.Herbenová and M.Lammarová   (Hamlyn Publishing Group, 1968)

Style in Costume   James Laver   (Oxford University Press, 1949)

Taste and Fashion   James Laver   (Harrap, 1945)

A Technical History of Costume   (Barnes & Noble)
> Vol.I *Ancient Egypt, Mesopotamia and Persia*
> Vol.II *Ancient Greek, Roman and Byzantine*
> Vol.III *Medieval Costume in England and France*

Costume Illustration: the Nineteenth Century   Introduction by James Laver   (Victoria and Albert Museum, 1947)

Costume Illustration: the Seventeenth and Eighteenth Centuries   Introduction by James Laver   (Victoria and Albert Museum, 1951)

Victorian Fashions and Costumes   From Harper's Bazaar, 1867-1898   (Dover Publications, Inc., New York)

Victorian People   Gillian Avery   (Collins)

A Visual History of Costume   (Batsford)

Other Valuable Sources

Catalogue of Rubbings of Brasses and Incised Slabs   (Victoria and Albert Museum, 1968)

Catalogue Raisonné des Peintures du Moyen-Age, de la Renaissance et des Temps Modernes. Peintures Flamandes du XVe et du XVIe Siècle   (Louvre, Paris, 1965)

Les Trè Riches Heures du Duc de Berry   (London,1969)

Peintures Ecole Française XIVe, XVe et XVIe Siècles   (Louvre, Paris, 1965)

The Golden Age: Manuscript Painting at the Time of Jean, Duc de Berry   (London, 1979)

The Medieval Monuments of Harewood   (Wakefield Historical Publications, Wakefield, 1983)

Churches, monuments, manuscripts, archaelogical museums and societies all provide fascinating material for the student of dress and fashion.

Costume Collections

AUSTRALIA
Melbourne
National Gallery of Victoria
180 St. Kilda Road, Melbourne, Victoria.

EUROPE
AUSTRIA
Vienna
Kunsthistorisches Museum
Vienna 1, Burgring 5.
Belvedere galleries
Paintings. Costumes at Hetzendorf Schloss,
19th Cent.

BELGIUM
Antwerp
Musée Royal des Beaux Arts
Paintings and Sculpture
Bruges
Musée Groenige
Brussels
Musées Royaux d'Art et Histoire
10 Parc du Cinquantenaire, Brussels

DENMARK
Copenhagen
De Danske Kongers Kronologiske
Samling Paa Rosenborg.
Nationalmuseet
Costumes from 14th Cent.
Rosenborg Palace
Royal family costume collection, 1600-1940.

FRANCE
Bayeux
Musée Tapisserie de la Reine Mathilde
Bayeux Tapestry
Paris
Musée de l'Armée
Hotel des Invalides. Arms and Armour
Musée de Cluny
6 Rue Paul Painlevé, 5e Odeon 24-21
Paintings, tapestries, accessories, footwear.
Musée du Costume de la Ville de Paris
Library, reference study.
11 Avenue du President Wilson, 16E.
Annex of Musée Carnavalet
Collection of costume from 1725
Musée de la Mode
Rue de Rivoli, Palais du Louvre.
Musée des Arts Décoratifs, Palais du Pavillon,
Louvre, de Marston, 107 Rue de Rivoli, 1Er

Rennes
Musée de Bretagne,
20 Quai Emile Zola, Ile-et-Vilaine.
19th Cent. costume.
Versailles
Musée National du Château de Versailles.
Paintings, Tapestries.

GERMANY
Frankfurt-am-Main
Historiches Museum
Untermainkai 14.   Costumes 1750 onwards.

Hamburg
Museum für Hamburgische Geschichte
Holstenwall 24
Munich
Bayerisches Nationalmuseum
Prinzregentstr. 3
Costumes, painting, sculpture

GREAT BRITAIN
Bath
Museum of Costume
The Assembly Rooms, Alfred St. BA1 2QH
Costume and Fashion Research Centre
The Circus
Bexhill
Bexhill Manor Costume Museum
 Manor House Gardens, Old Town
Birmingham
City Museum and Art Gallery
Congreve St., B3 3DH
Bradford
Bolling Hall Museum
Brompton Ave. BD4 7LP
Broadclyst
The National Trust Costume Collection
Pailise de Bush Collection, Killerton House.
Broadway
Snowshill Manor, Snowshill WR12 7JU
Cheltenham
The Costume Collection
Pittville Pump Room. Costumes, 1760-1960
Christchurch
The Red House Museum and Art Gallery,
Quay Rd. BH23 1BU

Hartlebury
Worcestershire County Museum
Hartlebury Castle, Worcs. DY11 7XX
Hereford
Churchill Gardens Museum
Venn's Lane   HRI IDE
City Museum and Library
Broad St., HR4 9AN
Ipswich
Museum and Art Galleries
High St. IPI 3QH
Leicester
Costume Museum
Wygston's House, 25 St. Nicolas Circle
LE1 5LD
London
Bethnal Green Museum
(affiliated to Victoria and Albert Museum)
Cambridge Heath Road E2 9PA
Horniman Museum and Library
100 London Road, Forest Hill SE23 3PQ
The London Museum
Kensington Palace W8 4PX
National Gallery and
National Portrait Gallery
Trafalgar Square. Paintings
Victoria and Albert Museum
Exhibition Road SW7 2RL
Wallace Collection
Hertford House, Manchester Square
Armour and paintings
Manchester
The Gallery of English Costume
Platt Hall, Wilmslow Rd, Rusholme M14 5LL
Market Harborough
The Symington Museum of Period Corsetry
R. & W.H.Symington & Co. Ltd.,
Church Square. LE16 7NB
Northampton
Central Museum and Art Gallery
Guildhall Road. NN1 1DP
Nottingham
Nottingham Museum of Costume and Textiles
51 Castle Gate
Salisbury
Salisbury and South Wiltshire Museum
The King's House, 65 The Close
Stratford-upon-Avon
Arms and Armour Museum
Poet's Arbour, Sheep Street
500 years of armour and accoutrements
Street
The Shoe Museum
C. & J. Clark Ltd., Street
Footwear from Roman times to the present.

Totnes
Devonshire Collection of Period Costume
10a High Street. Changed annually from
Collection. In interesting Tudor house.
York
Castle Howard Museum Y06 7DA
The Castle Museum
Tower Street. Folk museum.

SCOTLAND
Dunfermline
Pittencrieff Park
Fife KY12 7PB   Costume Collection,
c.1800 to present. May to September.
Paisley
Paisley Museum and Art Galleries
High Street. Paisley shawls.

WALES
St Fagans
Welsh Folk Museum,
National Museum of Wales.
South Glamorgan.   Welsh costume

ITALY
Florence
Museo Stibbert
via di Montughi 7, 50139
Uffizi Gallery
Paintings, sculpture.   Middle Ages on.
Milan
Pinacoteca di Brera
via Brera 28.
Raccolta delle Stampe
Achille Bertarelli, Castello Sforzesco
Naples
Museo e Gallerie Nazionali di Capodimonte
Palazzo di Capodimonte
Rome
Musei e Gallerie di Pittura di Vaticano
Venice
Galerie dell'Accademia
Campo delta Carita
Ca' Rezzonico
Museo Correr
Piazza San Marco, Procuratie Nuove
Volterra
Museo Diocesano d'Arte Sacra
Palazzo Vescocile, via Roma

THE NETHERLANDS
Amsterdam
Rijksmuseum
Stadhouderskade 42.
Costume collection, 18th Cent. onwards.
Paintings, tapestries.

The Hague
Koninklijk Kabinet van Schilderijen
(Mauritshuis)
Kostuummuseum
Collection, 18th Cent. onwards.
Utrecht
Centraal Museum
Collection, 1760 onwards.

NORWAY
Oslo
Kunstindustrimuseet i Oslo
St. Olavsgt. 1

PORTUGAL
Lisbon
Museo de Arte Popular
Pracado Imprevio Betern

SPAIN
Barcelona
Museo de Indumentaria
Costume collection, 17th Cent, onwards.
Museo del Pueblo Español
Plaza de la Marina Española 9. Costumes.
Madrid
Museo Arqueolôgico Nacional
Serrano 13. Paintings, mosaics,
sculpture. Medieval, Renaissance.
Museo Nacional del Prado
Paintings

SWEDEN
Gothenborg
Historiska Museet
Norra, Hamngatan 12. Costume Collection.
18th Cent. onwards.
Stockholm
Kungl. Livrustkammaren
115 21 Stockholm
Nordiska Museet
Djurgardsvagen Costumes 1600-1960

SWITZERLAND
Basle
Historisches Museums. Paintings
Berne
Bernisches Historisches Museum
Helvetia 5 18th, 19th Cent. costume, tapestries
Berner Kunstmuseum
Paintings
Schönenworp
Schuhmuseum,
Ausstellung Felsgarten. Footwear from early
times to present.

St Gallen
Industrie-und Gewerbemuseum
Vadianstr. 2.
Zurich
Schweizerisches Landesmuseum
Museumstr. 2. Costume and jewellery.

NORTH AMERICA

CANADA
Calgary
Glenbow-Alberta Institute
902 Ilth Avenue South West
Toronto
Royal Ontario Museum
University of Toronto, 100 Queen's Park.
Costume Collection

U.S.A
Boston
Museum of Fine Arts
Huntington Avenue
Los Angeles
Los Angeles County Museum of Art
Wilshire Blvd. Costume Collection
New York
Brooklyn Museum
188 Eastern Parkway. Costume Collection
Metropolitan Museum of Art
Fifth Avenue and 82nd Street.
Traphagen School of Fashion,
Museum Collection,
257 Park Avenue South
Philadelpia
Museum of Art
26th and Benjamin Franklin Parkway.
Fashions, costumes, textiles.
Seattle
Costume and Textile Study Collection
University of Washington,
School of Economics.
Washington
Smithsonian Institute,
National Museum of History and Technology.
Costume Collection

Exhibitions of Ancient Civilisations

EGYPT: Egyptian Museum, CAIRO

BABYLONIA, ASSYRIA:
British Museum, LONDON

CRETE, MYCENAE:
 1) Historical Museum of Crete, HERLKLION
 2) Chrysolakkos Museum, Crete
      (For jewellery)

GREECE:
Acropolis Museum, ATHENS
State Museum, Dept. of Antiquities, BERLIN

ETRUSCAN:
Etruscan Museum, CHIUSI
Musée du Louvre, PARIS
National Museum, TARQUINIA
Museo Archeologico, FLORENCE
Vatican Museum, ROME

ANCIENT ROME:
Vatican Museum, ROME
Museo e Gallerie Nazionale di Capimonte,
   NAPLES
Museo Archeologico, FLORENCE
National Museum, NAPLES
National Museum, DAMASCUS

BYZANTIUM:
San Vitale, RAVENNA   (For mosaics.)
Archbishop's Palace, RAVENNA
Musée du Louvre, PARIS
   (7th Cent. Lombardic)

ROMANESQUE:
Museum of Catalan Art, BARCELONA
British Museum, LONDON
University Library, PRAGUE
State Library, MUNICH.
Library of the Cathedral Chapter, PRAGUE.
Musée du Louvre, PARIS

GOTHIC: 1400 --
Museum of Catalan Art, BARCELONA
Museum of Fine Arts, BUDAPEST

LATE GOTHIC:
Kunsthistorisches Museum, BERLIN

Abbreviations Used

abbrev.	abbreviation	fem.	feminine	O.H.Ger.	Old High German
Aborig.	Aboriginal	Finn.	Finnish	O.L.Ger.	Old Low German
A.D.	Anno Domini	Flem.	Flemish	O.N.	Old Norse
	(in the year of Our Lord)	Fr.	French	O.S.	Old Saxon
Afr.	Africa; African			O.Sp.	Old Spanish
A.F.	Anglo French	Gael.	Gaelic	O.T.	Old Testament
A.L.	Anglo Latin	Ger.	German		
Amer.	American	Gk.	Greek		
Anglo-Ind.	Anglo-Indian	Gk.Myth.	Greek Mythology		
A.N.	Anglo-Norman	Goth.	Gothic	Paint.	Painting
Ar.	Arabic			Pers.	Persian
Arch.	Archaic	Heb.	Hebrew	Peruv.	Peruvian
Archit.	Architecture.	Her.	Heraldry, etc.	Pg.	Portugese
A.S.	Anglo Saxon	Hind.	Hindustani	Phoen.	Phoenician
		Hung.	Hungarian	pl.	plural
b.	born			Pol.	Polish; Poland
B.C.	before Christ	Ice.	Icelandic	Print.	Printing
Bib.	Biblical	Ind.	Indian		
Boh.	Bohemian	Ir.	Irish	Rom.	Roman
Br.	British	It.	Italian	RomMyth.	Roman Mythology
Braz.	Brazilian			Russ.	Russian
Bret.	Breton	Jam.	Jamaican		
Bulg.	Bulgarian	Jap.	Japanese	S.	South
Burm.	Burmese	Jav.	Javanese	Sax.	Saxon
Byz.	Byzantine	Jew.	Jewish	Scot.	Scots: Scottish
				Sem.	Semitic
C.	about (Latin: circa)	L.	Latin	Singh.	Singalese
Can.	Canada; Canadian	LL.	Late Latin	S.B.	single breasted
Carib.	Caribbean			Slav.	Slavonic
Celt.	Celtic	M.	Middle (languages)	Sp.	Spanish
cent.	century	masc.	masculine	St.	Saint
Chin.	Chinese	M. Du.	middle Dutch	Sw.	Swedish
Class. Myth.		M.E.	Middle English, 1200-1500		
	Classical Mythology	Mid.	Middle Ages, 1000-1400	Teut.	Teutonic
Copt.	Coptic	Mex.	Mexican	Turk.	Turkish
cp.	compare	Mil.	Military		
Cym.	Cymric	mod.	modern	U.S.(A)	United States (of
		Myth.	Mythology		America)
Dan.	Danish			usu.	usually
deriv.	derivative, etc.	N.	North; Norse		
Dor.	Doric	Norw.	Norwegian	W.	Welsh
D.B.	double breasted	N.T.	New Testament	W.Afr.	West Africa(n)
Dut.	Dutch			W.Ind.	West Indian
		O.	old (languages)		
E.	English	obs.	obsolete		
Eccl.	Ecclesiastical	O.E.	Old English		
E.Ind.	East Indian	O.F.	Old French		
Eur.	European				